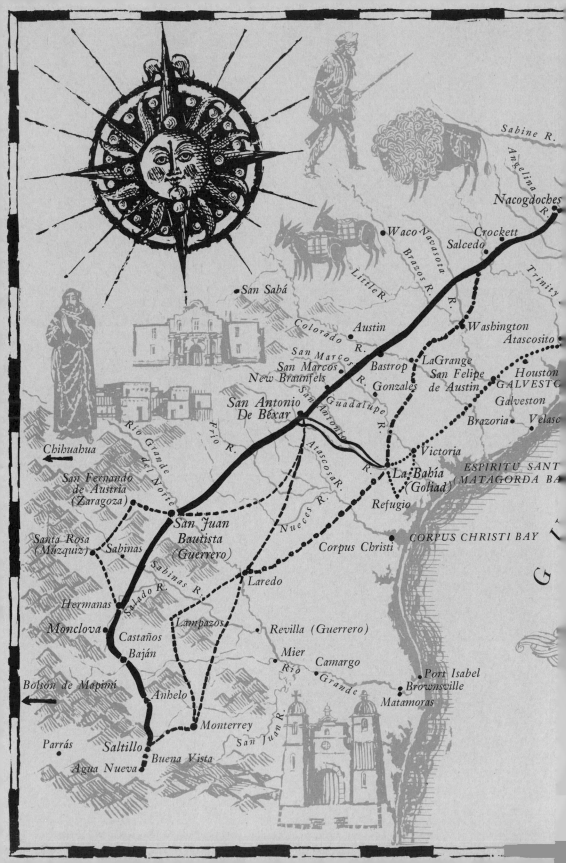

R.

*Los Adaes
(Robeline)*

• *Natchez*

Milam
Natchitoches
Gaines' Ferry
ustine

Mobile •
Pensacola

Neches R.

Baton Rouge •

Opelousas

*Lake
Pontchartrain*
BILOXI BAY

R. • *New Orleans*

• *Beaumont*
huac

O   F

F

M   E   X   I   C   O

SPANISH
TRAILS

from

NEW
SPAIN

to

TEXAS

T R A I L S

Camino Real ━━━━━━
La Bahía ━·━·━·━·
Atascosito ·············
Béxar to La Bahía ━━━━━━
La Bahía to Laredo ━●━●━●━
Alternate Camino Real ━ ━ ━ ━

And some towns prior to 1848

DOOMED ROAD

The Spanish Trail of Conquest by

McGRAW-HILL BOOK COMPANY, INC

OF EMPIRE

HODDING CARTER

WITH BETTY W. CARTER

Illustrations by Don Almquist

NEW YORK   TORONTO   LONDON

For my wife, Betty,
without whom this book
could not have been written

CONTENTS

DOOMED ROAD OF EMPIRE

CHAPTER ONE

SOME NOTES FOR A ROAD MAP

No GEOGRAPHIC DESIGNATION in the New World is more evocative than the Spanish Trail. None is more misleading. For *the* Spanish Trail never was. Instead, there were many. The buffalo course, the warpath and the blazed trees which were the wilderness signposts of the Spanish southwest and west were metamorphosed into rude thoroughfares upon which rode the friar and the *conquistador*. The Spanish ox team and mule train criss-crossed wearily the sand and dust and mud, the pine needle bed and flinty crust throughout the lower American reaches, and wherever a meandering route persisted, it became a *camino real,* a highway of the Spanish king.

The king's highways, with their dubious promise of protection for those who used them, attested to the Hispanic glory and power which would be evanescent, and to the greed and lust and cruelty and courage and vision of man. And each bore witness to the message preached beside the Spanish trails by the missionary brothers, who told the Indians of God the Father and the Blessed Virgin and the fruit of her womb.

Of all the trails of the Spaniard in the Americas none would become as significant an instrument in the shaping of North American destiny as that royal road which swung northward from Saltillo in today's Mexico, through what would become Monclova, then eastward to Guerrero, before crossing the Río Grande and on to San Antonio, and Nacogdoches and its ending at French-born Natchitoches.

Five Christian nations—Spain, France, Mexico, the Republic of Texas, the United States—and a nomad scattering of Indian nations which were submerged in the white man's flood brought to the *camino real* diverse national purposes and the single intent of possession.

The story told here of the road to Texas is essentially a tale of nearly 200 years of conflicting ambitions, cultures and faiths. It concerns itself with New World reflections of the power struggles of the old: of France against Spain and Bourbon against Bourbon, and Protestant England intermittently against each; and, more lastingly, a contest among Americans, with eventual victory going to the lank men of North America, the descendants of Anglo-Saxons and Celts, over the Spanish and Spanish descendants, settlers and soldiers of New Spain and Mexico. The *camino* itself today bears testimony to the outcome of the contest that shaped North America's southern and western boundaries.

When it was first opened, the *camino real* lay entirely within the borders of New Spain. Today two-thirds of the trail lies within the United States, and to the west of Texas, as far as the Pacific, the banners of Spain are but a memory. Because of the North American frontiersmen who settled along it, Mexico eventually lost more than a third of the territory she had inherited from Spain.

The trail ran a thousand miles in four topographical divisions: through cactus and mesquite valleys bordered by bare mountains and scarred by ravines; then down the Sierra Madre slope to the undulant Río Grande plain, to the verdant banks of the San Antonio River; through islands of trees in long-grassed prairies and across rivers which spread for miles in flood; and finally through the rolling hills of the redlands and, along a turning ridge, to the Red River's cypress swamps and moss-misted forests.

Sometimes the road wandered in a manner which seemed meaningless: northward by as much as 5 leagues—13 miles—because a newly discovered ford was better than the old; 3 leagues to the south where high boulders gave the lookout against Apache attack a better vista; 2 leagues west to where ungrazed pastures provided more forage for mule train and *caballada*. The road was marked and charted by old and abandoned campfire sites, by astrolabe readings, by the pioneer's knowledge of tall peaks and dry *arroyos*, by the mark of the ax on oak and gum and pine.

The trail bore more than one name. The wide-ranging Spaniards named the Indian trails which they joined together *El Camino Real para los Texas*, the royal road to the Texas. The Anglo-Americans who came later gave another name to that part of the Spanish Trail which they followed, at first furtively and in small numbers, then by the hundreds and thousands. The Road to San Antone, they nicknamed it. To the Spaniards who served His Catholic Majesty and to their heirs, the North American frontiersmen's designation was the sound of the heretic's tocsin.

Before the white man came, savage folk lived here whom the intruders collectively termed Indians: the Hasinai and other Caddo, Apaches, Coahuiltecans, Karankawas and, later, Comanches. In the shrouded past of pre-history, there had been others who left behind tall ceremonial mounds as proof of their cultural ties with Mexico.

To these savages, the craggy-headed brown bison provided the only guarantee of survival. These buffaloes were the first blazers of this trail. Pounding their way in thirsting thousands across plains and prairies, along wooded ridges, they chose the swiftest paths to the watering places. In search of food and water, the first men followed these buffalo paths and the circling bison, southeast ahead of winter's winds, northwest to the unsheltered plains whose rich grasses gave them an easy summer home.

The buffaloes were more than meat. Their tanned hides were blankets and tents, shirts and leggings and footwear; their tendons became the thread that sewed the skins together. Their burning dung warmed the lodges. The stretched, dried skin of the buffalo was a shield against enemy arrows. The soft brown wool of their bodies was fashioned into garters and belts and ornaments. The black, curving horns were carved into spoons and drinking vessels. The shoulder bones became plowshares with which to dig and clear the cornfields.

For the Apaches and Comanches to the north the buffalo was almost the sole provider. The Plains Indians kept close to the buffalo and were perforce nomads.

Far to the southwest of the plains—on the high plateau between the great sierras which constitute Mexico's divided spinal column, and down the eastern slope of the Sierra Madre Oriental to the Río Grande and beyond—another people, the Coahuiltecan tribes, made their equally mobile homes. Roots and cactus fruit, fish and wild rats constituted the basic diet of their poor existence in a land where trees grew only by rivers and great stretches of barren land separated these oases. Like locusts swarming into a food-rich area, they would remain long enough to strip it of edibles, then, driven by hunger and necessity, move on to another green haven.

Along the Gulf Coast littoral the gigantic Karankawas found fish, oysters, shrimp, crabs and alligators to their liking. For meat they ate buffalo and deer, and made their captives a source of food.

To the east, in the rolling East Texas woodland home of the Hasinai, the bison was not as fundamental to existence as to the Apaches, for here in the forests deer were plentiful. The Hasinai waited for the season of the buffalo migration southward, cutting and drying the meat, and loading the winter bounty on traverse poles pulled by dogs. They left their villages along the Neches and Angelina and their tributary streams only for the killing and returned from west of the Trinity in time to sow maize, beans and calabashes. They were a comparatively settled people in this land of movement.

The Hasinai called all their allies "Techas," or friends, and to the Spaniards it sounded like "Texas." Only later did the Dons discover that the Hasinai were not speaking of their tribes alone when they used the word. Among other Indians the Hasinai were almost a legendary nation, a strong confederation of people who built towns and raised so much grain that when they acquired horses there was enough corn left over to feed their mounts. Theirs was a well-organized clan ruled by a priestly chief. In time white men would hear of this mighty Kingdom of the Texas, worthy of conquest and conversion.

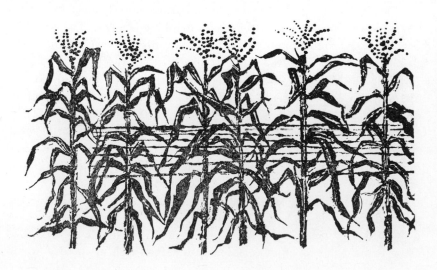

From the beginning the Spaniards sought to make the Hasinai their friends. This friendship between the Hasinai and the white adventurers from the Iberian peninsula proved, a century later, to be a mistake for Spain—an error which resulted in murder and terror. For the alliance with the Hasinai, upon which was based Spain's Indian policy east of the Río Grande, brought down upon the Spaniard and his decimated wards the vengeance of the fiercest of the warriors of the southwest, the Apaches and Comanches. The war whoop, plunging knife and trade musket tormented the ranches and settlements along the trail to the olden land of the Hasinai. Nor did the bloodletting end until, in the waning years of the nineteenth century, a chief named Geronimo was brought to heel far from the road to the Texas. Even then it was not the "yellow-legs," the American cavalrymen, who could take primary credit for the humbling of the Apaches. Instead, it was the buffalo gun, the Sharps rifle of the hide and meat hunters, which brought starvation and surrender.

What were they like, the travelers on this road, who gave it meaning, changing its being with every footstep and hoofbeat that scored the marl and shale and pebbly sand? To what purpose did they journey?

Here ventured treasure-seeking nobles and gentlemen and peasant soldiers, their minds ablaze with dreams of silver and gold and of

tawny women whose bodies would join with theirs to create a new race. With them, in that strange communion of Spanish purpose, went the Franciscan friars—iron-willed, steel-sinewed and single-minded.

Here moved in peace, on the hunt and at war, the eleven tribes of the Hasinai; and the Bidais, the Ais, the Adaes, the Natchitoches and their other allies in the Caddo confederation; the assorted Coahuiltecan tribes and the Karankawa of the coast; the Apache and, later, the Comanche, and later still the Cherokee and the rest of the displaced Indians of the east.

Here traveled the emissaries and traders of the French kings, whose kinship with Spain of religion and even of blood was no guarantee against their own hunger for the spoils of empire. And after them came the rough, relentless men of the north, as leathery as the skins that clothed them, the American hunters and settlers, soldiers and soldiers of fortune, planters and Negro slaves, all unknowingly joined in a tidal force which would one day be described and defended as "manifest destiny."

Along the *camino* they came, for a thousand miles, for 150 years, from Saltillo to Natchitoches, and from Natchitoches back to a bloody appointment of Mexican and Anglo-American in 1847 at a ranch near Saltillo named Buena Vista, and the final wresting away.

So, for all men to see and to follow was etched the Spanish Trail to the Texas, the most meaningful of all such which the probing Spanish columns clawed in Mexico and Florida and the Missouri and Louisiana country, and through the vast, tinted deserts of the Southwest, to California, to the Pacific, and into the shadows of the Spanish twilight.

CHAPTER TWO

THE TREASURE SEEKERS

I n 1519, the burnished gold disc which blinded Hernán Cortés as it shone in the Mexican sun dazzled Europe with the vision of the treasure of Toltec and Aztec. The scales of fortune in the New World were delicately balanced. Had not Montezuma, emperor of the Aztecs, feared the portents of the return of the white god, Quetzalcoatl, he would not have offered to Cortés the golden riches of Quetzalcoatl's temple. But the gifts of peace, the turquoise-encrusted, plume-surmounted mask of the high priest—the great golden sun disc whose matching silver moon was as large as a cart's wheel—and the Spanish soldier's helmet overflowing with gold dust which were given to Cortés in propitiation and sent by him to the Spanish king, changed the history of two worlds.

Cabeza de Vaca, seeking such treasure as Cortés had grasped, was the first white adventurer in the land of the future *camino real*. The story of his survival and of that of his companions is perhaps the most incredible of all the tales of endurance in the history of the Americas. More exciting to his contemporaries were his gilded reports which spurred on not only Coronado but many who came later.

Coronado, resplendent in gilded armor, saw the great plains and the buffalo. He met Hasinai Indians, tattooed and painted their characteristic red, far from home on the buffalo plains. He understood that they came from the Kingdom of the Texas, not far from the fabulous realm he sought. Parts of today's Arizona, New Mexico and Texas Coronado had surely seen, but nowhere gold.

Another Spaniard, Hernando de Soto, armed with a grant to

those countries awarded earlier to Narváez, crossed the Mississippi river in June, 1541, searching for yet another fabled land, Pacaha. Its gold turned out to be yellow maize, welcome but not rewarding. So close did the *entradas* of Coronado and de Soto come at one time they may have been no farther than a day's journey apart. An Indian maiden, seeking to escape the attentions of Coronado's soldiers, fled for several days through rough desert country only to be taken by the second group of predatory Spaniards.

When de Soto died on the banks of the Mississippi, his successor in command, Luis de Moscoso, led the cavaliers westward again, this time in search of their own kind at the Pánuco River, farthest east of New Spain's settlements. Whatever tales Moscoso's men told when they encountered their fellow Christians in New Spain in 1543, the elusive golden will o' the wisp which had lured them to seek rich kingdoms was soon to be forgotten in favor of a rewarding substitute —silver. The protection of that substitute was to be the primary secular and military function of the yet unblazed trail to the Texas Indians.

In 1548, in a windy mountain gorge near what would become the city of Zacatecas, four Spanish soldiers came upon a silver lode so extensive that their own fortunes were quickly won and the North American continent's first mining boom was on. The silver was mined in such quantity that from this first excavation and the others that were soon opened throughout New Spain's provinces of Nueva Galicia and Nueva Viscaya would come eventually two-thirds of the world's supply. It was silver enough to bury the feudal system of Europe beneath the inflationary effects of four billion dollars in ingots and coins—so great a trove that the geography of the silver country became Spain's state secret. Silver made mandatory the building of missions and *presidios,* and the establishment of roads to connect them.

The history of Saltillo, the first point on the future *camino real* to the Texas, began in 1568. North of San Luis Potosí's rich mines stretched a desert plain without water or tillable soil, so inhospitable to man that even the Indians avoided it. Above this the mountains came together and beyond—who knew?—more silver lodes might lie concealed. Francisco Cano, an obscure lieutenant, and fifteen men came searching from the mining town of Mazapil to the southwest. They returned, disappointed. But they were the first white men to descend through the narrow pass of La Angostura to what would in time become the Mexican state of Coahuila and the point of departure for the *entradas* to the Texas.

Seven years later Spain planted a settlement north of the pass. This first little town, which became the southern terminus of the future road to the Texas, was founded by Alberto del Canto who, with twenty families, reached the Valley of Saltillo, the "high land of many waters," in 1575. Little Saltillo, clinging to the side of the enfolding mountain, looked down on a valley that spread uninterrupted for 50 miles to the Sierra Galena range. The 275 springs nearby assured copius water with which to make the valley fertile. Del Canto distributed to the families the first *mercedes de tierra y agua*—grants of land and water—assigning to each family its own field and water rights, which the Spaniards considered just as important. With loaded muskets beside them and a prayer to Santiago, the patron saint of soldiers, the pioneer founders of Saltillo cleared and defended their fields and constructed irrigation ditches from the springs which were "as many as the days of the year."

Soon they were producing such crops of Spanish wheat and Indian corn and beans that the all but waterless mining areas around Zacatecas and Mazapil looked to Saltillo for foodstuffs. Fruit trees flourished in the well-watered orchards of the cool valley 6,000 feet above sea level and, just south of La Angostura, Alberto del Canto's *estancia,* Buena Vista, became the first pasturage grant in that area for breeding horses and mules for the mines of Nueva Galicia. From Saltillo, the farthest north-central outpost of Spain, the trail ran southward to the viceregal city of Mexico. Northward from Saltillo, the staging area for Spain's advance upon the Texas, the king's highway would run its thousand miles.

To this outpost, in 1580, came General Luis Carabajal y de la Cueva, a Jew, governor of Nuevo Reino de León, a new province created by the Spanish court. But what were the limits of Carabajal's jurisdiction? Portions of Nueva Galicia to the south of Saltillo, parts of Nueva Vizcaya to the west, land as far north as today's San Antonio, lay within the immense tract, ranging west and north from the Pánuco River, so vaguely delineated by His Catholic Majesty. The viceroy protested to the king that Carabajal was claiming parts of other provinces. The settlers of Saltillo feared for their property rights. Were their fields to be turned over to a Portuguese and he an apostate Jew?

Reports and rumors flew from this headquarters town, which would one day be Monterrey, while Carabajal and his family, his soldiers and settlers moved 46 leagues northward from Saltillo in search of minerals. Carabajal was the first explorer of northern Coahuila. The *camino real* from Saltillo to the site of what would be Monclova, the principal post on the road to the Texas, was blazed by this unbeliever. But Carabajal's road would soon be abandoned and the way of its going forgotten. To another would go even the title of "founder of Coahuila." Carabajal was an interloper, so the viceroy decided, as well as a backslider. He was brought to heel by Captain Diego de Montemayor and a small detachment, including representatives of the Sacred Office of the Inquisition. They bore accusations of treason and of heresy.

The hapless Portuguese was hauled in chains to Mexico City, disclaimed by his followers, many of whom deserted his town of Nuevo Almadén. His captors threw him into Mexico City's prison of the Corte, then into that of the Inquisition. Carabajal, deserted and broken-hearted, abjured and was let off in 1590 with a sentence of six years of exile from the Indies, the term cut short by his death "of a broken heart."

In the meantime, Captain Montemayor stamped out uprisings of the Indians of Nuevo León, who had rebelled against the Spaniards because Carabajal's colonists had made slaves of their fellow tribesmen and sold them to the mines. One of their attacks was halted, it is written, only because of the Samson-like strength of a Spanish soldier who picked up his horse when it balked at taking another step and carried it—saddle, bridle and war load—the remaining 3 leagues to Saltillo. Montemayor restored peace to the region and refounded Monterrey, bringing settlers east from Saltillo, the mother and nourisher of colonies.

But the expansion of New Spain northeast of Saltillo had halted. There was still no need for a road to the east. West of Coahuila and the high, dry sink-hole of the Bolsón de Mapimí, Juan de Oñate carried Spain's gold and red banner north to Santa Fé. In what is today's Coahuila, only Santiago del Saltillo remained as a feeble northern outpost for the protection of the pass of La Angostura and the mining lands beyond.

To the south, on the plains of Nueva Galicia, the Gran Chichimeca Indians had to be pacified if the mines were to be safely worked.

Ever since the days of Cortés the viceroys had clung to the ways of the first *conquistadores: guerra a fuego y a sangre.* But "war of flame and blood" begat only more bloodletting and destruction. After each expedition the Indians, mourning their captured women, children and brothers, only fought the harder. In 1585, the viceroy Alvaro Manrique de Zúñiga announced a plan which was to have consequential meaning for the Christian friar and Spanish soldier who later traveled the road to the Texas. His program was a sort of "peace by purchase." The price might be high but the cost would be less, he argued, and the results more efficacious and lasting than peace by the sword. Under Zúñiga's scheme the missionaries, clamoring for protection so that they might be able to go out and preach the faith to the Indians in Nueva Galicia, were to be allotted the soldiers they sought.

The pacification of the Indians was to be achieved by conversion, but the material basis of the new policy was the promise of food and clothing if the Indians came into the missions. In the past, these savages had raided the Spanish mining settlements and carried away what necessities they could find. Now they were to be trained to produce food for themselves. The Spanish war treasury was to provide for them while they learned. In time they could harvest such an abundance that their excess foodstuffs and cattle could be sold to the settlements. Such was Zúñiga's theory. His was, perhaps, the first technical assistance plan.

The missionaries had been urging such a policy for many years. Now, in pairs, protected by only two soldiers and taking as attendants some of the Tlaxcalan Indians who had become Spain's allies in the time of Cortés, Franciscans and Jesuits set up missions in the wilderness plains of Nueva Galicia. The friars and priests already spoke, or soon learned to speak, the languages of the natives. They came as friends, offering gifts, wooing by peaceful talk the Gran Chichimeca and telling of the crucified Christ. Molasses from Campeche, butchers' knives, hoof parers, iron shoes for horse and mule, medicines, thread, cheese and dried shrimp were the weapons in the Spanish strategy. Sometimes arrows and death were the reward. But more often the Indians came docilely to the missions to learn how to assure themselves of plenty in this life while the missionaries taught them the *doctrina* of salvation for the next. They lived in *pueblos,* Indian towns set up according to Spanish law on specially assigned lands, with their own *alcaldes* and officers supervised by the missionary fathers.

In twenty years, "peace by purchase" had quieted all of Nueva Galicia and much of Nueva Vizcaya. So astounding was the mission system's success in its initial phase that in the years to come the friars applied it unquestioningly as they moved along the *camino real*.

Zúñiga envisioned the founding of key settlements in the passes through which marauders might ascend to the silver plains—not simply fortified *presidios* but agricultural communities producing sufficient corn and meat to feed potential enemies and encourage them to settle down nearby.

His successor, Luis de Velasco, continued the policy of peace by purchase. In December 1590, Velasco and the Tlaxcaltecan chiefs arrived at terms by which 400 families of these Christianized allies would establish eight Indian *pueblos* as models for the frontier. Velasco promised that the head of each family which entered upon a contract would carry the title of *hidalgo*, a lesser nobleman, and be forever free from taxes. The Tlaxcaltecans would live in their own *barrios*, in which no Spaniard or Chichimeca would be permitted to dwell. Their *pueblo* markets would be free of the distasteful *alcabala*, the sales tax, the *sisa* or excise tax, and other taxes for thirty years. And as the supreme rewards for pacification and fidelity, they and their descendants, unlike the uncivilized non-Christians, would be permitted to bear arms and ride saddle horses without penalty.

In July 1591, four imposing wagon trains streamed northward from Tlaxcala, near the San Juan River. One was bound for the vicinity of San Luis Potosí; the destination of the second lay beyond Zacatecas; the third headed for Colotlán; and the fourth, with destiny as an unrecognized load, drove toward Saltillo under the command of Captain Francisco de Urdiñola. There, just west of the villa of Santiago, Urdiñola, a famed Indian fighter and pacifier, founded the Indian *pueblo* of San Esteban de Nuevo Tlaxcala. Side by side, the twin settlements of Saltillo, the Spanish *villa*, and San Esteban, the Indian *pueblo*, marked in symbolic unification the place of departure for the future royal road to the Texas. Geographically, they were indeed *la llave de la tierra adentro*, the key to the land inside, the heartland of Mexico.

For eighty years little was done to push the frontier farther into Coahuila. Then, unexpectedly and in dramatic manner, came the delayed extension of New Spain's frontier.

A Father Juan Larios intended only to call on his sister **at** Durango, then, being a Franciscan of the Province of Jalisco, to return to the Jaliscan headquarters near Guadalajara. But after he had left Durango, his short visit over, a band of long-haired Catzales, naked except for their maguey-fiber sandles, crowded around the benign blue-habited Franciscan and, through sign language, begged him to accompany them to their *ranchería* far to the northeast. There, said Father Larios' captors, thousands of natives awaited the placing of water on their heads. Their weapons and numbers were persuasive. Father Larios decided it would be best, with or without the authorization of his superiors, to heed these urgent pleas for conversion. He soon found himself ministering to the Catzales and other Coahuiltecan Indians far north of Saltillo.

Father Larios' first mission moved from its original site near today's Sabinas and found its permanent home near the springs on the north bank of the Sabinas River at the former Santa Rosa, today called Ciudad Múzquiz. From here, Father Larios crossed the Río Grande north of Eagle Pass, as we now call it, returning with many hundreds of Indians who desired to live in the mission *pueblo*. His establishment at Santa Rosa and of other missions in Coahuila in the 1670s gained for him in time the deserved title of "founder of Coahuila." The site of Santa Rosa became a point on the *camino real*.

But his Indians wearied of civilization. Supplies for the distant missions were erratic in arrival. Some of the Indians drifted back to their ancient river haunts. Others rebelled against the disciplines of church and state. A severe smallpox epidemic swept through the mission *pueblos*. The society which Father Larios founded began to fall apart. He who had begged that soldiers remain far south so as not to frighten his Indians now urged their coming to round up and bring back his errant children.

In answer to his plea, Antonio Balcárcel de Rivadenyra, newly appointed *alcalde mayor,* the principle civilian officer of all the territory north of Saltillo, set out from Saltillo in 1674 to re-establish the clerical, military and political authority of Spain. In the footsteps of Carabajal, the persecuted Jew, Balcárcel re-established the Indian *pueblo* of San Pedro y San Pablo, 20 leagues north of Saltillo, adding de Anelo to its designation. Ten leagues farther he established Santa Isabel and, 13 leagues beyond, Santa Cecilia de Castaño. Less than a day's march later he came upon the ruins of Nuevo Almadén, its two riverside smelters abandoned. Here, at the site of the future city of Monclova, Balcárcel founded the Indian *pueblo* of Nuestra Señora de Guadalupe on December 8, 1674. Then, God's and the king's will having been effected, he subdued the fickle Indians of Santa Rosa.

Father Larios, accompanied by Balcárcel's deputy, Fernando del Bosque, recrossed the Río Grande. But the required missionary effort was greater than the Jaliscan friars could make. Each of the many warring tribes would need a mission of its own, so Father Larios reported. What could a handful do with tribes, each of which was accustomed to eating its captive enemies? Father Larios returned to his mission in Coahuila.

What meaning does this have for us?

Because of Father Larios and Balcárcel, the *camino real* had begun. Indian *pueblos* marked the route from Saltillo all the way to Santa Rosa, 100 leagues away. But its function as a road across the Río Grande and to the Texas lay in the future.

CHAPTER THREE

THE SECRET PURPOSE OF
M. DE LA SALLE

CONSIDER NOW the interwoven destinies of two sons of the New World, a Canadian of high courage and distant mien, and a Spanish renegade. They were to set off an explosive chain reaction which would make the road to the Texas seemingly mandatory to the survival of Spain in Mexico. The one was René Robert Cavelier, Sieur de la Salle, the restless explorer of the Ohio, discoverer of the Illinois and the first white man to travel the Mississippi to its mouth. The other was Diego Dionisio de Peñalosa, one-time governor of New Mexico, a wretched traitor given to absurd pretensions and possessed by the desire for revenge. Together, though not in concert, they were to be directly responsible for the coming of the French to the Gulf Coast. The settlement which La Salle established there as a poignard at the throat of New Spain hastened by many years the reality of the *camino real*.

Later generations of historians thought the settlement's site unintended—for when the Sieur de la Salle set out on what was to be his last journey of exploration he announced publicly that he sought only the mouth of the Mississippi, the river down which he had earlier traveled. The great La Salle, the old chroniclers insisted, simply lost his way.

Nothing could be farther from the truth, as Peñalosa could have told anyone. Nor did the Spaniards of New Spain believe at the time or later that La Salle had gone astray. They warned each other that he had planned to come to the Río de las Palmas, and from there move upon the mines of the west. We must confront him, they said;

we must scotch his plans; we must establish a *presidio* of our own.

But first, Peñalosa. He had been governor of New Mexico from 1661 to 1664, a powerful representative of Spain who subsequently dubbed himself the Count of Santa Fé. But he was not as powerful as Mother Church and, after he had ordered his soldiers to violate the law of sanctuary by seizing a prisoner before a church altar, he was brought before the Holy Office in Mexico City. There, after hearings by the Inquisition, the Church passed sentence. The defier of the Church's protecting arm was ordered to dress in penitent's garb and, barefooted and bareheaded, to carry a lighted green candle through the streets of the city, to make other attestations of humble contrition, then to be forever exiled from New Spain and the Windward Islands. Had this penalty not been imposed, the fever for a descent upon the mines of Mexico might not in time have coursed so hotly in the veins of the great Sun King, Louis XIV of France.

Peñalosa sailed first to England with rage in his heart. There he tried to interest Charles II in an expedition which he himself would lead to Teguayo and Quivira, almost legendary regions which he swore he knew like the back of his hand. His English Majesty showing scant interest, the Spaniard moved on to Paris where he repeated at the French court his claims to vast knowledge of New World geography and of the whereabouts of gold for the taking.

By coincidence La Salle, the fabulous fur trader, had returned to Paris after having planted the Bourbon flag at the mouth of the Mississippi on April 9, 1682. The Canadian had not been unmindful of Mexico even as he possessed the new territory of Louisiana for Louis XIV. Indeed the patent from the king, under which he had been authorized to explore, build forts and trade in buffalo hides, had read in part: "We have received with favor the very humble petition made us in your name, to permit you to labor at the discovery of the western parts of New France; and we have the more willingly entertained this proposal, since we have nothing more at heart than the exploration of this country, through which, to all appearance, a way may be found to Mexico."

Standing at the marshy mouth of the Mississippi, La Salle had intoned the limits of Louisiana. Perhaps he looked boldly to the west, toward the Río de las Palmas, the river he set as the western border of the land of which he had taken possession in the name of his king. But his immediate plans were only for a colony on the great river

Colbert—the Mississippi—and from there to expand France's holdings into an empire in the heart of the continent.

By the time La Salle reached Paris to seek royal support for his colony, Spain and France were at war. The persistent traitor, Peñalosa, had already drawn up plans for a colony to be established on the Río Bravo, from where the mines of Nueva Vizcaya could be attacked. As the war progressed, Peñalosa became more and more bellicose. He boasted that he could lead Gramont, the fearsome corsair, and 1,000 men directly from Santo Domingo to Pánuco. From there he could easily conquer all of northern New Spain.

La Salle had sought only support for a colony. But there were not enough funds for two expeditions. In the months of court negotiations, the salient features of his and Peñalosa's plans were combined. La Salle now proposed to locate his colony 60 leagues beyond the mouth of the Mississippi. From there he would direct 15,000 Indians toward Nueva Vizcaya. With them would march 200 continental Frenchmen, 50 buccaneers from Santo Domingo and 4,000 warriors from La Salle's Fort St. Louis on the Illinois. With this formidable army he would conquer all of New Spain. All he needed from Louis XIV, he said confidently, was one vessel of thirty guns, a few cannons for forts, permission to raise the 200 Frenchmen, and the money to arm and maintain them for six months.

Impressed, the king commanded the explorer to visit him in private audience. What Louis had to say there was only for loyal ears; he did not trust Peñalosa. He used the Spaniard's ideas as part of his plan. But the king did not include Peñalosa in the venture his scheming contributed to. The king's orders were to La Salle alone, and they were not made public. But a private patent authorized La Salle to lead an army of Frenchmen and Indians in "the enterprise with which we have charged him ... below Fort St. Louis on the Illinois river and ... as far as New Biscay" (Nueva Vizcaya), a penetration considerably west of any French claim.

As far as was generally known, the purpose of the expedition was that which La Salle had suggested on his return from America. Since France and Spain were at war, the king of France felt no compunction about entering the Gulf of Mexico, which Spain had declared to be her own. On the other hand, details and destinations were military information to be withheld from the enemy. La Salle's orders remained a secret in France's official files.

It was a disparate and generally unworthy group which assembled on the docks of La Rochelle in the summer of 1684 to board the expedition's four ships, two provided by the king and the others by La Salle and private investors in the venture. The soldiers for whom the king had agreed to pay salaries and supply provisions for six months had been hard to come by, mostly the dregs of the streets of France, "mere wretched beggars soliciting alms, many too deformed and unable to fire a musket." La Salle had rounded up a blacksmith and some carpenters, masons and joiners but, as it turned out, they knew little about their trades. A number of young women were making the ocean journey to find husbands with whom they would begin to populate the New World. There were the religious, among them La Salle's brother, the Abbé Cavelier, two other Sulpicians and three Recollects, two of whom would live to write of their experiences. Two nephews of La Salle, one only 14 years old, and the Canadian, Talon, who had his family with him, were enrolled, as was La Salle's Canadian Indian hunter, Nika. And there were thirty gentlemen and burghers who had invested in the scheme and were going along to make their fortunes. Among these were the Duhaut brothers, the surgeon Liotôt, the dissolute Marquis de Sablonnière, and Henri Joutel of Rouen, a veteran of seventeen years' service in the French army, whom La Salle made his lieutenant.

La Salle sailed with Captain Beaujeu on *Le Joly,* a royal ship of the line with forty guns, her white standard flying smartly, the blue central shield and three gold *fleurs-de-lis* open to the wind. The rest of the little fleet was made up of the frigate *La Belle,* which the king himself had presented to La Salle, the flyboat *L'Aimable* of about 300 tons burden, owned by a rich merchant of Rouen and laden with all the effects necessary for the settlement, and a small ketch, the *Saint François,* carrying 30 tons of ammunition.

By September 11, the boats were in the latitude of the Island of Hispañola. The hurricane season was upon them and they had been separated by bad weather. The *Saint François,* bearing the expedition's ammunition, put into the harbor of Port de Paix, previously agreed upon as the first stopping place, and was captured by pirates. Had Beaujeu also made for Port de Paix, the ketch might not have been lost. But he argued that Petit Gouave was a safer harbor and deliberately sailed past the rendezvous, as was his right as naval commander if he decided that the weather required a change of course.

By the time *Le Joly* and the other two ships reached Petit Gouave, many of the men were ill. Sleeping on deck had been uncomfortable enough at sea. It was unbearable in the tropical port. La Salle sickened and nearly died. He ordered the men to be removed to shore and housed in whatever dwellings could accommodate them. During the weeks of La Salle's illness and convalescence, Beaujeu refused to assert authority over the soldiers, the Abbé Cavelier didn't know how to, and Joutel doubted that he had the right. The men fell into the dissolute life of the French buccaneer town. What discipline had existed at sea was forgotten. By the time La Salle recovered and the journey resumed, he had lost control of his men. Many had deserted. The soldiers and sailors were riddled with syphillis. A few recruits partially offset the losses. To the roster was added the buccaneer, Hiens, who had been in the English navy and was known as "English Jim," and young Jean L'Archevêque, whom the elder Duhaut hired as valet.

La Salle decided to board *L'Aimable*, the slowest ship. It carried the pilot light which the other two ships had to follow. In effect, he thus took over the naval as well as military command.

The winds, which earlier had blown so wildly, refused to rise. The sails drooped listlessly. The ship's planking felt as if it were afire and there was no shade for the men and women who crowded the decks for relief from the heat below. By December 3 the ships had sailed only as far as the Isle of Pines. Then came days of fog during which booming cannon served as the sole means of keeping the ships together.

When the dispirited expedition reached the latitude at which La Salle had charted the mouth of the Mississippi, the search for it began. La Salle announced that through errors in his earlier record he did not know the longitude. At one point, near the coast, he put out a few men in a small boat to discover if the river was nearby. A heavy fog rose, and when the crewmen returned to *L'Aimable*, they reported that they had seen nothing. But, as Joutel commented: "The master of the bark said he believed there was a river opposite to those shoals, which was very likely; and yet M. de la Salle took no notice of it, nor made any account of that report."

A little farther to the west, when boats were put over to search for drinking water, natives on the shore gestured vigorously to explain that a big river lay behind the white men. La Salle ignored them.

Did La Salle really take no notice? Or was it that at this point that he began operating under the secret clause of the king's instructions—namely to approach the Spanish colonies, establish his colony and from it undertake the conquest of Nueva Vizcaya? If so, why did he not tell the volunteers, or at the least, his lieutenant? Is the mystery explained by his personality? No one can ever know.

Evia's map, a hundred-year-old Spanish chart, showed *La Bahía del Espíritu Santo,* the Bay of the Holy Spirit. About fifty years before La Salle's and Peñalosa's time, some Franciscan fathers had recommended that a port be opened there for communication with Santa Fé and Nueva Vizcaya. La Salle, who might have seen this early map, sailed his ships to the longitude of Espíritu Santo but, discovering that its almost continuous roadstead lacked a protective lee, he turned back to where Evia's map had shown the large Bay of San Bernardo. Skirting the coast carefully and putting out exploratory boats, La Salle approached this bay, which he named St. Louis and which today is called Matagorda. After taking soundings, he discovered a channel between long, low-lying islands.

The frigate cleared the sandy bar. La Salle ordered *L'Aimable* to lighten ship by unloading her cannons, then to wait for the captain of *La Belle* to pilot her in.

Undoubtedly, Captain Aigron of *L'Aimable* had had enough of La Salle and his orders, and resented the implied slur on his own ability. He decided that he would wait only long enough to unload the heaviest items aboard, then take *L'Aimable* across the bar himself. Meanwhile, La Salle had sent ashore the Marquis de Sablonnière and a small party to fell a large tree from which to fashion a canoe. Hardly had the group reached shore when they were surrounded by 7-foot-tall, tattooed Karankawas, stinking with alligator grease and mud with which they covered their bodies as protection from mosquitoes. They were taken forcibly to the Indians' village, whereupon La Salle marched to their rescue. Only then did he notice that *L'Aimable* was under way and that if she continued on her course she would be wrecked on the shoals.

It was too late to do anything about the impending disaster. Besides, the men in the hands of the Indians had to be saved. As he and his party reached the cluster of oven-shaped Indian huts, the report of a cannon frightened the Karankawas so badly that they fell flat on their faces. At the same time La Salle, looking seaward, witnessed the wreck of *L'Aimable.* After seeking hurriedly to make friends with the Indians, who acted cordially enough for the moment and even offered the Frenchmen dried buffalo and porpoise, he hastened with the rescued men to the water's edge. But no gifts from the savages could make up for the disaster which had befallen the flyboat *L'Aimable* which carried the remaining ammunition and tools for the settlement. Because she lay high on the shoals, her supplies might have been salvaged except that her ship's boat was stove in. Worse, a sudden storm hastened her disintegration, the heavy surf opened her side at night and, before the gap was detected, most of the supplies were washed away. During the three weeks before she broke up entirely, the Frenchmen and the Indians competed angrily for the flotsam floating ashore. During a skirmish over a bale of Norman blanketing, a volley of Indian arrows killed two men and wounded Moranget, one of La Salle's nephews, and another volunteer. The following night two more members of the expedition were slain.

But matters were not yet hopeless. Some grain, Indian corn and beans for planting, a quantity of meat and meal, and 30 casks of wine and brandy had been recovered. The timbers of the wrecked ship were used to construct a temporary fort near the shore to shelter the married couples, young women and children. Hunters brought in wild game. Fish was plentiful, and a hasty pudding of corn and water helped assuage the hunger of the French.

In a matter of days, Beaujeu announced that the approaching spring storms made it imperative for him to leave immediately. This he did, taking with him the captain of the wrecked *L'Aimable* and several members of the expedition who saw nothing but ill-fortune ahead. Only *La Belle* remained as a means of communication with the French West Indies. Ashore were 180 disconsolate men, women and children with whom the commander must establish his colony and go about the secret business upon which he had been dispatched. If Gramont and his buccaneers were to join him from Santo Domingo, they had failed to arrive.

For weeks, the members of the colony explored the many rivers opening into the bay and the marshlands of giant reeds, cattails and sedges before La Salle selected, on the highest point of the plain, a site for the permanent fort. No reason remained to delay the removal of the colony from its temporary location. The grain, planted in April, had failed to sprout, possibly because of damage from salt water.

The building of the fort exhausted the workmen. There were

trees, indeed, but at a distance of a league from the site, and the cut logs had to be dragged over the matted prairie grass. Some of the timbers of *L'Aimable* were floated upstream behind *La Belle*. A main building of several rooms was erected, separate quarters for the men and the women arranged, a powder magazine provided and the whole surrounded by a palisade. Even the strongest men gave way in the intense summer heat. Many of the soldiers died of maladies contracted in Santo Domingo, "not withstanding all the relief afforded by broths, preserves, treacle and wine which were given them." The foul-smelling Karankawas sporadically attacked isolated groups or individuals. The crosses in the cemetery within the palisade increased, and La Salle, his plans all but hopelessly awry, became ever more peremptory, his harshness alienating his men almost to the point of insurrection.

With the fort completed and a crop of grain coming on, La Salle determined to set off in search of what Joutel was to record as his "fatal river." Leaving Joutel and thirty-four others at Fort St. Louis, La Salle led out a scarecrow force of sixty men, among them his young nephew, Cavelier. Five cannons boomed a salute in honor of the departure of the company.

Because none of La Salle's chroniclers accompanied him, exactly where the party went must forever remain a mystery. Had the expedition traveled east, La Salle would have reached the recognizable Mississippi. He would not have found any Spaniards in that direction. He traveled westward instead. When he returned to Fort St. Louis five months later he told of crossing and exploring many rivers, of coming upon more and more Indians who seemed better and better acquainted with the Spaniards, and of leaving a number of his men in a fort on a great river. He had claimed all the territory as far as the Río de las Palmas for Louis XIV. If his instructions were to raid Nueva Vizcaya, would this not have been the time to scout the land? Some scholars believe he did go as far up the Río Grande as a week's journey from La Junta de los Rios, today's Presidio in Mexico.

Whatever the direction and whatever the distance, La Salle's expedition ended with the return of only twenty of the sixty men who had started out. From the roof of the fort, Joutel spied La Salle and the haggard survivors and went out to meet them. The cassock of the Abbé Cavelier was so torn "there was hardly a piece left large enough to wrap a farthing's worth of salt." La Salle himself "had an old cap on his head, having lost his hat by the way." The rest were in no better case, for their shirts were in rags. Some of them carried loads of meat "because M. de La Salle was afraid that we [at the fort] might not have killed any buffalo."

On his return, La Salle sent messengers to the bay to tell *La Belle* of his safe arrival back at the fort. They returned with the disconcerting news that the expedition's last ship was nowhere to be seen. Earlier, her captain and six men had been murdered by Indians as they slept on shore. Perhaps her remaining crew had deserted and sailed for France.

Conditions at the fort had been good, Joutel assured his commander, for the lieutenant had ruled that all who would eat must work—friars, women and soldiers alike. With so many of the colony away with La Salle, it had not been too difficult to kill enough game. Buffalo grazed nearby during the winter and Joutel had learned that to kill buffaloes one must shoot them in the spine. He had put out nets to catch the fish which teemed in the river. A cellar for storing meat had been dug within the palisade. Only one untoward incident had occurred, said Joutel. When La Salle left he had instructed Joutel, as insurance against desertion, to permit no member of the expedition to re-enter the fort unless he came with La Salle's written permission. But one night a voice had been heard outside the palisade calling softly, "Dominic, Dominic." It was the voice of the elder Duhaut, who had accompanied La Salle, signaling to his brother within the fort. Duhaut told so plausible a story of having been inadvertently separated from La Salle that Joutel had permitted him to enter and go unpunished. Later the lieutenant would mourn his lack of foresight.

But Fort St. Louis, as well as the handful of men left on the distant, unidentified river, needed more equipment. *La Belle,* which could have carried a message from La Salle for supplies and more men, had disappeared. La Salle made the only possible decision. He decided to go to Canada himself to send to the king a report of what had been accomplished and what was needed.

For a few weeks La Salle recuperated from his exhausting explorations, then with a force of twenty men he set out on April 22 toward the northeast. Among his retinue were his brother, the abbé, the Friar Douay, a Sieur Bijorel, his nephew Maranget, the surgeon Liotôt, the one time buccaneer Hiens, and a Ducler and Hurier.

Just where he went on this first journey in search of aid is as obscure as are aspects of his earlier explorations. Scholars agree that he reached the Indians of the Texas and established a friendship which proved invaluable to France in later years. Only three days northeast of the fort he came upon peaceable natives, some on foot, some on horseback "booted and spurred and seated on saddles." Already the Spanish horses had come this far from the settlements of New Spain to change the life of the Indian.

Beset by accidents and hazards, the hardy group of Europeans slowly made their way toward Canada. As they crossed what we now know as the Trinity River, La Salle and his men came upon that branch of the Caddo people whose strategic location and cultural development was to make them a pivotal tribe in the contest between Frenchmen and Spaniards. La Salle called them the Cenis. The Spaniards would mistakenly name them the Texas. They called themselves the Hasinai.

Father Douay was astounded at the extent of the Cenis' establishment, stretching out along forest trails. "This village, that of the Coenis, is one of the largest and most populous that I have seen in America. It is, at least, 20 leagues long, not that it is constantly inhabited, but in hamlets of ten or twelve cabins, forming cantons each with a different name. Their cabins are fine, 40 or 50 feet high, of the shape of beehives."

La Salle was surprised to find Spanish dollars among these friendly natives, many types of lace, pieces of European clothing and a Papal bull exempting the Spaniards in Santa Fé from fasting during the summer. Especially was he amazed by the number of horses, of which the Cenis had enough to trade him one for an ax.

The Spaniards themselves had not come among the Cenis, he learned, but the Indians who lived near the missions of New Mexico and northern New Spain made frequent trips to the Red River. At this very time, in the Cenis villages, La Salle found six Choumans, as he called them—Jumanos to the Spaniards—allies of the Cenis who had journeyed from their homes six days away from the Spaniards. Father Douay recounted that these Choumans urged the French to join them in a war against the Spaniards who, they said, butchered the Indians cruelly and "were a cowardly race, had no courage and made people walk before them with a fan to refresh them in hot weather." La Salle promised to join the Choumans at some later time in an attack on the Spaniards. They were allies he might well have employed had he then been ready for his descent upon the mines. Instead, after five days among the Cenis, west of the Neches River, he started out for the village of the Nasoni on the other side of the river. At this point the journey was to be interrupted and, ultimately, abandoned.

The land of the Cenis was a pleasant country, the long trip from Fort St. Louis had been arduous, and difficult miles lay ahead. One night, four of La Salle's men deserted. Soon thereafter La Salle and his nephew, Moranget, fell victims of violent fever. For two months the French remained among the Cenis while La Salle convalesced, relapsed, then began a slow recovery. By the time he had regained sufficient strength to go on, his retinue had improvidently used up most of the gunpowder in indiscriminate hunting. The expedition had traveled no more than 150 leagues in a straight line from Fort St. Louis. The desertions had weakened it. There was nothing to do but to return to the fort for more powder and more men. Before the return journey began, however, La Salle had crosses and the arms of France emblazoned on a giant oak, proof that the French had traveled the future *camino real* and left their mark upon it.

Despite the horses which the Cenis had traded to the French, only eight of the twenty men who had started from Fort St. Louis returned to it on October 17. One man had been lost, four had deserted, one had been "carried off with his raft by a crocodile of prodigious length and bulk" and six had been left along the route, too worn out to travel further. One of these, the nephew of Liotôt, the surgeon, was subsequently killed by Indians as he tried to make his way to the fort alone. For this Liotôt was to hold La Salle personally responsible.

The capable Joutel had continued to manage well at the fort. The older Duhaut had attempted to take over command but La Salle's faithful lieutenant had held him in check. Several babies had been born, and, soon after La Salle had left, the survivors of the vanished *La Belle* had straggled into camp with the woeful tale of what had happened to the frigate. Had she sailed for and reached the West Indies, the report of her crew might have brought help to Fort St. Louis. But *La Belle* had never sailed. As she lay at anchor out in the bay, the ship's boat had broken loose and drifted away. With no means to fetch fresh water, the crew had begun consuming the stores of wine and brandy. In an irresponsible moment, a drunken crewman had hoisted anchor, and a swift tide and strong breeze had set the ship on the shoals before the befuddled crew were aware of their danger. By good fortune some of the men had been able to swim to shore, but all hope that *La Belle* might bring aid had been lost.

For another two and a half months La Salle explored the rivers emptying into the bay. He expanded the fort's stockade and prepared to make another effort to reach his stronghold on the Illinois where his aide, Henri de Tonty, anxiously awaited word of his commander.

That Christmas was a bleak one for the men, women and children of Fort St. Louis. But the holy feast day was observed. Joutel recalled, in the English translation, that ''Monsieur de la Sale being recover'd from his Indisposition, Preparations were again made for his Journey; but we first kept the Christmas Holy-Days. The Midnight Mass was sung, and on Twelve-Day, we cry'd The King drinks (according to the custom of France), tho' we had only Water: When that was over we began to think of setting out.''

On January 12, La Salle and sixteen companions, their five horses bearing such supplies as could be assembled, began a final attempt to save the colony. In the group were La Salle's brother the abbé, his two nephews, Moranget and the young Cavelier, the Duhaut brothers, Joutel, Hiens, Liotôt, Nika the hunter, La Salle's footman Saget, the young L'Archevêque, who was Duhaut's valet, the Sieur de Marle, Teissier, Ruter, Father Douay and the sons of the Canadian Talon, the latter two to be left among the Cenis to learn their language. Of La Salle's eloquent farewell address to the colony, Father Douay, who loved him, wrote: ''The whole colony was present, and were almost moved to tears, persuaded by the necessity of his voyage and the uprightness of his intentions.''

La Salle and his men left on January 7, 1687. There were only enough horses to carry the equipment. The men had to walk. Because there had been no decently cured buffalo hides or goatskins at the fort with which to make shoes, they suffered from the start from aching feet and the excruciating pain of blisters. Green skins, fashioned into crude boots, dried hard in a day's march. They ''hurt us so very much and we were often obliged to set our feet in the water to soften those buskins.'' Joutel was the lucky one. He managed early to trade four needles to an Indian for a well-cured skin, with which he fashioned some more comfortable shoes. Suffering as did the others, but without complaint or comment, La Salle led the way into the wet

cold of the Texas winter. Upon him converged all the tensions, disappointments and tragedies of many a month.

There is little agreement among scholars about the route of La Salle's last and most desperate venture. It may have ended at the Brazos, at the Navasota, or on a southern branch of the Trinity. But whatever his course, it took him through the general area that the later road from the Trinity to La Bahía, a branch of the *camino real,* would traverse. But if the place of the journey's ending is obscure, the tragic manner of its conclusion, two months after La Salle set out from Fort St. Louis, is unquestionable. The tragedy stemmed from a dispute over the marrow of a buffalo bone.

On the eve of the dénouement La Salle remained in camp near some Cenis villages, together with most of his company, while Duhaut, the surgeon Liotôt, the Sieur de Marle, Hiens, Teissier and L'Archevêque went out to hunt buffalo and cure the kill for the next stage of the journey. The hunters did not return at the expected hour. La Salle sent Saget, Moranget and Nika to find them.

When the searchers came upon the hunters it was evident that they had been successful. They were carving and smoking the meat. In one small pile were the toothsome tidbits to which the men who had done the killing were by custom entitled—the udders of a cow, the marrow of a bull, the livers and tongues. Moranget knew the custom of the reserve. But at the campfire he placed in his pan a marrow

bone from the tidbits that had been set apart. It was Liotôt's bone.
The surgeon snarled his anger. Voices rose in angry altercation. Saget
and Nika defended Moranget. Duhaut, who like Liotôt, had invested
in La Salle's expedition, sided with Liotôt. So did his servant, L'Archevêque, Hiens and their companion, Teissier. Moranget was becoming
more like his uncle every day, they grumbled, an arrogant man with
no regard for the rights of others. Anger, fed principally by Liotôt,
flamed throughout the day. That evening Liotôt conspired with Hiens
and Duhaut to murder Moranget, Saget and Nika. This is the friar's
account:

> They waited till Night, when those unfortunate Crea-
> tures had supp'd and were asleep. Liotôt the Surgeon was the
> inhuman Executioner, he took an Ax, began by the Sieur
> Moranget, giving him many strokes on the Head; the same he
> did by the Footman and the Indian, killing them on the Spot,
> whilst his Fellow Villains, viz. Duhaut, Hiens, Teissier and
> L'Archevêque stood upon their Guard, with their Arms, to
> fire upon such as should make any resistance. The Indian
> and the Footman never stirr'd, but the Sieur Moranget had
> so much Vigour as to sit up, but without being able to speak
> one Word, and the Assassins obliged the Sieur de Marle to
> make an End of him, tho' he was not in the Conspiracy.

Back at the camp, La Salle was disturbed because the hunting
party and the searchers were overdue. With two Cenis guides and
Father Douay he tracked the missing men. Later, Father Douay felt
that his leader had a presentiment of death. Before leaving camp,
La Salle had made his confession and, as they searched, the ordinarily
close-mouthed explorer talked at length of the mistakes he had made
in his life and of matters he wished he could correct.

As the four men approached the river bank La Salle fell silent.
Above them, buzzards were already circling. In the grass lay something white, spotted with red. La Salle picked up Saget's blood-stained
cravat. To advise any of his men who might be alive that he was near,
he fired his musket.

The shot was the signal for his death. The murderers, knowing
that La Salle approached, took cover—Duhaut in the high grass,
L'Archevêque nearer the path that feet had beaten to the riverside.
Discerning him, La Salle asked where the rest of the men were. The

youth pointed. La Salle walked forward into the trap. Duhaut's gun blazed and La Salle fell mortally wounded, unable to speak.

It was March 20, 1687. The most intrepid of France's New World explorers lay dying. The astounded Indian guides cringed at the sight of the white men's slaughter. Fully expecting the fate of his dying leader, Father Douay nonetheless took La Salle's hand and put to him the final questions of the Church. By the answering squeezes of the stiffening hand the friar felt that La Salle had forgiven his enemies. As the murderers crowded close, La Salle expired. The conspirators dragged his body into the bushes, leaving it there for the coyotes to eat. They then assured Father Douay that they would not kill him and that they had murdered La Salle only because they knew what their fate would have been when he discovered the death of his nephew, Saget and Nika.

When the cursing killers burst into the Cenis hut where Joutel had remained in charge, La Salle's lieutenant was certain he had but a few moments to live. The old Abbé Cavelier fell to his knees. But, inexplicably, Duhaut only assumed command, announcing that there would be no resumption of the journey, no return to civilization and justice.

The survivors divided into two camps, the conspirators controlling the food and ammunition. But the fever of killing had not burned out. Before the death of La Salle, Hiens had questioned whether he had to be killed. Now, unsatisfied and conscience-stricken, the former pirate began to berate Duhaut for the slaying and for what must necessarily be perpetual isolation from the world they had known.

In the mad finale, Hiens, arrayed in La Salle's scarlet coat, killed Duhaut, while Ruter, so Father Douay chronicled, "fired his piece upon Liotôt, the Surgeon, and shot him through with three Balls." The dying Liotôt made his confession to Father Douay, then, in what he thought would be an act of mercy, Ruter "put him out of his pain with a pistol shot." But he fired at point blank range and the flashing powder set Liotôt's hair and shirt afire, and Liotôt died enveloped in flames. A common grave was dug for Duhaut and Liotôt, "doing them more honor than they had done to Monsieur de La Sale and his nephew Moranget, whom they left to be devour'd by wild Beasts. Thus those Murderers met with what they had deserv'd, dying the same Death they had put others to."

Of the survivors, a few deserted to the Indian towns. But Joutel,

Father Douay, the Abbé Jean Cavelier, La Salle's nephew and a few others who had been guiltless of La Salle's murder, resumed the journey, plodding through the Nabedache village, the Nasoni village and on to the Red River.

Months later, the survivors reached the Illinois post. There they learned that Tonty had searched for La Salle at the mouth of the Mississippi and along its shores. None of the survivors reported the fact of La Salle's murder. Perhaps they feared that they all might be suspected and punished. Tonty, heading a sizable force, made another effort in the spring of 1689 to find La Salle. He followed the buffalo trail westward through the Cenis towns but nowhere did he find either Frenchmen or Spaniards. With his men deserting him, he turned back.

Had there been any usefulness in La Salle's colossal misadventure? He died without opening the way to Mexico for France. But he had lived among the Texas, made friends with them and followed their trails, which later became part of the *camino real*. In their country he had been struck down by brutal assassins. Some of his men had remained among the Texas to father half-breed children. And many years later, La Salle's coastal fort would be used to reinforce France's claim to territory westward to the Río Grande. Now, in the last decade of the seventeenth century, Spain could no longer postpone physical occupation of the land she held to as her own. The *camino real* had to turn east.

CHAPTER FOUR

THE WOMAN IN BLUE

T HE F RANCISCAN HABIT had been familiar to the savage infidels of the New World since 1524. Cortés had welcomed the first Franciscans, ordering the roads swept clean before them from Vera Cruz all the way to Mexico City and coming out himself from the imperial city to kiss their hands and their robes.

But in the century and a half that followed, the missionary effort had slowed down. There were not enough friars in New Spain. There might never have been enough had it not been for the additional inspiration of the holy mystery of María de Agreda, the Woman in Blue, exemplar of the saintly miracle of bilocation, who, as all good Catholics and especially the Franciscans knew, had mysteriously appeared to the Jumano Indians in 1625. They had read her *Mística Ciudad de Dios,* the *Mystical City of God,* posthumously published in 1670. And almost certainly it was the spiritual beckoning of the Woman in Blue which drew Father Damián Massanet to New Spain to work as she had, according to her revelations, among the Indians.

The skeptical can scoff at the Woman in Blue but all of Spain believed her story—most implicitly did the Franciscans. Dead since 1665, as legend or miraculous truth, she drew fresh bands of Franciscans to the New World, where they would be as useful as the adventurer and the soldier to the spread of the empire and the building of the Spanish trails.

Two compelling forces brought the Spaniards to the Texas. One was the revelations of the beautiful and dedicated Woman in Blue. The other was their fear of La Salle and his fellow Frenchmen. The

31

one meant the salvation of souls; the other the protection of silver.
One advanced the Holy Church; the other placed the something-less-
than-holy captains and soldiers in the *presidios* which were to be
strung thinly along the trails that threaded north and east.

This is the tale which became, near the end of the seventeenth
century, a magnet which drew the Franciscans to the distant wilderness of the Texas.

In 1629, fifty Jumano Indians appeared at the convent of Isleta
in northeast Mexico to ask that missionaries be sent among them. They
told Father Esteban de Peréa and Father Juan Salas of a marvel. A
white woman had appeared to them, the Jumanos said, and instructed
them in the truths of the Faith. To each tribe with whom she had
mingled, she had spoken in its own tongue. She had been dressed in
a habit similar to that of the fathers but wore, in addition, a blue
cloak. It was she who had told them to seek out the missionaries.

The fathers showed the Jumanos a painting of Mother Luísa de
Carrión, who was known for her saintly deeds in Mexico. The Indians
emphatically said that this woman was not their mysterious visitor.
The Woman in Blue, though similarly dressed, was younger and far
more beautiful.

It was strange that the Jumanos should tell this story. Only a
year before, the Archbishop of Mexico had asked the missionaries in
New Mexico if they had any evidence of instruction in the Faith
among the natives to the east. He had received reports that a young
abbess in Spain, Sister María de Jesús, had told her confessor that,
while apparently rigid on her bed, she had been repeatedly transported
in ecstasy to work among the peoples of a distant country. Could it
be that the Woman in Blue was this same Sister María de Jesús?

The following year, Father Alonso de Benavides, the former
Custodian of New Mexico, returned to Spain and visited the youthful
Venerable Mother at her convent in the small Spanish town of Agreda
on the border of Navarre and Aragón. Later, Father Benavides wrote:

> *I arrived in Agreda the last day of April, 1631, and be-*
> *fore saying anything else, I will declare that the said Mother*
> *María de Jesús, abbess now of the Convent of the Immaculate*
> *Conception, is about 29 years of age, not quite that, handsome*
> *of face, very fair in color, with a rosy tinge and large black*

*eyes. Her habit was that of the Franciscans, of brown sack
cloth covered by a white one and over this she wore a cloak of
blue cloth, with a black veil.*

The blue cloak of the Immaculate Conception met the Indians'
description. Had she visited among the natives, Father Benavides
asked:

> *The first time she went was in the year 1620. She has
> continued ever since until 1631. . . . She told me also . . . that
> she had commanded the Jumanos to call on us and that she
> had instructed them during all this time. She gave me all
> their signs and she had been with them. She knows Captain
> Tuerto* [a one-eyed Jumano chief] *very well, having given
> me his personal characteristics and that of all the others. She
> herself sent the messages from Quivira to call the mission-
> aries.*

Among the people to whom the Woman in Blue had appeared
were some she called Titlas. She had been transported some 500 times
to these distant peoples, María de Jesús told her confessor. She had
talked to them in Spanish but they had understood her as though she
were speaking their native tongue. She had urged them to seek further instruction.

To people of the seventeenth century the phenomenon of bilocation was entirely credible, as it is to uncounted millions today. This
last century before the Age of Reason was an age of the highest exalta-
tion and of a belief in the supernatural which sometimes took cruel
form. English settlers were burning witches in Salem when María de
Agreda confessed her bilocation. For Spain, there was no question but
that the Venerable Mother María de Agreda was indeed the Woman
in Blue.

Even before the revelation María was beloved and revered. She
had become a religious at the age of fifteen when her father entered
a monastery, and her mother, her sister and herself converted their
home at Agreda in Castile into a Franciscan convent. María had been
elected abbess at twenty-five, a position she held until her death. Word
of her devoutness had already spread when she undertook the building of a convent with but 100 reales, the equivalent of about five dollars. Within fourteen years the building, which still stands in Agreda,

had been completed. Philip IV himself visited her for advice, and her visions guided him. Two hundred years before the proclamation of the dogmas of the Immaculate Conception and the Infallibility of the Pope, she urged that both be considered *de fides*. For a while her book, with its apochryphal history in support of her contentions, was placed on the Index of forbidden writing. Through the influence of the Franciscans and the Spanish king it was removed from that list. Today there are many who seek her canonization.

In March 1683, a band of twenty-four Franciscans, bound for the mission of Santa Cruz in Querétaro, south of Saltillo on the road to Mexico City, sailed from Spain for New Spain in a plate fleet of eleven ships which expected to load the annual hoard of silver at Vera Cruz. The missionary venture had been organized by Father Antonio Llinás of the province of Michoacan in New Spain, who had opened Christianity's first apostolic college in the New World for the propagation of the Faith. They knew of María de Agreda and the call of the Indians for instruction. The missionaries' destination was the ancient friary in the city of Querétaro, from which the group would take its name. They landed at Vera Cruz, and there they witnessed horror.

As the fleet neared the city of Vera Cruz, at May's end, turgid billows of smoke obscured the face of the afternoon sun. Along the waterfront, aimless specks, no larger at first than fleas, grew into men and women and children, their arms waving in hysteria. Soon to the undirected motions would be added the dimension of elemental sounds, the wailing and imprecations and mournful prayers of the people of Vera Cruz who had survived an ordeal which the Franciscans at first could only surmise. The veteran soldiers and sailors knew.

To the southeast, sails wind-crowded in flight, fled a pirate fleet across the blue waters of the Gulf of Mexico, its holds heavy with the pillaged wealth of New Spain. In cabin and forecastle and above deck, lay other treasure, desirable but impermanent, naked, ravished girls and women of Vera Cruz selected for comeliness, to be enjoyed as a bright trinket is enjoyed, until it is broken beyond usefulness. Chained below in sweating clusters or on deck under the merciless sun crouched captive Negroes, slaves still but to different masters. Three of the cruelest of the buccaneers of the Spanish Main had done well; how well the Spanish plate fleet from Cádiz would not discover until the contrary winds changed and they could approach closer to the low-lying city.

From a launch, a young officer from the *presidio* of San Juan de Ulúa, 15 miles across the bay from Vera Cruz, shouted the terrible meaning of the frigates which now dipped over the horizon. He told too of the plea of the survivors of Vera Cruz. Pursue the murderers. Regain our women and our wealth.

Admiral Diego de Saldívar would have liked to follow the marauders, but his men were weak from short rations and their water supply was low. The pirates were far away. He called a conference of his subordinates. They agreed that any opportunity for a successful engagement with the enemy had passed.

That was on May 31, 1683. Not until June 6 did favorable winds permit the plate fleet to enter the roadstead and the Franciscans to learn the enormity of man's sinfulness. The knowledge came within minutes after they put out in small boats to minister to the living victims of sack and rapine.

The gold and silver ingots from the mines of New Spain had lain stacked like cords of wood in the city of Vera Cruz. Beside them, cowhide bags by the thousands held pieces of eight, stamped out by the Casa de Moneda at the City of Mexico. Leather bags contained dried cochineal, which would give the hue of brilliant scarlet to the raiment of grandee and officer of the king and all else who might afford such finery. Throughout the 18 months since the plate fleet had last arrived from Cádiz, endless mule trains had been bearing the treasure to the sandy, tropic port where Hernán Cortés had established the beachhead from which he had marched to the halls of Montezuma. Through the port now flowed the greater part of the western world's silver from the mines of Guanajuato, Zacatecas and Santa Bárbara. It was a time when men's bodies were counted as nothing. Only their souls mattered, and those who counted the stacks of bullion left the souls to the priests.

In the humid heat of May, the people of Vera Cruz—the proudly untainted Spaniards, the *mestizo* children of the not-always-willing union of Spain and Mexico, the mulattoes, the Negro slaves and Indians, and the garrison in the *presidio*—had daily looked seaward for the galleons of Spain, which came each year with casks of wine and bales of silk, embroidered hangings for the homes of the wealthy, and the more mundane supplies for a colony whose principal purpose was to gather the treasure which the plate fleet would bear away. At dusk on Monday the 17th, two merchantmen from Campeche, which had been expected in port with a cargo of cacao, signaled from far beyond the reefs that sheltered the harbor. The ships were pursued by pirates, the signals read, and would need fires after nightfall to guide them to safety through the narrow passageway. The captain of the port gave the order for guide lights, and that night the ships slipped past the lighted beacons into the harbor and cast anchor.

But they were not honest merchantmen now. Crowded into them and the buccaneer fleet which the darkness hid were 1,200 men. Their commanders were Lorenzo de Graff, onetime gunner in the Spanish Navy; Nicholas Van Horn, a Fleming from Ostende, as notorious throughout the Spanish Main for his heavy pearl collar as for his prowess; and Miguel Gramont, the French corsair with whom La Salle, two years later, would hope to rendezvous. They operated from the island port of Santo Domingo under the protection of the French. The buccaneers had captured the merchantmen days earlier. Now they were using them as cover for a coup which was perhaps the boldest and certainly the bloodiest in the history of piracy.

At midnight the pirate vanguard came ashore in small boats. In a matter of minutes they had scaled the wall and killed or silenced the sentries and garrison. Three leagues to the north, 1,000 more buccaneers had disembarked from ten other vessels and marched unperceived to the walled city of Vera Cruz, their footfalls muffled by the sand. At dawn they battered open the city gates.

According to the ancient narrative, the buccaneers forced the principal citizens of the city, the priests and 6,000 people—the estimate seems unbelievable—into the cathedral on the main plaza. Once their victims were inside, the captors nailed the doors shut, piled gunpowder against them and threatened to blow up the building if any rescues were attempted. Wedged so closely that they could do nothing but stand, denied water, almost without air and overcome by the stench of the packed, sweating bodies, many of the townsmen lost their minds. Many others died while standing upright, held in place by the living bodies around them. The living who fell were trampled by those who could not bend to lift them.

After nightfall the pirates entered the pitch-black church by way of the sacristy door, which they had not sealed, and amused themselves by scourging the prisoners. Separating the women from the rest, they led them outside where, as a chronicler put it, "neither the Spaniard nor the Indian, neither the maiden nor the married woman" escaped the lust of the conquerors. All the women save the crones were publicly disrobed and from the youngest and loveliest the buccaneers made their selections.

On the second day de Graff, his blond hair curling damply to his shoulders, hewed through living bodies with his sword a path to the center of the church and, placing a keg of gunpowder at his feet, threatened to explode it if the prisoners did not surrender at once whatever personal jewelry they might have concealed about their persons. The parish priest made his way laboriously to the pulpit and from it exhorted the sufferers to give up whatever they owned and so appease their tormentors. In desperate obedience, the townspeople removed rings, pendants, earrings, gold chains, whatever valuables they had on them and from the dead, and placed the objects in wicker hampers.

Not for three days did the buccaneers open the doors of the cathedral. Before then they had made sure they could load their ships without interruption and quickly; they had transported the men of Vera Cruz to the Isle of Sacrifice to the southeast, where they were kept under guard.

As a final tribute, the pirate chief demanded a ransom of 150,000 pesos for Vera Cruz itself and for its chief magistrate, who had been found hiding under a pile of hay. There was no help for it. Lacking ships as transports, the garrison of the island fortress of San Juan de Ulúa could not assist the town. The Spanish fleet was not yet in sight nor had any succor come from Mexico City, some 300 miles away. The city fathers wrung from the people whatever else they had cached; the ransom was paid just as the sails of the deliverers appeared on the horizon far out to sea; and at about the same time an Indian runner brought word that the Count of Santiago was approaching from Mexico City at the head of a body of Spanish regulars. He might have arrived in time had not his Negro and mulatto auxiliaries been riding in slow-moving manure carts which held back the entire column.

The buccaneers hastened now to take leave of the city they had raped. At the harbor, in a quarrel over possession of a casket of jewels, de Graff, the merciless giant, ran his sword through Van Horn; leaving his dead companion where he lay, de Graff snatched up the casket and took over prime command of the expedition. He and Gramont would live to harass the Spaniards for years to come, their sorties encouraged by France which, whether there was peace or war in Europe, acknowledged no peace beyond the line south of the Tropic of Cancer and west of the Azores. Beyond the Line, anything went.

In the days that followed, the Franciscans attended, not to the savages of the wilderness, but to the dying and the despoiled and the bereft, picking their way among the putrefying bodies to administer the last rites and to give what solace they could, until, worn out from grief and fatigue, they slept at a Franciscan friary.

Such was the arrival of these Franciscans on the continent which awaited salvation. Among this destined group were five who would travel the trail which would become the *camino real:* Father Damián Massanet, a stubborn Majorcan, who more than the others brought about the opening of the road; Fathers Miguel Fontcuberta and Antonio Bordoy, who walked beside him; Father Francisco Hidalgo, whose letter would reopen the road; and Father Antonio Margil, an ascetic flagellant who would be considered for the sainthood.

In a few days Father Llinás, the leader of the missionaries, said they could tarry no longer. He despatched his friars, two by two, on the road to Mexico City, each with a staff, a crucifix and a breviary. The grey Franciscans carried no knapsacks. They would eat what was offered, find shelter where they could, make no provisions for the morrow. Their companions were muleteers. Their lodgings were stables or the outdoors, their food the almsgiving of stableboys. Along the way that was sometimes dusty, sometimes muddy, they preached as Father Llinás had commanded: at Cotaxtla, at Santiago Huatuaco, at San Lorenzo de los Negros, Córdoba, Orizaba, San Agustín del Palmar, at Amazok. The missionaries were reunited at Puebla, then separated again for the long climb to the continental divide on their way to Mexico City.

This was a legendary capital, whose grandees wore diamonds in their hatbands, and even the slaves could be adorned with a pearl neckchain or bracelet; a city of abominations where rollicked drunken and debased Indians, Negroes and mulattoes; where the good-hearted tossed golden coins to the *léperos,* the lowest caste of all; a cosmopolitan city to which were borne the spices and silks and ivories and brocades of Cathay. In this worldly, wicked place, there was especial meaning in the words chanted in Father Margil's loud rich voice, the words of the *Alabado* in praise of the Holy Eucharist, which the thin, barefoot man would make known from Costa Rica to a little log mission near the Red River in the eastern lands of the Texas:

> *Whoever seeks to follow God*
> *And strives to enter in His glory,*
> *One thing he has to do*
> *And from his heart to say:*
> *"Die rather than sin,*
> *Rather than sin, die."*

They would stay in this place of temptation no longer than was absolutely needful. They must hasten to Querétaro and to the friary of Santa Cruz.

Because of these Querétaran fathers, Querétaro would mark the spiritual beginning of the road to the Texas as surely as Saltillo was its geographic origin. From it would go the friars to join the soldiers in the *entradas* to the northeast in their search for the French, the Kingdom of the Texas, and the land of the Woman in Blue.

In their relationship to each other, missionary and fighting man —the one the guardian of the spirit, the other the physical protector of priest and layman—were a team of antagonistic work horses, neither able to draw the plow alone, neither happy at the needful teaming. That each entertained a grudging admiration for the fortitude and endurance of the other is beyond doubt, but among those who beat the cross and the firearm into the parallel Spanish plows that cut deep across the Americas, distaste and respect walked hand in hand.

The soldiers grumbled that the priests were too exacting, their thoughts elsewhere than on the trail save when they witnessed or suspected the weaknesses of ordinary men. The godly brethren couldn't understand, or pretended not to understand, the natural cleavage of man to woman, or even the relaxation that a game of chance or a plentitude of warming *aguardiente* could bring. Good men, yes, and brave, without whom the expeditions whose purposes were establishment of missions and *pueblos* would be meaningless. But these intense, sandle-footed, prayer-chanting men whose minds dwelt so exclusively upon heaven and the herding of all mankind toward it, were not the most delightful of companions.

In turn, the friars had no reason to applaud their protectors save for their willingness to face death for little more than an odd devotion to king and God, and the occasional largesse of loot and women. Here in northern New Spain the soldiery, by and large, were morally an uncommonly sorry lot. The rank and file were mostly drawn from the scum of the northern Mexican towns. Some were of Spanish background and blood. A majority were at least part Indian. Almost all were ridden with venereal diseases and other maladies so prevalent as to be almost endemic, but they were men of rare endurance. The survivors of the life of the town and the expeditions were hardy indeed.

The Franciscans inveighed often against the immorality of the soldiers, who were inveterate gamblers, wagering their meager salaries and even their clothing on the turn of the card or a roll of the dice. So reproachful were the friars that the gamblers had to hide in the forest for their card playing.

No matter how deep in the wilderness they pushed, they took with them the love of bull-fighting. When they hunted buffalo, they would often capture young bulls alive, and enrage them until the behemoths of the plains were exhausted and ready for the kill. They raced their horses and put them through their paces for the entertainment of the Indians, especially the Indian women.

What the Franciscans abhorred most of all was the debauched behavior of the troops, who "robbed the Indians of their wives, bothered their daughters and did not know how to keep Christian countenance." As a matter of course, throughout the history of New Spain, the soldiery possessed the Indian women whom they found in the native *rancherías,* whether willing or not; even around the missions themselves, it was not safe for a young woman to venture far from the *pueblo.*

The friars condemned also the indifferent manner in which most of the fighting men performed their religious obligations. They were ever ready to invoke the blessing and the protection of Santiago before going into battle, but they grumbled at the time which the Church demanded of them. On most of the expeditions mass was celebrated every day, two or three sermons were preached each week and the sacraments were frequently offered. All feast days were observed and church attendance was obligatory. It seemed to the soldiers that they were constantly being summoned to help the clergy in their duties. Even when a baptized infant died, the military had to fire salutes while on their way to the burial place, with the mission bells clanging and the friars preaching that this was a day of glory because a saved soul was entering the kingdom of God.

But whatever their morals and however indifferent they were to their religious duties, the courage and resourcefulness and combat skills of the fighters of New Spain were admirable. They learned the hard way not to follow Indian tracks in the mountain country nor to leave the villages at night nor ever to abandon their horses. They had to master the difficult, required chore of bathing their steeds in brackish pools where man and beast alike could drown in the suddenly treacherous depths. They were vigilant at the watch, for they had to be or die. If the hours of sentinel duty were long, the midnight drink of *aguardiente* when the guard was changed was both reward and soporific, and a like dram at the beginning of the dawn vigil put life into aching bodies.

They must have presented a fearsome sight to the Indians when first they disclosed themselves. Most of the ordinary soldiers wore what was termed a *terno de armas,* a set of buckskin clothing—trousers, a vest and a doublet or jacket—and carried on the left arm an oval leather shield, the *adarga,* to ward off arrows. Additionally some of the officers wore coats of mail, but by the latter years of the seventeenth century the visored helmets had been discarded.

On their shoulders, the Spaniards bore a flint-spark musket, the arquebus, or a long lance, and at their waists hung sword or saber and small daggers. If they set out on horseback, as was most often the case, they wore cruel spurs; and on the several horses or mules allotted to each soldier were carried powder and bullets, additional arms and provisions.

Barring mischance, members of the *entradas* ate well most of the time. The leaders of the expeditions provided all necessities; *mestizo* servants cared for the soldiers and hunted game and prepared flour and corn biscuits and made up the milkless chocolate, the *atole champurrado,* which was almost the most indispensable item of diet. Usually the streams held a sufficiency of fish. The bisons which almost always grazed near the waterholes provided fresh meat as needed, with the surplus to be dried and salted for the lean days which might lie ahead. The Indian villages usually offered corn, beans, *tamales* and *pinole,* a cornmeal made from parched corn.

All in all, not a bad life for a footloose, adventurous spirit, except for the nagging priests and the vagaries of the weather.

On a September day in 1685, two years after the sack of Vera
Cruz, His Majesty's viceroy in Mexico City knew he would have immediate need of priest and soldier, not so much for the good of the
Church as for the safety of New Spain. He had just received from
Vera Cruz the deposition of one Denis Thomas, a youthful French
pirate whom the Spaniards had captured during a devasting raid
upon Campeche by the buccaneer Gramont.

Denis Thomas had sworn to his Spanish captors that nine months
earlier he had deserted an expedition led by "Monsieur de Salas"
while its ships lay at anchor at Petit Gouave in Santo Domingo. Before Thomas had taken his leave, his deposition continued, Nika, a
Canadian Indian hunter who accompanied the French leader, had
told him that a French fort had been built during an earlier expedition, on a great river, and that the purpose of the present expedition
was to seize some mines near the "Micipipi."

The viceroy was appalled. Spanish control of the entire Gulf of
Mexico was threatened. The river beside which the French fort of
Denis Thomas' deposition had been erected must be the one known
to the Spaniards as the Espíritu Santo. The mines could be no other
than Spain's own. And for nine months this expedition had been
loose in the Caribbean. Where was it now? Where precisely was the
French fort? The viceroy knew he had to act quickly. He must ask
Havana for a naval force. The coast must be examined, the river fort
and the French intruders discovered.

Storms delayed until January the departure of the search fleet
from Havana. Then, methodically, from bay to bay, inlet to inlet, up
the western coast of Florida and on west sailed the ships of Spain.
They could only sail on to Vera Cruz to report they had found nothing.

Now Spain itself was disturbed. A new viceroy, the Count of
Monclova, who wore a silver arm to replace the limb lost in combat,
was warned that "a thorn had been thrust into the very heart of America." The annual plate fleet with which the viceroy sailed was augmented by two frigates to supplement the naval forces in the Gulf.
Spain's orders to Monclova were succinct. Find the French, destroy
them and their fort.

Monclova decided upon a second sea expedition. It would start
from the Pánuco on Mexico's east coast in February 1687, sail east and
examine the coastline diligently. Not until August did the searchers
return. This time the seamen had found evidence, a wrecked boat

bearing the *fleur-de-lis* of France, but no sign of a fort. The viceroy sent out two more expeditions, neither of which added any further confirmation of the presence of the French. A search by land must be prosecuted.

The settlements of Nuevo Reino de León, the farthest east of the provinces of New Spain, were the most exposed to any enemy thrust. So the frontiersmen of Monterrey and Cadereita were entrusted with the assignment. None of them had heard of the Espíritu Santo river or of nearby Frenchmen, but if the king and the safety of New Spain required it, they would· have a look. The governor appointed a professional soldier, Alonso de León, to head the expedition.

De León explored both the west and east banks of the Río Grande but found nothing. The viceroy rewarded his efforts by making him governor of the newly organized province of San Francisco de Coahuila and ordered him to establish a *villa* and *presidio,* Santiago de Monclova, which would be the capital of the province.

On his way from Nuevo León to establish the villa of Monclova, De León halted at a mission in the valley of Candela well eastward from the future villa. There he met its founder, Damián Massanet, who had sailed to Vera Cruz with the plate fleet in 1683. Father Massanet had not tarried long at Querétaro; within the year he had departed for Guadalajara, where he had served with the Franciscans of the Jaliscan house.

It was no simple matter to lead an expedition. The commander had to be able to draw maps of the regions he discovered. He must be versed in the use of astrolabes and declination tables to find the latitudes. He must take soundings of rivers and bays, observe the natural resources, set down in writing the life of the Indians and offer geological hypotheses. In the Indian *pueblos* and Spanish *villas* which rose in the wake of the *entradas,* the commander had the initial power to invest subordinates with authority, to administer oaths and erect civil governments. Upon him fell the supervision of official elections and the taking of testimony.

De León, now governor of Coahuila province, and the designated leader for the expedition to find the French, had a more immediate task than the establishment of a *villa* and *presidio.* The Toboso Indians of Coahuila had risen in revolt. The governor sent out an Indian named Agustín to enlist allies. Agustín's journey, which brought him some 20 leagues beyond the Río Grande, led to a pathetic, foreboding mystery. He came upon a large *ranchería* where ruled a mad white chief. The ruler, whom Agustín thought to be about 50 years old, sat naked on a bench covered with buffalo skins. His body was painted like an Indian, and on either side an Indian warrior stood fanning him. He said his name was Jean Géry and that he had been sent by God to establish *pueblos* among the Indians. Informed that Agustín served Governor De León, he expressed a polite interest in meeting the Spaniard and gave the Indian some pages of a French book to be delivered to the governor as proof that the story that Agustín would tell was true.

When Agustín related this tale, De León and a party of twelve mounted men traveled posthaste the 62 leagues to the *ranchería*. Jean Géry's story did not make sense and assuredly he seemed mad; but as De León and his party entered Géry's house, guarded now by forty-two Indians armed with bows and arrows, the strange man knelt and kissed the priestly robes of the chaplain, Bonal. He then shook hands with De León and his subordinate, Mendiolo, with great courtesy, crying out in broken Spanish again and again, "Yo Frances." De León persuaded Géry to return with him. Whoever he was, he was a Frenchman in Spanish territory. He must be interrogated.

After the viceroy's *Junta General* questioned Géry in Mexico City, it voted in July 1688 to send De León out again after the rainy season. The story of a French settlement must be run to earth. The viceroy ordered that fifty men be sent from the *presidios* of Cerro Gordo, Cuen Came, El Gallo, Conchos and Casas Grandes in Nueva Vizcaya, and another fifty be recruited in Coahuila and Nuevo León, and that De León should take beads, cotton blankets, bundles of tobacco and shirts as gifts for the Indians. The Spanish fences were in need of repair.

By the end of March 1689 more than 700 horses and mules, eighty-two packloads of flour and hardtack and other stores, and the gifts had been assembled. The men of Coahuila and of Nueva Vizcaya moved out from De León's *presidio* near the site of the present Monclova, following the banner of Our Lady of Guadalupe, the Virgin of the Christian Indians of New Spain. At the Sabinas River, they were joined by the men of Nuevo León, and with them, eager and impatient, was Father Massanet. As part of his duties he would keep the *derroterro,* the log of the expedition.

De León's force for this first *entrada* to the Texas numbered 115 men and the Frenchman Géry, who had been returned from Mexico to act as a guide. In each of the *rancherías* beyond the Sabinas the Indians gave honor to the mysterious Géry. Obviously the madman was known. But he was of no use to De León for he knew nothing of the direction the *entrada* should take.

Father Massanet remembered a Quems Indian who had come to him and who lived somewhere in this region. The Quems was found near the Río Grande. He told Massanet that he had visited the French fort and could find his way to it again. The expeditionary force crossed the Río Grande on the yellowish-gray bedrock of a ford 30 miles below today's Eagle Pass, henceforth to be called Paso de Francia, Frenchman's Way, thence traveled northeast across the Nueces to the Guadalupe. This river was not reached until April 14. There a High Mass was celebrated in honor of Our Lady of Guadalupe, who thus far had guarded the expedition well and for whom De León named the river. De León and Father Massanet, with the Quems guide and sixty soldiers, now pushed ahead of the main body.

Soon De León's vanguard captured an Indian who confirmed the presence of nearby Frenchmen. There were four of them, he said, living in his *ranchería.* When the Spaniards approached the *ranchería,* the Indians made for the woods, abandoning to the white intruders the *ranchería* and their dogs, which were so loaded down with buffalo skins that they had not been able to drive them ahead. The captive Indian went after his fellow tribesmen, bringing assurance that the Spaniards would do them no harm. Shortly the natives returned and, embracing the Spaniards, cried "Techas! Techas!"—their word for friends. One of the Indians was wearing the habit of a friar. Father Massanet recovered it by giving a blanket in exchange.

The four Frenchmen had left four days before for the villages of the Hasinai Indians, the natives said. They told De León of the destruction of the French settlement some three moons before, of the massacre of the French by the coastal Karankawas and of the earlier death from smallpox of many of the French fort's inhabitants.

No need now for haste. There had been a French settlement; now there was none. De León and his vanguard returned to the camp on the Guadalupe. But before leaving the *ranchería* he left with the

Indians there a letter for the four Frenchmen, suggesting that they join the white men at La Salle's fort. Father Massanet added a note in Latin in case any of the survivors were priests. With the letter went a blank piece of paper so that a reply might be written.

On April 21 the expedition left the Guadalupe. The next day it came upon the empty, ruined French settlement on the little river. Along the way the soldiers picked up more than 100 arquebus stocks without locks or barrels. The Karankawas had carried them off and stripped away the metal.

Now De León and thirty of his men began an exploration of the coast, searching as far as the bay which today is called Lavaca Bay. He decided it was Espíritu Santo Bay.

A letter awaited him when he returned to La Salle's fort. It had come from the Texas country and was written in red ochre on the paper he had left with the Indians. Signed by Jean de L'Archevêque de Bayonne, it noted that the writer and one other Frenchman were tired of living with the savages and would like to join the Spaniards. De León and Father Massanet and thirty soldiers continued to the Texas. There Jean de L'Archevêque and Jacques Grollet, their bodies tattooed in Hasinai fashion, awaited them. So were rescued two Frenchmen, one an accomplice in the assassination of René Robert Cavelier, the Sieur de la Salle, who had dreamed of creating a French empire far west of the Mississippi.

Young L'Archevêque and Grollet said they had been away from the fort at the time of the Indian attack and so had escaped death. But as for Jean Géry, they had never heard of him. Perhaps he had been stationed at the Illinois post. The mystery of his identity was never solved.

But even more interesting to Father Massanet was the principal chief of the Texas, who now accompanied the Spaniards back to the Guadalupe. The chief brought with him a portable altar adorned with religious emblems and the figures of four saints and Christ. Even more astonishing, he burned a sanctuary light before the altar night and day. True enough, the Texas Indians had trade communications with Santa Fé. But to Father Massanet, here was God-sent proof that he was among the Titlas whom Mother María de Agreda had visited so many times.

Titlas ... Techas ... Texas ...

The blessed Woman in Blue! Father Massanet knew that it was

she who had led him here. Here, among the people to whom she had appeared, the Querétaran friars of Santa Cruz must labor. Would the chief like instruction in the faith represented by the altar, asked Father Massanet. The chief answered that he and his people would indeed.

Military policy might have dictated that Spain place a *presidio* or mission in the vicinity of the destroyed French fort near the coast so as to contribute to the control of the Gulf of Mexico and its coastal approaches to Spain's empire. But this was the working of God's will, Father Massanet was convinced. The Spanish establishment should not only be a mission but it should be specifically a mission to the Texas. Father Massanet promised he would return. He did; and Damián Massanet, more than any man, became the father of the king's highway to the Texas, to the land of friends, to the Hasinai, to the waiting people of the Woman in Blue.

Armed with the viceroy's orders to establish a mission among the Texas and protected by De León and his soldiers, Father Massanet came back to the Hasinai with three accompanying friars, Fathers Antonio Bordoy, Francisco Casañas de Jesus and Miguel de Fontcuberta.

The *entrada* went first to the ruins of Fort St. Louis to make sure no Frenchmen had returned. Father Massanet set fire to the fort's timbers so they could not be used again. The Spaniards then moved northeastward to one of the most important of the Hasinai tribes, the Nabedache, who had their village on the banks of San Pedro creek. Here, 3 leagues southwest of the Neches, near today's city of Weches, the Nabedache and the soldiers planted posts upright in the ground as walls for the little chapel of San Francisco de los Texas. The next day, Corpus Christi—May 25, 1690—the Querétarans sang Mass at the little chapel 800 miles beyond the outer fringes of Spanish power.

The official occupation of the Texas country by Spain had been achieved. To hold that land would be another matter.

Damián Massanet knew that in New Mexico the witch doctors in 1680 had temporarily wrenched their people free from the iron hand of Spain. Now he began hearing about the powerful Gran Xinesi, the mysterious spiritual and temporal ruler of the Hasinai. The Gran Xinesi must be placated. So Massanet asked the Caddi, his friend the chieftain, to send some of his braves to the Gran Xinesi with an invitation to visit the Spanish settlement. For three days he waited, not knowing that the delay was caused by the ceremonial necessity that the braves dance long in the presence of their all-powerful priest before escorting him to the chief's lodge.

After this ritualistic interval, the high priest of the Hasinai and the servant of God and His Son confronted each other. The reaction of the priest of the Hasinai is not recorded. Father Massanet preserved the white man's version:

> *He came advancing slowly, and bearing himself with much dignity, and with him was a crowd of Indians, men, women and children. He appeared extremely serious and re-served, and as soon as he reached the place where we were, the governor had him kiss our robe. This he did, and we sat down to dinner. I asked the governor to let our visitor sit by his side.*

As he took his first mouthful of food from the common dish, the Gran Xinesi pointed with the vessel to the four winds, invoking a blessing. He was gracious about accepting the Spaniards' gift of clothing for himself and his wife, but it must have been wishful thinking that prompted Father Massanet to record that the priest then told the Texas: "Now you will no longer heed me, for these priests who have come to you are the true priests of Ayihit Caddi."

Whatever contest would develop between the gods of the white man and the Indians lay in the future. In these first days on San Pedro Creek Father Massanet was convinced that the mission was firmly founded. He himself would return to Mexico to arrange for a continuous supply line, while Fathers Bordoy, Fontcuberta and Casañas would begin the imposition of the civilization and faith of Europe upon these remote Indians; and since there existed the French as well as the heathen, they would maintain a visible Spanish settlement against all encroachers.

De León suggested that fifty soldiers be left as a permanent garrison. Father Massanet demurred. So many unmarried men so far from home would cause too much trouble among the Indians. In the end his objections prevailed. Only three soldiers were left for the protection of the mission.

And now, a last element of the supernatural. Just before Father Massanet left, he related, the Texas chief came to him with a special request. The chief's mother would die soon. When she did, he would like to have on hand a piece of blue baize to wrap her in.

Why *blue* baize, Father Massanet asked.

Because, the chief said, that was the color of the cloak worn so long ago by the beautiful woman who had come to the Texas to tell them of God. No, he had never seen her. It was before his time. But his mother and the old men of the tribe had known her.

Now, beyond all doubting, Father Massanet must have thought, María de Agreda had spoken truly.

CHAPTER FIVE

A SOLDIER BLAZES A ROAD

THERE IS GENTLE IRONY in the good use to which Father Massanet, back now in Mexico and impatient to get supply trains on the trail and new missions founded among the Texas, employed every tidbit of fact and rumor concerning the dreaded coming of the French to the fringes of New Spain. The presence of the redoubtable Tonty was grist for his dedicated mill. So was the continuous trickle of stories of French beads and French guns among the Indians of the northeast.

Father Massanet must have discussed these tales almost rapturously with the viceroy and the courtiers and the military in Mexico. See, the French know how rich is this land. It must not be abandoned. The best way to save it is to establish mission upon mission and so, by saving the soul of the pagan, save the land for Spain.

The viceroy agreed. In January 1691 he elevated the country around San Francisco de los Texas, a log cabin mission, to the Province of Texas. As governor he designated Domingo Terán de los Ríos, who for the previous four years had served with distinction as governor of Sonora and Sinoloa. Governor Terán had skillfully quelled Indian revolts in his province, as might be expected of a professional soldier who had served thirty years in the Indies and Peru. In the western interior provinces of New Spain, he had won royal favor by opening a valuable mine. A good man, seemingly, to whom to assign the military protection of this new *entrada* which Father Massanet had convinced the *Junta de Hacienda*, the viceroy's cabinet, should be undertaken. The purpose of the *entrada* would be to establish eight missions "for our Holy Father, Saint Francis"—

Damián Massanet was not one to keep his sights low—to explore and describe the country, and to take custody of any Frenchmen, layman or priest, who might be smoked out.

The command was to be divided; the results of such division would be unfortunate. Governor Terán would direct the military operations, name the rivers and explore the land. Father Massanet would be commissioner and prelate of the expedition, in full charge of all supplies, horses and cattle destined for the mission.

Father Massanet's hand was evident in the more explicit instructions concerning the expedition. He had been shocked at the way in which the soldiers and the Indian women consorted. He had denounced the ransacking of Indian huts for souvenirs. So his directions read that the soldiery must "avoid all carelessness in conduct and example. ... They must be anxious to prove their honesty, their religious faith and their charity by their acts, especially before the Indians."

The keystone of the Franciscan missionary program was friendship. The secular side of the government—the governors, the soldiers, the viceroy himself—might and often did lose patience with the Indians. But not the missionaries as a whole. They were backed by the idealistic royal instructions promulgated more than a century earlier, which declared that no Indian nation should be "reduced to royal obedience under the dominion of the king, or of the Catholic religion, or of the missionaries, by force or violence. They shall be controlled by persuasion, kindness, gentle and considerate treatment." The ghosts of Cortés and De Soto must have shuddered.

The directions were specific in detail. Arms should never be used first against an Indian, only for self-defense. Indians should not be set against Indians. Whatever His Catholic Majesty was to gain by conquest and exploration could be justified only by giving the aborigines something of value in exchange. That something of value, which justified much else in the king's eyes, was the Catholic religion. The *Junta* reflected the policy of the king.

The military and the missionaries were split almost from the start. Governor Terán and fifty soldiers departed from Monclova on May 16. Ten friars and three lay brothers with a smaller contingent of troops under Captain Francisco Martinez left Querétaro at about the same time for a rendezvous on the Sabinas River. They saw no reason to detour 40 leagues to Monclova. Father Massanet could not hide his disapproval of the soldiers on the night the two parties met, for these protectors, displaying an exuberance that would not last, drank wine around their campfires and, disregarding Terán's own orders, blew their trumpets and beat drums in drunken gaiety that kept awake those who would have liked to sleep, notably the religious. Many horses stampeded. In the morning the steeds which were used to round up the runaways almost foundered because of the long, hard chase. And even after the horses were recovered, the expedition failed to get underway. Terán explained that he must write letters to his excellency, the viceroy.

The expedition didn't reach the reed- and willow-bordered Paso de Francia until May 28. That night forty horses were lost. Governor Terán reported that they were drowned at the crossing. Father Massanet asserted that they had stampeded during the night—thanks, no doubt, to the carousing soldiers. And so it would go.

Governor Terán gave the name Río del Norte to the river. Beside it grazed, too distractingly, buffalo for sportive hunting and fresh meat. The full party did not cross the river until May 31 when, lacking wood for the construction of rafts, the members of the expedition swam the river on horseback, the soldiers and friars going back and forth carrying 1,700 goats, sheep and chickens in their arms, the cattle, oxen and horses breasting the river on their own.

On Monday, June 11, at the Río Hondo, "from this place, we started for the Texas, a route pursuing a direction different from the one followed by the two previous expeditions." The expeditions to come would travel somewhat north or south of Terán's campsites. In general the road of the future, the royal road to Texas, would follow the route of Terán.

June 13 was a date that would have meaning; the expedition came to the *ranchería* of the Payayas, one of the Coahuiltican-speaking tribes. Here a mission would be founded and from it would rise the city of San Antonio. "This is a very large nation and the country where they live is very fine," wrote Father Massanet. "I called this place San Antonio de Padua, because it was his day. In the language of the Indians it is called Yanaguana."

On again they rode with the Payaya chief as guide to and beyond a stream where the Indians told the Spaniards they secured their colors for painting their war shields. Now came surprise and suspicion. On June 18, some 3,000 Indians, united remnants of the Choma, Cíbola, Cantona, Chalome, Catqueza and Chaynana tribes, converged on horseback, in two long columns, seated on small saddles with stirrups, to meet the man with whose color and purpose some were already familiar. Their head chief, holding aloft a wooden cross, led them. Behind him rode lesser chiefs and to their rear a standard bearer who carried an image of Our Lady of Guadalupe which Massanet had given the Indians the year before. The leaders kissed the friar's robes and his hands.

The greeting was fervent almost to the point of obsequiousness, but the tribesmen also brought sad news, contained in a letter from Father Bordoy and Father Casañas. Their companion, Father Fontcuberta, had died during an epidemic. Father Massanet had wanted to push on with all speed even before the meeting. The soldiers and the overwhelmingly large Indian party were becoming overly fraternal and any small incident might lead to serious trouble. The disclosure of Father Fontcuberta's death gave added compulsion. So, after the distribution of tobacco, pocket knives and other cutlery to the men, and rosaries, earrings, glass beads and red ribbon to the women, and the dispatch of two loads of flour to their *ranchería,* the Spaniards took to the trail again on June 19.

It was almost time for a rendezvous at La Bahía del Espíritu Santo with ships to be sent by the viceroy with fresh supplies. Captain Martínez with twenty men, and 150 horses and forty mules rode to the ruins of Fort St. Louis, but when he returned on July 19 he was empty-handed save for the two young Talon brothers, another two survivors of La Salle's expedition, whom the Indians had turned over to him. There was no sign of the supply ships, he reported.

Terán, growing ever more discouraged, urged the captain to return to the coast to look again for the overdue bilanders, but the missionaries' anxiety about their fellow Franciscans was too strong. The royal standard moved forward, the usual rate of progress being about 6 leagues a day despite the intense heat of late July. On the morning of August 11, the impatient fathers, offering explanation to no one, left the governor and his soldiers behind them and hurried toward San Pedro creek.

The swift-moving Franciscans held a mournful reunion with their brothers before they reached the mission. The missionaries from San Francisco de los Texas, accompanied by the Caddi, and many of the tribe had ridden out to meet Father Massanet. They bore bad news in addition to what Father Massanet already knew. Many of the

Indians had become dangerously suspicious of the white fathers, they said. During the winter of 1690–91 an epidemic had struck the Texas. Some 3,000 of the tribesmen had died, more than half their total number. The mission fathers could not stand by while the pagans died without chance for salvation. Whenever word came that an Indian was stricken they had hurried to his hut to baptize him. Understandably enough, the Indians connected the deaths to the strange rites of the Franciscans, especially to the water which was placed on a sick person's head. As more and more Indians were baptized, and more and more died, the Gran Xinesi had only to point to the deadly results of the white priests' incantations. The Hasinai became intractable.

During the spring the Indians had refused to break the ground and sow the fields around the mission as the fathers requested. They had grown impudent and worse, the disheartened fathers said. What progress had been made was now completely wiped out. The late-arriving Governor Terán found the priests disheartened and the Indians truculent.

All the governor wanted to do was get back to Mexico. He turned over to the chief of the Nabedache the sheep, goats, horses and cattle he had brought. Terán invested the chieftain with the silver baton of authority as recognition of his obedience and his inclination toward the Catholic faith, and as a token of royal protection.

Having delivered the supplies and blazed the trail, Terán was hopeful that he could return to Mexico without further delay. But there was the matter of the supply ships. So, on August 24, he took leave of the missionaries and he and his soldiers headed toward the Bay of Espíritu Santo. If the vessels were not at anchor, he planned to continue directly to Mexico City. The governor must have prayed that there would be no ships at Espíritu Santo. But the relief vessels and the viceroy's orders were waiting for him. The viceroy wished him to return to the mission country, to go beyond the established center and to build boats and explore the rivers and openings into the sea. Only reinforcements of fifty men and a supply of powder and ammunition consoled him.

So back Terán went, arriving at the mission near the end of October. An early winter was already setting in. Fogs and rains delayed the soldiers' departure. The Indians were openly insubordinate, stealing stock and horses, and Bernardino, the chief, who had been helpful earlier, was the ringleader. When the reluctant governor and his men started on the ordered further exploration on November 6, rain and ice impeded them. By November 25 "the country was covered with snow to a depth of two spans without any exaggeration whatever."

Perhaps Terán, with no stomach for going ahead, exaggerated the conditions. In any event, when he reached the Red River, he explored it for 3 leagues only; on December 1 he gave the order for the return to Mission San Francisco. He had carried out little of what he had been ordered to do. The mules carrying the equipment for the boats he had not built could barely make a league and a half a day. The men walked and their tired horses were used as pack animals. Terán promised them that he would swap their exhausted steeds for fresh mounts from Father Massanet's supply.

But at Mission San Francisco, Father Massanet, now openly at odds with the governor, refused to surrender any of his horses. They belonged to the mission, he said, and those which the soldiers had been using were past reclamation anyway. Terán answered angrily that the mission didn't need the horses, that even those which were at the mission had been carelessly handled and that Father Massanet was, indeed, actually butchering some of them to give to the Indians for meat. Whatever the facts, the rift between the two was complete.

Over Father Massanet's opposition, Terán seized some of the mission's horses. Then, abandoning his heavy munitions at the mission and using pack mules to carry some of his men, he headed on January 9 for La Bahía. Six of Father Massanet's missionaries accompanied him. That Father Massanet permitted them to leave is sign enough that even then it was evident that the project had failed. The new missions had not been founded nor would they be. But not yet would there be any turning back for Damián Massanet.

Drought had been Terán's enemy on the journey to La Bahía del Espíritu Santo during the summer. Now came floods and bitter cold. When the party reached the Trinity it was so swollen that Terán could hardly recognize it as the same river he had encountered three times before. The only way the raging flood waters could be crossed was by a raft large enough to carry men and horses, a small load at a time, until all were on the far bank. The building of the raft offered no problems, but a towline had to be taken across and lashed to the far bank so that the raft could be manipulated. Three men who knew

how to swim volunteered. One turned back midway in the icy river.
The other two reached the far side, but "benumbed by the cold, lost
the line without knowing it..." Another volunteer sought to carry
a line across. He reached the far bank, half dead, after taking advantage of the upper part of a tree which the waters almost covered. He
tied the line to the tree, but the current was so strong that the three
men could not pull the line when the raft was attached.

Then, in the only stroke of good fortune of the expedition, a
hollow log was discovered. The Spaniards converted it, after three
days work, into a canoe. Now a crossing could be made, however
dangerously. Men took turns paddling across, "each trying, by sheer
force of will, to row across with animals tied by their heads to the
sides of the canoe. Thus a considerable loss in number was avoided."
All day long and far into the night the canoe ferried men and animals
until all were across.

Beyond the Trinity the countryside was so flooded that it re-
sembled an immense inland sea. An Indian guide tried to avoid the
marshes, but even the hills were boggy. When a horse mired down six
men were required to pull it out. Not until March 5 did the exhausted
expedition reach the vessels which had been waiting at La Bahía for
two months for their return. The spent horses were abandoned at the
seashore. Terán knew that he had failed. The expedition had not
carried out a single assignment. "This was not due to the lack of
courage of noble souls who are willing to obey the orders of His
Excellency implicitly," he reported. "But it seems that it must have
been so ordered by Divine Providence."

But he had wrought more than he knew. He had not been ordered
to find and blaze the direct route to the Texas, but this he had done.
The achievement would be lasting.

Father Massanet had failed too, in the immediate sense. At San
Francisco de los Texas, conditions grew ever worse. Floods washed
away the newly planted crops. The mission of Santa María, which
Father Casañas had opened as a nearby adjunct to San Francisco,
had been placed too close to the Neches; its sole hut was inundated
and swept away. The crops, replanted in mid-summer, died of the
drought. The Indian men, more and more angered by the behavior
of some of their women and the nine soldiers who had been left to
protect the fathers, shunned the settlement. A relief expedition from

Nuevo León and Coahuila brought emergency supplies. But without way stations, the pack trains could not be maintained.

Finally, the tough Majorcan himself confessed failure. The mission must be destroyed and abandoned. He and Father Francisco Hidalgo, who had been with him at Vera Cruz, and their fellow friars, together with the grumbling soldiers and a handful of faithful neophytes, buried the heavy bell and everything else which they could not carry with them. They loaded what remained on the backs of their horses and mules. Then the hand of the Franciscan who had put the torch to the fort of La Salle set ablaze the wooden chapel in the land of the Texas to which the Woman in Blue had summoned him.

CHAPTER SIX

A LETTER IS WRITTEN
AND ANSWERED

PERHAPS THE CONSCIENCE of Father Francisco Hidalgo troubled him as he poised his long quill pen over the fresh sheet of paper. What would the Spanish viceroy in Mexico City believe if he knew of this letter? But what would God think if it were not written? The saving of souls in the Texas country was paramount to all else.

Carefully Father Hidalgo wrote the date, January 17, 1711; then the inscription:

> *To the Governor of Louisiana:*
>
> *Did the French Governor have any information about the spiritual and material condition of the people of the Texas among whom Father Hidalgo had begun to labor a score of years ago? Would the Governor cooperate in establishing a mission among them? If so, the journey should be taken by way of the Mississippi to its confluence with the Red, thence up the Red to the abode of the Natchitoches Indians and westward on the buffalo trail leading to the Hasinai.*

Father Hildalgo made three copies of the letter and placed them in the hands of Indians who would be traveling eastward to barter, with instructions to give the copies to the first Frenchmen they met.

His Indians of the Texas had never been far from his thoughts. They had refused nineteen years before to remain near the two small Franciscan missions and the missions had failed at high cost to the royal treasury and to the givers of alms. But while others might be willing to put off the re-opening of the too-distant missions and the creation of new ones, Father Hidalgo was not.

His first ally after the Franciscans returned from the abandoned missions had been the saintly Father Antonio Margil, who was serving as guardian of the Missionary College of Santa Cruz of Querétaro after a preaching journey, legendary even then, to Guatemala. Father Margil readily discerned the principal reason for the failures. His brethren had tried to take too long a step from colonized New Spain to east Texas. The Querétarans must not make that mistake again. He gave the order that at least one new mission should be founded somewhere in between, in Coahuila and east of Monclova.

Gratefully, Father Hidalgo and Father Diego Salazar traveled to the mountains of Lampazos. There they found the perpetually hungry Coahuiltecans, who offered them rats. The fathers promptly planted corn. Soon a group of Chaguane Indians came to them requesting that a mission be established farther to the east. On San Juan Bautista Day Father Salazar chose for them a site across the Sabinas River. To this mission, San Juan Bautista, the Franciscans brought sixteen Tlascaltecan familes, Christian and domesticated, from San Esteban, the Indian *pueblo* next to Saltillo, to instruct the savages in the ways of civilization. The civilizing process was interrupted when the Chaguanes dispersed to the forest. Father Antonio Olivares received permission from Father Margil to seek them out and recongregate them at a new location. This he did.

Father Olivares re-established the San Juan Bautista mission 5 miles west of the Río Grande and close to the Paso de Francia. Other tribes, seeking protection from the Tobosos, besought the fathers for missions for them also. Accordingly, the Mission of San Francisco Solano and Mission San Bernardo came into being, and the Presidio del Rio Grande was established to protect the cluster of missions, which soon became the most important resting place east of Monclova, 250 miles beyond.

The sites of San Juan Bautista and the Presidio del Río Grande became today's Guerrero. San Francisco Solano was destined to be removed farther east and renamed San Antonio de Valero. As for San Bernardo, in time travelers would marvel at its beauty and wealth and at its 20-league irrigation ditch bringing a sure supply of water to its fertile fields and pastures. Built of the yellowish gray limestone of Coahuila, its triumphant dome a guide to the traveler plodding through winter mud and choking on the dust of summer, it would become by mid-century one of the loveliest missions in the New World.

But the country of the Texas was yet unredeemed. From San Juan Bautista and Querétaro Father Hidalgo wrote letter after letter, even to the king himself, explaining why a mission to the Texas was so greatly needed. Yet even though the Querétarans had founded in 1702 a new college at Zacatecas, dedicated to Our Lady of Guadalupe and staffed with eighteen younger and more vigorous priests and two lay brothers newly come from Spain, it was not until 1709 that the aging father had reason to believe that his prayers would be answered.

In that year heartening rumors came to the Franciscans that some of the people of the Texas had migrated farther west. If this were so it would be simpler for the missionaries to reach them. But Captain Pedro de Aguirre and fourteen soldiers, accompanying the veteran Father Olivares and young Father Isidro Espinosa, went as far as the Colorado, only to discover that the rumors were false. Father Olivares would remember the beautiful river of San Antonio de Padua. He would erect a mission there; its chapel would become the barracks of soldiers from the Alamo de Parras Company and by their name The Alamo would be known.

But Spain was now too preoccupied for further missionary excursions to the Texas. So Father Hidalgo wrote his letter to the French governor of Louisiana and prayed for its safe delivery.

No one can know through what hands and in what manner the copies of the letter passed for the more than two years before one copy was delivered at Mobile on the Gulf Coast in the spring of 1713 to Antoine de la Mothe Cadillac, founder of Detroit and now governor of Louisiana. Governor Cadillac had been a much-worried man.

The little colony of Louisiana had been founded in 1699 at Biloxi Bay by the Canadian Pierre Le Moyne, Sieur d'Iberville, during a short period of peace in Europe. About the time Father Hidalgo started his letter on its way, Louis XIV, disgusted with the nonproductivity of his feeble Louisiana—whose 175 soldiers were an expensive investment for the protection of only 300 inhabitants—had been happy to sign a contract with Antoine Crozat, a notorious war profiteer. By this contract Louisiana was Crozat's to exploit for fifteen years and the king was saved the bills. Crozat had appointed

Cadillac as his governor, with instructions to make as much profit as he could.

Profit, his master had told him, could best be gained through the discovery of mines, if possible, and in any case by the exchange of French goods for the minted silver or the silver bars of Mexico. The front door to Mexico through the port of Vera Cruz was firmly shut. How then could the harried governor begin to carry out Crozat's orders? Perhaps by a back door? The letter from Father Hidalgo might help open such a door.

But entering where Spain said "no" could be dangerous business, an adventurous enterprise which could be entrusted to few among the settlers of Louisiana. Already Cadillac knew that among the few, one man towered. That man was Louis Juchereau de St. Denis, one-time officer in the king's army, explorer and Indian trader. Governor Cadillac ordered a passport and instructions prepared for St. Denis. In response to Father Hidalgo's letter, St. Denis would go as far west as was necessary to reach the friar's headquarters. There he would purchase horses and cattle for the province of Louisiana. If all went as planned, Father Hidalgo would get his eastern Texas mission and Cadillac his foot in a door opened to contraband trade from which the colonists of Spain and France might profit alike. To the passport of his representative, Governor Cadillac appended Father Hidalgo's letter as proof of invitation.

Louis Juchereau de St. Denis was no simple Canadian *coureur de bois*. He had been born in the family *seigneury* of Beauport in Quebec in 1676, the son of a father who would be ennobled fourteen years later for gallantry at the siege of Quebec. A second *seigneury*, that of St. Denis, had been subsequently acquired and its name added to that of Juchereau. When he was only a youngster, St. Denis had attended the Royal College at Paris and after he returned to Quebec he had served France on Hudson's Bay as a naval officer. When he was ordered to return to France he took with him Medar Jalot, a barber and surgeon, who would be his faithful friend and valet for many years to come. In 1699, the twenty-three-year-old officer, his capacity for leadership already established, sailed from La Rochelle with Iberville on the second voyage of the founder of France's Louisiana colony to Biloxi Bay.

In the ensuing years St. Denis came to know the Indians of the

lower Mississippi and the Red better than any other white man. He
explored the Red. He traded with the Caddo, the Yatasi below them
and the light-skinned, flat-headed Natchitoches, and won their friendship and respect. When the crops of the Natchitoches failed and they
turned to him for help, he arranged for them to move closer to his
own holdings north of Lake Pontchartrain and dwell among the
Colopissas.

It was no coincidence that these were the years when muskets
began to appear among the Hasinai and even among the Apaches,
whom the French called Padoucas—muskets brought as items of trade
or offered as gifts when the peace pipe was smoked. To St. Denis, at
Fort St. Jean on Lake Pontchartrain, came pirogues, loaded with
buffalo robes and deer pelts. He had found no silver mines, but he was
acquiring a rich understanding of the Indians and their languages, a
valuable knowledge of the country west of the Red River, the affection
of the tribes among which he visited and the beginnings of a profitable
trade.

And now, at the head of twenty-four men and bearing 10,000
livres of trade goods, he would enter proscribed New Spain.

The people of Mobile gathered excitedly along the quai and the
wharfs that ran alongside the cedar fort built two years before: Jesuit
priests and Capuchin missionaries, soldiers and Indian house slaves,

carpenters and visiting Indians from the bordering forests, farmers and hunters and trappers; the young women from Brittany only recently come ashore as prospective wives of settlers; the governor himself and his wife and their sons and daughters. A great moment was at hand.

Out of his heavily shuttered, high-roofed cypress cottage strolled the fastidiously dressed St. Denis, his scarlet coat, too warm for wearing in this September of 1713, neatly folded for the ceremonial occasions that might lie ahead. With him walked his friend Medar Jalot, the barber and surgeon. Within minutes came the last of the farewells, the first rhythmic strokes of the paddles. Ahead lay Mississippi Sound, the Mississippi, the Red—and Spanish territory.

But there were Indian troubles to settle along the way and it was winter before St. Denis crossed the Mississippi. Then, 80 leagues up the Red River, the party came to a monstrous log jam; not even a canoe could travel through it at this season. Here, where the pine-studded hills rolled gently to the river, the Frenchmen disembarked. At this farthest point to which men could travel by inland waters in the direction of New Spain, the pirogues must be abandoned.

At the Red, the Frenchmen were among good friends. For fourteen years they had been trading with the Natchitoches who dwelt here for deerskins and buffalo robes, for bear fat so needed as cooking oil and as grease for soap, for the salt required in curing skins and preserving food and in cooking, and which the Natchitoches scraped from three nearby saline hills into calabashes and bartered, not only with the French, but from time immemorial with the Indians of the Río Grande. Their name meant persimmon eaters as contrasted with the pawpaw eaters, the Nacogdoches, their allies farther west. St. Denis had joined them often at their feasts of venison and smoked fish and astringent persimmon bread.

With added purpose St. Denis smoked the calumet with his foster brothers. This time he had brought them a new gift, a gift of grain and seed corn for planting. He told them that from now on their friends, the French, would never leave them; they could be counted on always to remain nearby to protect the Natchitoches against their enemies. He presented axes and hatchets to them, explaining that they were to be used to make larger clearings for plantings sufficient to feed their French brothers. Their red-dyed reed baskets would have to hold more than just enough for themselves.

In the next few days St. Denis and his men and the Natchitoches constructed two log houses in which he stored the greater part of his trading goods. He would need to return only this far for more supplies if the Spanish and Indian trade required them rather than go back to Mobile. In this manner St. Denis established in the winter of 1713–1714 the *magasins* to store France's goods and gifts for the protection and expansion of empire. These warehouses became the first permanent center of white settlement in the present state of Louisiana.

After completing the *magasins* St. Denis left ten men to guard them while he and the balance of his small force, accompanied by thirty Natchitoches as guides and companions, made their way westward along the oak- and pine-shaded buffalo trail where now in the January sun the red holly berries shone. For identification as members of his party, each man wore a strip of buffalo hide around his arm, holding in place an ear of corn.

The travelers ate well. In the forests between the Natchitoches village and the Sabine, 50 miles westward, buffalos and bear and deer and turkey were plentiful. The rivers and streams offered fish aplenty and upon the chill waters swam geese and ducks and trumpeter swans.

Twenty-two days from the Natchitoches, the traders reached the Hasinai. The Indians remembered Father Hidalgo well and were pleased that these white men would carry to him their request that he return. Even this early St. Denis had developed his scheme: he planned that when he met with some Spaniards, he would bring a number of them back to the Hasinai. A Spanish outpost would represent a means of present and later trading of cattle and horses.

St. Denis remained among the Hasinai for many weeks, leaving only when he had traded all his stock. He then returned to Cadillac, waiting at the Natchez fort on the Mississippi, to report on his activities and pick up more powder and guns to trade for cattle and horses.

It is improbable that any other European had such a knack for getting along with the Indians of America. St. Denis made friends of them easily. He traded in the goods that they desired. He did not try to change their way of life; rather he identified himself with it. The people of the forest revered and all but adored the tall Frenchman and, because they admired his long, beautifully muscled legs, identified him in their sign writing with that limb alone. Whether the Spanish returned or not, the Hasinai would continue to trade with the French.

Having made firm friends of this western branch of the Caddo, St. Denis, accompanied by Chief Bernardino, twenty-five braves and three of his own men, set out for the Río Grande. The rest of the party would shortly depart for Mobile, driving before them cattle and horses so imperative to the development of the Louisiana province. St. Denis' French companions were Jalot, Penicault, a carpenter who would report on the venture, and Pierre Largen, a hunter and woodsman. Thanks to the Indian trade, he and his companions were now well mounted. Traveling briskly, far enough south to avoid the brushy, miles-wide Cross Timbers of oak, hickory, elm and shin-oak and their nearly impenetrable mattings of grapevines and briars, the party experienced little trouble in fording the Brazos and the steep-sided Colorado.

Then came the expedition's first test of arms. At the San Marcos, the Hasinai were surprised by a band of their traditional enemies, the Apaches, 200 strong. Not until two in the afternoon did French powder and shot win victory for the Hasinai. Twelve Apache fighting men and one woman were killed. Two of the Hasinai were wounded. The victorious allies pursued the attackers to their *ranchería*, where they imposed a peace upon them.

The Hasinai chief, Bernardino, assured St. Denis that there would be no further trouble. Twenty-one of the Hasinai returned home. The much-diminished party was now made up of the four Frenchmen, the chief, two Hasinai chiefs and one other Indian who had been wounded by an arrow and whom the surgeon Jalot persuaded St. Denis to bring along as he wished to study this "Nicest and Genteelest of all injuries." St. Denis reasoned that the small size of his party would be disarming to any Spaniard they encountered.

Six weeks and 120 leagues from the Hasinai, St. Denis crossed the Río Grande and entered the *presidio* of San Juan Bautista. It was as if a man from outer space had arrived. One of the astonished friars wrote to Father Hidalgo, who was then at Querétaro, that the appearance of the French was the answer to Hidalgo's prayers.

Certainly in these hinterlands of Spanish empire, the arrival of Frenchmen in territory closed to all foreign trespassers was a matter of supreme moment, even though the Bourbons of France and Spain were for the time being allies in the War of the Spanish Succession.

For two years, Don Diego Ramón, the commander of the post at San Juan Bautista, had been aware of the policy so explicitly stated by the viceroy: no foreign merchandise and no foreigners were to be admitted on any pretext. Yet here was a confident Canadian who explained glibly that he was seeking Father Hidalgo and would like to trade for grain and cattle for the hungry settlements of Louisiana.

Ramón should have sent Denis packing. He had enough men to do so forcibly. Instead, he placed him and Jalot under comfortable house arrest in his own home and waited for orders from the governor of Coahuila. Perhaps the sight of the bundles of laces and linen opened his eyes to the profits that might be made at this post so far from the heavily-taxed port of Vera Cruz. Perhaps also, thinking of the merchants at silver-rich Boca de Leones, some 60 leagues away, Ramón saw that he could profit from illicit trade in silver. Or perhaps St. Denis himself explained how they could help each other in such a business. St. Denis wrote Cadillac of the "piastres" and "lingots" which the merchants and miners of Boca de Leones would happily pay for his wares. He and Ramón most certainly must have confided in each other.

St. Denis could easily have escaped from the amiable Captain Ramón's home, but, as he wrote Governor Cadillac: "As seeing a good fortune before my eyes and wishing to put my name in repute, I rejoice at all that may happen. For I fear nothing from these people or from Mexico." He added, however, that he hoped that the governor would recognize the risk he was running and reward him with fitting employment at Mobile. He dispatched this letter on February 15, 1715, probably through the carpenter Penicault and the Indians. By that date he had been in friendly custody for seven months. They had not been idle ones. French goods began to appear in the *presidios* and mining towns of Nuevo León, Nueva Vizcaya and Coahuila.

His persuasive charm had won more than customers for his goods. The flashing brown eyes of Manuela Sánchez, the commandant's seventeen-year-old granddaughter, fired the imagination of the thirty-nine-year-old Frenchman. Jalot devised ways for his master to avoid the chaperonage which custom demanded. An ardent courtship began.

Legend has it that when the governor of Coahuila, Don Gaspardo Anya, angrily sent a twenty-five-man cavalry escort to bring the prisoner St. Denis to Monclova in chains, his intent was as much to take the Frenchman bodily away from the lovely Manuela as to abide by the regulations of the viceroy. Legend also relates that with his grand-daughter's lover in the hands of a jealous rival, the fearful Captain Ramón sent to the viceroy a belated report of St. Denis' arrival and his removal under arrest. The viceroy, the Duke de Linares, responded promptly. The intruder must be brought to Mexico and there cast into the common prison.

But St. Denis' luck held. He was recognized in Mexico City by some French officers, long-ago friends from France's Royal College who were now in the service of Spain. They persuaded the viceroy to permit their compatriot to lodge with a Spanish officer who would be responsible for his person. And when Linares himself confronted the prisoner he was so impressed by his gallantry, gracious manner and excellent Spanish that he invited him to dinner.

The ornate silver plate from which St. Denis dined in the home of the viceroy, the heavy silver sconces, the silver encrusted chairs and armoires and tables did not escape the Canadian adventurer's attention. Linares suggested that his guest enter His Catholic Majesty's service. Other Frenchmen had done so. St. Denis declined. There were more promising approaches to Spanish silver than the king's annual pay. But, however charming St. Denis was, Linares was not impressed with his later guileless, hand-written explanation that he had simply been searching for Father Hidalgo and trading for food for the French colony. The adventurer had described to Linares in his deposition on June 22, 1715, the beautiful country through which he had traveled, emphasizing the "natural affection" the Hasinai had for the Spaniards—but he failed to mention his warehouses among the Natchitoches or his long months of trading with the Caddo.

Soon the viceroy discovered that he had an international incident on his hands. Governor Cadillac had heard a rumor that 800 Spanish cavalrymen had intercepted St. Denis and carried him off in irons to Mexico and from thence to the dank dungeons of Spain. He had written the French minister in Madrid to intercede for him, and in this roundabout way the Spanish court had learned of this latest threat to New Spain.

The viceroy turned over to the *fiscal*, the provincial treasurer of New Spain, St. Denis' statement, his passport and a map he had made of the route. The shrewd official pointed out that non-Spanish merchandise, introduced into Nueva Vizcaya, Nueva Estremadura—Coahuila's some-time name—and Parral, would divert the silver from their mines to foreign countries. Moreover, it was extremely dan-

gerous that the French had learned the route to the Río Grande. St.
Denis' map was better than anything the Spaniards themselves had
produced. And, added the *fiscal*, Father Olivares, Father Hidalgo and
the other religious should be sent east at once to reestablish Father
Massanet's ruined mission of San Francisco de los Texas, to prevent
further incursions and—as an afterthought—to assure instruction in
the Holy Catholic Faith for these Indians "to which the zeal of His
Catholic Majesty is so inclined." Father Hidalgo would have smiled.

Now the royal *Audiencia*, the *alcaldes*, the treasury officials, all
the ranking representatives of the government joined the viceroy in
a *Junta General*. Everyone agreed with the *fiscal's* recommendations.
By early September Linares had not only ordered an *entrada;* he had
increased the number of proposed missions from one to four. In a short
time their number would rise to six. He named as commander of the
entrada Domingo Ramón, son of the commandant at Presidio del Río
Grande, and, in an astounding gesture which may have come from a
forgiving heart but most probably from recognition of superior quali-
fications, he asked St. Denis to become the conductor of supplies, at a
salary of 500 pesos! St. Denis agreed. Even the bewildered Jalot was
to receive remuneration of 100 pesos for services rendered.

Linares looked upon the new missions as instruments to halt the
encroaching French. St. Denis, the wily, adventurous trader, foresaw
that the bringing of Spaniards closer to his trading post in Louisiana
would make greater trade and profits possible for him, even though
the move violated territory France claimed as her own.

Some historians believe that Linares did not have the wool pulled
completely over his eyes. Assuredly, Spaniards participated in illicit
trade no matter how much the colonial policy opposed it. Especially
did the Ramóns adhere to the principle—or lack of it—of live and
let live, and a handsome profit to all. And throughout the lifetime
of the *camino real* to the Texas under Spanish domination the traders
who would travel it illegally would greatly outnumber those who came
with credentials. The royal road would become the contraband route
without peer. One can almost see the expressive Latin shrug from
both sides of the Río Grande.

Graciously St. Denis accepted from Linares a wedding present
of 1,000 pesos—how else could a Frenchman come into sufficient Spanish money for a wedding?—a fine bay horse and an escort of ten soldiers to accompany him to San Juan Bautista. There he would await
the coming and the passing of the winter rains, and the assembling

of the *entrada,* and prepare for his wedding to the lovely Manuela.

At San Juan Bautista, St. Denis and his companions found the missionaries and soldiery tense and nervous. The *pueblo* Indians were sullen. There had been grave trouble the spring before. Now there was trouble again. The friars had been marching the Indians to the graveyards, there forcing them to kneel to receive the lashes their wicked attitudes required. Then one morning all the Indians were gone. A thousand men, women and children had forsaken the Spanish outpost for the less disciplined if also less assured tribal life. To turn back this mass exodus, more than the *presidio* soldiers and their guns would be needed.

St. Denis knew well the psychology of the Indians. He volunteered to go after them. Alone, except for the omnipresent Jalot, he forded the Río Grande, where, on the east bank, the fleeing Indians lurked. There he lifted high his white lace handkerchief as a flag of truce and approached the deserters. He told them he knew what they would find farther east. The Indians there would not welcome them if they intruded upon their hunting grounds, and would kill them all. He promised that if they returned to the mission they would receive no further punishment. The *pueblo* Indians had been domesticated long enough to fear the insecurity of the hunter's life and the enmity of rival tribesmen. Docilely they followed St. Denis back to the sureness of corn and beans and an occasional piece of meat.

While the relieved Domingo Ramón organized his *entrada* and the jubilant Franciscans hastened back and forth between Querétaro and Zacatecas, deciding which missionaries should accompany the expedition and what they should undertake, more romantic preparations were also being made. The handsome St. Denis would soon wed his adored Manuela. Her father, the younger Diego Ramón, and Jalot, with an escort of soldiers, rode to Monclova—Ramón to buy a wedding gown for his daughter, Jalot to select the groom's costume and the soldiers to attend a bullfight.

The wedding mass was celebrated early in the spring of 1716. To each soldier in the *presidio,* St. Denis gave three pesos and a yellow cockade to be worn in his hat during the ceremony. The gay celebration of the wedding itself lasted three days, with much firing of muskets and drinking of wine and dancing. So was the relationship of the Ramóns and St. Denis sealed with a bridal kiss. It was to be a happy union for more reasons than one.

And ahead, the Ramón *entrada.*

CHAPTER SEVEN

AN OPENED TRAIL

T HE GRIEVING FRIARS whispered to each other that Father Antonio Margil, their most sainted associate, did not have long to live. On the cot in the adobe-walled cell of the mission of San Juan Bautista to which they had carried him, Father Margil lay on what must surely be his death bed. It had been twenty-five years since this man of once magnificent physique had landed at the tortured city of Vera Cruz. Now his body, from the sweating brow which spoke eloquently of his suffering to the thick soles of his feet, almost as tough as a mule's hooves, was wasted and ridden with pain.

Within and outside the cell crowded other missionaries. Some had hurried in this spring of 1716 from the nearby Río Grande camp of Captain Domingo Ramón's expedition. Here also were the brothers of the three missions surrounding Presidio del Río Grande—San Juan Bautista, San Francisco Solano, San Bernardo—praying in these waning hours for the apostle. However much Captain Ramón might fume, the eight priests of the expedition had no thought of leaving until they had done all that was possible to man. Even Father Hidalgo, impatient almost to the point of frenzy to return to his beloved Texas, knelt sorrowfully in the cubicle where Father Espinosa administered the Holy Viaticum.

The man whom the friars believed to be dying had wandered far in these twenty-five years. Barefooted, he had penetrated the jungles and scaled the mountains of southern Mexico, and trudged through Guatemala and as far as Costa Rica, taking the Holy Evangel to the Indians. His associates and the people among whom he moved had loving tales to tell. Once, when he had eaten a meal prepared by a farmer's wife in her home she marveled at the amount that a friar so famed for his spirituality could consume. She related that his answer was: "If we do not feed the burro, he will let us down on the way." The wayside crosses he had erected in the mountains remained to remind his converts of his coming. The great *Alabado*, the chant in praise of God and the saints, which he sang so lustily as he marched, had become the best-loved song of the Indians whom he had won to Christ.

Recently he had been stricken by what was surmised to have been a double hernia while helping to drive a herd of goats given as alms to the mission at Zacatecas, where he was to take charge. However much Captain Ramón might object, Father Margil's illness would further delay the Ramón *entrada*, already two months on the way from Saltillo and now only at the Río Grande.

For seven days the encamped train waited near San Juan Bautista while the missionaries prayed. At the end of that fretful week, Captain Ramón gave the order to resume the *entrada*. No one could have been more delighted than Louis Juchereau de St. Denis, who had his own ideas as to why the Texas should be Christianized. He was leaving his young and pregnant bride behind, but surely he would soon return to fetch her.

Father Espinosa, who would be in charge of the Querétaran missions in the Texas country, led the expedition out of the camp. Behind him rode Father Hidalgo, his white-maned head high, his mind fixed upon the opening of the promised land that his letter of invitation to the French—and the worldly manner in which the French had answered it—had all but assured. Behind them followed five more Franciscans and two lay brothers, then twenty-five mounted musketeers, each with a newly made and carefully bored weapon. Ahead ranged the Indian guides; behind in indiscriminate order, moved the remainder of the expeditionary force: settlers-to-be, mounted musketeers, soldiers and artisans and herdsmen, a Negro—seventy-five in all, afoot, on muleback, on horseback, or in big-wheeled ox carts, each with an appointed task for the weeks and months ahead.

The carts were crammed with blue and red woolen cloth, tobacco, butcher knives, beads, medals, ribbons and hats for the Indians; hardtack and flour and chocolate for friars and soldiers and muleteers; hoes, axes, hacksaws, hammers, chisels, oxen yokes, seed and cook pots for the projected mission. Securely loaded too were the special adjuncts of the spiritual life of the missions: amices and albs and chasubles, chalices and pattens, brass candlesticks, copper fonts for holy water, bells and surplices and pure wax for candles, sacramental wine from Saltillo, flour for the communion wafers and heavy black irons in which to bake them. The mules, bearing gunpowder from the royal arsenal, and luggage and tents and personal supplies, picked their way, patiently, serenely, without harness, in single file. And all around, more than a thousand goats and sheep under the eye of the Indian drovers, and nearly a thousand horses and mules raised the enveloping cloud of dust. None of the livestock was in the best of condition, for the countryside had been drought-ridden. The Río Grande itself was low, so low that only twelve goats were lost in the crossing at Paso de Francia.

Northeasterly to the Nueces River moved the *entrada,* beset with drought and depressing heat. The dry Frío and the Hondo were easily traversed. At the San Antonio River, where the flax grew nine feet tall, Captain Ramón came upon the springs which his predecessors had named San Pedro; he estimated that they could supply a city. The men explored the crystal clear San Antonio to its nearby source. Father Espinosa recorded in his diary that "this river is very desirable and favorable for its pleasantness, location, abundance of water, and multitude of fish." And St. Denis, ever the French soldier and opportunistic trader, observed that if this site could be occupied by 500 trained troops and the Bay of Espíritu Santo by a hundred, they could control the Texas, the San Antonio River and the Río Grande, which he called the Río del Norte.

At the Salado River St. Denis and Jalot quit the main body to range ahead in search of the Texas. After the barrier of the Colorado was mastered, Captain Ramón sent ahead an officer and two soldiers to scout the country.

For almost a month not an Indian had been sighted, but at Las Animas Creek, now Brushy Creek, a Mescal and a Yerbipiame Indian were cornered. Their *ranchería* was near, they said. Not for two weeks did the Spaniards come upon it, for instead of impressing the Indians as guides, they permitted them to leave. They entered a green wilderness country of enmeshed willows and vines and brambles through which Diego Ramón could find no path. Waist-high briars pulled at horses and men. Meandering streams were forded, then forded again later on. For a while the expedition seemed hopelessly entrapped. Even St. Denis, returned from the Texas, could recommend no sure way out.

Relief finally came. Forty Indians, who had been told by the Mescal and the Yerbipiame of the Spaniards' proximity, came to welcome them to their *ranchería*, an unusual one because of the inhabitants. In the large village dwelt remnants of many different Coahuiltecan tribes—Yerbipiames, Ticmamaras, Mesquites, Pamayas, Payayas, Mescals, Xarames—decimated by disease and the Apache, and now bound together by common need and a common language in the tent village which the Spaniards designated the *Ranchería Grande*. Their behavior was friendly. They constructed a bower in honor of Captain Ramón, St. Denis and the friars, and knelt there before them and kissed their hands.

But Ramón was apprehensive for the safety of his party. There were too many tribes represented for any one chief to have authority over the unstable group. The friars had recognized the chief who had the largest following. He had come often to the Río Grande on thieving forays. They recognized also others who had briefly tarried as neophytes in the missions before returning to the wild state and were suspect because they knew enough of the range limits of Spanish guns to be dangerous. Ramón ordered his men to pitch camp a musket shot beyond the *ranchería* and to be most circumspect when trading beads and blankets for buffalo and deerskins.

But no fighting broke out; sixty Indians even chose to accompany the white men eastward. Save for their help, the Brazos would have been a far more difficult river to cross. The Indians carried the goats and sheep across in their arms, one by one. At the second branch of the Brazos they helped build the rafts on which men and supplies could be ferried. A huge alligator scattered them for a while but, when Captain Ramón put a ball through the creature's eye, they praised him loudly and went back to work.

At last, at the western border of the Hasinai country, the Trinity was reached. St. Denis and Diego Ramón, the captain's son, pushed ahead to make sure that the prospective converts and barterers would be receptive to the coming of the Spaniards. Captain Ramón pitched camp on the western bank of the Neches to await word of what greeting he could expect. Two months from the day the expedition had left the Río Grande, the Indians of the Texas, in ceremonial attire, entered the Spanish camp in welcome.

St. Denis had prepared an impressive pageant. Resplendent in his brilliant red coat, its gold braid shining in the sun, he rode to the Spanish encampment at the head of twenty-five mounted Hasinai chiefs in full regalia. A gunshot away from the camp all of them dismounted, leaving their bows and arrows and horses, and marched in single file toward Ramón and his people.

The captain was ready for them. Lining up his soldiers to the right and the left, he marched between ranks toward them, holding aloft a banner with the image of Our Lady of Guadalupe. Behind him followed the Franciscans, bearing a crucifix. When the vanguard had passed through the avenue of troops, these fell in behind. The procession then advanced to greet the oncoming Indians.

When the two groups met, each halted. St. Denis dropped to his knee before the sacred banner. Ceremoniously he kissed Ramón and the missionaries. With infinite dignity, the Hasinai chiefs followed his example. Together, Spaniard and savage marched into camp, where blankets had been spread in a great circle on the ground. Again, before they all sat down in the council ring, the Indians embraced Captain Ramón and the happy friars.

The brightly daubed and decorated calumet, white feathers adorning its yard-long stem of cured wood, was brought forth. From his own pouch each Hasinai took a pinch of powdered tobacco to add to the bowl until it was filled. The tobacco was then lit and puffed by the principal chief. Meticulously, each Indian performed the pipe ritual, blowing smoke first to the sky, then to the east, the west, the north, the south and, finally, toward the ground. These were the signs of enduring peace. When the last chief had finished, he passed the pipe to Captain Ramón. Gravely he repeated the six puffs before handing the pipe to Father Espinosa. Each Spanish man and woman had his turn.

Next the Indians placed tobacco from their pouches in the center of the ring and invited the white men to accept their gift. Ramón ordered tobacco from the Spanish supply distributed to these friends. A young boar, roasted over hot coals, was sliced up for the feast. The Texas seemed happy to see the Spaniards. Many had felt a genuine affection for Father Hidalgo years before and had not forgotten him.

The following day, St. Denis brought in 150 more Hasinai braves. This time the chiefs were accompanied by their squaws. The women fed the Spaniards green corn, watermelons, melons, *tamales* and beans cooked with corn and nuts. The gorged Spanish presented the Hasinai with 100 yards of flannel, forty light blankets, thirty hats and three bundles of tobacco. The soldiers marveled at the fairness with which the leaders distributed the largesse.

Captain Ramón addressed the Texas ceremonially. He had come as the representative of the Spanish viceroy. The viceroy himself had despatched these presents in the name of his master, the king of Spain. The Spaniards were among them to save their souls and, in order for all to work together, the Indians should elect a captain-general with whom the white men could treat. After a short consultation, the Hasinai elected as their representative Bernardino, the son of the Indian who had visited Coahuila. He probably had the longest number of years ahead of him, they explained. Captain Ramón gave the proud young chief the silver baton of authority and dressed him in one of his own fine lace-trimmed coats. In a few days the more distant Nazonis and Nacogdoches rode expectantly into camp. Again the proper ceremonies were observed.

The Texas had welcomed the Spaniards back. The Spaniards must now try to change the Hasinai way of life, and civilize and convert them.

Accompanied by Ramón and a small guard, the missionaries crossed the Neches to a site 3 miles away, near some ancient mounds. Like the first Texas mission, which had stood 4 leagues farther west, they named the mission established here San Francisco de los Texas. Father Espinosa selected Father Hidalgo as missionary in charge. Any other choice would have broken the elderly priest's heart. One other friar and two soldiers would remain with him. Land for a *pueblo* would be officially set aside.

There were certain recognizably bad portents if anyone looked for them. The indifferent response of the Indians to the Franciscans' invitation to learn their way of farming could have been interpreted as an indication of vexations to come. Angelina, a friendly Texas woman whose name was given a river, relayed the benevolent summons. The answer of the Hasinai was that they could not leave their huts until the crops had been harvested. Might there not always be a reason that the time was not right? But no one gazed into a crystal ball. The Spaniards rejoiced and their joy was greater because of what they considered a miracle.

For Father Margil, who had been left sorrowfully *in extremis* at San Juan Bautista, had not died after all. Instead he had recovered his strength and with a Father Patrón and a lay brother, together with a few Indians, turned up at the Spanish camp. They had started out from the Río Grande on June 13. This spiritually and physically indomitable man was as purposeful a missionary as the New World would know. As his only concession to the flesh on his journey he had traveled on muleback instead of afoot for the first time in his career.

The happy reunion over, the Zacatecan and Querétaran Franciscans sat down in a rough shanty, built by the Indians, to divide the field of their missionary labors. Father Margil, as president of the Zacatecan missions to be opened in East Texas, spoke for his friars; Father Espinosa was president of the Querétarans. Above a line roughly corresponding to the route of the future *camino real*, the Querétarans would work; to the south of it, the Zacatecans.

Beyond the Angelina River, some 8 leagues northeast of San Francisco de los Texas and in the middle of the largest Hasinai village, the Querétarans established their second mission, Nuestra Señora de la Purísima Concepción, 6 miles south of today's Douglass. As with the first, it consisted only of a simple church of logs placed postwise in the ground, with a nearby hut for the friars. Father Margil and Captain Ramón established the first mission of the Zacatecans to the Texas, Nuestra Señora de Guadalupe, in the Nacogdoches village 9 miles southeast.

Far-spreading forests of oaks and walnuts, delectable plum trees, laurel and sky-reaching pines surrounded the small hill on which Father Margil's mission rose. On either side of the hill two creeks, La Nana on the east and El Bañito on the west, flowed through a maze of brambleberry and wild grapevine. From the west bank of La Nana bubbled two cold, crystalline springs, each filling a circular basin about a foot and a half in diameter. These springs would be known as the springs of Father Margil, *Los Ojos del Padre Margil*. And because the Spanish word for eyes is also *ojos* and there were two of them, the springs would in time be known as "the eyes of Father Margil." And so are they called in Nacogdoches today.

In a short time Captain Ramón joined Father Espinosa and St. Denis at the Nasoni village 15 miles northeast of Purísima Concep-

ción. There they established Mission San José for the Nasonis and the Nadaco Indians on the present Bill's Creek at the north of Nacogdoches county. With this task Captain Domingo Ramón had fulfilled his official orders.

St. Denis had also accomplished what he had in mind. He had brought the customers closer. When he left for Mobile he was accompanied by his father-in-law, Diego Ramón, and two other Spaniards. They took with them many more horses than they required for remounts. The horses so needed by the French settlement would be converted into silks and laces which in turn might become Spanish silver in the hands of wily traders.

We can only conjecture whether Domingo Ramón was truly surprised at the news that reached him from the Natchitoches while the others were away. To disbelieve that he had some part in the contraband dealings of his dashing nephew-in-law is all but impossible, but he made a convincing pretense of alarm when some Natchitoches tribesmen told him that Frenchmen were living in their village on the Red River.

Summoning to him Father Margil and the other Zacatecan friars, and a few soldiers, the captain hurried from Nuestra Señora de Guadalupe to the Red River. There he beheld with his own eyes a well-built log house surrounded by a stockade and situated on a small island in the middle of the stream. Only two Frenchmen presently were there, but even these represented encroachment on land claimed by Spain.

The two Frenchmen told Captain Ramón that they were expecting ten men as reinforcements; thereupon Ramón erected a cross, and Father Margil and his brother Franciscans intoned a Mass before it. It was a sign that Spain had not surrendered its claim to the Red River. Returning toward the Nacogdoches, the Ramón group rested among the Adaes Indians, some 7 leagues from the Natchitoches, their allies in the Caddo confederation. It would be well to have a mission here, as close to the French as possible. As was the prescribed procedure, the Spaniards asked if the Adaes desired a mission of their own. Yes, of course. Ramón named one of the Indians as governor, drew up a title to the lands of the *pueblo* and thus officially established Mission San Miguel de Linares de los Adaes, where Robeline, Louisiana, is situated today. It was the only Spanish mission along the *camino real* ever to lie within the limits of the present state of Louisiana; soon it would be the capital of the province of Texas; and for more than a hundred years it was Spain's outpost on the border between Texas and Louisiana.

Midway between Los Adaes and Nuestra Señora de Guadalupe de los Nacogdoches, the energetic commander and the priests founded still another mission, one for the 300 pierced-nosed Ais whose language differed from all the rest. This mission, Nuestra Señora de los Dolores de los Ais, was established at the site of the present day San Augustine, Texas. With its creation, the Zacatecans had the three missions they had been promised. Father Margil chose the mission at the Ais bayou as his own headquarters. The locations of all three Zacatecan missions would remain important in the history of the *camino real*.

With the six frontier missions established and evenly divided as agreed upon between the Querétaran and Zacatecan Franciscans, Captain Ramón removed his camp from west of the Neches to a creek only a league from Mission Concepción. There his men and their Indian helpers built a small number of cabins and enclosed them with a stockade. To this guardian fort on the *camino real,* just west of today's Douglass, he gave the title of Presidio de Nuestra Señora de los Dolores—Our Lady of Sorrows Presidio.

Single-minded Father Hidalgo might glory that he was back among his Texas. Father Espinosa and Father Margil might rapturously undertake their labors in these distant missions. The viceroy and the king and grandees in Madrid might celebrate the planting of the six missions and the *presidio* at the eastern borderline of Spanish empire as barriers to their intermittent foes and constant rivals, the French. But St. Denis' sturdy warehouse on the island in the Red River would in time sway the Indians of the Texas and beyond more than would all the missions the precarious road united.

In Mobile, St. Denis conspired with Governor Cadillac to widen the crack he had opened in the Spanish trade wall. The door to Mexico was now sufficiently ajar for certain people to whisper through. Captain Domingo Ramón was protecting the eastern border of the Spanish lands. Diego, his brother, prolonged his visit in Mobile. The elder Captain Diego Ramón, St. Denis' grandfather-in-law, commanded Presidio del Rio Grande at San Juan Bautista. It was what later inhabitants of Texas would have described as a set-up.

This time St. Denis' *modus operandi* must be different. On his first trip Cadillac had given the assured adventurer a proper passport, together with Father Hidalgo's letter, and had stressed the need of the Louisiana colony for cattle and horses. Henceforth St. Denis must operate as a completely independent smuggler. France and Spain were still allies in Europe, but New Spain's trade could be only for the benefit of Spain. The Spanish viceroy had informed the French that they intended to keep the back door as tightly closed as the front. Were Governor Cadillac to try to kick the back door open, the ministers of the French and Spanish Majesties would take exception. Yet if Cadillac did not move some of the merchandise which still filled Crozat's warehouse, the scheming lessor of the colony and the king himself would incur tremendous losses. So St. Denis must return to New Spain's northeastern frontiers as a trader without any apparent official backing. He could owe Crozat the cost of the warehoused goods until he had traded or sold them. The risks, though considerable, were worth the gamble. The chances of profit were tremendous.

But such an incursion could not be kept secret. Frenchmen, Spaniards and Indians visited back and forth between French Mobile and Spanish Pensacola; and from Pensacola Captain Gregorio Salinas Varona wrote the viceroy in Mexico that rumor was that 70,000 livres of goods were being taken to Mexico from French Louisiana. Varona added, conservatively, that he did not believe the value exceeded 30,000 livres. That was more than enough to bestir the court.

That fall of 1716 St. Denis made the plans which northers and winter floods would prevent him from carrying out until springtime. In the meantime he intended to keep in touch with the new missions and with Captain Domingo Ramón, the useful Spanish in-law.

Late in November he and an Indian retinue paddled up the Mississippi and the Red to the stockade at the Natchitoches. There he traded for horses and rode to the Spanish mission where Father Margil, weak from malaria, was in sore need of help. The French group aided in building additional structures at Dolores de los Ais and San Miguel de los Adaes. They comforted the other ailing missionaries, dejected over the poor response of the Indians to their ministrations and the desertion of some of the soldiers at the *presidio*. As a matter of course they had taken with them the best horses. No supplies had come for the priests and the garrison. Gratefully, Father Margil accepted the grain which St. Denis had brought from the Natchitoches.

At winter's end, eleven Frenchmen joined St. Denis at Domingo Ramón's camp. Somehow Domingo failed to mention their arrival in his official report to the viceroy. Nor did he report that they were traveling with His Catholic Majesty's mules, which he was returning, ostensibly unloaded, to Coahuila. He listed as making the trip only St. Denis, Diego Ramón, *Alférez* Francisco Hernandez, who was Domingo's dispatch carrier, and the necessary muleteers. But the mule train of undisclosed size bore the wares and the hopes of St. Denis, and his French and Spanish collaborators. St. Denis traveled ahead, impatient to see the infant daughter of whom an Indian had told him.

What happened to the convoy on the way to Coahuila was never made clear, but not much freight arrived, according to the official record.

Was a story of an Apache attack the one told to St. Denis? Was he short-changed? Or was the story one to cover up for loads diverted to Boca de Leones? Was it the same story that was told to Captain Diego Ramón, commandant of the *presidio,* who may also have been surprised at the small amount of goods that he finally seized? Was his report of the impounding of a number of *cargas* his way of telling the viceroy that he had done his duty, failing to mention the rest of the trade trove which officially he never came upon? Who can say now? But with all of Coahuila gasping about the *cargas* of French goods headed that way and with the viceroy alerting the frontier governors to many thousands of livres of contraband, Captain Ramón ostentatiously did his duty and seized seven loaded mules bearing thirteen bundles and a box of thread.

Certainly the Ramón family seems implicated if, from east Texas, Domingo Ramón had permitted the mules to set out with the illicit loads. But this was no time to sit quiet and wait for what might happen next. Captain Diego Ramón gave St. Denis permission to make a personal explanation to the viceroy of the thirteen bundles that had been seized. He probably urged his kinsman-by-marriage to hurry.

St. Denis, stripped of what remained of his trade goods, hastened toward Mexico City with a stop at Querétaro. There Father José Diaz was pleased to write for him a letter of commendation and confidence; after all, St. Denis had done much for the Franciscans. So St. Denis carried this supporting letter with him to present to the recently arrived viceroy, Baltasar de Zúñiga, Marquis de Valero.

The marquis was courteous. But there was more than enough smoke to indicate fire. From Coahuila, Governor Alarcón's reports concerning St. Denis were far from favorable. At San Juan Bautista, Father Olivares wrote that not only were Frenchmen in evidence but that three of them were even opening a mine of their own! In mid-July the marquis ordered St. Denis thrown into prison.

From his cell St. Denis argued that he was a resident of San Juan Bautista. He had married a Spanish subject. He had risked his life for Spain in leading the expedition to establish the eastern-most missions. He had gone to Mobile only to gather up his personal possessions so that he would have the wherewithal to enter the cattle business in his new homeland. The thirteen bundles and the case of thread were worth, all told, 5,500 pesos at Mobile, no more. He asked that the bundles be returned to him. As for those Frenchmen who had accompanied him—the viceroy knew of but two—they were his cousins and had probably already returned to Mobile. Emphatically he told the viceroy that instead of being thrown into jail he should be rewarded for his services to Spain.

On September 22, the plausible, intrepid Frenchman was out on bond, a free man as long as he remained within the City of Mexico. Soon thereafter he talked the viceroy into permitting him to return to San Juan Bautista to recover and sell his property. But the viceroy ordered him never to return to east Texas.

Whether St. Denis recovered the thirteen bundles and the thread is not known. After all, these were unimportant if he had shared in the profits from the mysteriously-vanished bulk of the mule loads. Neither is it clear when and under what conditions he departed from San Juan Bautista. Again he left Manuela behind him, with little Luisa Margarita.

A free man, though with all of New Spain's officialdom alerted against him, he made his way across the plains and down the buffalo trails to the Natchitoches village. During his absence the French had strengthened the stockade and garrisoned the outpost with twenty "beardless boys." The place was now known as Fort St. Jean Baptiste. From now on St. Denis, as commander of the fort, would guarantee France's border—and, as an inveterate smuggler, make capital out of the nearby Spanish settlements he had helped restore among the Texas.

Meanwhile, the viceroy had reported to Spain on the affair of

Monsieur de St. Denis. As soon thereafter as a galleon could bring the message, there came to Mexico in 1719 an order from the Spanish monarch. If Frenchmen attempted to send out another *entrada* by land or sea, the viceroy must imprison its commander in the castle of Acapulco; the rest of any such encroachers would work in the mines of Mexico.

The king also gave another command. Deport St. Denis and his wife to Guatemala. But it arrived too late. St. Denis was already safe in Louisiana. Manuela and his child were left undisturbed.

CHAPTER EIGHT

THE MISSION THAT BECAME
THE ALAMO

MORE AND MORE FREQUENTLY NOW, aged Father Antonio Olivares, who had helped found San Juan Bautista mission, bewailed his years. Even more often he protested that Spain was dragging its heels in the matter of a mission at the lovely river of San Antonio de Padua. His mind dwelt both carefully and angrily upon returning to that God-given stream beside which he had rested in 1709 when he and young Father Espinosa and Captain Pedro de Aguirre had searched for the Indians of the Texas.

But when the Ramón *entrada* had set out for the east, Father Olivares was not among the Franciscans who accompanied it. Father Hidalgo himself had seen to that. He had protested that Father Olivares, whom he had known well at San Juan Bautista, was too troublesome. The old man, anticipating his exclusion and salving what he could of his pride, had already requested the viceroy to excuse him from going because of "his age and infirmities."

But within the year Father Olivares had his chance and forgot the handicaps. No sooner were the east Texas missions established than alarming letters from them began to reach Querétaro. And Father Olivares, chafing over his uselessness, was delighted when he was ordered to bear the messages personally to the new viceroy, the Marquis de Valero, and to impress upon him the missions' extreme need of assistance. What better way to aid the eastern outposts than through the establishment of a way station close by the San Antonio River? Not only would he give the viceroy the direful reports from

Captain Ramón and Father Espinosa and Father Margil, he would suggest his own remedy.

The letters from the east which Father Olivares took to Mexico City were alike in their pleas for more soldiers and provisions. They related that French influence was everywhere apparent and that without more military aid the Spaniards could not combat the swift and furtive traders. Captain Ramón wrote that a *presidio* among the Caddo would help and that more troops were needed to protect the missionaries if they were to smash the idols that still decorated the temples of the Hasinai. Grain was in short supply. All in all, unless relief came quickly, the money and energy that had been expended in the past would go for nothing.

The letters delivered, Father Olivares began building up the case for a mission on the San Antonio or its tributary, the San Pedro. Hundreds of pagans were waiting there to be converted. The place itself was ideal for a *presidio* and warehouses, the grazing lands were rich, the soil fertile, the water supply abundant. Drawing upon the reports of previous *entradas* as much as from his own burning desire to found yet another mission where the pagan raw material could be fashioned into Christian souls, Father Olivares poured out to the viceroy a warmly persuasive catalog of merit:

"It is impossible to exaggerate the pleasant character, the beauty and the fertility of the province of the Texas from the Río Grande, where our missions begin, to the new ones which the zeal of your excellency desires to establish." Here grew flax in untold quantity, grapes of supreme richness, mulberry trees surpassing those of Murcia and Granada in Spain itself, nuts more abundant and sweet than those of Castile and with shells so thin that the Indians cracked them with their teeth. Here too were birds of infinite variety, and countless wild turkeys and deer and buffalo. The Indians, representing more than fifty tribes, have always been friendly to the fathers and are fond of Spanish goods and especially Spanish clothes, he said. They have repeated many times that they would like to be Christians and, as they have no serious vices and many virtues, their conversion to the Holy Faith would be relatively easy.

Subtly Father Olivares touched upon the possibility of mineral wealth as well as the presence of eager unbelievers. There were strong indications of a mountain of silver. Tracings of gold had been discovered; the green rock from which the Indians mixed their paint must contain not only alloys of copper but silver as well. To establish a mission would be simple. Father Olivares begged the viceroy to permit "this useless person" to gather together the remaining neophytes in his little mission of San José, renamed San Francisco Solano, which he had himself established sixteen years before near San Juan Bautista, and to employ them at the new mission as a training cadre, so to speak. No more than ten soldiers would be needed for protection and these only for a short time, for about the mission would congregate goodly numbers of peaceable Payas and Sanas and Pampoas, all of Coahuiltecan stock, long friendly to the Spaniards and all speaking a common language. Father Olivares pointed out that he too spoke the tongue of the Coahuila Indians.

The Marquis de Valero was more than convinced. A mission, a warehouse and a *presidio* would provide the answer to many problems. Through the neophytes at the mission the fathers could learn of French incursions among their savage brothers. A warehouse would store goods to be transferred to the east as needed. And from the *presidio* soldiers could be sent at periodic intervals to La Bahía del Espíritu Santo to make sure that no new French fort rose on the strategic bay to control Gulf shipments or cut the thin line of the road connecting the missions.

On December 7, 1716, the *Junta General* recommended the immediate occupation of the San Antonio River area and the establishment of Father Olivares' mission.

This time Father Olivares proposed that the mistakes of the past not be repeated. He asked that only married soldiers should be sent so as to insure against the excesses of the licentious bachelor troops such as those of Captain de León and Captain Terán. On the positive side, married troops and their wives and children would form the beginning of a truly Spanish settlement. Father Olivares would bring Indians of proven rectitude from his established mission to teach their newly congregated, uncivilized brothers to plant and cultivate crops. A master carpenter, a blacksmith and a mason should be employed to build the church and dwellings, and to instruct the Indians; a capable weaver should teach the weaving of flax and wool and goat hair.

And so, once more, the assembling of supplies: tools and provisions and gifts for the Indians, livestock and, for the chapel, a good picture of St. Anthony, 2 *varas* or 6 feet long. Set aside for the personal use of Father Olivares and his Franciscans were sackcloth, a box of soap for washing their clothes, a ream of paper, a dozen shaving knives, two guns for defense in an emergency and chocolate for their almost indispensable beverage.

The viceroy next appointed a governor and captain-general for the province, a position which had not been filled since the abortive penetration of Captain Terán and Father Massanet. His choice was the strong-minded governor of Coahuila, Martín de Alarcón. Governor Alarcón was ordered to proceed with fifty soldiers, all of them to be of pure Spanish blood and, if possible, married, to the San Antonio River site.

Understandably, time was the most vital factor to Father Olivares. He wanted to get underway at once. For a man long past his prime, he showed remarkable agility and determination. Promptly he went from Mexico to Querétaro to report, from there to Saltillo to begin assembling supplies, and from Saltillo to Monterrey, driving livestock before him. At Monterrey he was given military escort from Nuevo León to accompany him as far as San Juan Bautista "because of the well-known dangers of this part of the road." By May 3 he had reached the Río Grande, where he requested of Captain Diego Ramón and the governor of the Monclova *presidio*, José Múzquiz, the ten soldiers whom the viceroy had promised him. But these independent-minded officials refused. Already their forces were inadequate, they said. They would not turn over to the old priest a single man.

Without this minimum of military protection Father Olivares had only one alternative. He must wait. He drove his assembled livestock to his old mission, San José, 4 leagues distant, not to protect them from Indian raiders but from the meat-hungry *presidio* soldiers.

Meanwhile Governor Alarcón was taking what seemed to Father Olivares an inordinately long time to prepare his *entrada*. The crops in the eastern missions failed dismally that summer of 1717. Father Espinosa learned to eat an Indian delicacy, mustard greens, seasoning them with salty earth. Father Margil found the black flesh of the crow nourishing if not delectable. The missionaries at the six little log missions ran out of wax candles and flour for bread and wine for the celebration of the Holy Eucharist. Ill with malaria, they lacked the tamarind and *cassia fistula* which they believed provided a cure. The supplies of *huisache* and *copperas*, indispensable for making ink, were so low that soon they would not be able to write the urgent requests for help. In December, Governor Alarcón at last sent Father Miguel Núñez de Haro and an escort of fifteen soldiers into the raging winter storms with a small supply train. To Father Olivares' repeated entreaties, he said brusquely that he had much more to do than prepare for the *entrada*.

And in fact he did have something else on his mind. The viceroy had notified him of St. Denis' second trading expedition. Alarcón took depositions at Saltillo and San Juan Bautista. But no one apparently knew anything definite about the elusive Frenchman, no one that is except the busy-body Father Olivares, who had reached San Juan Bautista a few weeks after St. Denis had passed that way. The father reported that four Frenchmen had actually been at San Juan Bautista itself.

The governor could find no supporting testimony. Too many Spaniards and Indians were already involved in what was a potential if not an already lucrative trade with the French.

From the beginning the friar and the governor rubbed each other the wrong way. Father Olivares was aghast at the type of soldiers whom Governor Alarcón finally enlisted. He complained that the men actually enrolled were unfit to settle among the Indians as examples to them. They were the worthless, immoral offspring of worthless, immoral Spaniards: some half-white, half-Negro *mulattos;* some half-Negro and half-Indian *lobos;* some half-Spanish and half-Indian *mestizos;* some half-*mestizo* and half-Indian *coyotes,* human beings so low that they even attended the Indian dances and *mitotes* "just to get deer and buffalo skins from them." The governor's excuse, that it was next to impossible to obtain volunteers who were married and of pure Spanish blood, didn't satisfy Father Olivares.

Not until April 1718, was Alarcón prepared to leave. Even then he had enlisted but thirty-three soldiers, he said, and only seven of them were married men with families. He would claim in a later report to the viceroy that he had established thirty families on the San Antonio. Perhaps some followed after him. So irritated with the governor was Father Olivares that he refused to leave with the *entrada*, preferring to accept the ten soldiers assigned to him and follow after the larger party nine days later. But he was encouraged because 150 Indians from the San Antonio country had ridden past his Mission San José and there had promised that they would be awaiting him on the San Antonio, as prospective converts, when he arrived.

On April 9, the Alarcón *entrada,* which counted seventy-two persons, crossed the swollen Río Grande at Paso de Francia. It suffered little loss of the livestock, which included some 550 horses and six droves of supply-laden mules.

Six leagues west of the Medina they came upon the gaunt, emaciated Father Núñez de Haro and four of his soldiers who had been ordered to take supplies to the beset missions. They had struggled to beyond the Navosota River, but there floods had halted them. They had waited through February and March for the high water to subside, exhausting the food they had brought for their own use.

Some friendly Texas brought them corn; other tribes gave them roots which could have been potatoes. Then, when the friendly Indians left to plant their spring crops, the Spaniards decided to withdraw rather than remain and consume the food intended for the missions. Father Núñez gave up his tent for use as cover for part of the *cargas;* the soldiers cached them on the wooded banks of a lake, which was thenceforth called Laguna de las Cargas, the lagoon of the mule loads. Before leaving its banks, Father Núñez gave a Texas Indian a letter to the eastern missionaries, telling where the supplies had been hidden. Father Núñez had no way of knowing whether they had received the letter or not. But, acting on the probability that they had not located the desperately needed foodstuffs and other supplies, Governor Alarcón sent orders to San Juan Bautista for the dispatch of more supplies to the missions.

The Alarcón *entrada* arrived at the San Antonio river on May 1. Probably because of spite, Alarcón did not wait for Father Olivares to participate in the legal forms of establishing the mission of San Antonio de Valero, a little to the west of San Pedro Spring. But his triumph was a hollow one. Spry Father Olivares arrived later that same day in time to put his signature to the Act of Possession of the land given to the Indians by the king for their mission and *pueblo.*

Three faithful Xarames Indians who had accompanied him built for him a *jacal,* a thatched hut of mesquite wood. Here he waited all summer for the Indians who had promised him so faithfully at San Juan Bautista that they would join him at his mission on the San Antonio. The friar had his mission but no Indians except for the few he had brought with him.

Four days after the establishment of the mission, Alarcón took formal possession of a site three-fourths of a league upstream for the *presidio,* which, together with the mission, would become the most important points on the long *camino real.* The *presidio* was named San Antonio de Bexar for the viceroy's brother, the Duke of Bexar, who had fallen in the defense of faraway Budapest in Hungary against the infidel Turks. To the group of mission and *presidio* buildings Alarcón gave the collective name of San Antonio de los Llanos, St. Anthony of the Plains.

The governor had carried out that much of the viceroy's instructions. But he had not yet gone to the bay. There were strong rumors that the French planned a large colony on the Mississippi—which indeed they planted that same year and called New Orleans—and hoped to seize Espíritu Santo again. Alarcón found it all but impossible to reach La Bahía. His guides deserted for fear of the giant Karankawas, the cannibals whose fathers had wiped out La Salle's settlement. Cloudbursts and thunderstorms impeded his progress, storms "so frightful that all those who have experienced them in Spain as well as in these parts say that they have not seen any like them, for the shortest lasted six hours, with thunder pealing like arquebus shots in battle."

Having failed to reach the bay, Governor Alarcón returned to the Río Grande for more supplies. He came back to San Antonio in late August, just before the arrival from the east of Father Espinosa, Captain Ramón, Father Matías Sáenz and some soldiers. The three said they intended to go to Mexico to present to the viceroy the problems of the missions. In what seemed almost a miracle, taking into account the Indian wars and the high water and heavy rains, they had found at the Laguna de las Cargas the cache concerning whose whereabouts Father Nuñez had written his letter of direction. They had also passed, on its way eastward, the second supply train ordered by Alarcón.

Governor Alarcón, heartened by the presence of the soldiers who had come with Captain Ramón, decided to try to reach the bay again and from there to go to the eastern missions. This time he did reach the bay, but his visit proved simply that the French had not reoccupied the area. Hundreds of wild Castillian cattle, descended from some abandoned by De León, were unexpected proof of earlier Spanish visits. Alarcón's arrival in east Texas with only sixteen muleloads of food did little to alleviate the missionaries' needs. However, Alarcón, like others after him, followed trails to the Trinity that became the La Bahía Road.

On his mind these days more than before were the French. He had learned that two Frenchmen dwelt among the Caddo on the Red River. These Frenchmen, the friars told him, were "the ones through whose hands the French acquire slaves and other things of that land from the Indians. Since the Indians are so interested in muskets, powder, bullets and clothing, which they exchange for young slaves, wars are maintained and even brought about among the Indians themselves, causing many tribes to be destroyed who would otherwise be converted to Christianity."

Alarcón proposed an immediate attack on Fort St. Jean, the Natchitoches' post. The reckless scheme frightened the missionaries. They knew that if Alarcón and his fifty men were to attack the Natchitoches' stockade, the Hasinai might well come to the support of the French traders and kill them all. They had never liked or even trusted this high-tempered man. Soon they would let the viceroy know their fears, emphasizing that France and Spain were at peace and that the governor had no authority to break that peace.

A good omen heartened the Franciscans. In the early fall of 1718, the Jarames and Payayas and Pamayas, who had promised Father Olivares that they would come to him, began to gather at San Antonio. Father Olivares would maintain that they had put off congregating because they feared Alarcón. The governor had sent word that he would come after them with the sword if they didn't submit peaceably and soon to the civilizing forces of Spain and the Church.

Mission San Antonio de Valero now began to prosper. In January 1719, when Alarcón returned from east Texas, he appointed Indian *alcaldes* (justices) and *regidores* (councilmen) and an *alguazil* (sheriff) required for the simple form of self-government which Spain had instituted for the mission *pueblos* to replace the tribal structure. He ordered the digging of irrigation ditches for the mission and the *presidio*.

That spring the mission acquired its bell. Governor Alarcón had found it at the site of San Francisco de los Texas, the first mission which Father Massanet had established and later set afire when it was abandoned. That same bell may still have been hanging in the later church of San Antonio de Valero when it was turned over to the military and became known as The Alamo.

In the spring the neophytes planted watermelons, pumpkins, chile peppers and melons, and vines and fig cuttings transplanted from the orchards and vineyards of Coahuila. The process of civilizing them had begun.

At dawn the bell summoned the *pueblo* Indians to early devotions and instruction in the *doctrina*. It was then that the *fiscales* appointed by the friars took note of absences. Later a *fiscal* would lead any who had absented themselves willfully to the mission's cemetery, where they were made to kneel before the cross in penitence. Habitual offenders received lashes on their naked backs.

After devotions and instruction, the neophytes went about their appointed chores, so different from what the ranging hunters had known in their nomad life. They plowed with the single-handled wooden plow which the missionary or soldier-guard or one of the Xarames showed them how to use, or opened the long irrigation ditches that brought water to the fenced farm. They learned to guide the ox carts, put out salt for the cattle and horses, brand them and drive them from the mission's ranch to nearer the mission. At harvest time they brought the corn and beans into the communal granary near the chapel, from where Father Olivares would distribute these staples to the newest neophytes daily, and weekly to those who were learning to manage their supplies better. Once every two weeks he ordered a head of cattle slaughtered as a special treat. In the weaving and sewing rooms the women fashioned the garments of cotton, mohair and wool that took the place of the skins the Indians were taught

to despise. And, forever, work on the mission buildings continued, and through it carpentry and masonry became skills of men who had known best how to handle the bow, the arrow and the stone hatchet.

Not yet had Indian labor, supervised by the friars, produced the stone structures, the happy blend of the functional and beautiful, which stand today as reminders of the heyday of Church and Spain along the *camino real*. San Antonio de Valero's chapel, the friars' cells, the continuous rows of arch-portaled huts around a central plaza for the Indians were still built of adobe, their roofs thatched with reeds from San Pedro Creek.

To add to the beauty of the church service, voices that had previously chanted loudest around a victim tied by his hands to a tree, learned the liturgical hymns of the Church under the direction of *cantores* imported from longer-established missions. Apt pupils played the guitar or violin as accompaniment. Love of a new culture gradually won the hearts of the neophytes.

These folk whom Father Olivares and his assistant instructed were a simple people who would need time to learn the ways of European civilization. They gave up their roving ways principally for the mission's security, but, with the coming of spring and word that the buffalo hunting was good, the ancient excitement would triumph over the regular and dull regimen of farming and ranching demanded by the friars. The call of the roving life would triumph. Family by family, many would depart, their minds reeling with the remembered orgies of buffalo meat and the dancing of the wild *mitote*.

In the mornings the *fiscales* would report their absences and a missionary would leave for the distant hunting grounds where the neophytes,
replete with feasting, would usually greet him meekly and return to
the disciplined life.

In the establishment of San Antonio de Valero and the city which
rose upon the banks of the San Antonio River, Alarcón indeed had a
part. But he did not earn the affection or respect of the missionaries.
It was they who had the ear of the viceroy. So when he wrote that
he would resign unless he were given 175 more soldiers to strengthen
the province, his resignation was accepted.

CHAPTER NINE

A MARQUIS-BY-MARRIAGE
PROVES HIMSELF

THE WAR OF THE SPANISH SUCCESSION had put Philip V on the throne of Spain. But Philip himself was dominated by his second wife, Elizabeth Farnese, daughter of the Duke of Parma. Interested in Italian territorial advantages for herself and her children, she sent Spanish troops against Sicily in 1718. Promptly war spread through Europe again, aligning England and France against the Spain which had provoked the new conflict. The English destroyed the Spanish navy and the French overran the Basque countries before peace came again, in 1720, for a short while to Europe.

Europe's wars had their extensions to the Americas.

On a scorching mid-June day in 1719, the Franciscan lay brother and the lone soldier who protected him at Mission San Miguel de los Adaes could not have had much more on their minds than their daily religious and secular chores. Certainly they knew nothing of Elizabeth Farnese or Louis XV's retaliatory declaration of war against his cousin of Spain. So, to say the least, they must have been astounded at the sight of friendly young Lieutenant Blondel of the French fort, St. Jean Baptiste, at Natchitoches and six soldiers riding toward the log quarters of the mission.

But Lieutenant Blondel knew and, as he politely explained, he had been ordered to seize all Spaniards at the mission. Possibly he added with Gallic pride that just a month ago St. Denis, striking from Mobile, had captured the Spanish stronghold of Pensacola.

This was a delicate matter, the seizing of a religious. Lieutenant

Blondel tactfully requested the two Spaniards to saddle up. Next he ordered his soldiers to gather up the mission's sacred vessels to prevent their falling into the hands of Indian thieves who might discover that the mission was empty. On their own account, his men also saved the mission's chickens from possible mistreatment at the hands of the Indians. They tied the chickens to the pommels of their saddles. But as the soldiers mounted, the frightened fowl flapped their wings and squawked violently. The unusual sound and behavior frightened in turn Lieutenant Blondel's horse so that the mount reared and threw his rider. As the soldiers dismounted to help their commander, the lay brother escaped. Riding full tilt for Mission Dolores de los Ais, he reported to Father Margil the harrowing turn of events. The panicking of pot-bound chickens thus sped the tidings of war through east Texas faster than might otherwise have been the case. The flailing wings had done Spain a good turn.

At Mission Dolores the lay brother sputtered to Father Margil all that the Frenchmen had told him. The most meaningful bit, aside from the news of war itself, was that Lieutenant Blondel had boasted that a hundred French soldiers were at this very moment on their way from Mobile to drive Spain from Texas.

Prudently and in haste Father Margil, his mission padres and the fugitive brother withdrew to Mission Concepción, only a scant league from Captain Ramón and his twenty presidial troops. Father Espinosa of Mission Concepción, the frontier captain and Father Margil were alike satisfied that here they were safe from the French, at least for the time being. But eight of the presidial soldiers had wives as well as the oncoming French to contend with. Their spouses tearfully urged a further retreat before the enemy, preferably to San Antonio, or at least to Mission San Francisco on the Neches. The panic of the womenfolk infected the soldiers and even some of the missionaries. To quiet them Captain Ramón ordered a withdrawal to the Neches.

Father Margil and Father Espinosa protested. The mission Indians, who had accepted the protection of Spain, were begging the fathers not to abandon them to the Frenchmen. We will remain, said the fathers. Readily they signed a release for Captain Ramón, stating that they had chosen to stay of their own volition and absolving him from responsibility for their safety. Remain they did, for a while, but when Captain Ramón sent word from the Neches that he was retiring even farther, to the *presidio* on the San Antonio, the two fathers reluctantly joined him at the Trinity. From there, just before the winter's rains and floods, the harried Spaniards struggled into San Antonio de los Llanos, weary of the road and of meat without salt and of flour that was mostly husks from the bottom of the sacks. Only two of them had yet seen a foeman.

Warmly Father Olivares welcomed the Querétaran and Zacatecan fathers to Mission San Antonio de Valero. The soldiers found shelter in the thatched-roofed *jacales* of the *presidio* along with troops sent from Coahuila for the emergency.

These Coahuilan reinforcements provided for most of the Spaniards at San Antonio their introduction by proxy to José de Azlor y Virto de Vera, second Marquis de Aguayo—a second son of a noble Spanish family who had married his title and the fortune that went with it. Because he was a rich woman's husband, Aguayo had to prove something to himself and to his wife. It was well that he did, for he planted Spain's standards firmly only 7 leagues from France's Natchitoches post. The pointed stakes of his hexagonal fort would give the lie to the later claims of Napoleon and Thomas Jefferson to an extension of Louisiana's southwest boundaries beyond a bayou, the Arroyo Hondo, just west of Natchitoches. For more than eighty-five years after Aguayo's coming no official suggested that the *camino real* belonged to France. The Marquis de Aguayo had settled it, with the unenthusiastic help of Louis Juchereau de St. Denis.

The mythical treasure of the Gran Quivira and a love of country and adventure animated this able Basque soldier, who nine years earlier had married in Spain the twice-widowed Doña Ignacia Echever Subiza y Valdes. Doña Ignacia possessed most of the then Coahuila, Zacatecas and Durango. She was a great-granddaughter of Francisco de Urdiñola. All the descendants of Urdiñola, the Indian fighter and founder of San Esteban de Nueva Tlaxcala near Saltillo, were girls and all of them were rich. Doña Ignacia's own father had lent 6,000 pesos to the archbishop of Durango. He had then sailed to Spain with the record of the services performed for the crown by his wife's family and his own. He returned with the title of Marquis de San Miguel de Aguayo. The title was passed on through his daughter Doña Ignacia to her third husband, the proud and sensitive Basque, Azlor y Virto.

The marquis enjoyed the title, but how fitting it would be to make a fortune in his own right.

Four years before the reopening of hostilities between France and Spain in 1719, the marquis-by-marriage had thought that he had found a quick road to riches. José de Urrutia, a soldier who had remained in east Texas when Father Massanet burned Mission San Francisco, was certain that Gran Quivira, the fabulous country of gold, lay just northeast of the Kingdom of the Texas. He told the marquis so.

In 1715, Aguayo had presented a lengthy memorial to the viceroy in which he recommended the formation of an *entrada* to seek out the treasure land. But other matters occupied him until the declaration of war provided good reason—or excuse—to push beyond the eastern limits of Spanish territory and into France's empire to the east of the land of the Texas. Urrutia could not accompany him. All the better. Aguayo would gamble alone to win Quivira. That would make his wife proud.

Even before the outbreak of war, Viceroy de Valero had received from the king the necessary orders for such an expedition as that which the Marquis de Aguayo proposed. These *cedulas* had authorized him to increase the military guard at the frontier, to send out additional missionaries and to establish a *presidio* at La Bahía del Espíritu Santo. Now that war had been declared a mighty *entrada* would be needed to confront the French among the Natchitoches and along the Red River; perhaps, too, at the feeble post of New Orleans. The viceroy welcomed the aid of the rich marquis, whom he named Governor of Coahuila.

It took the Marquis de Aguayo months to prepare for the *entrada,* as well it might. The logistics of providing for 500 men who would travel overland for more than a thousand miles might have dismayed a less determined man. The *entrada's* success would be his gift to Spain. As for himself, and the wealth of Gran Quivira, that was another story.

More had to be gathered together than the instruments of war and supplies for an army's survival. Aguayo ordered from Mexico the rough sack clothing to be presented to the ordinary Indian braves, beribboned Spanish suits for friendly chieftains and many another gift as well—but no guns. France gave muskets to her Indian allies; Spain gave clothes and blankets and missions.

Aguayo's *entrada* would also need hundreds of muleloads of corn at 360 pounds-to-the-load. The marquis ordered that no one in his province of Coahuila sell corn to anyone save himself or his agents until his needs were filled. And horses—his aides estimated that at least 3,500 horses would be required. So Aguayo waited at Monclova until June 1720, for horses and horsemen and supplies to be rounded up. Five hundred men enlisted from Nuevo León, Coahuila and Parras, and 3,600 horses were collected. That was the tally when the recruits started from Saltillo. But when they reached the rendezvous at Monclova, they drove only 560 horses before them. The rest lay dead or abandoned by the wayside. Drought and unbearable heat had almost wiped out the herd on the way.

The Marquis sent messengers to every *hacienda*. They must supply him with 3,400 more horses. While he waited, his army began to melt away. The deserters were court-martialed and shot in the main plaza of Monclova as a lesson to the rest, many of whom had been taken from prison. Others were young boys signed up by their fathers, who kept most of the 450 pesos advance pay.

Not until November 16, 1720, did Aguayo's *entrada* leave Monclova. The marquis could count 500 men, nearly 4,000 mounts, and a train of 600 mules loaded with clothing, foodstuffs and arms and powder from Mexico. The six brass cannon of the expedition had been dragged through La Angostura, the pass above Saltillo, and on down the valley into Monclova.

Inevitably, floods soon slowed the *entrada*. It was Christmas before Aguayo began crossing the Río Grande. He had expected to use Indian canoes fashioned of skins pulled taut over wooden frames. At the Sabinas crossing the canoes leaked because of a lack of resin. New ones were built at the Río Grande, but they too were leaky. Makeshift rafts of ten beams attached to barrels were constructed. Fifteen of the best swimmers were selected to draw the mule-laden rafts across the river, a task they performed in a winter so cold that only on rainy days did the temperature rise enough for them to take to the water. No more than six loaded mules could be crossed over at a time. The marquis stood on the bank to encourage the swimmers with brandy and hot chocolate and food, but the last of the *entrada* did not reach the

eastern shore of the Río Grande until March 23, almost two months
after the crossing was undertaken.

Four months had elapsed. The marquis had spent thousands of
pesos. Then he received disconcerting news from the viceroy. A truce
was being negotiated between Spain and France. The marquis' operation could accordingly be only defensive. He must hold only what
Spain had always claimed.

But however specific the orders of the viceroy, the Marquis de
Aguayo wore the mantle of the last of the *conquistadores,* who fought
for Spain but sought gold on their own account as well as the king's.
And whatever was happening in Europe, the French to the east still
had to be reckoned with. Of this the marquis was sure.

From Captain Matías García at the *presidio* at Béxar came a
message to Aguayo, relaying a report from friendly Sanas Indians
that St. Denis had called a convocation of all the Texas tribes north
of the Texas road and between the two arms of the Brazos. García had
sent the loyal Chestengal Indian, Juan Rodríguez, to ascertain the
truth of the story. Rodríguez could not find any Indians in their
accustomed haunts even though he had gone almost to the Brazos
itself. The story must be true. St. Denis was planning to lead the Indians against Spain.

The marquis sent a strong force ahead under Lieutenant-General
Fernando Pedro de Almazán to reinforce Béxar. He ordered the well-
tried Captain Domingo Ramón to go down from Béxar to La Bahía del
Espíritu Santo with forty men. The last of the Spanish *entradas*
through Texas resumed its march toward Béxar.

There was no doubting now where the *camino real* ran. From
Saltillo to Monclova, from Monclova to San Juan Bautista and Paso
de Francia, from the Río Grande to San Antonio de los Llanos, the
trail was well marked. In the Aguayo *entrada* was many a man who
had traveled the way before: Father Espinosa, who had kept a diary
himself, and the other missionaries; such soldiers as Captain Ramón,
who had written a long report; common militiamen who had also gone
all the way to east Texas and back, not once, but twice and even three
times as escorts for mule trains and missionaries.

But even though the way was known and clear, the army knew
excitement and tension. The last *entrada* was moving east to assert
the inviolate borders of Spain, to return its missionaries to their log

chapels near the shaded streams in the pine lands of east Texas, perhaps to discover dazzling mines of silver and gold and precious stones as Urrutia had predicted.

But no *entrada* was ever free from the whims of the Texas weather. During the two days before the arrival at San Antonio, storms scattered the horses and mules of two of the companies. Afterward came a 9-league march without water. But the *entrada* arrived safely at San Pedro Creek. In gratitude the Marquis de Aguayo marched his army straight to the San Antonio de Valero Mission so that "the soldiers might offer their hearts to God from the time they took their first steps in the province of Nuevas Filipinas."

Shortly, he conferred with Father Margil who, while waiting to return to the east, had organized a new mission under the marquis' sponsorship. This mission of San José y San Miguel de Aguayo—San José for the patron saint of a Spaniard who had given Father Margil a statue of St. Joseph, and San Miguel for the new governor's patron saint, Saint Michael—was destined to become one of the most stately in New Spain. Partially restored, Mission San José stands today as a reminder of the saintly priest and the courageous marquis.

Soldier and priest and muleteer rejoiced again on April 18, when word came from Captain Ramón that he had taken possession of Espíritu Santo Bay without encountering a single Frenchman.

The bay was the key to the province. The marquis immediately sent a petition to the viceroy, asking permission to transport supplies from Vera Cruz to La Bahía. Without waiting for an answer, he ordered his agents to purchase a bilander, a freight boat, to transport corn and other provisions for his men by way of the port. But this logical employment of La Bahía was sanctioned only as a war measure. A few months later, with the border established and the threat of war ended, Spain ordered the port closed. It was the old and eventually destructive Spanish policy of denying the development of ports for fear they would be used to the advantage of other nations.

On May 13 the *entrada*, reinforced by two more cavalry units, left Béxar. It was guided by Juan Rodríguez, who suggested a more northerly route than had been taken in the past. It would be better, he said, to cross the many smaller tributary streams which made up the arms of the Brazos, one after another, rather than conquer the Brazos farther to the south where, grown great at this season, it would be unfordable.

There was an Eden-like quality to the flower-carpeted plain along which the *entrada* now moved and to the small hills whose closely-spaced wild flowers gave the semblance of a single great bouquet. But every day the itching soldiers found "as the ant among the flowers, the chigres that annoyed us more than mosquitoes, and also many ticks and snakes." But Aguayo had little thought of beauty. He had become greatly disturbed, for he still had seen no Indians. Anxiously he sent some of Rodríguez' braves to seek their brothers, whose *ranchería* usually was situated west of the Brazos. For more than 30 leagues the Indians scouted the countryside. They found only deserted huts. Wherever he was, St. Denis was bound to have many Indian allies with him. Aguayo doubled his watches.

On July 8, after days of heavy going, the first Indians were seen, members of the *Ranchería Grande* whom Juan Rodríguez and his scouts had sought. They were discovered by Father Espinosa, another missionary and a few soldiers south of the *camino real* some 12 miles west of the Trinity. The fathers reported that the Indians had been friendly. But when the marquis entered the camp of these elusive *Ranchería Grande* tribesmen, with royal standards unfurled, he was once again perturbed. The Indians came out to meet him in well-drilled ranks. Worse, they held high a white taffeta flag with a blue ribbon, obviously a gift from the French. Most alarming of all, their salutes in honor of the Spaniards were fired with French guns and powder. It was well for Spain that Aguayo had arrived.

The governor of Coahuila met the French challenge head on. At his forthright command, the chiefs affixed the white taffeta flag beneath a Spanish standard. In token of Spain's suzerainty, Aguayo placed his hands on the heads of each of the 200 chiefs present and urged them to return to their usual haunts west of the Brazos, where the might of Spain could better protect them. He promised to build the mission at San Antonio which Juan Rodríguez had said they desired. He distributed beads and pocket knives, rings, mirrors, clothing and bright blankets, which were the coveted substitutes for buffalo robes or deerskins—but no muskets or gunpowder. Then, at the suggestion of some of his captains, the marquis put his splendid stallion through its paces in matchless Spanish horsemanship. Never before had the Indians seen so skilled a rider and so well-trained a steed.

Afterward, the marquis placed himself at the head of his battalion and rode for the rampaging Trinity, where the tribesmen had promised to help him with the crossing. At the river an Indian raft of dry logs and reeds proved to be unusable. So did a more cumbersome float of trees and boughs which the Spaniards built. After the *entrada* had lost two days trying to cross, a missionary remembered that he and other Franciscans had hidden a large canoe at a creek when they had fled westward. Two more days were required to find the canoe, another four for oxen to drag it to the Trinity on log rollers. At last, after sixteen days, the river lay behind the *entrada*. Somewhere ahead lurked St. Denis. Two vital questions remained unanswered. Did St. Denis know of the negotiations in Europe? Was he already leading his Indians to battle?

The blood of the Spaniards quickened. They were nearing the land of the Texas, the land of Father Massanet, of Father Margil, Father Hidalgo and Father Espinosa. The missionaries were returning to their pagan children for whom, so far, they had been able to do so little. The soldiers anticipated a fight.

To them came the first Texas, led by the great chief of all the Hasinai, eight lesser chiefs and four women—among them Angelina —bringing presents of flowers, watermelons, the parched corn flour called *pinole,* and corn in the ear; again not a war party but friends, happy and surprised to see so many Spaniards. Aguayo gave the chief a long green coat, a jacket, woolen breeches and a silver-headed baton of authority as Captain and Governor of the Texas Indians. The other Indians received smaller but gratifying gifts. During the day sixty braves of the Neches tribe entered the Spaniards' camp firing salvos in salute. Once again the greeting was that of friends, but they carried French guns, always an ominous sign. The chiefs sat down in the council ring, mixed their tobacco with that of the Spanish captains and smoked the calumet.

Already St. Denis knew of the approach of the Spaniards.

That evening a French emissary arrived at the Spanish camp. He said that St. Denis had sent him from the French camp at the site of Mission Concepción, where St. Denis was holding a convocation with his Caddos. The messenger also informed Aguayo that if St. Denis were granted safe conduct, he would lay before the Spanish governor the orders which, as commandant of the French forces on the frontier, he had received from Mobile.

The next morning Aguayo gave the messenger his written assurance of safe conduct for St. Denis. At last he would know whether

war or peaceful occupation of the land would be the lot of his *entrada*.
He then moved his camp to the banks of the Neches, over which he
decided to build a bridge. The span, roughly 100 feet long and 4 feet
wide, was finished in six days, and so substantial was it that the missionaries blessed what they believed would be a permanent bridge on
the *camino real*.

More than the building of a physical bridge marked those six
days. To Aguayo's camp came a hundred Nacono Indians, behind the
chief priest of the Hasinai, who had torn out his own eyes when he
assumed the sacred office. The high priest also professed friendship.
In an eloquent, poetic welcome he said that his people most esteemed
God, the sun, the moon, the stars and the Spaniards, and that neither
earth nor water nor air nor fire could compare with the men of Spain.
He promised that his people would ever live as friends of the Spaniards, ready to stand by them in any war. The Naconos then presented
the marquis with *tamales,* watermelons, ears of corn, *pinole* and beans
in the ritual of gift exchange.

In answer to the high priest, Aguayo explained why His Majesty
had sent so many Spaniards to the Texas. They had come to establish
peace, to protect the Texas from their enemies and to implant the
Christian religion among them forever. After this reply, he distributed
coarse woolen garments and small cloaks to the men and women, together with the trinkets and other gifts. To the priest he gave a silver-
headed baton and an elegant Spanish suit, and to the high priest's
wife "raiment fit for a marquessa."

That evening Louis Juchereau de St. Denis swam his horse across
the river and rode into the Spanish camp.

The marquis received him with every courtesy. After some polite
small talk, St. Denis withdrew to spend the night with his old Franciscan friends, Father Margil and Father Espinosa. He was tired
from his long ride on this last day of July in 1721. Like the marquis,
he wished to be fresh and ready for the conference the next day.

In the morning, after Mass, the Marquis de Aguayo, governor of
Coahuila and savior of east Texas, summoned his captains, the principal missionaries and St. Denis to his tent.

"Why are you come among us?" he asked the Frenchman. "And
what do you propose?"

St. Denis answered frankly: "I am now post commander at
Natchitoches in charge of this entire frontier. As such, I have been

informed by dispatches from Mobile that a truce has been published in Spain between the two powers. I believe this truce has now been established. I would like to ask your Lordship if you propose to honor it. If you do, I will do so likewise.''

Aguayo had ridden these many leagues, not only to reestablish Spanish power to the Red River, but to drive the French from Louisiana itself and to find the treasure of Gran Quivira. He had known of the truce, but he had hoped for war. He answered carefully.

''I will observe the truce as I was instructed to do by the viceroy, provided that you and your men immediately evacuate the country of the Texas and withdraw to the Natchitoches post, without impeding directly or indirectly the reoccupation of the land up to and including the former mission of Los Adaes.''

Now it was St. Denis' turn to hesitate. He had been criticized for guiding the Spaniards across Texas to the Red River. Adroitly he suggested that the Spaniards would not want Los Adaes. The area was not at all healthy. The soil was so poor.

But the Spaniards had been at Los Adaes. They knew the place at least as well as did the French. Aguayo held his ground and when St. Denis rode back to Mission Concepción it was to lead his Caddo Indians eastward to the Red River. His careful campaign had come to nothing. He had planned to use the Caddo and the Texas to take La Bahía del Espíritu Santo in conjunction with a naval attack and from there move upon San Antonio. As Juan Rodríguez put it, ''that cloud had cleared away'' with the coming of so many Spaniards.

Moving more quickly and surely than ever before had a Spanish leader in the Texas country, Aguayo reestablished the six missions, either at their former sites or at somewhat different ones, and with their names altered where necessary to correspond to the new locations: San Francisco de los Texas, in the Neche village near the prehistoric mounds, became San Francisco de los Neches; Mission Concepción; San José de los Nazonis; Nuestra Señora de Guadalupe de los Nacogdoches; Mission Dolores de los Ais, rebuilt a half mile south of today's San Augustine, at the edge of a bayou which the Americans would miscall Ayish Bayou; San Miguel de Cuellar de los Adaes. Of all the earlier structures, only the church of Mission Concepción had not been razed. All save San José de los Nazonis were on the main road.

A special ceremony heralded the reoccupation of Mission Concepción. Aguayo presented the nearby chief with the best raiment he had, a blue suit beautifully braided with gold and a jacket trimmed with gold and silver. He then ranged his companies in three files in front of the church; between them he placed the six brass cannon which had been pulled so far. Three general salutes were fired during the Mass sung by joyful Father Margil.

So did the Franciscans return to the Texas.

When the *entrada* actually crossed the San Francisco de las Sabinas, today's Sabine River, on August 25, its waters reached the horses' girths. On the far side a long stretch of muddy trail had to be covered with boughs to keep the cannon from bogging down. No matter. Soon, in the very face of the Frenchmen, Aguayo erected the *presidio* which for half a century was to be the capital of New Spain's Province of Texas.

As site for this *presidio* of Nuestra Señora del Pilár, the marquis chose a hillside 7 leagues from Natchitoches, near a spring, and half a league beyond where the old Mission San Miguel had stood. On the ground he drew the outline for a hexagonal fort. He planned a stockade of pointed logs with three bastions, each named for a saint: San Miguel, San José, Santiago. From these the six brass cannon, two to a bastion, could dominate the walls. He planned to reinforce the stockade with adobe walls. But Los Adaes remained a wooden *presidio* as long as it stood, an outpost of New Spain from which no shot was ever fired at an enemy.

On November 11 the triumphant *entrada* of the Marquis de Aguayo was ready for departure early the following day. Rounded up from the wide ranging pastures, the mules and horses waited in the shelter of the woods around the *presidio* to be loaded and saddled at dawn. The soldiers who would leave bade farewell to the hundred who would remain. The men made sure their gear and their weapons were in shape for travel. The marquis, worried by shortages brought about because mules from the Río Grande and La Bahía could not be ferried across flooded streams, totted up the supplies he had bought from two Frenchmen secretly at night so that the Natchitoches post would not know of his dependence upon the countryside.

And again the Texas nemesis, the weather.

During the afternoon the temperature dropped precipitately. A norther, with no mountain barrier to impede it across the great sweep east of the Rockies, howled down upon the *entrada*. Numbing cold and sharp-pointed sleet, intermixed with heavy hail, fell upon the Spaniards and their horses. As the icy downfall accumulated on oak and pine branches, its weight snapped great limbs from the trees beneath which the horses were hobbled. All through the night the crackling of branches foretold the desolation the morning would reveal. At dawn hundreds of the unsheltered animals lay dead and hundreds more heaved dying on their sides. Those still standing were all but unconscious from their night of exposure.

For five days the unseasonable weather continued. Who could say that winter had not come for good? The winter's heavy rains would make the rivers more difficult, even impassable, on the march to the west. The marquis decided that he would have to risk the journey from Los Adaes to San Antonio without waiting for supplies or fresh mounts. On November 17 the battalion headed home. For many hours each day, every man of the expedition, including the marquis himself, walked to save the weakened horses.

At the Trinity, a second provision train from La Bahía, on its way to Los Adaes and making its way by a route which would be known as the La Bahía Road, met the spent army. The Indian muleteers told Aguayo that the Brazos was still fordable by the old *camino real*. It was the shortest way back and he took it. His men had to cut their way through 17 leagues of heavy brush. In the woods where icy rains dripped through barren branches little pasturage remained. More horses died.

Two months later the *entrada* clumped wearily into the *presidio* of San Antonio de Béxar. The brave expedition, which had departed from San Antonio with nearly 4,000 horses, returned with only fifty. Of the 800 mules which had carried provisions eastward, only a hundred still lived.

But not a man had been lost. Of that, and much more, Aguayo, broken in health from the long ordeal, could be proud. The husband of a wealthy and titled widow had won the right to speak for himself.

Sick as he was, the Basque soldier mustered the strength to do what needed to be done.

He realized that the *jacales* of dry grass which housed the *presidial* soldiers could easily be fired by unfriendly Indians. The marquis therefore ordered the construction of a new *presidio,* an adobe square fort with two bastions. Within its walls a church, a powder magazine and barracks would be constructed of wood. Since its founding, San

Antonio de Valero mission had been moved to the east of the San Antonio river. The marquis chose the site for the permanent *presidio*
on the west bank of the river. "It would be better to have not only
the barrier afforded by the river but the wall of the Great Tartary as
well, in order the better to keep apart the soldiers and the Indians,"
he said.

Then he turned to the matter of a royal *cedula* which had reached
him at the Guadalupe. Until now, because of the condition of his men
and the dearth of horses, he had not tried to carry out its orders. The
directive was simple enough as far as directives go. Captain Ramón
had taken Espíritu Santo. Now, so the king ordered, a fort must be
built there.

Aguayo sent down fifty of his strongest men. He followed with
forty others and reached La Bahía toward the end of March. On April
6, 1722, the Spaniards began excavations for the *presidio* of Nuestra
Señora de Loreto at the spot designated by the marquis, a league and
a half inland on the west side of the Lavaca River.

As the soldiers dug, they began to turn up iron nails, broken
gunlocks, French gun barrels. Thirty-seven years before, La Salle had
chosen this very site for his hapless fort! The man who guaranteed
Texas for Spain built his monument on the ruins of France's hope.

And then, each objective accomplished save the two of which he
had dreamed earliest and longest—the discovery of the wealth of Gran
Quivira and the conquest of Louisiana—Aguayo returned at last to
Monclova. There he mustered out the veterans, most of whom had
started with him as boys and former convicts. In a gesture rare for the
day, he paid them for the extra time they had spent in his and the
king's service. He returned then to his Doña Ignacia. The expedition
had cost many thousands of pesos. Never again would the Marquisate
of Aguayo be as prosperous as in the past, even though its great properties would not be divided until long after a distant revolution.

For his services to Spain, Aguayo was elevated to the rank of
field marshal by a grateful monarch. The one-time José de Azlor, the
Basque soldier who became a marquis by marriage, had done enough
in his own name.

A grim footnote to the story of the Spanish *presidio* at La Bahía
has some meaning, for it concerns the way in which Captain Domingo

Ramón, sure of himself after his years among the Indians, lost his life there.

The Indians who dwelled near the *presidio* and mission at La Bahía were not changed. They were the Karankawas, the butchers of the French and the eaters of human flesh. Upon their spirits the veneer of Spanish civilization and Christianity lay thin and brittle. Inevitably, they quarreled with the often presumptuous and overbearing presidial troops.

A year and a half after the founding of the outpost, a mission Indian entered the house of a soldier and asked for a portion of a cow which had just been butchered. As he waited for the meat to be prepared by the soldier's wife, he shook out his blanket. Some of the dust fell in an unpleasant cloud on the *metate,* the stone upon which the soldier's wife was grinding corn. Angrily she summoned her husband, who ordered the Indian to leave. When the Karankawa refused to depart until he had received a piece of meat, the soldier threw him out of the house. Fleeing from the Spaniard, who would have whipped him, the Indian took refuge in some woods near the mission.

When some presidial soldiers searched for him almost all the mission Indians rose in defense of their brother. A rearguard of about forty warriors, armed with bows and arrows, withdrew to a thicket, while the rest of the tribesmen, including the troublemaker, slipped away.

This breakdown of Spanish authority could not be tolerated. Captain Ramón and a detachment of soldiers surrounded the armed Indians and their families, and at gunpoint herded them back to La Bahía, as the *presidio,* from its location to control the bay, was called. There Ramón crowded men and women and children into a prison hut. It was his intention to remove the leaders of the insubordinates, one by one, from the prison and, after allowing them a suitable time to repent of their sins, try them and hang them for their defiance of Spanish authority. As an added fillip Ramón ordered that a beef be barbecued immediately in front of the hut and a cannon trained on the door so that any hungry brave who emerged from the hut without permission could be blown to pieces.

The Indians, peering through the small windows, saw not only the meat but the cannon. They stayed where they were. This irritated Captain Ramón all the more. He decided to taunt them for cowardliness. He walked to the door of the hut and began mocking the prisoners. The door opened and an Indian dragged him inside. Pushing and remonstrating, Ramón pulled himself free and, running outside, shouted to his nearby soldiers: "At them, friends! Get them!" and jumped out of the line of fire. The cannon roared, but though the ball tore a gap in the wall of the cabin, no Indians were wounded. Instead they escaped through the hole. On his way to freedom one of the Karankawas speared Ramón with a blade of a large pair of scissors.

Eight days later, Captain Domingo Ramón, soldier of Spain, friend and kinsman by marriage of Louis Juchereau de St. Denis, and probably a fellow smuggler, died of his wounds.

CHAPTER TEN

OF ISLANDERS AND APACHES

WHEN THE FAR-RIDING APACHES began early in the 1730s to loot and murder in earnest, the Franciscans came up with a scapegoat. He was Brigadier Pedro de Rivera, the viceroy's *visitador,* who, having inspected the twenty *presidios* of New Spain's long northern frontier between 1724 and 1727, had offered certain suggestions to the king, all but one of which were approved. Don Pedro probably made mistakes, yet it is only fair to conclude that the Apaches would have struck again and again even had not this penny-pinching official sought to save money for His Catholic Majesty.

The first error of Don Pedro, so the priests and many another believed, was his recommendation that Spain halt the importation of Canary Islanders at the king's expense for the colonization of Texas. Governor Aguayo had recommended that they be brought. Civilian farmers and ranchers, he said, would defend their fields themselves at less cost to the king than would soldiers. But the viceroy's inspector, in agreement at first, changed his mind when he discovered how much the colonists were costing; also, he had begun to suspect that Governor Aguayo's real interest was to protect his own lands. Reversing himself, he reported that such a scheme should never be tried again. Unfortunately, it wasn't.

A second recommendation was as distasteful. Don Pedro proposed that the presidial forces along the whole border be drastically reduced. All hell—meaning the Apaches—did break loose soon thereafter, but it was only by coincidence, a coincidence which was the doing of the Comanches.

Don Pedro never saw an Apache on his tedious inspection trip. As he jogged along on muleback with his two assistants, his secretary and military convoy and the necessary muleteers, the Apaches were still more or less settled in their lairs above the *Lomeria Alta,* the Balcones Escarpment. These ancient enemies of the Texas and the Coahuiltecan tribes, who on the buffalo hunts penetrated Apache country, rarely rode southward down the passes save to follow the buffalo. Certainly Don Pedro would not willingly or knowingly weaken a line of defense longer than Rome's ancient Danube border and as important to New Spain's security and prosperity as Rome's own distant barriers had been. But the Apaches were quiet and Don Pedro was here to save pesos.

The friars complained also of another recommendation, this one indisputably justifiable. Until the coming of Don Pedro, no supply convoys operated along the road under fixed schedules. When a presidial pack train or the friars' commissaries wished military escorts, they requested and expected them. Don Pedro limited the supply trips from Saltillo to Los Adaes to only four a year, setting out respectively on the 1st of January, the 1st of April, the 1st of July and the 1st of November. Those who wished military protection must join the trains at these stated times. He suggested that ten soldiers and an officer from the garrison at Monclova should come to Saltillo and from there lead friars and supplies back to Monclova and on to Presidio del Río Grande. There a fresh escort of ten mounted soldiers would guard the train to San Antonio de Béxar and on to Los Adaes.

The friars disliked being bound to fixed dates. They disliked even more a fourth recommendation. Rivera, who had been commandant at San Juan de Ulúa, was shocked by the lack of discipline among the soldiers at Nuestra Señora de los Dolores de los Texas and disappointed that the Texas Indians had not congregated at the three Querétaran missions, which the *presidio* near the Angelina was built to protect. He recommended the abandonment of this oldest *presidio* in Texas, a step which would automatically force the removal of the missions. Understandably, the missionaries felt further aggrieved. As it turned out they fared better among the Coahuiltecans than they had among the Texas. They would maintain the old missions at the new sites chosen in 1731 for more than sixty years. The ancient buildings still stand along the San Antonio River for all to see: San Francisco de los Texas, renamed San Francisco de la Espada, farthest down the San Antonio River, its dam and portions of the aqueduct which carried water to its fields still standing; San José de los Nazonis, renamed San Juan Capistrano because of the proximity, just down stream, of Father Margil's San José; and Nuestra Señora de la Purísima Concepción de los Hasinai, with the end designation changed to de Acuna in honor of the viceroy. Of the three missions, Concepción's history would be the most closely entwined with that of the *camino real*.

But it was Don Pedro's recommendation to cut the military strength of the Texas *presidios* from 269 to 118 men that most aroused and frightened the friars. They predicted Apache raids and, when the raiders struck, they interpreted them as the result of the weakening of the garrisons. But cutting the size of the force at Los Adaes, for instance, could not have inspired Apache depredations. No Apaches dwelt near the *presidio*, nor could added soldiers there prevent the Apaches from riding around them to trade with the French. Don Pedro, a tactful man, pointed out that the garrison at Los Adaes could safely be reduced from 100 men to sixty. No matter what its size, should war with France occur, St. Denis could readily overcome the garrison by bringing troops from Mobile. Any force there was simply a token one, to mark the frontier. As an afterthought, he observed that in any case French rifles outranged the Spanish arquebuses.

The frugal Don Pedro looked for other ways to save money for his king. With little thought of morale he proposed that the presidial soldier's pay be cut from 450 to 420 pesos a year. To make the reduction more palatable, he set up a standard price list above which the captains, who were also the paymasters and suppliers, could not charge for their goods. His list fixed the prices at 5 pesos a bushel for corn; 16 pesos a head for cattle; 6 reales for brown domestic from Puebla; 4 reales for good quality powder puffs; a peso and a half for sweetened chocolate; 20 reales for rebozos, the 3-yard-long shawls; 4 pesos for fully-lined black hats of finest quality; 25 pesos for Mexican saddles; 10 reales a pound for *comales,* the iron pans on which *tortillas* were cooked; 11 reales for a bundle of tobacco of good quality. Out of their reduced pay the soldiers would continue to provide themselves with broadswords and lances, firearms, six horses, a pack mule and whatever kind of uniform the captain designated.

The *visitador* also proposed another location for the *presidio* of La Bahía, which the Marquis de Aguayo had established. It had been removed in 1726 from the low tidal flats 14 leagues up the Guadalupe. Here Don Pedro found the best-drilled soldiers in all New Spain. His recommendation that it be further removed to the Medina was not accepted. Perhaps this was a victory for the friars, for they wished protection for Nuestra Señora del Espíritu Santo de Zúñiga Mission, which they had located among the nearby Xaranames.

But by 1731 most of the *visitador's* recommendations had been approved and were in force for good or ill.

In 1731 the complex of *presidio* and two missions—the *presidio* of San Antonio de Béxar, the Queréteran mission of San Antonio de Valero and the Zacatecan mission of San José—was a small and peaceful patch of civilization. Within the adobe walls of Béxar drums summoned the soldiers to the prosaic duties of the day. Beyond the walls, in the deep bend of the river, grazed the soldiers' horses, guarded night and day, the sentries bearing the heavy hide shields, the *cueras*, which could ward off the arrows of Indian raiders. Two or three soldiers were assigned to each of the missions officially for their protection and to train the Indians in defensive warfare, but unofficially to help the friars instruct the neophytes in plowing and the care of the livestock.

The arrival in the spring of 1731 of the Querétaran missionaries from the closed east Texas missions, together with their livestock and equipment and a few faithful neophytes, must have saddened yet also made glad the fathers of San Antonio. The removal of the missions was a blow to the Church, but it was good to have help among the Coahuiltecans. Save for the continuing quarrels between the soldiers and the friars because of the interest of the troops in the Indian women, life continued serene.

Then into this quiet life by the San Antonio River there infringed that same year two new elements, the Canary Islanders and the Apaches—the one to vex even as they strengthened, the other to kill and, together with the Comanches who descended later, to put an end to the expansion of Church and Spain north of the *camino real*. Had Spain continued to settle civilians in Texas, much of the New World's history could have been different.

On the sunny morning of March 9, 1731, a tired, contentious and demanding group of fifty-six men and women and children arrived under special escort at the military plaza of San Antonio de Béxar. No vision of gold or silver had drawn them to this place which the viceroy had selected for them to settle. These *Isleños* were for the most part God-fearing peasants who had scratched a living from the mountainous soil of the Canaries. They had been glad to volunteer for a new beginning under the auspices of their king. The choice of the king and his advisers had been wise; the Canary Islanders were known throughout the Spanish peninsula for their piety, frugality and energy, and for their devoted family life. Spain badly needed such qualities in her colonies.

Even though their minds were not dazzled by the thought of treasure, these *Isleños* would have been less than human had not their heads been just a little turned by the king's munificence. Theirs was the first civil settlement Spain created in Texas and it would prove to be the only one. The royal treasury had not only paid all expenses of the trip but had guaranteed the colonists funds and materials to build their homes, plant their fields and maintain themselves for a year. Perhaps most gratifying of all to these peasants, as original founders of a villa the heads of families would become, by decree under the Laws of the Indies, *Hijos Dalgo,* lowest in the ranks of the nobility but nonetheless aristocrats.

They had taken thirteen months to reach the warm plaza in front of the *presidio* of Béxar. Some had died and some had married, and children had been born in these months since they had awaited at Teneriffe the forming of the fleet with which their ship had crossed to Havana—thirteen months to the completion of the march from Vera Cruz, the springless ox carts weighted down with the tents and provisions for the journey.

Francisco Duvall, who had been sent to Mexico City to conduct the train from Vera Cruz to Béxar, started his charges north from Cuatitlán on November 15, 1730. The viceroy expected them to reach Saltillo in 29 days. But this was wintertime. The mothers and young children tired easily. Along the way they may well have seen grim evidence that others beside themselves were protected by the king in the crucified bodies of *mestizos* and Indians hanging beside the road as warning to other brigands that the justice of the *Acordada* had been meted to these highwaymen; the *Isleños* would have blessed the *Santa Hermandad,* the Sacred Brotherhood, which had cleared Spain's roads of robbers.

On January 28 they left the Río Grande behind. Couriers on horse-back could travel from the Río Grande to Béxar in three and a half days. But in winter rain and wind, the slow-moving train took a month and a half.

No wonder that the Islanders were tired and quarrelsome when they reached the *presidio* of San Antonio de Béxar. Captain Juan Antonio de Almazán welcomed the settlers personally. Others were not so cordial. The presidial soldiers grumbled at having to find shelter for these newcomers until homes were built. The *vecinos agregados,* the families of soldiers living outside the *presidio,* were discomfited because the lands they had been occupying without legal title would be taken over by these wards of the king.

The *Isleños* were too busy with their own affairs to care. This was the season to break the land for the basic corn crop. They planted their corn and beans, barley, cotton, melons, chiles, watermelon and calabash and squashes, all supplied by the king. The settlers' cattle were placed on the best pastures to recuperate from the long journey. Their horses were kept with the presidial herd, guarded by fifteen soldiers. Until such time as they could build a church of their own, they could worship at the presidial chapel or at Mission San José so that they would not have to cross the ford to Mission San Antonio. Nothing, in the eyes of the government, was too good for the *Isleños.*

Not until the beginning of the harvest in July was there time for the laying out of San Fernando de Béxar, the only civil settlement Spain would ever foster formally along the *camino real* in Texas— San Fernando in honor of the Prince of the Asturias, who would later become King Ferdinand VI of Spain; Béxar, as with the *presidio,* for the viceroy's heroic brother.

The instruments and tools for the occasion were a sundial, a chain 50 *varas* long, ten stakes for each family, thirty cartloads of large rocks, a yoke of oxen and a plow. Since the church was the center of Spanish life, its site must first be chosen; all else would be measured from it. Directly across the plaza should rise the *casa real,* the government building. Heavy rocks and stakes were set out to mark the corners and the center of the plaza, and the two principal squares. Late the first evening oxen opened a furrow which outlined the perimeter of the squares. On the next day a lot for the customhouse and others for the principal families were similarly marked, each lot 80 *varas* square and separated from the others by streets 13 *varas* wide, the plan conforming in general outline to the layout prescribed by the Laws of the Indies. Beyond the plazas and squares and homesites were outlined the *ejido,* or common lands, and beyond this, on three sides, the pasture land. To the south, the *sitios,* the measure of lands allowed for pastures, abutted those of Mission San José.

But floods soon required the removal eastward, nearer the river's bend, of the villa of San Fernando and the town grew up without the straight streets so carefully laid out. With the king's gold the church was finally built. It was not begun until 1738 nor finished until 1758; the location was to the east of the *presidio.* The plaza in front of this parish church of San Fernando was from the outset the principal plaza, rather than the one which had been laid out in the summer of 1731.

The spokesman for the *Isleños* did not endear himself or his people to the local officials or soldiers or priests. Juan Leal Goraz, at 54 the oldest of the group which landed at Vera Cruz, was a cantankerous champion of a cantankerous band. It was he who went to Mexico City to demand of the viceroy an allowance of 4 *reales* a day for food, rather than the three which the viceroy had thought sufficient for the journey. It was he who later returned to Mexico City to request, respectfully but plaintively and persistently, fresh horses to replace the exhausted mounts the train had abandoned by the wayside. The king had probably not planned to give these tired horses to the settlers anyway; they were intended only for the journey itself. But to quiet Goraz the viceroy agreed to the substitution and warned the governor at Los Adaes by courier to see to it that the Canary Islanders stayed where the king had paid for them to be—out on the frontier. So the horses were added to the family allowance of a yoke of broken oxen, ten female goats, one male goat, ten ewes and a ram, five mares and a stallion, five cows and a bull. Goraz—he was called the Old One— was steeped in his own new importance. Captain Almazán appointed him first *regidor,* principal among the five-man council. His fellow *regidores* subsequently elected him First *Alcalde,* the justice of the peace, in the initial election to be held on the Texas side of the *camino real.* He reveled in his honors and his title. He signed himself "Juan Leal Goraz, Spaniard and settler by order of His Majesty (whom may God guard) in his Royal Presidio of San Antonio de Vexar (sic) and villa of San Fernando, province of Texas or New Philippines, and present senior *regidor* of the said Villa and farmer."

The Islanders were as overzealous in protecting their rights as they were arrogant in proclaiming them. No sooner was Juan Goraz assigned his land and water rights than he had to be placed under technical house arrest to keep him from fighting with a neighbor over a fence line. At other times, when presidial horses strayed onto the unfenced Canary Island *labores,* the Islanders maliciously cut their tendons to teach the owners a lesson. The mission cattle had a way of appearing barbecued on the settlers' tables. Later the Islanders sought to induce the well-trained Tlaxcalan Indians, who taught the mission neophytes, to leave the friars and work for wages in their homes. A direct order from the viceroy was required to keep the Indians in the *pueblos*.

But whatever the fault of the *Isleños,* they provided, through their daughters, Spanish wives for the Spanish soldiers at Béxar. That had been one of the reasons the king had brought them over. How else could a Spanish civilization be built? Throughout New Spain a new race made by a crossing of Spaniard and Indian was being created, but at least at this place on the *camino real,* as in other instances, a strong nucleus of all-Spanish families would endure.

And the *Isleños* would fight for their homes. This was good, for six months after they arrived the *presidio* of San Antonio de Béxar and the villa of San Fernando stood off the first of the many serious Apache raids that were to come.

The Zuñi Indians, the friends of Spain who lived far to the west at Santa Fé, had taught the Europeans their word for the Navajo and all the unknown, related tribes to the north. That word was *Apachu,* the enemy, and later Spaniards realized there were five major groups of the Apaches. Along her eastern reaches New Spain had chosen to make allies of tribes which called themselves collectively *Texas,* friends, united in resistance to foemen. Because of its friendship with the Texas, New Spain won the enmity of their enemies, the Lipan Apaches. But there were other reasons, too, for the deadly Apaches' outbreaks along the *camino real*.

In the first quarter of the eighteenth century the few *presidios* and missions were remote from the upper waters of the Colorado and the Brazos, the Red, the Nueces and the Medina, where ranged the buffalo-hunting Apaches. There was little occasion for the paths of Apaches and Spaniards to cross. But after Aguayo assured Spanish domination of Texas, Spanish soldiers and friars moved closer to Apache country.

The Apaches had been very little in evidence when Aguayo marched eastward in 1721. Soldiers and missionaries were then astounded and horrified that the Apaches had dared kill the lay brother Pitá when he went hunting for buffalo for the missionaries' table, north of the *camino* and without a soldier escort. The avenging expedition from San Antonio de Béxar, the first to move against the Apaches, had to go 105 leagues to the north and west before joining battle with the tribesmen.

But in that same year, Apaches waged and lost a mighty battle which raged for nine days against another foe, the well-disciplined Comanches, themselves moving southward ahead of encroaching tribes which the white colonists of the Atlantic seaboard were displacing. That decisive battle and subsequent ones drove the Apaches ever south and west, down the San Sabá, the Chanas, the Pedernales and, in time, all the way to the Río Grande. The Apaches, hounded from the north, would drive the Coahuiltecan tribes south, where the remnants would finally take refuge along the coast of the Gulf of Mexico or, in desperation, enter the missions for protection.

Don Pedro de Rivera, inspecting the *presidios* and calculating how best to save money for his monarch, did not know of the conflict. Nor could he pierce the veil of the future. He may have been aware, as were the Spaniards in Santa Fé, of the Apaches' consuming love and need of the horse. But he did not understand that this love and need made imperative horse-stealing raids upon the Spanish settlements.

The Apache's mount was not his chattel; it was a part of him. Only the horse could overtake the buffalo. Only the horse could take the place of and improve upon the dog and travois as carrier of tents and robes and supplies. From the back of the horse the Apache could wage a different war of cunning surprise and swift retreat. The herds of Apache horses, descended from abandoned, strayed or stolen Spanish stock, changed the Apache's manner of living and his reasons for existing almost from the day in 1660 that he first came upon the strange steed loose on the plains. From then on the horse was the Apache's passion, for the mobility it afforded and for the superiority over more sedentary tribes which it assured.

He gave his horse the same protection in battle that he provided for himself. Each wore armor of thick, hard buffalo hide. His was fashioned into breastplates and shields, his mount's into body armor draped low and painted as brightly as the warrior's own shield in reds and whites and greens and blues. When he learned the artifices of the white man, he fashioned wooden saddles with iron stirrups, making longer hours on horseback possible, and he plaited horsehair into reins for surer control.

And the mustang was also Apache food, a meat to be killed and roasted, still warm, hide, and entrails and all.

But with the coming of the French to the Illinois country and the Mississippi at the end of the seventeenth century, the horse became in the New World a form of negotiable and easily-moved specie for which the French would exchange guns and ammunition.

By the middle of the eighteenth century the Apache badly wanted the white man's weapons, for the Comanches, geographically closer to the French, had them. And at the same time that the Apache's need of guns increased, France's need of horsepower for the plantations of the New World rose. To get the gun, the Apache required horses, not the wild horse of the plain, but the branded, partially broken horses of the ranches. The Apache could justify his attack on mission and presidial herd by reasoning that as the Spaniard was the ally of the Coahuiltecan and Texas tribes, his enemies, a foray against Spain was legitimate war. From Saltillo to the Trinity there would never be real peace with the Apache along the *camino real.*

Even in the 1730s, before they acquired guns, the Apaches dared their thieving raids. Their spears and darts and iron-tipped arrows discouraged settlement. When a coyote howled in the mesquite thickets beyond San Fernando, who could say whether it was wild animal or wilder Apache? When the horses neighed nervously in the Potrero, the horse pasture in the bend of the San Antonio, was it the moon that stirred them or a bedaubed prowler ready to drive the *cavallada* across the ford? Who could sleep when Cabellos Colorados, the chief with the bright red hair, was loose on the border he ravaged for more than four years?

Settlers and soldiers relaxed a little when Colorados and his small daughter were captured and lodged in the guardhouse at Béxar, she to be placed with a family which would rear her in the Christian faith but as a servant, and he and his fellow captives to be sold into slavery in the West Indies. But there would be others to take his place. The

Apache depredations would not end. More and more commonplace along and above the *camino real* became the hideous sight of the Apache victim, head scalped, body naked, flesh ripped from the bone to be taken away for feasting, the arrows still embedded in stomach and back, the gaping death wound of the spear.

The year the *Isleños* arrived, a band of fifty Apaches attacked two *padres* and other travelers under the escort of four soldiers on the road from San Juan Bautista to San Antonio, killing two of the Indian women in the party and carrying off a little boy. The emboldened marauders next raided the corrals of San Antonio de Valero and drove off fifty burros. Then, while the missionary was absent from one of the new missions along the river, Apaches raided it and put the Indian neophytes to flight. A month after the Canary Islanders arrived, eighty Apaches captured the horses which a squad of soldiers were driving from San Antonio to Presidio del Río Grande.

Six months after the arrival of the Islanders, the Apaches dared to raid Béxar's presidial pasturage at high noon and drive off sixty horses. Captain Almazán left his sickbed to order five soldiers in immediate pursuit. Soon thereafter he and twenty men were spurring along the trail marked by the galloping herd. A league from the *presidio* the captain caught up with the five-man Spanish vanguard just in time to save it from being overrun by a party of forty Apaches. The Indians retreated as Almazán and the main body reached their countrymen, but within minutes 500 hidden Apaches swooped down in the characteristic wide crescent, which, in a two-hour battle, grew ever smaller as it tightened around the outnumbered Spaniards. When two of his men had been killed and thirteen others of the force of twenty-six Spaniards had been wounded, Captain Almazán ordered the soldiers to dismount for what must have seemed a last-ditch stand. And then, in what the soldiers could interpret only as a miracle, the Apaches galloped off as swiftly and unexpectedly as they had appeared.

It was well for San Antonio de Béxar and the *Isleños* of San Fernando that they did. Of the reduced force which Don Pedro de Rivera had allotted to Béxar fourteen soldiers were away on a mission to Monclova. The few who remained at the *presidio* could not have held out against an attack in strength. But the Apache retreat was no heaven-sent miracle, simply a calculated policy. The Apaches did not believe in incurring high losses to win an objective. When casualties began to mount, they would always withdraw. There would always be another day—or another night.

From the Guadalupe to the Río Grande the smoke signals billowed. Along the *camino real* the symbolic red cloth attached to the Apache arrow spoke war. Aguayo's expedition had circled northward to avoid the bramble-choked thickets of the *Montaña Grande.* Now no man dared to travel the upper road; the old way farther south would have to be used, and the old Spanish Road which the early Anglo-Americans would know was clearly marked. Spain's New World officialdom even talked seriously at one time of abandoning the missions, the *presidio* and the Canary Islanders' settlement on the San Antonio. The Apaches were too numerous, too implacable, too deadly, the more faint-hearted said.

By the end of the 1740s the Apache attacks became less ferocious and came at wider intervals. Some thought they wanted to make peace. The Apaches who came to Father Santa Anna's Mission Concepción in 1749 to trade the fat rendered from wild cattle for tobacco and *piloncillo* and corn gave the priest a reason for their more pacific behavior. They told him of the Comanches. Perhaps the time had come, reasoned the president of the Querétaran missions, when the eastern Apaches needed the friendship of Spain. If Spain would forgive their past depredations, the Lipan Apaches might be ready for an alliance.

Captain Toribio de Urrutia was now captain at Béxar. He was not sure that Father Santa Anna's surmise was correct, but he was convinced that punishment through military expeditions had not worked. Then, early in 1749, the Apaches drove off a large herd of cattle from Father Santa Anna's own mission. Here was the opportunity to prove that magnanimity and patience were weapons superior to the sword and the gun. The father made certain suggestions to which Captain Toribio agreed before setting out in pursuit of the Indians with a combined force of 300 soldiers and Indians from Mission Concepción. They came upon the Apaches at the Guadalupe where they were encamped. Had the full Apache force been waiting, any gestures would have been all but impossible. Fortunately, most of the braves were on a buffalo hunt. Without bloodshed, Captain Urrutia was able to take prisoner thirty men, ninety women and forty-seven children. His men also rounded up the stolen cattle.

At Béxar the Apache captives were placed in missions and homes, and treated almost as guests although closely guarded against escape.

Captain Urrutia chose two Indian women from among them to return to their people with gifts and the message that if the Apaches would live in peace with the Spaniards, the Spaniards would release to them not only the prisoners taken on the Guadalupe but all others who languished at Béxar. He exacted a promise from the messengers to return.

Within three months, the Apache envoys were back, accompanied by a brave of great distinction. He told Captain Toribio de Urrutia that four Apache chiefs, each with 100 men, waited at the Guadalupe River and would remain there, so that no misunderstanding would arise, until the Spaniards set a date for their entry into San Antonio. Then they would come happily to make peace and arrange for the release of their kinsmen.

Within a week the prescribed smoke signals rose against the August sky. Toward the *presidio* cantered the Apaches, no longer enemies but friends. The soldiers, missionaries and citizens of San Fernando went out to greet them 2 leagues from San Antonio de Béxar, there to suffer the embraces of the odorous Apaches and to lead them to the *plaza*. Before the *presidio* a bower had been constructed for the *fiesta*. The Apaches and their hosts dined together upon barbecued beef, squash, corn and fruit. That night the principal chiefs of the Apache slept as honored guests in the *presidio* and the missions.

The next morning the Spaniards and the Indians attended Mass. Then, with the Spanish and Apache spokesmen seated together in the bower, the great council began. To prove their good intent and friendship the Spaniards first delivered up the hostages who had been taken on the Guadalupe. It would take time to separate the earlier Apache prisoners from the *vecinos* and Islanders whose servants they had been for so long. This too would come about.

That day a hole, wide and deep, was dug in the center of the plaza. The next morning the Apaches placed in the hole their principal instruments of war: a terrified live horse, a tomahawk, a lance and six feathered war arrows. Then, before the soldiers and missionaries and the tribesmen and the *Isleños*, Captain Toribio de Urrutia and the four Apache chiefs, all in military finery, grasped hands and circled the hole three times in ritualistic dance. The other assembled Spaniards and Indians clasped hands and followed suit in a larger circle that all but filled the plaza. At a signal from the captain all rushed to the perimeter and threw dirt into the hole, burying the struggling

horse and the weapons to the Apache whoop and the *Viva el Rey* of
the Spanish soldiery. Peace had come.

But not precisely peace. Horse theft was still a part of the Apache
way of life. The declaration of Apache-Spanish friendship made it
easier to steal. More than an occasional cow or a horse seemingly wandered off, and sugar cake and tobacco disappeared from the storehouses.
Even so, Father Santa Anna's policy and the Comanche threat had
apparently made friends of the Apaches. The priests began to talk
of a mission among them.

Epidemics had given impetus to such talk. What almost no one
realized at the time was that the surest way to kill off Indians was
to congregate them in a mission, where the white man's diseases were
more effective than on the plains. In their accustomed habitats the
Indians would build fences of thorns around a smallpox victim and
leave him isolated, with food and water, believing that the thorns
would pierce the postule sacs of the smallpox spirit and halt the epidemic. The fences didn't seem to work inside the *pueblos,* where men
lived close together, and smallpox and measles swept like angels of
death through the adobe cells. The epidemic of 1739 almost wiped
out the Coahuiltecan neophytes. Ever since then the friars had been
begging for permission to find new pagan tribes to build missions for;
now Father Santa Anna thought the time had come for a mission high
in Apache country.

The father had a persuasive argument. From San Juan Bautista
to Los Adaes there was not a single Spanish post north of the *camino
real.* It was not beyond possibility, he argued, that the Apaches might
form an alliance with their old enemy, the Caddo, who were the friends
of the French, and with the Texas and so open wider the region north
of the presidial road to the traders and the soldiers and even the settlers of France. Prophetically, he said that unless this were done Spain
might find its trans-Río Grande holdings confined to a small triangle.
A mission among the Apaches might avert this unwanted eventuality.
It would help halt any French encroachment toward Santa Fé and
encourage direct communication between San Antonio and Santa Fé
as substitute or supplement to the present route by way of San Juan
Bautista or Monclova. If the Querétaran fathers were afforded a *presidio* for their protection, they could establish a mission to perpetuate
the newly-won friendship of the Apaches.

The royal permission for some new missions was granted, but not for one among the Apaches; rather, they should be situated among the Indians of the *Ranchería Grande,* their enemies. The sites must be on the San Xavier River, today's San Gabriel, near the present Rochdale.

The San Xavier missions got off to a bad start. No one but the Franciscans wanted to leave civilization so far behind. The projected missions were 270 leagues from Los Adaes and 75 from Béxar, and too close to Apache country for safety. The seventeen soldiers who were removed from Los Adaes and the thirteen who were reassigned to the new *presidio* from La Bahía raged at being separated from their families. They told the *Ranchería Grande* Indians that the missions would soon be abandoned and that they would be at the mercy of their enemies, the Apaches. The *Ranchería Grande* tribesmen began losing their taste for mission life. But the specific reason for the abandonment of the missions only five years after their beginning in 1750 and the retreat of Spanish power to the *camino real* line had its origins in the character of a dissolute sadist whose name was Felipe de Rábago y Terán.

Don Felipe came to the San Xavier with fifty soldiers, recruited in Coahuila, Nuevo León and Texas, to relieve the original garrison. As always happened, the missionaries and the enlisted men had been bickering over the immorality of the troops. The Franciscan fathers

were willing to overlook much to insure a peaceful climate. But long before Rábago arrived with his men and the twenty families from San Antonio who had accompanied him as settlers, the gossip of the entourage, with truth to back it up, was that he himself was sleeping with the wife of Juan José Ceballos, a San Antonio recruit. Juan protested the captain's relationship with his wife. Don Felipe ordered him to be put in chains, and when he arrived at the stockade, with its guardhouse, barracks and commander's hut, the outraged husband was thrown in the guardhouse, staked hand and foot and head. At least once he was freed of his bonds and carried into the captain's hut while Rábago possessed his wife. Upon the insistence of Father Miguel Pinilla, chaplain to the soldiers, the woman returned to San Antonio.

On Christmas Ceballos managed to escape to Father Pinilla's mission, where he claimed the right of sanctuary. The next morning Rábago and a squad of soldiers rode into the church itself and recaptured the prisoner. Father Pinilla put the lecher under censure. After ten days Rábago submitted to the Church and returned Ceballos to Father Pinilla.

But the commander's lascivious conduct had encouraged imitation by his soldiers. Soon they were bringing Indian women into the barracks at all hours of the day and night. A soldier complained to Father Pinilla that an intimate of Captain Rábago, one Corporal Carabajal, was having an affair with his wife. All the garrison was talking of it. The corporal accused Father Pinilla of defaming his character and violating the seal of secrecy of the confessional. Rábago backed up his fellow seducer and persuaded thirty soldiers to sign a document which accused the friar of revealing what the wife had confessed. Promptly Father Pinilla nailed on the *presidio* door a notice of the excommunication of Captain Rábago and the thirty soldiers. Meanwhile, the Coco Indians, for whom one of the missions had been founded, had fled the establishment in a body after one of them was severely beaten for an infraction of a rule.

On the night of May 11 there came the murderous, consequential denouement. Father Pinilla, another missionary, Father Gonzábel, and the cuckolded husband, Ceballos, supped together in the mud hut which housed the two fathers. A noise from outside disturbed them. Ceballos went to the door and peered into the darkness. A moment later a blunderbuss roared and he fell dead. Beside him knelt the dying Father Gonzábel, pierced by an arrow.

Blandly Captain Rábago announced that rebellious Coco Indians had committed the crime. But a Savoyan Indian whom Father Gonzábel had raised from childhood at Mission San Juan Capistrano on the San Antonio told another story. He had been angry with Father Gonzábel at the time, he said. When Captain Rábago ordered four soldiers and himself to murder Ceballos and the priest, he had consented. No Coco Indians were involved.

Rábago was taken to San Antonio and from there to Mexico for a trial that lasted seven years. He was eventually acquitted.

But Mexico City had had more than enough of the San Xavier missions. In 1756 the presidial troops were withdrawn. The missions closed their doors. The missionaries who had served them fretted to go into the Apache country, but no one save the fathers themselves were interested until Captain Bernardo de Miranda returned with the news that silver had been found near the San Sabá River. His report to Governor Jacinto de Barrios at Los Adaes was electrifying: "The mines of Cerro del Almagre are so numerous ... that I pledge myself to give all the inhabitants of the province of Texas one each, without anyone being prejudiced in the measurements."

Some seventy years later a knife fighter from Opelousas in Louisiana named James Bowie would seek those fabulous Los Almagres mines.

Miranda had been sent far north of the *camino real* to run down persistent rumors of silver in vast quantities there. With twelve soldiers, four San Fernando citizens, some servants and an interpreter, he traveled through the Llano River region and past today's Honey Creek to Cerro del Almagre, a hill a half-mile north of the creek, its red ochre composition a telltale sign. The soldiers sank a shallow shaft, which yielded fistfuls of the hematite. The San Antonians staked out ten claims to five mines. As they returned to San Antonio, an Apache at the Guadalupe River buoyed their enthusiasm. Pointing to the silver buckles on Captain Miranda's shoes, the Apache said that mountains of solid silver rose six day's journey above the Llano, in Comanche country.

Along the *camino real* the mining fever began to run high.

A mule train carried Miranda's samples of ore to Don Pedro de Terreros, the owner of the silver mines of La Viscaina, to assay at Mazapil. This Don Pedro was a philanthropist and founder of the National Pawn Shop in Mexico City. He was also a cousin of Father

Alonso Giraldo de Terreros, the much-venerated president of the Río Grande missions. Father Alonso had discussed with Don Pedro, his cousin, the possibility of financial aid for missions to the Apaches. Don Pedro had assured Father Alonso of his willingness to help.

But the offer which he made to the viceroy of Mexico in July could scarcely have been entirely a philanthropic gesture. It bound his wife and himself "to equip, provide and maintain every mission that may be established in said [San Sabá] territory, under the direction of Father Giraldo de Terreros," for the ensuing three years. Don Pedro estimated that the cost would be around 150,000 pesos. The government would bear the expense of the necessary presidials. Because of his munificent gift, Don Pedro became Count of Regla. The missionaries rejoiced at the imminent establishment of missions among the Apaches. And, not incidentally, silver prospectors were delighted. No doubt, some of them were identified with the interests of Don Pedro de Terreros.

Father Terreros planned the founding expedition carefully. He had established one mission for the Apaches near San Fernando de Austria, a new *presidio* south of the Río Grande at what is now Zaragoza. Within a year, the unreceptive neophytes had reverted to their old ways and burned the mission building down. He conferred now with the commissary general at Querétaro about what was needful. The cost was not important.

Then he set out for San Antonio, with four other missionaries, nine Tlascaltecan families from Saltillo, who would serve as his assistants in training the Apaches to become herdsmen and farmers, and a richly laden mule train.

At San Antonio he met the valiant Spaniard whom the viceroy had appointed captain of the proposed *presidio* of San Sabá, Colonel Diego Ortiz y Parrilla, who in the seven years since he had landed at Vera Cruz had made a name as an Indian fighter. No selection could have made Father Terreros and his fellow friars happier. With the captain were twenty-seven recruits who had joined him along the way from Mexico City, and a number of settlers and prospectors lured by silver and secure in the protection which a man of Colonel Parrilla's stature guaranteed. The force which set out from San Antonio in early April 1757, was formidable enough. Colonel Parrilla had under him his twenty-seven recruits, twenty-two soldiers from Béxar and most of the former garrison of San Xavier.

The journey to the north side of the San Sabá River was made without incident. There, near today's Menard, Colonel Parrilla located the *presidio* of San Luis de las Amarillas, named for the viceroy, but more often to be called Presidio San Sabá. At a ford 3 miles downstream the first mission, Santa Cruz, was constructed. It was in the form of a square stockade enclosing huts for the fathers, a church, and quarters for the expected neophytes. A cannon protected it.

By June the prospectors near the Pedernales and the settlers around the *presidio* numbered some 400 civilians, among them 237 women and children, principally Canary Islanders drawn by the talk of the wealth that lay beneath the earth. But the mining boom lasted only a year. No fortunes were made. Later the excavations would be known as the lost mines of the San Sabá.

Father Alonso was not concerned with the making of fortunes. But he was disturbed at the cool reception the Indians were according him. Back at San Antonio some Apaches from the San Sabá country had assured him that their people were looking forward to his coming. But, in the summer of 1756, the Lipan Apaches who had been so cordial failed week after week to appear, until one morning Father Terreros awoke to find 3,000 Apaches camped nearby. Joyfully he went out to welcome them. The Indians were sullen, explaining that they were there by happenstance. They were on their way to a buffalo hunt, they said. They would probably meet some Comanches and would be glad to have the soldiers go with them as protectors. They didn't have time to enter the mission until they returned from the hunt.

At the end of the summer a Lipan chief and his men rode up to the mission, their horses laden with buffalo meat. But the chief could not tarry; he and his men rode hurriedly southward. Others from time to time also came to the mission, but stayed only long enough to receive food and gifts. Colonel Parrilla became certain that the Apaches did not intend to give up their nomad life and enter the mission. He recommended that the one mission already established be closed, that the missionaries should be escorted to San Antonio, and that the *presidio* itself be moved nearer the Pedernales, where the miners needed protection.

The colonel was soon to have reason to be concerned for the miners. During the winter disconcerting tales began reaching the *presidio,* the mission and the prospectors' tents. All the Nations of the North, including the Comanches and the Taovayas and the Wichitas, were meeting in council, the stories went. They were planning a concerted attack on San Sabá, the Lipan Apaches and the Spaniards who were their friends. In the spring, some Indians raided the *cavallada*. The pursuing soldiers failed to catch them, but on their return they gave a foreboding account of the many Indians, all in warpaint, whom they had seen along the trail. That spring, too, Indians wounded four of the prospectors on the Pedernales. The thoroughly alarmed Colonel Parrilla urged Father Terreros to return to San Antonio.

At the least Father Terreros should take shelter in the *presidio,* the colonel begged. Only five soldiers guarded Father Terreros, Father Santiesteban, Father Miguel Molina and the nine Tlascaltecan families. Father Terreros declined; he would take every possible precaution, he said, but he would remain at his post. The stockade was well built and protected by a cannon and the seventeen adults within it. But seventeen persons, however courageous, could not hold out against an attack of the magnitude of that which was to come. The *presidio* itself, 3 miles away, had no soldiers to spare.

Early on the morning of March 16, just as Father Alonso finished saying his Mass and Father Santiesteban was beginning the second service, there came from the river the warning cry, "Indians, Indians!" The soldiers and priests hurriedly closed the gate just as the main body of attacking Comanches and their allies, firing in the air, rushed upon the stockade.

Since the Spaniards were ready for them, the Comanches resorted to subterfuge. Through signs and broken Spanish they told the soldiers that they were friendly. The corporal of the guard recognized in the crowd beyond the gates a number of Texas, Bidais and other Indians whom he had known as friends. He told Father Terreros that the Indians had come in peace even though they were garbed and painted for war. He opened the gate.

Ominously these were the first Indians who had ever menaced the Spaniards with guns. There were nearly 2,000 of them, half of them armed, their faces painted black and crimson. Most of them were Comanches. As the fathers entered into the patio, some of the Indians removed the last bars from the stockade gate and pushed into the mission compound. The *padres* ordered the distribution of tobacco and other gifts, with four handfuls going to the principal chief of the Comanches, dressed in a bright French uniform, who remained mounted. A few of the Indians began shaking hands with the white men but their companions began pillaging the mission. Others took from the corral the few horses that were within it.

Next the invaders told Father Terreros that they wished to go to the *presidio* but that they were uncertain of their welcome. The father, trying to be conciliatory, replied that he would write a letter to the captain which would win them friendly treatment. He wrote a brief note and gave it to a Texas chief who, mounted on Father Terreros' own horse, rode with a number of the warriors toward the *presidio*.

The fathers, pretending that nothing was amiss despite the open plundering, asked questions of the Texas Indians who told them that they did not intend to hurt the Spaniards. They were seeking Apaches who had killed their people.

Within a few minutes the Texas chief returned. He had not really had time to ride to the mission and back, but he declared angrily that Spaniards at the *presidio* had fired upon him and his men, killing three and wounding another. Father Terreros offered to go with him to the *presidio*. The chief accepted. The courageous father ordered the last horse in the corral to be brought to him and, accompanied by a mounted soldier, José García, rode toward the gate. As they reached it, an Indian fired and Father Terreros fell mortally wounded. A volley killed García and a general massacre began.

Father Santiesteban was slain at the foot of the altar as he prayed. Two soldiers were shot and cut to bits in the patio. Father Molina, his arm broken, and eight survivors, most of whom were wounded, fought their way to the president's room, where they barricaded themselves. The maddened Indians set fire to the stockade and the buildings where the survivors had taken refuge. The Spaniards, peering through the loopholes in the walls, saw the savages strip the bodies of Father Santiesteban and Father Terreros, cutting off the head of Father Santiesteban and tossing it about to each other. In the orgy, they smashed the images of the saints in the chapel, killed the cattle in the corral and destroyed everything that they could not carry away.

The Indian servants had fled at the first warning. One of them reached the *presidio* and told the dreadful story. Colonel Parrilla sent nine soldiers to the aid of the mission, but an ambush party of Indians, lying in wait against such an eventuality, attacked the small band, killing two and wounding several others, one of them so badly that he fell to the ground to die later of his wounds and burns suffered when the savages threw him upon the flaming stockade of the mission.

In the burning building in which they had taken refuge, the nine survivors withstood the terrible heat as long as they could. By noon they could remain no longer. Father Molina and his companions dashed into the adjoining building. The Indians set fire to the second refuge. Before nightfall the bedeviled Spaniards ran into the chapel, itself already on fire. The Indians, confident that their victims would soon be burned to death, did not attack. The chapel still stood after nightfall. Under cover of night a sergeant and fourteen men from the *presidio* approached the burning mission. They were discovered by lurking Indians, who shouted to their companions that Spanish soldiers were approaching in undetermined numbers. Quickly the savages abandoned the destroyed mission. The soldiers found only three survivors: Father Molina, a mule driver named Nicolás and a soldier.

For days the invaders laid waste the countryside. Then, despairing of surprising the *presidio* and reluctant to make a frontal attack, they rode north again.

On March 16, the night of the massacre, Colonel Parrilla had sent two messengers to San Antonio and two more on the 23rd. A fugitive soldier reached Béxar first. His story reduced most of the people along the river to terror; their turn would come next. The *Isleños* and missionaries protested violently when a lieutenant and eighteen men were dispatched to San Sabá. Were they to be left exposed to the savages? The Spanish settlers, missionaries and soldiers on the Guadalupe hurried to the town. The governor at Los Adaes learned of the attack and started promptly for San Antonio, but floods delayed him. Soon panic ruled every *presidio* along the *camino real*.

The determined Don Pedro Terreros, grieving for his cousin, paid for the establishment of two other missions to the Apaches, each farther west than San Sabá. These also failed.

In August, 1759, Colonel Parrilla led a punitive expedition of 500 soldiers and 500 Indian allies from San Antonio. Moving north and east to the Red River, near what is now Ringgold, he came upon hundreds of Taovoyas, allies of the Comanches, encamped within a moat-surrounded stockade above which flew a French flag. Colonel Parrilla sought to storm the fortifications. Counter-attacking, the Taovoyas ignominiously routed the Spanish army, which abandoned baggage, weapons and cannon in their flight. Parrilla believed that Frenchmen were inside the stockade, but some Apaches who escaped from the Taovoyas told of other white men—Parrilla deduced they were Englishmen—who were teaching the Nations of the North the use of some kind of "explosive bombs."

For as long as it was maintained, the San Sabá *presidio* remained in a state of siege, the only fortification along the frontier which had no missions to protect. The prospectors, unable to work their claims, returned to San Antonio or Coahuila. The French continued to trade with the Nations of the North, exchanging guns for horses. The Texas, enemies of the Apaches, felt drawn to the Comanches. As for the San Sabá *presidio,* an inspector for the king would observe of it in 1767: "It affords as much protection to the interest of His Majesty in New Spain as a ship anchored in mid-Atlantic would afford in preventing foreign trade with America." And so the *presidio* was abandoned, the troops which manned it were assigned to the *presidio* of San Fernando de Austria, established west of the Río Grande to block Apache raids, and Spain's northeastern limit became, in effect, the *camino real,* as Father Santa Anna had feared.

Don Pedro de Rivera, who had reduced the border garrison for the benefit of the king's treasury, actually had little to do with the debacle. Spain simply did not have the manpower to defend all her *presidios.* But the Franciscans were still blaming him as late as 1781, when Father Juan Agustín de Morfí, noted historian of the work of the order along the *camino real,* wrote his *Memorias para la Historia de Tejas.*

The alliance of Spaniard and Apache fell apart, for as much as they might need the Spaniards as friends, the Apaches needed horses and guns, and more horses and guns. Above them the relentless Comanches were riding down from the north, and the Comanches had all the guns and the horses they required. So the Apaches began again to acquire arms and mounts where and how they could. The pack trains and groups of travelers who followed the lonely trail from San Juan Bautista to the missions and *presidios* of Texas heard more and more often the war shrieks of Apache and Comanche alike—and more and more often those who heard the terrifying cries died to their echoes. And as the Apache attacks increased in the San Juan Bautista area, the soldiers and priests and officials and ordinary citizens who traveled to La Bahía, San Antonio and Los Adaes gave thanks that an alternate road now ran from Saltillo to Texas.

This road was greatly the doing of José de Escandón, one of the most efficient organizers New Spain was to know. In 1748 he began the exploration and settlement of the vast area from the mouth of the Pánuco, where Tampico is now situated, to the *presidio* of La Bahía on the Guadalupe. The area would be named Nuevo Santander and would have its own governor apart from the governors of Coahuila and Texas.

With the pacification of the country, José Vásquez Borrego, a Coahuila rancher who owned a large hacienda near San Juan Bautista, moved his family beyond Apache danger to the east bank of the Río Grande in Nuevo Santander. Borrego and his son-in-law had been granted fifty *sitios de ganado mayor,* the grazing land for horses and cattle. The acreage lay on high, level ground by the riverside. It was a stockman's paradise, as ranchers 200 years later would agree, and the twenty-five families who accompanied Borrego prospered. So many royal couriers and officials, missionaries and convoys crossed the river at the *población* of Dolores that five years later Borrego placed two canoes at the riverside with four peons to paddle the travelers across. Five years later he was allowed another fifty *sitios* for his services and received permission to charge a reasonable ferrying fee. It was the first time that such a convenience was afforded anywhere on a road to east Texas.

In May, 1755, another stockman, Tomás Sánchez, who had pastured some cattle across from Dolores, was granted the right to establish a villa of his own 10 leagues up the river. His Villa de Laredo was officially established close to the Paso de Jacinto. The perceptive Sánchez also began to operate a ferry. The site was advantageous, for some 3 leagues below this Villa de Laredo the Río Grande spread out to form a wide ford, shallow enough for sheep and goats. Soon the advantages of the Laredo crossing made it the principal one on the way to the Texas.

Dolores ceased to grow and Laredo became the center from which trails were marked to San Antonio, Monclova and the towns of the Río Grande which Escandón had established: Camargo, Reynosa, Revilla, Mier. To protect the outer limits of his Nuevo Santander, Escandón received permission to remove the Presidio of Nuestra Señora de Loreto from the Guadalupe, to where it had been moved in

1726, to its final site on the right shore of the San Antonio, where the river narrowed as it passed between two hills. This new La Bahía, as the *presidio* continued to be called, was built of lasting stone and lime.

The Apaches were responsible for the use of the alternate road through Coahuila and Nuevo Santander. From Monclova it ran 50 leagues to Laredo and another 50 to the new site of La Bahía. From there travelers could go up either side of the San Antonio river to Béxar or northeast to the Trinity crossing of the old *camino real*. There the La Bahía Road joined the *camino real* trending eastward toward Los Adaes.

Apache and Comanche made the new roads almost as important as the old.

CHAPTER ELEVEN

THE RIFLES OF ATHANASE
DE MÉZIÈRES

H U M I L I A T I N G I N D E E D was the trouncing of Colonel Parrilla's punitive expedition when the Taovayas routed him from their fortifications. More disturbing in the long run was the rumor that even then, in 1759, Englishmen peered from behind those Taovayan low mud walls many hundreds of miles west of England's Atlantic seaboard colonies.

That same year the battle at Quebec's Plains of Abraham ended what North Americans called the French and Indian War. The Seven Years War, the larger struggle of which it was a part, would not be settled until the Treaty of Paris in 1763.

While war still raged, Louis XV of France transferred Louisiana, west of the Mississippi River, and the Isle of Orleans, east of it, to his cousin, Charles III of Spain, to keep England from getting them in the subsequent peace treaty. By that Treaty of Paris, Spain traded her rights to the Floridas for Cuba, which the English had captured, and France surrendered to England all her holdings on the North American continent.

The transfer of Louisiana to Spain required changes in Spanish defense and policy. The English, not the French, were now at the Mississippi and their traders were not to be stopped by its waters.

If the Spaniards, listening to their priests, had not traded guns among the Indians, the French had. And if the French of a Louisiana that was no longer Spanish could not traffic in weapons because of the old Spanish proscription, others, meaning the English, would. These were the facts of life.

The Spanish horse had changed the culture of the Indians immeasurably, and for the better. The rifle in the hands of the Indian, astride his horse or afoot, altered his standards and way of living even more dramatically, and for the worse. As long as the bow and arrow was the Indian's principal weapon, he was self-sufficient. He could manufacture the armament that almost alone produced his food, his clothing and even his shelter. But when he accepted the musket and the fusil rifle, he incurred an immediate and continuing need for powder and shot. These he could procure only through bringing to the gun-rich white man the buffalo hides, the deerskins, the horses and the wild mules which were demanded in exchange.

In turn, the greater efficiency of the rifle ran down the price of skins and hides and, in only superficial contradiction, reduced the number of animals in a given area. The hunter now had to go farther afield to slay the buffalo and the deer. This wider ranging encouraged his nomadic bent. Even those tribes which had learned the subtler ways of an agricultural existence deserted the missions in the hunting season so that they could earn the wherewithal to secure for themselves more new weapons and the needed ammunition.

The first victims of the rifles, though in a bloodless sense, were the missions. As long as the tribesmen were satisfied with the axes and knives, the beads and the blankets—all of which the Spaniards were willing to barter or give them—the Franciscan missions had a chance of settling them permanently in the *pueblos*, but, even before the coming of gunpowder into their lives, only a small chance. The missions depended upon the imposition of the habit of daily attendance at services, the discipline of learning by rote, the quotidian responsibility for tilled fields and domestic herbs. The life of the American savages had been attuned to a more exhilarating cycle of seasonal, not daily repetition. Here in or near the land of the buffalo they lived by the buffalo and found it exciting. Why give up the freedom of the chase to the restrictions of the missionaries? The question was asked from the beginning. The answer which the questioner would give to his own query was more convincing after the coming of other white men with the weapons which would make the chase more thrilling yet.

So, while the missionaries at Los Adaes, on the Ais bayou, and at Nuestra Señora de Guadalupe de los Nacogdoches tolled the mission bells and hurried to baptize those about to die, the number of neo-

phytes shrank until they virtually disappeared. In the agony of failure, the Franciscans saw the French traders as the agents of the devil
himself. Spain had brought one inducement to civilization, the Cross
of Christ, which the grey-robed men offered to the savages. The system had worked in Mexico, it was working in California. But it failed
in east Texas. And the Spanish friars, looking over the Gran Montaña
which separated Texas from French Louisiana, perceived there the
horns of Satan, the guns. From French Louisiana, into which the
camino real officially should not enter but nevertheless did, and
demonstrably from Natchitoches, the nearest settlement of the French,
the Indians received their guns. Guns, as the friars tried to teach un-
availingly, were the tools of the anti-Christ.

And now, following the Family Pact of the Bourbons, the French
gun traders would be under Spanish rule throughout all Louisiana,
and by the 1770s the most urgent question on the frontier, in mission
and *presidio* and *ranchería,* was whether the change in suzerainty
would affect the Indian policy. Would His Catholic Majesty cut off
the flow of arms to the Indians?

On moral and spiritual and traditional grounds the question
could not be debated; the trade in guns must end. But at the eastern
end of the *camino real* an overriding consideration had to be faced.
If the French traders did not provide guns to the Indians, the English
would.

For the daring English were everywhere. Now that Florida was
theirs the Englishmen were making more and more frequent appear-
ances among the Indians along the Gulf. Shortly they were to paddle
up the Mississippi in canoes loaded with trade goods. And soon they
might even press into the heartland of New Spain. They were not
men to be held back by Spain's royal decrees. So the Indians must be
taught to distrust these intruders in Louisiana and Texas. They must
learn that the French and the Spaniards were now one and that old
allegiances to either now meant alliances with both. Tribes remote
from the French and Spanish centers also had to be brought into
closer touch with Louisiana's and New Spain's authority to remove
them from any possible English orbit. Inevitably, the mind turned to
the guns that the Indians craved.

In what had been French Louisiana, there was a more personal
decision to make, in Natchitoches as well as in New Orleans or wherever
Frenchmen had been citizens of France before the scratching of royal

pens. Many of them had been born in France, had fought for France in the Old World and the New. What should their attitude toward the Spaniards be?

In New Orleans six Louisianians who refused to accept the authority of the Spanish king had answered the question with their lives. They were the first martyrs to political freedom on the North American continent. But for most Frenchmen, wherever they dwelt, the wiser solution seemed to be to accept as gracefully as possible the situation in which Louis XV had placed them.

This was the decision of a remarkable Frenchman, Athanase de Mézières y Clugny, a Parisian of noble lineage whose sister had married the Duc d'Orleans and who had served France at Natchitoches since 1733.

De Mézières had entered Louisiana as a naval ensign. Under Governors Bienville, Vaudreuil and Kerlerec, he had been steadily promoted and was now a captain. Immediately after the transfer of Louisiana he had requested and been awarded the Cross of St. Louis for his long service.

But a man's time on a quiet frontier was in considerable measure his own. Like most of the officers at the post of Natchitoches, De Mézières was also a planter; moreover he was a successful purveyor of supplies needed in the Indian trade. Several times he had been sent as an emissary to the Indians; he knew the Caddo, the Petit Caddo and the Yatasí well. In 1746, a seasoned officer in his thirties, he had married the daughter of St. Denis. After her death he took as his second wife Dame Pelagie Fazende. His home, his career and more than thirty-five years of his life were one with Louisiana. He could not give them up.

The Spaniards were slow in coming to Louisiana in force. But one month after Governor Alejandro O'Reilly arrived in New Orleans he sent for De Mézières, having been told that the French officer and trader was "better able than anyone else to give me correct information regarding everything in your district." De Mézières made the trip to New Orleans and awaited the governor's pleasure. After a single interview in September, 1769, O'Reilly named De Mézières lieutenant-governor in charge of the Natchitoches district.

Before his death ten years later, the aging De Mézières was to ally the Nations of the North to Spain, circumventing the English. He, a Frenchman, would be appointed governor of New Spain's prov-

ince of Texas. But in the years that lay between, more than once did
Spain's viceroy in Mexico City wonder what was going on in Texas.
It was difficult for Spanish officialdom to believe that Frenchmen could
be loyal to Spain. It was even more difficult for them to accept the
French policy of providing arms for the Indians. Athanase de Mézières
made Mexico City believe the one and accept the other.

An anomaly of the administration of Spanish Louisiana was that
while it was administered by the captaincy general at Havana, the
Spanish colony of New Spain to which it was immediately contiguous
was under a different authority. The citizens of one colony could
not travel legally to the other without proper passports. In explanation, the Spanish king said that as Louisiana was not included in the
provisions of the Law of the Indies, he desired that his Louisiana
subjects remain in Louisiana and not trespass into New Spain. Thus
even properly accredited French traders who appeared among the
Indians of New Spain were watched warily.

De Mézières epitomized the Spanish contradiction. He was suspect
at the western end of the *camino real*. At its eastern terminus, the
Spanish governor of Louisiana endorsed his trading. In between, at
San Antonio the practical Governor Juan María Vicencio de Ripperdá
approved and understood. Some whispered that his endorsement of
De Mézières had more than political motivation, that because he himself was profitably involved in the Indian trade there was no wonder
he was willing to let French traders settle even at Béxar.

Hugo Oconór, commandant inspector of *presidios*, disagreed with
Ripperdá. Soon after the cession, he had threatened to put to death
any Frenchman trading in Texas, but he too had learned a lesson.
When, at his orders, a French trader was prevented from making his
accustomed visit to the Yatasí, the entire tribe rebelled and only immediate action by De Mézières pacified the aroused savages.

De Mézières, under O'Reilly's orders, in 1770 renewed the li-
censes of such bonded traders as Alexis Grappé, Dupain, Fazende,
Morière, Barré, Gagnée and Lemoyne. They were to return to the
Indian villages after reporting to the Spanish authorities as they
had in the past to the French. Then, in a maneuver which must have
appeared strange to Indians inured to ancient and continuous tribal
feuds, he sought to gain for the Spaniards the friendship of the tribes

which had always been loyal to the French. To Natchitoches he summoned Tinhiouen, the chief of the Caddo, and Cocay, chief of the Yatasí. For the solemn ceremonies which would confirm their friendship he requested the presence of the aged commandant at Los Adaes, Lieutenant Gonzales, so that the Indians would understand that the two districts were now as one, that where there had been enmity there was only brotherhood and that the road between the two posts was open.

Captain De Mézières, resplendent in his light blue, gold-braided uniform and surrounded by his military associates, received the two chiefs in the audience chamber of the post. The chiefs, puffing on the pipes of peace, listened to him carefully. They accepted the great shining medal of Charles III and the Bourbon flag bearing the cross of Burgundy. Approvingly they examined the presents of tomahawks, awls and pickaxes, hatchets, hunters' knives and pocket knives with dog-head handles, Limbourg cloth and blankets, mirrors and copper wire for bracelets, beads of sky blue and white and black, combs and pure vermillion for their faces—and lastly what they wanted most, fusils of good caliber, French gunpowder and bullets to fit the rifles. De Mézières announced that they would receive annually other gifts from the Spanish king. In turn, they promised to accept the traders as they had in the past and to bring them their buffalo hides and deerskin and pots of bear fat, the lard of the French frontier. They signed over title to their land to the Emperor of the Indies, His Catholic Majesty Charles III, as they had already done to the French Bourbons.

These two greatly respected chiefs had accepted the change of suzerainty, but the tribes with which they were allied must also be won over. The safety of the road from the Red River to the Sierra Madre depended on pro-Spanish alliances in the country above it.

Now De Mézières encountered opposition from New Orleans. Governor Unzaga, who had replaced the man whom the French hated as the bloody O'Reilly, was suspicious of all Frenchmen. Only with misgiving did he permit De Mézières to visit the chiefs of the Nations of the North, who had had little contact with the French.

In the undertaking the Caciques Tinhiouen and Cocay were to prove staunch friends. They summoned their tribesmen and their allies to a great inter-tribal conference with the Spaniards and De

Mézières to be held in October in the Caddo village far up the Red. Then they returned to Natchitoches to escort Captain De Mézières and his party to the parley.

This was to be an Indian gathering in the grand style, and De Mézières and the Spaniards prepared to live up to their roles. In the party was a lieutenant of militia and five soldiers. At Los Adaes they were joined by a sergeant and four soldiers, who were to assure the protection of the old and recently ill Father Miguel de Santa María y Silba, president of the missions of the Los Adaes district.

Such was De Mézières' hold upon the tribesmen that, as the colorful procession of white men and Indian chieftains passed through the villages of the Yatasí and the Petit Caddo, the Indians abased themselves before the flag of Spain; the caciques and head men and principal chiefs of the villages joyously joined in the expedition. Obviously, the tribes with the longest history of allegiance to France had accepted the new overlordship of Spain.

But the major work to be done was with the northern tribes the Spanish lumped together under the name of the Nations of the North, far up the Red River. A hundred leagues from Natchitoches De Mézières reached the Caddo village, a place surrounded by pleasant green groves and large pastures with ample salines for cattle. Here De Mézières expected to parley with the chiefs of the Taovayas, the Tuacanas, Iscanis and Quitseys.

All had gone well up to now. But unknown to De Mézières, the chiefs and some tribesmen of these nations had arrived at the Sabine River a few days before De Mézières reached the Caddo village. At the Sabine they became panicky. What if the conference were in reality an ambush? Perhaps when the warriors were all assembled in the village, the Spaniards would fall on them and destroy them in reprisal for the massacre at San Sabá and for less bloody raids upon the *presidios* and ranches.

Once again Chief Tinhiouen served his new Spanish masters well. After hours of urging and exhorting he persuaded seven of the chiefs to accompany him to the village. De Mézières placed the representatives of the Los Adaes post in the ceremonial circle of the conference so that all present would know that the Spaniards and French were as one. Next to himself he sat the Father President of the east Texas missions, Father Santa María.

De Mézières first told his listeners that he had come at the command of the Captain General of Louisiana, the father and protector of the Indians, who would have only benevolent regard if his authority were recognized. Until a friendly attitude was made known, aid would be suspended. The new emperor was the most powerful in the world. He would forgive the Indians for their past misdeeds, and look with love and compassion upon them if they showed their devotion and desisted from robberies and hostilities.

"Profit now from the example of the Cadodacho," De Mézières exhorted. "You Nations of the North are surrounded by enemies, the Osages to the north, the Comanches to the west, the Apaches to the south and, to the east, the Spaniards of Louisiana if you want it that way . . . Think well. Consider your decision, but do not move your lips to invent excuses which sooner or later your deeds will belie. You can only receive aid if you accept the terms we propose. There are no French to turn to. The very name Frenchman has been erased and forgotten; we are all Spaniards now. As such we are sensitive to the outrages you have committed in the past. But even the grave and venerable man by my side, wearing the same gray habit as that of the priest you beheaded at San Sabá, far from being angry, has come to invite you to merit his pardon. Repent now for what you have done to the Spaniards. Agree to live in peace with our great king."

Affectionately, De Mézierès took the hand of each Spaniard in his own. Chief Tinhiouen and Chief Cocay soberly approved his oration. But the other caciques remained seated, their eyes averted. Finally the only chief among them who knew the Caddo language spoke:

"What we have done against the Spaniards, even at San Sabá, was done because we have found them acting in friendship with the Apaches, our enemies. Until this was so, we had nothing against the Spaniards though we knew well the location of the ranches, villas and *presidios*. Our anger became greater when the Apaches aided the Spanish army in its march to the Taovayas. But today this is over. Already in answer to the wish of the great captain of Louisiana we have quitted our establishment near San Antonio and San Sabá, and have moved near San Pedro, where we will leave the Apache in quiet rather than take the chance of offending you."

This was better. But now De Mézières turned to the most meaningful issue. To the chief who had just spoken he answered:

"That is well. But your nations have committed so many insults,

robberies and homicides in and about Béxar that you chiefs must go
at once to that city with two Spaniards and an interpreter I shall
provide you, carrying the flag I will give you as protection. There
you must humble yourselves in the presence of a chief of the greatest
power who resides there and who will ratify the treaty of peace which
I propose and you desire."

The chiefs demurred. They protested that the season was too late
for such a lengthy journey.

"Go then to Los Adaes," De Mézières said.

Again they refused. There were shelters to be built for the winter
in the new San Pedro location. They lacked sufficient horses. It could
not be done.

De Mézières concealed his disappointment. It was better to continue with caution and gentleness. Again he assured the suspicious
chiefs that all he had said was true. Because he knew that the chiefs
would eventually see this to be so, he would keep on deposit against
a future meeting the presents he had brought. Relieved, the chiefs
replied in concert that they would assemble again in the spring.
Meanwhile they would hunt only game.

The vital conference was ended. What had it accomplished?

Frenchmen and Spaniards differed. The Spanish soldiery from
Los Adaes had seen no Spaniard take the hand of an Indian in friendly
gesture. The Indians had expected the gifts usually presented at such
a time. They had not received them. Lieutenant José de la Peña of
Natchitoches, spying on De Mézières for Governor Unzaga, thought
that more harm would come of this expedition than good.

As for De Mézières, he was willing to wait in patience. The
Indians' ammunition would soon be exhausted. They would have to
turn somewhere for more. It was only a matter of time, he thought,
before they would go to Béxar.

Or would they? Soon the Spanish governor in New Orleans was
not so sure. Reports of what had been accomplished at the Caddo
village conflicted. Besides, who could vouch for the loyalty of a
Frenchman? Rumors ran throughout the colony: at Los Adaes, where
Lieutenant Gonzales was displeased because De Mézières had not sent
him a copy of his report to the governor; at Pointe Coupée and Natchez and Natchitoches itself. De Mézières would resign, some said.
The Spanish authorities were incensed because he was spending too

much time at his plantation with its scores of slaves and hundreds of acres in tobacco.

De Mézières heard this criticism and sold the plantation. No longer a planter, he was living on his small military pay and needed his job. But how could he quiet the suspicion as to his loyalty? He wrote to Unzaga that he would prove his allegiance to Spain. He placed his sons in the service of Spain. Zealously, he entered into the routine administration of the post and he even undertook to build a new church for the Spanish priests. He sought other funds to replace the 80-peso tax which had been used to pay the *alguaciles* who had ended the illicit liquor dealings among the Indians and Negroes. Income from the tax no longer existed because the only two legal dealers in spirits had given up their privilege.

During the winter De Mézières devoted much of his energy to the development of crops that might supplement the tobacco economy which was now threatened with ruin because its normal export to France was cut off and export to Mexico had not yet been permitted. He asked Governor Unzaga for wheat and barley and rye from the Illinois country to plant experimentally. He suggested hopefully that ale might be made from the barley and whiskey from the rye. If the experiment succeeded, Louisiana would have to pay only half as much money for imports as it did.

Again came spring, the time for a second visit to the Nations of the North. Governor Unzaga, still suspicious, hesitated. What did the Governor of Texas think? Ripperdá replied that he could not as yet give Unzaga an opinion about De Mézières. He himself was busy fighting the Comanches and trying to hold off the raiding Apaches. De Mézières had written him most cordially when he had assumed the governorship in Béxar, but he didn't really know the man.

Unzaga sought the opinion of the president of the Zacatecan missions, Father Pedro Ramirez, who was about to leave the beautiful confines of mission San José to inspect the missions in east Texas. Father Ramirez would be happy to investigate. Father Francisco Sedano, who for twenty years had been father conductor of the supplies to the eastern missions and knew the country well, would accompany him. They conferred with Chief Bigotes of the Texas. The Texas Indians, while failing to congregate at the missions, had remained the friends of the Spaniards through thick and thin. Chief Bigotes said he would go to the Nations of the North to see what was going on and to try to win their friendship.

Bigotes succeeded. The chieftains with whom De Mézières had unsuccessfully conferred gave him two buffalo skins, a white one which signified that the roads were open and free from blood, and another with four crosses, the symbol revered by the white men, meaning that many nations were willing to make peace. Bigotes and the fathers, joined at Los Adaes by Lieutenant Gonzales, then proceeded to Natchitoches to give De Mézières the good news. And, hesitant no longer, the chieftains soon accompanied Bigotes to Natchitoches. In the council chamber Indian and Spaniard and De Mézières, who was neither, covered themselves with the royal banner as a sign that all were united under the Spanish king.

Bigotes placed himself at the head of the pacified chiefs and, with the friars, they all rode over the *camino real* to Béxar. There, as the soldiers of the *presidio* stood at attention before the portrait of the king, Governor Ripperdá designated Bigotes as the paramount chieftain of all the Indians he represented, decorated him with his second royal medal and changed his name to Sauto, buckler of peace.

Soon the tribe of the Taovayas, next to the Comanches the most numerous of the northern nations, sent their chiefs to De Mézières at Natchitoches under the guidance of Chief Tinhiouen. Here were represented more than 2,000 warriors. Their geographical location was as important to the Spaniards as were their numbers. They were neighbors of the Comanches. They promised now to try to keep those warlike folk at peace. They would even return the two cannon abandoned by Parrilla when they routed him from their village.

By the year's end almost all of the Nations of the North had been consolidated under the red cross of Burgundy. Meanwhile, wherever the Spaniards had posts or ranches, the elusive, omnipresent Lipan Apaches used their avowed friendship for the Spaniards as cover for their thievery.

To ratify the peace, it was still imperative that the Taovayas also go to Béxar. Accordingly, De Mézières set out from Natchitoches in mid-March 1772, this time with Governor Unzaga's blessing, to strengthen the alliances already formed in the north and to bring the chiefs to Béxar to demonstrate their loyalty. He would also study the strength and weaknesses, and the customs and the lands of these in-

terior tribes. To all this De Mézières added another objective: he would
encourage the tribes to move closer to the Spanish missions and
presidios so as to form a cordon of mutual protection and to leave
only empty space between them and English influence.

On this notable journey all the white men were of French descent:
De Mézières' nephew, who carried the royal flag, six other Frenchmen
from Natchitoches and one from Los Adaes. Westward along the
camino real they traveled as far as the site of old Mission San Francisco, then turned toward the mysterious north. Eighty-seven days
after the little group departed from Natchitoches, De Mézières would
enter Béxar in triumph. Meanwhile he would have visited the Kichais,
the Quitseys, the Iscanis, the Tuacanas and the Tankawas. Even a
delegation of Comanches would have parleyed with him.

His mission concluded—he had conferred with the leaders of
every tribe on the periphery of Spanish power—De Mézières and his
party, increased now by some seventy Indians from the several tribes,
began the 150-league journey southward to Béxar. Perhaps now the
Spaniards would believe him loyal. Perhaps also they would agree that
fire must be fought with fire, or to put it more straightforwardly, that
English rifles must be forestalled by weapons of French manufacture.
While among the Nations of the North he found an Indian who had
been Christianized in Quebec and who, having been present at the
fall of the city, was awed at the power and strength of the English.
This man, whose name was Joseph, was now the intermediary between
the Panis-Mahis, who as allies of the English could get English guns
for trade, and the Indians of the interior provinces. De Mézières
brought Joseph with him to Béxar as proof of the English threat.
De Mézières' advance scouts brought Ripperdá word that De Mézières
and the northern chiefs were camped in a large cave near today's
New Braunfels on their way to Béxar. The governor prepared for
their ceremonial reception.

In the plaza outside the *presidio* were assembled the presidents
of the Querétaran and Zacatecan missions, and two other reverend
fathers, the captain of the *presidio,* the *cabildo* of the villa of San
Fernando, and Governor Ripperdá himself, all in dress uniforms or
official trappings. On either side of the officials were ranged the presidial soldiers. The visiting Indians, with De Mézières' nephew carrying the royal flag before them, followed by De Mézières and his men,
entered the plaza. The Indians wore long headdresses of dyed and

beaded feathers, and bore bright lances and guns. In the sunlight of
the plaza they performed the great feather dance in honor of the
governor. At its end they gave him the feathers and wrapped him
in buffalo skins, as was their custom on high occasions. Then the chiefs
made their grave harangues, calling on the creator of all things to
make the alliance a success. They promised to watch over the Comanches, even to declare war against them if they broke the peace. Evea,
high chief of the Comanches, agreed for his part to put to death any
transgressor rather than have his tribe as a whole blamed for any
misdoing. Evea knew that shortly before De Mézières' party reached
the *presidio,* a Comanche band had entered the area under a flag of
truce and had killed several Spaniards and stolen some horses. Peace
with Comanches was something no man could really guarantee.

But as far as any man could assure peace, De Mézières had assured it.

In the subsequent days, Governor Ripperdá and the visiting
Frenchman conferred on the many problems confronting Spain on
her borders. Ripperdá became convinced that not only gifts but trade
in guns and ammunition among the Nations of the North was basic
to the security of his district. So did he write the viceroy, Bucareli.
But the viceroy later warned him six times to end the traffic. Ripperdá said that he would, but afterward he sent at least two embassies
among the Nations of the North, one from Los Adaes and another
from San Antonio. It is more than likely that among the presents and
trade goods were guns. He, like De Mézières, believed they were the
only answer.

Now came intrigue. Governor Ripperdá learned that the Apaches
feared that the treaties being signed by the Nations of the North would
produce a coalition which might seek to destroy them. Through the
Bidais, a separate tribe who lived south of the *camino real* and to
whom they had long traded horses for guns as intermediaries, the
Apaches suggested to the Texas that the three nations meet to form
an alliance of their own. De Mézières, from his own vantage point and
not fully cognizant of conditions at San Antonio, might have looked
upon such a treaty with favor. But Governor Ripperdá feared even
wider coalitions. Let the Apaches unite with the Bidais and the Texas,
and they in turn with the Nations of the North, and Spain would
not have the power to protect either the *presidios* of Texas or even
Coahuila itself. Something would have to be done.

And that something, whatever it was, would have to be done by De Mézières.

It was true enough that De Mézières was ill with the ague and exhausted by his trip, but the governor considered it imperative that De Mézières hasten to the Bidais and the Texas and see to it that they turn down any overtures from the Apaches. His health prevented that, however, and De Mézières left on July 13 for his home at Natchitoches.

But when De Mézières learned in Natchitoches that four Apache chiefs and their bands were on their way to the Texas and the Bidais Indians to draw up the proposed treaty, he had no time to lose. Unable to go himself, he sent Alexis Grappé, the trader and interpreter, to Sauto-Bigotes with a pertinent suggestion. Bigotes and his Texas should feign friendship with the visitors, but they should never forget that the Apaches were truly their enemies and must be treated as such.

Bigotes took the hint. When the Apache chiefs entered his tent they were attacked by Texas tribesmen. Three Apaches were slain. The Bidais danced over the dead bodies. Thus was the potentially dangerous alliance among the Apaches, the Texas and the Bidais avoided. At Natchitoches, Mass was said and the Te Deum sung in the new parish church, resplendent in its glittering silver ornaments, for the success of Spanish arms and the beneficial results of the tour of Captain De Mézières.

The next spring, Athanase de Mézières, now completely trusted, was granted a passport to visit France on private business. While in Europe he was graciously and affectionately received at both the French and Spanish courts, and he returned to Natchitoches a lieutenant-colonel.

While De Mézières was abroad, the New Regulations of 1772 came into force and the task of justifying his policy had to be done all over again. The New Regulations were based on the findings of His Catholic Majesty's representative, Cayetano María Pignatelli Rubí Corgera y Climent, who had made a 6,000-mile journey up and down and back and forth between New Spain's northern *presidios* in 1766 to investigate their condition and make recommendations. He was accompanied by a thousand *gente de razón*—Spaniards and *mestizos*—and additional hundreds of Indians. Along the way, Rubí visited the *presidios* of Monclova and San Sabá, traveled the *camino real* from Béxar to Los Adaes, went down the Trinity to a recently established post among the Orcoquisa Indians, and on to La Bahía.

The field marshal was not impressed with what he saw in east Texas. The Orcoquisa post could be closed because New Orleans could keep much better guard against the English on the Gulf of Mexico. The three Zacatecan missions, like the Querétaran ones thirty-five years earlier, had failed to congregate the Indians. And the *presidio* of Nuestra Señora del Pilár de los Adaes, which guarded them, was no longer needed as an outpost against the French.

Rubí's over-all recommendations to the king had to do with shortening and strengthening the entire presidial line in realistic recognition of what Spain could actually hope to hold, and the appointment of a commandant inspector of *presidios*. In June 1773, the order for the closing of Los Adaes arrived. Governor Ripperdá brought the royal *cedula* himself. *Presidials,* missionaries and *vecino agregados* were commanded to leave east Texas within four days.

Delay their departure as they tried to, the settlers finally had to comply with the order and in the hot sun of August, September and October they toiled along the way to Béxar. Forty of the 300 or more men, women and children died on the way or shortly after their arrival.

One of the east Texans, Gil Ybarbo, born of Andalusian parents and brought up on the frontier, did not accept the order as final. He wanted to get back to his ranch, El Lobanillo, half way between the Ais bayou and the Sabine. Under his leadership, the Adaesanos would return within six years, not quite as far east as Los Adaes, but to where Father Margil's abandoned mission of Nuestra Señora de Guadalupe de los Nacogdoches still stood. For them even to start back, Ybarbo had to circumvent the direct orders of Viceroy Bucareli and the violent protests of red-headed Hugo Oconór, commandant inspector of *presidios,* who argued that if the frontiersmen returned to the east they would simply reestablish a contraband center comparable to Los Adaes.

Ybarbo first built a little town at the Trinity crossing of the *camino real*. When floods and Comanches made this site, Bucareli, untenable, he directed his neighbors to go farther east. He joined them to become the founder of today's Nacogdoches. It soon became a center for contraband trade, as Oconór had feared. The stone house there, which Ybarbo is reputed to have built, was presumably the warehouse for the supplies.

De Mézières found in Oconór an honest but irascible and suspicious official. Oconór trusted few Spanish frontiersmen and no Frenchmen. From the start, the commandant inspector made it plain that he did not put any faith in "the false peace agreements entered into with the Indians at San Antonio." His suspicions mounted when, on a February night in 1774, Comanches drove off more than 200 of the Béxar presidial horses as the sixteen presidial guards slept.

All through the spring similar forays were reported. The citizens said the signs were those of the Nations of the North. Ripperdá vowed that the raiders were Comanches. His theory seemed to be that it was better to pretend to believe that the Comanches were the offenders rather than jeopardize the pacts with the various Nations of the North simply because a few individual Indians were stealing horses and mules. Travelers along the *camino real* going to Ybarbo's Bucareli or on to Natchitoches still arrived at their destinations without incident. At any rate, said Ripperdá, since the forces had been cut under the New Regulations, he didn't have the manpower for all-out retaliation anyhow.

But the Indian unrest continued. The Comanches made trouble. The Lipan Apaches stole and re-branded horses while pretending friendship. Oconór ordered Ripperdá to have no communications with De Mézières. By viceregal order, emissaries bearing gifts from Ripperdá to the Nations of the North had been halted. And the English were coming closer and closer.

Then to Louisiana there came as governor in June 1777 the brilliant young Bernardo de Gálvez. Ripperdá, who would leave soon for Honduras, wrote him in welcome and to beg that he tell De Mézières to keep the Panis-Mahis Indians, the allies of the English, under close survelliance—for these Indians "in great numbers are approaching us" and increasing their pressure on the Plains Indians, and to be sure that the traders furnished nothing to the Comanches.

In Chihuahua, Don Teodoro de Croix, knight of the Teutonic Order, Brigadier of the Royal Forces and governor and first commandant general of the Interior Provinces superseded Oconór. He advised Ripperdá that no matter what slander had been spoken of him, he should have done what he knew was best, namely to continue to send emissaries to the Nations of the North. Until 1776 the *Provincias Internas* had simply meant the frontier provinces. After that year, and subsequently at irregular intervals, they were separated from the control of the viceroy at Mexico City. The new commandant general had political as well as military power in the Interior Provinces.

Don Teodoro, El Cavallero de Croix, called a council of war at Monclova for December 11, 1777, to consider frontier matters and especially the Indian problem. To the meeting he invited only officers and officials of the *Provincias Internas*. De Mézières of Louisiana was not of his jurisdiction and was not included.

It was just as well. In the six days between December 11 and 17, the brave Frenchman lost his wife, a son and a daughter in the great epidemic of influenza or measles which took the lives of fifty citizens of Natchitoches alone as it swept from one end of the *camino real* to the other, felling soldiers, neophytes and settlers, cutting the Bidais tribe in half and killing 17 at Bucareli.

It was the sense of this council of war that the removal of the *presidios* from the settlements under the New Regulations had made the Indians a worse menace than ever. The council agreed that the Comanches and the rest of the northern Indians were implacably hostile to the eastern Apaches. It agreed also that the treaties which the Lipans "have made on this frontier have been, are, and will always be false and deceitful, proving it by various events, well and publicly known."

Spain had not sufficient strength to attack or even to defend effectively the frontier. Along the entire presidial line of 2,000 miles were stationed only 280 men. Six hundred more troops were needed. If such reinforcements could be sent from Spain, a campaign against the Apaches would be feasible. But its timing would have to be determined by the governors of Texas and Coahuila.

Then, coldly and deliberately, the beleaguered leaders of New Spain undertook to plan a campaign against the Apaches. Necessary to its success must be the enlistment as war allies of the Indians of the North. In the meantime, the Spaniards must persuade the Apaches that everyone was friendly. Until reinforcements arrived, the troops and militia must be strategically redistributed. So, with cynical evaluation the Spaniards made their decision. The Nations of the North were stronger. The Nations of the North were well-armed with English and French guns, with pikes and axes and lances. They must be Spain's allies.

It was agreed that Captain De Mézières should be consulted;

more, he should be placed at the head of the troops if Governor Gálvez of Louisiana were willing. And Gálvez must be requested to send De Mézières to Béxar for immediate conferences on how best to consolidate and encourage the Nations of the North. De Mézières should be asked when the attack should be made, how many Indians he could gather under Spain's banner, what Spanish troops should accompany them—in short, to advise Spain "with respect to everything which the zeal, intelligence and honor of the commandant of Natchitoches may consider adapted to the successful outcome of the enterprise."

What greater proof of the Frenchman's value? What greater testimony to his loyalty?

As early as September, Croix had asked Gálvez for 300 to 400 *chasseurs*. But Gálvez had decided that because of the American Revolution he couldn't quit New Orleans for a distant Apache war. History proved his wisdom. As an ally of the Americans, he captured Pensacola and Mobile from the English and restored the Floridas to Spanish power. But he did instruct De Mézières to proceed to San Antonio, place himself at the disposal of Ripperdá and answer whatever questions were asked him. The middle-aged Frenchman, his spirit broken by his recent bereavement, arrived at Béxar in the dead of winter with a small escort. Already he had sent to Croix his analysis of the complex Indian relationships. The details must be worked out.

De Mézières and Ripperdá agreed that he should first pay a friendly visit to the Nations of the North and, on the way, confer with any Comanches he might meet.

Sick at heart and tired in body, De Mézières nevertheless set out at once. At a stockade on the Cíbolo, pretentiously named Presidio de Santa Cruz, he left the *camino real* and headed straight north through the rough and all but trackless regions where the Comanches preferred to situate their corrals and dwellings. Finding no Indians he returned to the *camino real* at the Guadalupe crossing.

Croix had complete faith in De Mézières, whose high position among the Nations of the North would be so needful when the Spanish pincers would be applied to the Apache. In September 1778, Croix wrote De Mézières that he was needed in San Antonio to serve as acting governor during the absence of Governor Domingo Cabello and also to "treat of the matters previously discussed." By now the indefatigable Frenchman was completely trusted. Croix promised

De Mézières that he even might win a proprietary appointment as governor with its perquisites and high pay. He did not know that the Frenchman did not want to leave Louisana nor to be transferred out of the jurisdiction of Governor Gálvez, whom he had come to love as a son.

Croix went further. He wrote an unusual letter to José de Gálvez, an uncle of Governor Gálvez and the powerful *visitador general* sent by the king to Mexico City to prepare a complete reorganization of New Spain. To the *visitador general* Croix praised "the zeal, tact, prudence, aptitude and efficiency with which De Mézières had fulfilled his important commission."

In the meantime, De Mézières sought out young Governor Gálvez to ask to be retained in Louisiana. To this Bernardo de Gálvez replied that it was beyond his power.

Would the governor be so kind then as to write Croix and tell him something of De Mézières' social position? Croix, so De Mézières feared, knew only that he was a frontier soldier and trader and a successful emissary to the Indians. Perhaps the governor could advise Croix that De Mézières' sister was the Baroness d'Andelot, that another sister had married the Duc d'Orleans, that two of his uncles were generals in the French army and a cousin had served as minister of state. This, said Gálvez, he would be glad to do for the older man whom he so much respected. Further, he would speak to Croix about employing De Mézières' sons in the province of Texas. In this way De Mézières could have his family with him in his new home in San Antonio de Béxar.

The Louisiana French had already virtually absorbed their Spanish rulers, culturally and even politically. The Spaniards of Texas, unlike the French, lived under Spanish authoritarianism. The reluctant De Mézières sought excuses for delay.

Not until May 1779 did De Mézières leave Natchitoches to take his position as acting governor of Texas. With him were twenty-seven veteran militiamen, together with servants and passengers—forty-three men in all, most of them mounted on stallions or mares grown thin because of the poor fodder during the river's Spring overflow. But now they must hasten. De Mézières wanted to make one more visit to the Nations of the North before proceeding to Béxar. He knew that almost everywhere the Indians were possessed by war fever. That January the Comanches had destroyed Bucareli. But before his party had traveled far northward, De Mézières was stricken with an almost fatal illness, perhaps influenza. After resting for two weeks for the malady to pass, he gave up. Four seizures wracked him in quick order. From the Sabine he returned to Natchitoches, sending the gifts he was bearing to Bucareli so that the Indians would know he had planned to come.

Making another start, he was breaking camp at the Sabine, heading west, when a messenger from Gil Ybarbo informed him that the Comanches had attacked some of his people on the way to Béxar, that all able-bodied men at Nacogdoches had hurried after the aggressors and that he was urgently needed there for the protection of women and children.

As De Mézières hastened toward Nacogdoches, his horse stumbled and fell at the brow of a steep hill, throwing him. Fever and delirium followed. He tried to go on. He had himself carried to the Attoyac River but when, after five days, his pain worsened, he had his servants put him on a stretcher and carry him back to Natchitoches where, for two months, he was confined to bed. He left most of his company at the Attoyac so the Indians would believe that news of his departure was a false report.

Finally, on August 21, 1779, he started out again. He went to San Antonio, but not before a swing well north of the *camino real*. The Nations of the North were on the verge of a neighborly war; this was no time for an unscheduled conflict. The final plans for the Apache operation were not yet ready. He would have to visit the tribes and settle their differences.

When he arrived at Bucareli a messenger from Louisiana overtook him with the welcome news that young Gálvez was to be commandant general of the Interior Provinces—thus, if De Mézières was to serve as governor of Texas he would still have him as his superior. In the courier's pouch was a commendation from the king of Spain, reported in a letter to De Mézières from the *visitador general* José de Gálvez. The letter read:

> *I have made known to the king the important service which you have performed, and His Majesty has regarded it with much complacency and gratitude, commanding me to give you, in his royal name, due thanks. This I do with the greatest of pleasure, assuring you that His Majesty will keep in mind your merits and services.*

De Mézières' visit to the Nations of the North quieted them. He was also assured by the Comanche chief that the Comanches, who had been attacking along the *camino real*, were not doing so under any concerted war plan but simply as bastard, undisciplined groups.

On September 30 De Mézières arrived at San Antonio, presented his passport from Governor Gálvez to the outgoing governor of Texas, Don Domingo Cabello. To his unhappy surprise Governor Cabello informed him that because of the fine work he had done, Croix had appointed De Mézières not interim but proprietary governor of Texas. It was an honor the Frenchman didn't want. From San Antonio he sent his excuses by messenger to Croix: He didn't know Spanish law and there would be no one at Béxar with whom to consult. At Béxar he would have to pretend friendship for the Lipan Apaches, which would weaken his position with their enemies, the Nations of the North. There was no provision for gifts to the Nations of the North when they would come to call on him, no money for the feasts that would have to be given them. The Revolutionary War was approaching Natchitoches. He should be free to go to its assistance if the English were to approach that post and try to mobilize the Indians of the area against Spain. If left unhindered, the bloodthirsty Englishmen would turn, after their own war, from killing each other to killing others. He should be at Natchitoches to stop them.

But if he must become governor of Texas, what of his sons, who were still in Natchitoches? One son was a captain, another a lieutenant of the militia cavalry. Of the two youngest, the fourteen-year-old was already a cadet. He wanted his twelve-year-old to be a cadet also. If the boys went to New Spain, what of *their* preferment? He would like the lieutenant to be made standard bearer of the Béxar company, and the oldest a commander of the troops or of the militia of the province of Texas.

There was a growing weariness in the tone of the gallant De Mézières' letters. At the end of October he wrote the new viceroy: "I am only awaiting to die and my ills cause me to desire it." He was dying in poverty. His last journey had occasioned heavy debts. No new trade had yet been developed and the ill-fated excursion had caused the malady from which he was dying.

Feebly he wrote Croix in French: "I can write you only very little and that very badly and in my own language." He was too weak to translate. He commended his children to Croix and asked that his two daughters be made participants of the *Monte Pio Militar,* a pension for the military.

Athanase de Mézières y Clugny died on November 2, 1779, at San Antonio after receiving the Sacrament of Penance, the Viaticum, and Extreme Unction from the parish priest. His burial certificate described him as Don Athanacio de Micieres, Knight of the Order of St. Louis, Commander of the Post of Natchitoches, Province of Luiciana, widower by second marriage. It might have added "heroic servant of New Spain." The Frenchman had served Spain well, but at heart he remained a Frenchman.

Croix's plan for the Apache war was not confirmed by the Spanish court. He must have been glad of it. De Mézières, who best was able to manipulate the strings of war and peace on the Indian frontier, was dead.

CHAPTER TWELVE

PHILIP NOLAN AND A GENERAL

AS THE EIGHTEENTH CENTURY WANED, the young American giant had already outgrown his Atlantic coastal abodes and westward extensions of the original colonies—or so some of the sons of the giant believed.

The men of the western frontier were land hungry. They felt cramped and put upon and neglected. If the giant lifted his head too high, he bumped upon the floor of Canada. He could not move eastward except to swim in the Atlantic. If he stretched his legs too far beneath him, he violated the East and West Spanish Floridas or nudged the Spaniards beyond the Mississippi.

From Peru to California and southeast to the tip of Florida and the islands of the Caribbean, Spain's all-but-dead hand still grasped, save Brazil, most of the empire the hot-blooded conquistadores and hardy friars had won for His Catholic Majesty in the great years of Spanish expansion. In 1621, Philip III had ruled the greatest empire, territorially, the world had ever known. But in the intervening years —despite her apparent might—war, misgovernment and corruption had brought Spain to exhaustion and bankruptcy.

By 1790 the might of Spain was no fearsome deterrent. And no one knew this better than did Hector, Baron de Carondelet, governor of Spanish Louisiana in the last decade of the eighteenth century. The now free, English-speaking revolutionaries—whose tongue and faith and mode of government were alike alien to all that Spain represented —were streaming through the Allegheny passes, settling in the western country, producing a variety of goods which cried out for purchasers and demanding a southern outlet for their produce through Spain's port of New Orleans.

The governor showed that he was an observant man when he wrote this about the Americans:

> *A carbine and a little maize in a sack are enough for an American to wander about in the forests alone for a whole month. With his carbine, he kills the wild cattle and deer for food and defends himself from the savages. The maize, dampened, serves him in lieu of bread. With some tree trunks crossed, and one above another, in the shape of a square, he raises a house, and even a fort that is impregnable to the savage by building on a story crosswise above the ground floor. The cold does not affright him. When a family tires of one location, it moves to another, and there it settles with the same ease . . .*
>
> *If such men succeed in occupying the shores of the Mississippi or the Missouri, or to obtain their navigation, there is, beyond doubt, nothing that can prevent them from crossing those rivers and penetrating into our provinces on the other side.*

And on the other side, to the southwest, waited the rich silver mines of the *Provincias Internas.*

Carondelet's predecessor, Governor Esteban Miró, had also seen the approaching challenge. He had thought of a way to meet it: encourage the separation of the western country from the eastern seaboard states. The Scots-Irish frontiersmen needed New Orleans as an outlet for their tobacco—their principal commodity—whose warehouse receipts for thousand-pound hogsheads, brought by flatboat down river, were as negotiable as cash along the western waters during the short periods that Spain opened the port to river trade. The westerners could expect little from their seaboard compatriots. Their government wasn't even able to negotiate and preserve the right of deposit at New Orleans for western goods awaiting trans-shipment by sea to the East. Only the Spanish had hard money to pay for the tobacco. A trans-Allegheny country, independent of the Atlantic states and bound by economics and alliance to Spain, would assure an outlet for the American frontiersmen and some guarantee of safety for the Spanish lands and the Spanish mines beyond the Mississippi.

So Miró and Carondelet alike believed. Their machinations produced no separate country. But the Spaniards did find Americans who would listen. Among these was General James Wilkinson, George Washington's quartermaster of the Revolution, who was living in Kentucky in the 1780s and who in 1796 would become commanding general of the United States Army.

But General Wilkinson's story will come later. Here is the tale of a personable, adventurous and ill-fated young Irishman, Philip Nolan—protégé and sometime agent of the general—who rode into the Spanish lands to trade for horses and returned with geographical information about the country beyond the silver curtain and of trails that led to Mexico. Frightened even of traders, the dons were to fear especially this intelligent, persuasive horseman, who first of all Anglo-Americans mapped their woods and plains and brought his armed compatriots into Spanish lands west of the Mississippi.

Philip Nolan was born in Belfast, Ireland, in 1771. As a boy in his early teens he had been befriended by Wilkinson, who was then living in Maryland, where Philip had emigrated with his mother. His intelligence and persuasive Irish ways and unusual charm impressed the general. So did his strength. With one arm he could hoist a silver saddle bag bulging with 2,000 silver pesos. Soon he was virtually a member of the Wilkinson household and moved to Kentucky with the family. He was only 18 when, dressed in the westerner's leather pantaloons and coonskin cap, he floated down the Mississippi with a convoy of flatboats piled high with tobacco, tallow, butter, pork and smoked beef consigned by Wilkinson for sale in New Orleans. This first venture into Spanish Louisiana lined Wilkinson's pockets. But when his trade monopoly was superseded by a short-lived permission to all Americans to trade in New Orleans and his land speculations in Kentucky all but ruined him, the Revolutionary officer rejoined the American army as a lieutenant-colonel in charge of military affairs on western waters. The young Irishman had to look then for other employment. He sought the help of Wilkinson's Spanish friends, went through the forms of becoming a Roman Catholic and took the oath of allegiance to the king of Spain.

Whatever the relationship between Wilkinson and Governor Miró, it was through Wilkinson's intercession that Miró gave Nolan a passport to enter Texas to procure horses for Spain's troops in Louisiana and to trade with Indians for skins and furs. Ostensibly it was simply

as a trader, his goods packed on his horses—three barrels to a horse—
that Philip Nolan entered Nacogdoches in 1790. But the Spanish officials at Nacogdoches refused to recognize the Louisiana Spanish governor's passport and order. Nor did Nolan's wit and ready smile
persuade them. They took away his trade goods and his passport.

But Nolan didn't leave the country of the Texas. Stripped of his
possessions, he roamed the wilderness for two years, making friends
of the Indians and learning their ways, especially their manner of
corralling and breaking wild horses, conditioning them and driving
them in herds to market. Official Spanish interference or no, Philip
Nolan returned to Louisiana late in 1793 with fifty partly-tamed
horses. He had fulfilled the Louisiana governor's contract.

He had done much besides. His observant eyes had recorded the
place and direction of the streams and rivers that crossed the western
lands, where the forests ended and the plains began, where Spain had
her settlements and who her Indian allies were.

In the Indian country he had thought often of the profit to be
derived from trading Spanish horses in the more distant and long-
settled sections of the United States, especially in Virginia, where such
leaders as Patrick Henry took great pride in their Spanish mounts.
Good money could be made in horses. So in June of 1794 Philip Nolan
returned to Nacogdoches with five Louisianians and a Negro slave,
and soon thereafter presented himself and a fresh passport from the
Baron de Carondelet to Governor Manuel Muñoz in San Antonio. In
the last two decades of Spanish authority in Louisiana, a limited trade
in horses between the two Spanish provinces was permitted, under
strict control by the governor. This time the passport was honored.
But another obstacle developed.

To collect the horses he wanted, Nolan must trade with the Indians, and he was not an authorized trader. So the governor looked
the other way while the Irishman rounded up 250 horses from down
near La Bahía. He and his *rancheros* drove the mounts from there
to Nacogdoches and thence into Louisiana. Perhaps Philip Nolan had
once kissed the Blarney stone. Not only had he made a friend of Governor Muñoz, but the governor somehow actually believed that Philip
was a relative of Hugo Oconór, the commandant general! And, near
Nacogdoches, Philip made another friend, fifty-year-old Antonio Leal,
a trader among "the friendly Indians of the Nations of the North."
Leal's 4-league-square ranch, La Teguitana, lying just north of the

camino real on either side of the Ais bayou, where San Augustine is now located, provided ideal pasturage for his horses before the final drive into Louisiana. And it offered something else as well. Antonio Leal's comely, dark-eyed wife, Gertrudis de los Santos, was seventeen years younger than her husband and she liked to ride; especially did she like to ride out with Philip Nolan, whose mistress she became.

But if Nolan made friends, he also made some enemies. One of these was William Barr, an Irish citizen of New Spain, who was licensed as a purveyor to the Indians of Texas. Barr resented Nolan's competition with his warehouse at Nacogdoches and told himself that one day he would do something about it. One day he did.

Up to now there was scant doubt that young Nolan had simply been a trader in horses, a hunter and, on his own behalf, a close observer of the Indian country. Little doubt exists also that from now on he would be, in whosever behalf, something more. He had traveled over trails never mapped and unknown to any white man. Now he drew a map of these trails that criss-crossed Texas and Louisiana, and showed it to Wilkinson before presenting it to Governor Carondelet. Soon Wilkinson employed Nolan as his agent and sent him to Gayoso de Lemos, commandant at Natchez, with a significant letter:

> *This will be delivered to you by Nolan, a child of my own raising, true to his profession [of loyalty to Spain and the Roman Catholic religion] and firm in his attachment to Spain. I consider him a powerful instrument in our hands should occasion offer. I will answer for his conduct. I am deeply interested in all that concerns him, and I confidently recommend him to your protection.*

As with most of his correspondence with the Spaniards, Wilkinson wrote the letter in code. All we know for certain is that Gayoso cordially welcomed the Irishman.

Now came the turning of wheels within wheels. In 1795, the Treaty of San Lorenzo settled the line between the United States and Spanish territory east of the Mississippi at the 31st parallel. This meant that Natchez, which had been Spanish since the American Revolution, was now in American territory. The western men could legitimately move closer to New Orleans and Natchitoches and Nacogdoches. But Governor Carondelet began playing for time. Much might happen to keep Natchez in Spanish hands if he could defer the actual surrender of the town and the lands beyond the parellel. He and Gayoso made it continuously difficult for the Americans to survey the boundary.

So angered did President Thomas Jefferson become that he suggested to his aides that if the land could not be acquired by treaty, an alternate solution would be to encourage American migration. The plum, thus ripened, would fall easily into the hands of the United States.

Meanwhile, in 1796 the government ordered Andrew Ellicott to journey down the Mississippi River and run the boundary line. And, either by happenstance or upon instruction from General Wilkinson, young Nolan made the acquaintance of the surveyor at the mouth of the Ohio. As did almost everyone, the Quaker Ellicott took to the soft-eyed traveler and invited him to join his party for the remainder of the trip South. Philip Nolan accepted. During the slow float voyage, the surveyor taught Philip astronomy. In turn Nolan gave Ellicott valuable information about the people he would meet in Natchez. Perhaps this shared knowledge would counteract, ahead of time, the rumors concerning Wilkinson which Ellicott was bound to hear when he reached Natchez. The frontier and the southern reaches buzzed with stories of intrigue.

But Ellicott's eyes were too sharp and his mind too keen. After a few months in Natchez he wrote to Jefferson at Philadelphia that Wilkinson was in Spanish pay, that his object was to detach Kentucky and Tennessee from the Union and that, leading troops along a route which had already been explored—he did not say by Nolan—Wilkinson's plan was to create a new empire with Mexico City as its center, perhaps in cooperation with Spanish officials.

We cannot say what schemes were in the making; but if the route was already explored, Nolan had done the exploring and the mapping. That year the young man was heard to say that the United States would conquer Mexico and that when the expedition was organized, his patron, the general, would give him a conspicuous command.

Late in July 1797, Philip Nolan again left Natchez for the *camino real*. This time he was probably looking for more than horses. His passport from Governor Carondelet authorized him to "secure more horses for this province, where, on account of the increasing population, the cold and the floods, there is scarcity." With him was a partner, John Murdoch—a Natchez businessman who had put up $2,400

—William Escot, four Spaniards and two slaves. Nolan brought with him $7,000 worth of merchandise and twelve rifles to trade. He bore a letter from some New Orleans priests to Texas priests which might come in handy. He carried also a portable sextant given to him by Gayoso, Andrew Ellicott's own field glasses, and a good timepiece, important for astronomical observations. He wrote Wilkinson that he intended to make an even more perfect map of the area, a task not generally considered an adjunct to horse trading.

Passing through Natchitoches and Nacogdoches, Nolan found time for conversation with his friend Antonio Leal and for dalliance with the dark-eyed Gertrudis. Later she would admit to "illicit intercourse [with Nolan] as a frail woman."

From Nacogdoches, Nolan proceeded to San Antonio to present his passport to Governor Muñoz. The passport was in order and Governor Muñoz was courteous. But Philip Nolan here requested more than simply the privilege of trading for horses in Texas. He had been commissioned to get remounts for the Louisiana regiment, he said. To do this he would have to travel beyond the province of Texas into Nuevo Santander, to the region between the Nueces and the Río Grande. There the mustangs ranged wild in their thousands. Unfortunately, he added, he had lost the copy of his order to proceed into Nuevo Santander as well as a letter of introduction to its governor. Would Governor Muñoz get him the necessary permission?

Governor Muñoz was sympathetic. He forwarded Nolan's request and his passport to Pedro de Nava, commandant general of the Interior Provinces at Chihuahau. Nolan himself wrote the commandant general in friendly vein offering Nava a new kind of gun, a short fowling piece, known as a *retaco*. Nava accepted the weapon, commenting that it might be a useful type for his troops. As for entry into Nuevo Santander, that was up to the viceroy and the governor of that province, he replied. Nava recommended that Muñoz treat the young man with firmness and, to keep him from ranging too far, offer him the use of the Béxar presidial pasture for the Louisiana governor's horses.

For the next few months Nolan fared well. Without permission from commandant general or viceroy he even went down to Nuevo Santander. Its governor failed to report the incursion. There and in San Antonio Nolan secured 1,200 horses. He built pens on the Trinity in which to condition them. And he explored the land south of the *camino real* from the Río Grande to Opelousas in Louisiana.

And then he ran into a snag. Before he left Natchez he had written to Francisco Rendón, a Spaniard whom he had known in New Orleans and who was now the intendant at Zacatecas. In the letter he had sought Rendón's aid in securing a passport for Nuevo Santander; he added that he had a letter of introduction from Governor Carondelet to Carondelet's counterpart in the distant province. The letter aroused Rendón's suspicions.

If Governor Carondelet already had authorized the project, why did Nolan need help? So Intendant Rendón wrote Carondelet, who had now been succeeded as governor by Gayoso. The former Louisiana governor promptly denied ever having given Nolan such a letter. Governor Gayoso had also developed suspicions of Nolan. The new governor had lost confidence in the Spanish adviser, General Wilkinson, who, in the last few weeks before Spain reluctantly turned Natchez over to the United States, had brought troops to Fort Adams near Natchez to assure American possession of the land. It followed that Gayoso also had no faith in Wilkinson's "child of my own raising," Philip Nolan.

So Gayoso forwarded to the viceroy in Mexico City a recommendation that all foreigners in Texas be arrested and that Philip Nolan, suspect citizen of Spain, be carefully watched. After a lengthy exchange of letters, the viceroy instructed Pedro de Nava tactfully to order Nolan to quit Texas. Because Nava assumed that Nolan had already left, he failed to forward the instructions to Governor Muñoz. Not until April, 1799, twenty-two months after Philip Nolan had entered Spanish territory, did Nava learn that he was still in the Interior Provinces. What had he been doing all this time?

The worried Nava recalled that Nolan had offered to draw a map of the land in the Interior Provinces and "especially of the large, uninhabited region between your government and that of Louisiana." The adventurer had assuredly been up to more than horse trading. Belatedly, Nava wrote Muñoz to check on Nolan's whereabouts and behavior and actions as a prelude to his immediate expulsion.

In answer, Muñoz told Nava that he would send Nolan packing, but that Nolan was "a very enterprising young man of good education, who had acquired more than an ordinary knowledge about the country of both provinces [Texas and Nuevo Santander], not only because of his long residence in them, but because of his industrious nature, his natural comprehension, and his knowledge of geography.'' Muñoz ended with the statement that he would await further orders.

Meanwhile, Nolan went in May to his huge pasture on the Trinity and, when Nava's explicit order to Muñoz to expel him reached San Antonio, Muñoz was dead. The provisional governor who succeeded him failed to open Nava's letter or another from Governor Gayoso warning that Nolan was one of the most dangerous men ever to enter the country. So, thumbing his nose at Spanish officialdom, Nolan rode unhindered out of Texas with 1,300 horses. Behind him he left a few hundred more with his agent, John Cook, at Nacogdoches.

The enterprise had been a tremendous financial success, so much so that Philip Nolan began making plans to return. To the lively, wanton Gertrudis, he sent Irish linen to be given to the commandant at Nacogdoches and a double-barrel shotgun for Father Gaeten, a Franciscan friend. In the autumn he ordered that those of his horses which remained near Nacogdoches should be marked with Gertrudis's brand and placed in the Leal pasture for safekeeping.

His comings and goings had thoroughly frightened and aroused Commandant General Pedro de Nava. Nolan had remained in Texas and Nuevo Santander for a far longer period than was necessary to round up horses for the Louisiana regiment. Worse, he had not received an order to go as far as Santander and he was not even acting under the direction of the governor of Louisiana. Couriers galloped along the *camino real,* their pouches laden with questions from Nava to Governor Gayoso or with Gayoso's suspicions indited to the commandant general. It was well known that Nolan had previously lived with and had great influence among the Indians. He knew all of the tribes and the trails, and this and all other information he carried in his head was dangerous to a New Spain which had always kept such knowledge secret. Governor Gayoso characterized him to Nava as a hypocrite who professed to be a Catholic when among the Spaniards, but scoffed at their religion when among Americans. In 1800, Nava ordered the immediate arrest of Nolan if he tried to reenter Texas.

In Natchez, Philip Nolan's exploits were a prime topic in the coffee houses and barber shops and along the riverfront. The leading Americans of Natchez boasted of how he had made fools of the Spaniards and listened avidly to his stories. So listened also the lovely young Frances Lintot, daughter of William Lintot, who was a rich planter and the father-in-law of Don Esteban Minor, one-time Spanish commandant at Natchez. Although William Lintot admired the Irishman as a man's man, he didn't want his daughter to marry a horse trader and protégé of James Wilkinson, whom most of the prominent Natchez Americans mistrusted. But when the planter learned that his daughter was so much in love with the adventurer that she was meeting him secretly despite her father's opposition, he finally consented to their marriage so as to forestall the inevitable elopement. Philip Nolan and Frances Lintot were married on December 19, 1799.

In the summer of 1800, leaving his bride at Forest Hill, the plantation of the noted one-time Tory, William Dunbar, and his horses in the lush swamplands, Philip Nolan went to Philadelphia, bearing a letter of introduction from General Wilkinson to Thomas Jefferson. All that is known is that the pair conferred for hours. That they talked only of wild horses is improbable, for, during Nolan's long stay in Texas a letter had come for him in New Orleans from Jefferson.

Another of Wilkinson's former business partners, the enigmatic Daniel Clark, opened the letter. In it, Jefferson said that he had heard of Nolan's earlier journeys and asked for information about the wild horses of the west. The nervous Clark assumed that if the Spanish authorities knew of the contents of this letter, they would certainly become suspicious of Nolan. So Clark suggested to Thomas Jefferson that he inquire of Andrew Ellicott what Nolan knew of the West, but not to quote the information as coming originally from Nolan himself as "the slightest Hint would point out the Channel from whence it flowed and might probably be attended with the most fatal Consequences to a man, who will at all times have it in his Power to render important Services to the United States, and whom Nature seems to have formed for Enterprises of which the rest of Mankind are incapable." Clark knew well the suspicions Spain entertained for all outsiders.

Nolan participated in another unexplained conference while in the East, this time with British diplomats. It is likely that they too talked of more than horses. At this juncture, Great Britain would have been glad to see both Spain and the young United States weaker than they were.

Whatever his motivation, when Philip Nolan returned to Natchez he began to prepare for what was the first armed entry of Americans into Spanish territory.

Was he to enter simply as a horse trader hopeful of bringing vast numbers of the valuable animals into the United States? Was he to go as an American agent to make a geographical study of an area so carefully shielded from foreign eyes? Did he intrude in the interest of Great Britain?

Two facts are certain. He went at the head of twenty-eight armed men and he entered without a passport. He had been denied one by the Marquis de Casa Calvo, Louisiana's governor since the recent death of Gayoso, who died from eating too much at a banquet in New Orleans.

Across the Mississippi River from Natchez, José Vidal, Spanish consul for the Natchez area, heard with anxiety of Nolan's preparations. He warned Casa Calvo that Nolan had a more perfect knowledge of Texas than did its natives, that he planned to enter Spanish territory from the old French post of Bayou Pierre—50 leagues northwest of Natchitoches—there to recruit the Indians whom he planned to use. Nolan must be stopped, said Vidal, not only because of the harm he might himself effect, but also because the men he was recruiting were the sort who could become leaders of future expeditions.

The anxious consul also urged the American governor of Mississippi Territory to forestall this armed expedition across a friendly border. He even requested the Supreme Court of the Territory to act. But the court blandly accepted Nolan's explanation that his armaments were but for defense against thieves and for hunting, and that he was returning to Texas only to get the horses he had left there. Vidal was certain that the government of the United States was giving the expedition its tacit approval.

By the end of October 1800 Nolan's party was ready. Among its members were twenty-four-year-old David Fero from near Albany, New York, second in command; Mordecai Richards of Natchez, third in command; Mordecai's young son, Stephen; Charles King and Simon McCoy, both Natchez carpenters; Joseph Reed of Kentucky; Solomon Cooley, a Connecticut tailor; John Waters, a hatter from Winchester, Virginia; Thomas House, a Tennessee blacksmith; seventeen-year-old Ellis Bean from Kentucky; and a few other Americans, making nineteen in all; seven Spanish subjects; and two of Nolan's slaves, one named Robert, the other César, in whose veins ran as much French and Spanish blood as African, and whose ability as an interpreter had already brought his master $30 a month when Nolan leased him to Don Esteban Minor. The Americans provided their own horses, carbines and pistols. Nolan supplied the food and ammunition. The men would be paid with the horses they caught, at the rate of $1.25 a day. If longer than three months were required for the round trip, each man would receive a dollar a day for the extra days.

Whether trading goods were included has never been ascertained. But among the supplies were extra arms and provisions, axes, shovels, a knife with which to make ax handles, leather for saddles and cotton to put in the horses' ears to muffle the sound of gunshots and so keep them from stampeding. Nolan brought with him his treasured double-barrel shotgun. All his subordinates were sure that they were entering Spanish country for horses; some thought they might also look for mines. They were surprised when from the start Nolan began making maps and charting distances.

As fast as Vidal received reports of Nolan's plans, he reported them to Miguel de Músquiz, commander at Nacogdoches. Almost as fast, Nolan changed his plans. One of his letters to John Cook, his agent, fell into Vidal's hands. In it he said that he had hoped to travel just south of Nacogdoches but, now that the Spaniards knew of his intentions, he would try another route. He added:

As you value my friendship, keep the secret.

I take with me a large stock of goods and they all think I am going to run mustangs.

I expect to be back in January.

I know from certain information, that, if you do not, as soon as you receive this letter, gather up all your stock and mine, and drive them off, we shall lose the whole of them. Mind my advice, dear friend, and do not lose one moment to leave the place. I have heard that Vidal has some information about my intentions, and did forward it to Nacogdoches. But I have no fear; I have good men with me, and I will never be caught.

I am so well acquainted with the coast from Opelousas to the Rio Grande that they will never be able to overtake and attack us. I have everything so well arranged at Revilla [Today's Guerrero in Tamaulipas] *that I shall not be detained two days in that place.*

As soon as you read this letter, burn it.

The letter never reached Cook. And learning that Vidal had read it, Nolan changed his route, leading his men up the Mississippi to Nogales—the present Vicksburg—across to the vicinity of the Ouachita post. As he neared this post he encountered nineteen *mestizo* auxiliaries who had been sent out to look for him. But these searchers, noting the resolute looks of the adventurers, asked no questions and pretended to be seeking Indians who had stolen some horses.

Next, Músquiz dispatched fifty men from Nacogdoches northward to look for the intruders. At about the same time Antonio Leal and Gertrudis, together with John Cook, the agent, and Nolan's servant, Pedro Longueville, wisely fled toward Louisiana, driving Nolan's horses as fast as they could move them. Músquiz' soldiers overtook and arrested them. They denied knowledge of any armed expedition or contraband trade. They had simply been exchanging goods for horses, they said, under the legal authorization which had been in effect since 1780. Although they swore that they had had no secret correspondence with Nolan, they were kept under surveillance in Nacogdoches.

But somewhere north of the *camino real* Philip Nolan himself was still at large.

Early in January the Spanish authorities received more information about what was happening. Mordecai Richards had deserted the Nolan expedition. Turning on his companions he told the officials all he knew. The traitor swore that he had not known that Nolan lacked a passport. His first intimation came, he said, when Nolan showed concern at the approach of the Ouachita troops. When he asked Nolan why the troops had been sent after them, Nolan had sought to reassure him by promising that whatever happened, Mordecai himself would be paid well for each six months he served and that his wife would be well provided for.

Richards told the Spanish interrogators that he and two companions had then quietly deserted. The three of them had hidden in the woods until Nolan quit looking for them. His son was still with Nolan. Richards also said that Nolan planned to build a fort in the Caddo country and there look for mines and round up horses. These he would remove in the summer to Kentucky, where he would meet friends, accept a commission as a general from the British and return to take over New Spain. All this and more the Spaniards were ready to believe.

Far to the west, Pedro de Nava ordered all posts alerted against the coming of Nolan and his desperadoes. The governor of Nuevo Santander searched for them between the Río Grande and the canyons of San Sabá. Governor Antonio Cordero of Coahuila ordered the troops at Monclova to prepare to repel instant attack and called upon the militia to be ready to march at a moment's notice. Indian agents brought word from the Caddo country that Nolan had built three small forts. He was running mustangs. He was parleying with the Comanches, perhaps organizing them to attack the Spanish settlements. The agents were instructed to offer forty horses in exchange for Nolan, dead or alive. William Barr, the trader whose enmity Nolan had earned by competitive trading activities, and a man whom the Indians knew and trusted, sent word to the tribesmen that Nolan was "a bad man."

Forth from Nacogdoches rode Commandant Músquiz with his forty regulars, augmented by thirty soldiers who had come on the double from Béxar, and by fifty militiamen, all heavily armed. With them Músquiz brought along a swivel gun, loaded on a mule. Beside him rode William Barr as a volunteer, determined to capture his irritating competitor.

It was still dark on the morning of March 21 when Indian guides led the Spaniards to the vicinity of Nolan's stockade near today's Waco. In the first light of dawn they could make out the 5-foot stockade of logs which protected saddles and supplies and men. Nearby were two similar "forts" and corrals in which mustangs milled. All through the night they had been restless. Nolan had believed that Indians were trying to steal them. In the morning light he could make out the sombreros of the Spanish soldiers. Unknown to him, five of his men who had been guarding the horses at the corral had already been captured. Spain had run him to earth.

There had been other harbingers of disaster before now. Mordecai Richards and his companions had disappeared. Twenty-one-year-old Thomas House was spreading rumors of imminent capture. Nolan had silenced him by warning that "if anyone flees, Luciano [García, a native of Real de Charcas and a resident of Nacogdoches] will catch him, even if he hides in the woods, and will hang him afterwards like a dog." The Comanches, whom he had hoped to win as allies, were suspicious of him because of William Barr's message and the warnings of the Indian agents. Nolan had brought provisions for only two months. He had been gone five and the supplies were exhausted. Afraid to waste powder in hunting for game, the men had been eating horsemeat for weeks.

Bearded and gaunt, Nolan and nine of his remaining twenty men left the stockade to meet the Spaniards, forty of whom were advancing under a flag of truce. As the two groups approached closer to each other Nolan shouted: "Gentlemen, come no farther, for one of us will be killed!"

The Spaniards halted. Músquiz and Barr came forward, demanding of Nolan that he surrender in the name of the king. Nolan refused, warning that this was to be a fight to the finish, and retired with his men into the fort.

Suddenly, two of Nolan's Mexicans ran out of the stockade, taking Nolan's carbine with them, and surrendered. Nolan and his men continued to fire as rapidly as possible in the hope that the Spaniards would retire temporarily and thus enable the filibusters to escape.

But at nine o'clock in the morning a cannonball struck Philip Nolan, killing him instantly.

Inside the stockade, the survivors debated what to do. Seventeen-year-old Ellis Bean, who had joined the expedition without even a word to his relatives in Natchez, said only two alternatives were open. They must capture the deadly swivel gun or retreat. To seize the cannon from the superior force of Spaniards was all but impossible. The men filled their powder horns to the brim and gave the remaining

powder to Nolan's slave, César, to carry. Then they sprinted across a prairie and into the woods.

César was caught at a little creek. From a nearby cave the rest of the filibusters fought on until their ammunition gave out, then they made another run for it. One of their number surrendered. Another, though wounded, slid into a deep ravine with the remaining survivors. But here the wounded man, tormented by thirst, could stand no more. He climbed out and surrendered. Soon he returned with a promise from Músquiz of immunity to all those who would surrender now. Músquiz promised that since Nolan was dead and the danger over, the Americans would be sent home.

While the men pondered what to do, William Barr approached under a flag of true and confirmed the offer. David Fero, in command with Nolan's death, accepted the terms and surrendered the men to Músquiz. The filibusters gave up their knives and pistols. Músquiz permitted Nolan's two slaves to bury their dead master, but not before William Barr, in keeping with Spanish custom, cut off Nolan's ears to send to the governor at Béxar as proof of his death. The still vindictive Barr volunteered to carry Nolan's papers and ears and Músquiz's report of the affair to the governor.

The Spaniards marched their captives southward down the Trinity, which they found in flood, and into Nacogdoches, where the Spanish citizens of Nolan's party were lodged in the stone fort. The others were kept under surveillance in private homes. Captain Músquiz assured these foreigners that they would be liberated as soon as Nava had sent the authorization from Chihuahua.

But the weeks of waiting were long and ominous. Even before the preliminary hearing at Nacogdoches on June 8, three of the Anglo-American group—Robert Ashley, Thomas House and Michael Moore of Ireland—induced a trader to bring them a file and almost broke out before they were discovered. News of the attempted flight aroused the governor at Béxar. The commandant general would not understand how such things could happen. He ordered Músquiz to march the prisoners, in chains and under heavy guard, to San Antonio. At the Angelina fifty soldiers from Béxar reinforced Músquiz' fifty men. Despite this precaution, David Fero escaped at the crossing. But, weighted down with shackles, he could not go far. He asked some friendly-looking Texas Indians to help him free himself. Instead they returned him to Músquiz.

For three scalding summer months the Americans were imprisoned in the Casas Reales at San Antonio and the Spaniards in the old, leaky *carcel*. Then came the long awaited orders. The captured trespassers would not be granted the freedom that by now they scarcely expected. Instead they would go to the prisons of Mexico City.

Of them all, it can be said with certainty that only two ever walked the *camino real* again. One was young Stephen Richards, whose turncoat father would procure his freedom and who would serve as a Spanish soldier at Nacogdoches. The other was Ellis Bean, who later would fight for the Mexican Revolution as a Catholic with Spanish citizenship.

As for Antonio Leal and his faithless wife, they were ordered to leave Nacogdoches, where they were too close to the Americans, and take up residence in San Antonio. There Antonio Leal died and the lonely Gertrudis married the commandant of the *presidio*. Back in Natchez, heartbroken Frances Lintot gave birth to a son six months after her brilliant swashbuckler had kissed her goodbye. She died shortly thereafter, convinced that her husband had abandoned her. The son died at twenty-one of tuberculosis.

The hateful memory of the incursion from the United States persisted. The new commandant general, Nemesio de Salcedo, was often heard to say that if it were in his power he would stop the birds from flying over the boundary line between Texas and the United States. It was not to be in his power to halt either bird or man from east of the Mississippi. The Nolan expedition was luckless. But others would follow.

CHAPTER THIRTEEN

THE DILEMMA OF GENERAL WILKINSON

FOR GENERAL JAMES WILKINSON, ranking officer of the United States Army and Spanish agent for many years, the moment of irrevocable decision came in the pre-dawn hours of the morning of October 9, 1806, in his room in the headquarters of Camp Claiborne at Natchitoches. He could betray his country. Or he could betray his friend, Aaron Burr, recently vice president of the United States and a man of no small vision. Whatever the choice, the golden coin of Spain might reward a friend or be loot for a victorious foe. Where lay the surer profit?

Six years before, while the Spanish consul across the Mississippi river from American Natchez maneuvered through legal channels to block Philip Nolan's projected entry into Texas, Spain and France had come to a secret understanding in the Treaty of San Ildefonso by which Louisiana and the Isle of Orleans had reverted to France "with the same extent that it now has in the hands of Spain and that it had when France possessed it." In return, France promised support for the Queen of Spain's uncle, the Duke of Parma, in his effort to add Tuscany to his Italian duchy, and assured Spain that Louisiana would not be transferred to any other power.

Napoleon, remembering La Salle's claim at the mouth of the Mississippi to all the territory westward to the River of Palms, thought the border, though never agreed on with Spain, to be the Río Grande. When, in 1803, he sold the province to the United States for $12 million and a settlement of $3 million for debts owed by French to American citizens, his minister Talleyrand refused to fix the border, but

advised the Americans that the United States had made a good bargain and should claim all the land she could get. President Jefferson
preferred to believe that the border was the distant Río Grande. An
expanding nation needed space for future growth.

Within three years of the purchase, American regulars and militiamen and Spanish presidials and auxiliaries were bivouacked within
25 miles of each other near the Sabine crossing on the *camino real*,
most of them convinced that a march toward Mexico was about to be
attempted.

Who wanted that march? Who stopped it, and why?

The most favorable comments that can be made about General
James Wilkinson, one-time rebel officer in the American Revolution
and, from 1796 to 1814, commanding general of the United States
Army, is that he was courageous, that his family loved him and that
his descendants have loyally defended his reputation. Against these
champions have been arrayed relays of scholars who in later years
have produced evidence enough to convince themselves and many a
reader that Wilkinson was, to say the least, a devious, high-living and
greedy double-dealer—perhaps a triple-dealer.

Yet, in his behalf, it is indisputable that he was never found
guilty of treason or even of conspiracy against his young country. And
whatever his reasons and however inept or self-aggrandizing his tac-
tics, he did bring to the inflamed attention of the American people
the land that, in the early years of the nineteenth century, waited
almost supinely across the Sabine River.

One side of the Wilkinson coin is bright. Time and historical
investigation have given a tarnished look to the other side—an appropriate metaphor, since the general had an almost compulsive affection for coin of the realm, any realm, so said and say his critics. He
performed favors for Spain for pay, but not as a traitor in the meaning of the accursed word in his own time. He did conspire to detach
the neglected settlers and traders and frontiersmen of the West—
notably his own Kentuckians and the Ohioans and Tennesseans—
from an American confederation too much dominated by the shrewd
if proper Bostonians, the gentry of Virginia and the other established
citizens of the Atlantic seaboard. James Wilkinson and Aaron Burr
prodded and aroused many of their fellow countrymen, hungry for
land, starving for trade and Papist-hating, to feverish awareness of

what beckoned resolute men in the land of the Texas and in the halls
of Montezuma. Had Wilkinson or, more grandly and single-mindedly,
Aaron Burr, succeeded, another nation—perhaps an empire—might
have been created on the North American continent. Such notions as
theirs were not then treasonable. The first association of the late colonies of George III was loose and even after the Constitution of 1789
Thomas Jefferson had said, as President of the new United States,
that if the western folk were discontented with the union, they should
be permitted to leave it.

But what is also certain is that Wilkinson did betray Aaron Burr,
the friend to whose rash vision of a western empire he was early privy.

No soothsayer would have thought the young James Wilkinson,
professional soldier, ill-starred. His father, a substantial Maryland
planter, left him an orphan at seven. A medical student at the outbreak of the Revolution, he obtained a captain's commission in the
Revolutionary Army. He was unruly, but he fought well when fighting was required: at the siege of Boston; with Benedict Arnold at
Montreal; at Trenton and Princeton under George Washington, who
promoted him to lieutenant-colonel in 1777; as deputy adjutant general
for the Northern Department; and as brevet brigadier-general by order of Congress in November 1777.

Intrigue was his passion, drinking his delight, extravagance his
goad. He joined the Conway Cabal that sought to topple Washington.
In the wake of the failure of the cabal, he was forced to resign his
several high posts. With his uncanny ability to land on his feet he
sought and was awarded the money-making post of clothier-general,
but, when his extravagances were reflected in irregularities in his
accounts, he resigned early in 1781. Meanwhile he had married Ann
Biddle, sister of Clement Biddle of Philadelphia, which made for an
impeccable alliance.

The restless, bold and avaricious man turned in 1784 to Virginia's
growing and discontented district of Kentucky. Commanding and
handsome in person, glib of tongue and pen, he readily supplanted
George Rogers Clark as spokesman for the region. By mid-1785 he was
writing fervent memorials in support of the separation of Kentucky
from Virginia. So overwhelmingly did the Kentuckians back him that
he turned to more grandiose—and more remunerative—objectives. He
ingratiated himself with the Spanish authorities in Missouri and in
1787 he took an oath of allegiance to Spain as prelude to a trading

monopoly in lower Louisiana. His fellow Kentuckians, economically stifled, gladly assembled their produce to entrust it to him for shipment to New Orleans. The young Philip Nolan floated down the river on this history-making trip.

During these years, Wilkinson, who dreamed of being the Washington of the West, convinced the Spaniards in Louisiana that he was seeking to separate the frontier territories from the United States. For his efforts Spain ultimately granted him an annual pension of $2,000, delivered in thick leather pouches borne by Spanish mules or packed in barrels along with sugar and coffee being shipped from New Orleans to Kentucky.

When Spain opened the river trade to all Americans, Wilkinson's monopoly lost any meaning. Wealth remained the will-of-the-wisp and, failing in his commercial and land ventures—among them the founding of Frankfort—he returned to the American military service.

James Wilkinson was a good soldier and, when Mad Anthony Wayne died in 1796, he became the highest-ranking officer in the American Army.

The President appointed him, together with William C. C. Claiborne, governor of Mississippi Territory, to accept the transfer of Louisiana after the purchase in the official ceremonies at the Cabildo in New Orleans on December 20, 1803. In the festivities accompanying the event, the general entertained lavishly, at government expense. His account of expenditures included 844 bottles of claret, 196 gallons of madeira, 4 gallons of sherry, 144 bottles of champagne, 260 bottles of white wine, 100 bottles of "hermitage" wine, 580 bottles of red wine, 6 bottles of cordials, 27 gallons of brandy, 81 bottles of porter, 1 case of gin, 258 bottles of ale, 5 gallons of rum, 2⅛ gallons of whiskey, 3 barrels of cider and 11,360 "Spanish Segards."

He took advantage of being in the city to submit a memoir to the Marquis de Casa Calvo, now Spanish boundary commissioner, concerning American designs on other Spanish territory. He suggested to him and to the governor of West Florida that Texas be fortified against possible United States attack. Frightened and impressed, Casa Calvo paid him $12,000 due on his pension, and asked for further recommendations. To protect himself, Wilkinson arranged that correspondence between the Spaniards and himself should be coded, not too unusual an agreement when the mails were far from dependable. He added that he should be referred to only as Number Thirteen.

He then left for New York, and there began his involvement with Aaron Burr.

The pair conferred often in the winter of 1804–05 in Washington. Burr met with Wilkinson in June at the mouth of the Ohio, from where Burr proceeded downstream in a river craft supplied by the commanding general of the United States Army and bearing Wilkinson's fulsome letters to people of importance in New Orleans. Three months later Burr was Wilkinson's guest at his headquarters in St. Louis. Everyone in the government and many outside of it had begun to speculate on the possibility that the two intriguers were plotting an invasion of Mexico.

In addition to his other duties, Wilkinson was now serving as governor of the Upper Louisiana Territory in 1805, with headquarters in St. Louis, and with great civilian as well as military authority. From here he dispatched Lieutenant Zebulon M. Pike westward under orders to find a military route to New Mexico. His fellow citizens later believed the action was part of the Burr conspiracy. Ultimately, because of his unpopularity and the strong opposition to his governorship, Jefferson relieved him of his high civilian office.

Meantime, in the summer of 1806, a bitter critic, Joseph Street, publisher of the *Western World* at Frankfort, began openly attacking Wilkinson's ties with Aaron Burr and speculated in print upon his earlier conniving with Spain.

General James Wilkinson began to grow desperate. His moment of decision was near.

That moment came to James Wilkinson in the dark, early hours of the morning of October 9, 1806. All night he had debated with himself in the room at headquarters at Camp Claiborne in Natchitoches. He could betray his friend, Aaron Burr—who hungered to rule an all but limitless empire in the Americas—or he could do grave disservice to his country, if not betray it, by opening hostilities against Spain. If, in the interests of Aaron Burr, he created an incident which would bring about war with Spain, the grand plot might succeed, for Burr and his own projected army of filibusters, perhaps with Wilkinson and at least some of his militiamen aiding them, could strike on their own. James Wilkinson would be Burr's commanding general in an empire based on Mexico and reaching from there through New Orleans to the Alleghenies. But if Burr's probable plan failed, what then?

During that night, momentous for the United States, for Spain, for Aaron Burr and for James Wilkinson, the distraught general must have reviewed everything which, taken together, had brought him to Natchitoches. Where had the money gone, the Spanish pesos that mules had twice carried to Frankfort, the $9,000 hidden in flour and sugar barrels, the years of Spain's pensioning? Why had the ultimate in personal fame eluded him? How had he failed to persuade his countrymen that he was a patriotic and honest soldier?

And what of the confrontation of Spain and the United States that had brought him here to the Natchitoches post with orders to hold to the Sabine but to avoid war if possible?

Let us review now the past as Wilkinson most surely did that night.

The Louisiana Purchase made imperative a difficult adjustment. For the Creoles of Louisiana, Spanish since 1762, the news had been incredible. Forty years before, it had been difficult enough to shift allegiance from Bourbon to Bourbon. It was far more difficult to accept the rule of an English-descended, Protestant nation. The priests at Natchitoches, as elsewhere in the territory, had assured their parishioners that Spain would not permit such a tragedy and that social intercourse with heretics dishonored their forebears.

For the United States there were also worries. Not only had Napoleon stated no boundaries in the purchase treaty but he had promised Spain that he would not transfer Louisiana to any power. As long as Spanish soldiers remained in New Orleans, Secretary of War Dearborn feared that Spain might seek to prevent American occupation of the region. The Marquis de Casa Calvo helped spread the rumor that Spain would soon reclaim her own.

The United States moved softly and slowly. Not until April 20, 1805, did Claiborne, now governor of Orleans Territory, send a sixty-four-man force to Natchitoches under Captain Edwin Tucker to take over the strategic point for the United States. The thirty-two-man Spanish garrison stood at attention as their flag was hauled down and the French tricolor raised for a brief hour before it in turn was lowered and the flag of the United States hoisted in its place.

The ceremony enraged Nemesio de Salcedo, commandant general of the *Provincias Internas*. He sharply reprimanded the Spanish commandant at Nacogdoches for his diplomatic mistake in attending. By his presence at the ceremony the commandant had signified acceptance of the transfer. By the time the reprimand reached the commandant, he and his men had withdrawn to Nacogdoches and the Americans were building a Natchitoches fort of their own—Fort Claiborne—on a hill overlooking the Red River.

But Governor Claiborne was nervous. The hostile behavior of the Creoles of New Orleans, Casa Calvo's casually dropped remarks that Spain would retake the country and the belligerent reaction of the viceroy in Mexico City and of Commandant General de Salcedo were not reassuring. Moreover, the Spaniards were making it clear that they objected to the boundaries between Louisiana and New Spain as designated by Charles Pinckney, the American minister to Spain, and James Monroe, envoy extraordinary. At no time had Spain considered what the Americans were suggesting—namely that the Río Grande, the Colorado, or the Sabine marked the northeastern limits of New Spain.

The preposterous Americans, who had first proposed a neutral ground between the Sabine and the Colorado, then more impudently, one between the Colorado and the Río Grande, finally sought on May 12, 1805, the exchange of all Spanish holdings east of the Mississippi in return for a border on the Colorado. The proposal, insufferable to Spain, would mean that she must give up East and West Florida and the greater part of the Texas buffer lands. Spain felt herself forced to act.

During the months of tedious negotiation, Spain ordered out of Nacogdoches all Americans who did not profess the Catholic religion. Those who did remain under those terms must remove west of the town itself. Salcedo invited Louisianians loyal to his country to enter Texas with all their possessions, duty free. He asked six Indian tribes unfriendly to the Anglo-Americans to settle between the Sabine and the Trinity. He opened a port at San Bernardo Bay, the better to provision the interior—a measure Spain never took save in time of extreme danger. He founded two new towns: Santíssima Trinidad de Salcedo on the Trinity, its population made up of ninety-one Louisianians and a small number from San Antonio, and another on the San Marcos composed of settlers from San Antonio and La Bahía. When the United States in May made her proposal that Spain surrender her lands east of the Mississippi, Spain ordered a build-up of her troops in the border province of Texas.

Tension mounted.

That fall of 1805, under orders from Salcedo, Antonio Cordero, acting governor of Texas and a renowned forty-eight-year-old soldier of the king, marched with three companies to the Trinity. There he was joined by Governor Simón de Herrera of Nuevo León, also an experienced soldier, who had brought both regulars and militiamen with him from Monterrey by way of the La Bahía Road. Governor Herrera, who assumed command of the defense—a soldier whom Zebulon Pike would later praise as one of the "most gallant and accomplished men I ever knew"—fortunately knew and liked the United States. The tall, black-haired Spaniard had married an Englishwoman. During Washington's presidency he had lived in the United States for a year. He spoke French well and English slightly. Under him were 700 men. Together with Cordero's troops the Spanish force numbered more than 1,000. It was the first time since 1722 that Spain had gathered so many troops together in Texas. Captain Porter, with only 200 men, was outnumbered five to one.

Salcedo instructed the governors to strengthen Nacogdoches, restore the long abandoned Orcoquisa and Atascosito posts and establish new ones where the *camino real* crossed the Trinity, the Brazos and the Colorado; to reoccupy Los Adaes; to place an outpost on the trail at LaNana 7 leagues east of the Sabine; and to occupy Bayou Pierre, northwest of Natchitoches, where the French had once had a post.

Captain Moses Porter rushed a courier from Natchitoches to the new capital of the United States at Washington. But he could not wait the two months it would take from the time the courier departed to his return with instructions from the War Department. To Captain Porter the occupation of Los Adaes represented an outright act of aggression against his country. He could not have known that more than eighty years before the Marquis de Aguayo had faced down Louis Juchereau de St. Dénis and secured Los Adaes again for Spain. The captain sent an officer and sixty men to Los Adaes, where the Spanish garrison of one officer and twenty men was persuaded to withdraw to Nacogdoches. For the first time American troops had marched on the *camino real* and evicted Spanish soldiers from land claimed by Spain.

Porter's first messenger returned from Washington with the order that if the Spanish commandant at Nacogdoches assured him that no aggression was planned, he was to leave the Spanish garrisons in possession. But the size of Herrera's command indicated aggression might be contemplated. Again Captain Porter rushed a messenger to Washington.

The War Department acted swiftly. Colonel Thomas H. Cushing was ordered to Natchitoches with three companies of regulars and two field pieces. The department also ordered General Wilkinson to proceed from his headquarters at St. Louis to Orleans Territory to repel any invasion and to hold to the Sabine River. But Wilkinson, who had only recently received his appointment as governor of Upper Louisiana, tarried in St. Louis.

In October, Casa Calvo traveled the *camino real* to Los Adaes, where he studied the old mission records. He returned to New Orleans in February. There he asserted that the line between Louisiana and Texas had always been the Arroyo Hondo, in the environs of Natchitoches, and not the Sabine. In his absence, President Jefferson had directed Governor Claiborne to oust all Spanish officers from Orleans territory. Reluctantly and before he could do any further mischief, Casa Calvo, the last representative of Spanish dominion over Louisiana, departed for East Florida. General James Wilkinson, commanding general of the United States Army, Spanish agent and confidant of Aaron Burr in plots that, if successful, would help neither Spain nor the United States, must have felt relieved.

Aaron Burr needed a war between Spain and the United States, a conflict which he, his westerners and his other promised forces could turn to their own advantage. A border incident could provoke it. The contest would be popular among the frontiersmen, who looked upon the Spaniards as their enemies. But Burr also needed money and the British had not agreed to aid him. Very discouraged, he wrote Wilkinson in April 1806 that he was suspending all action until fall.

Wilkinson went ahead on his own. He was still in St. Louis, despite the orders from Washington for him to go to Natchitoches. He already knew much about Texas from the maps and information Philip Nolan had supplied. That summer, he sent Lieutenant Zebulon M. Pike from St. Louis to explore the upper waters of the Arkansas and Red Rivers, with orders to penetrate as close to New Mexico as practicable. With the Pike expedition was a civilian volunteer, Dr. John Hamilton Robinson, whose presence was never explained. It seems possible that Wilkinson planned that Pike and his men should be captured by the Spaniards and that Robinson could thereby give

Salcedo a message that the general was working in Spain's interest to prevent hostilities.

Incidentally, on the mission, Pike discovered the peak that bears his name. After his capture, the Spanish would take him to Santa Fé and Chihuahua: there Salcedo would liberate him, and Pike and his companions would be the first Americans to travel from west to east along the *camino real,* from Monclova to Natchitoches, and Cordero and Herrera would entertain him. Whether Wilkinson had secret designs in sending out Pike is a matter for speculation. Another is whether Wilkinson delayed his own departure from St. Louis only because his beloved wife was ill. Or was he also waiting to see if Burr would find enough money and supporters for his scheme to assure its success?

In August, Governor Herrera crossed the Sabine. The Spanish patrols moved back and forth along the *camino real* to Los Adaes. Governor Claiborne arrived at Natchitoches with such militia as he could bring to the aid of Colonel Cushing. Acting Governor Cowles Mead of Mississippi promised reinforcements. At the end of September, Claiborne passed General Wilkinson coming up the Red River at last as ordered by the War Department. He had waited overlong for unclear reasons of his own.

The situation at Natchitoches at the time of Wilkinson's delayed arrival was well summed up in a letter which a remarkable American in Natchitoches wrote his son on September 26. He was Dr. John Sibley, a Revolutionary War hero who, after the Purchase, had moved to Natchitoches from North Carolina in 1803. Dr. Sibley had soon recognized the need for American conferences with the Indians to assure their loyalty to the United States. In February 1805, he had sent to the War Department detailed reports on all the tribes from the Mississippi to the Río Grande. Now he was the Indian agent at Natchitoches. Governor Salcedo was irate that this American had dared to negotiate with the Indian tribes under Spanish domination. He had requested 150 additional soldiers to cope with the Indian intrigues of "the revolutionist Dr. Sibley." Here is Dr. Sibley's eyewitness account of conditions at the time of Wilkinson's arrival:

The Spaniards resenting being removed over the Sabine
by the officer commanding here last winter have returned
with 1,200 under two officers of rank and experience,

equipped with cannon, 4,000 horses and frequently patrol within 5 or 6 miles of Natchitoches and have turned back an exploring party ascending Red River by order of the president, have captured and taken away prisoners three American citizens, and two others made their escape from them, have cut down and carried away the flag of the U S with other insults and outrage not to be borne.

General Wilkinson arrived here last Sunday and is making every preparation to attack them in their camp. He has here now nine companies of Infantry and two artillery of the U S, what cavalry can be raised in this part of the Territory and I expect from Natchez. There will be in the course of ten days from 800 to 1,000 militia. Gov. Claiborne went from here about a week ago, he is now in the turning out and organizing of militia and probably will be here again in a few days. Sibley is in command of what cavalry can be raised and I shall join Gen. Wilkinson day after tomorrow. The Spaniards will probably stand three or four fires. Whether this will bring on a general war or not is uncertain—but it probably will.

What Wilkinson's sentiments were, for public consumption, he expressed in a letter to Secretary Dearborn:

I shall drain the cup of conciliation, but a blow once struck, it would seem expedient that we should make every advantage of it; and if means and men are furnished, I will soon plant our standards on the left bank of the Grand River.

More privately, he wrote Senator John Adair, a fellow Kentuckian who had also taken part in the old so-called Spanish Conspiracy, the plot for western secession: ''The time longed for by many and wished for by more, has arrived for subverting the Spanish government in Mexico...unless you fear to join a Spanish intriguer, come immediately. Without you I can do nothing.''

Governor Claiborne had promised 400 militiamen. Five hundred rushed to Natchitoches from Kentucky, from Mississippi, from Orleans, all spoiling for a fight, bearing whatever arms they possessed— blunderbusses, pistols, fusees and long rifles—and identical in their desire for an incident which would provoke war. An incident, and proper timing, was what Aaron Burr also required.

Soon after General Wilkinson arrived at Natchitoches, he sent Colonel Cushing to Lieutenant Colonel Herrera with a lengthy document. Its tenor was that the United States claimed the whole of Texas as part of Louisiana, but that he would agree upon the Sabine as a temporary border. Herrera took Colonel Cushing to Governor Cordero at Nacogdoches. The governor told the American that his orders were to remain at the Arroyo Hondo. When Cushing reached the Sabine on his return to Natchitoches, he discovered that Herrera had prudently withdrawn his men from Bayou Pierre and had crossed to the west bank of the river. Again the Spaniards had avoided an incident.

Wilkinson now notified Cordero that he was moving to the Sabine, not as an act of hostility but "only as signifying the pretentions of the United States to the east bank." He moved only to within 25 miles of the Sabine. A full-scale advance of the American troops to the river bank itself would almost surely precipitate war. Wilkinson had not yet made up his mind what was best for himself.

On the night of October 8, a weary young man, his fashionable eastern clothing covered with the grime of hard travel, arrived at Fort Claiborne in Natchitoches. There, in the temporary absence of the general, he was welcomed by Colonel Cushing. The traveler introduced himself as Samuel Swarthout. He was ten weeks out from Philadelphia, he said, and had come to volunteer to serve under General Wilkinson.

When the general returned to the officers' barracks and met the young volunteer, he knew at once from whom the young man had come and why. Samuel Swarthout's brother had been a second for Aaron Burr in his duel with Alexander Hamilton. Soon, and without being detected by Colonel Cushing, Swarthout gave Wilkinson the packet of letters which was the real reason for his trip to Natchitoches. General Wilkinson retired early to his quarters. There he sat down with his code book to decipher messages from Aaron Burr and United States Senator Jonathan Dayton of New Jersey, another plotter. He was certain that the Burr communication was an answer to a letter he had written the previous May, when, beginning to entertain strong doubts that Burr could succeed, he had asked for more specific details and assurance that all was arranged. He wanted no part of a revolution which might fail. Wilkinson first deciphered Dayton's terse note. It contained ominous information: "It is now well ascertained that you are to be replaced at the next session [of Congress]. Jefferson will affect to yield reluctantly to public opinion, but yield he will. Prepare yourself therefore for it.''

The rest of Dayton's note was more revealing: ''You know the rest. You are not the man to despair or even despond, especially when such prospects offer in another quarter. Are you ready? Are your numerous associates ready? Wealth and glory! Louisiana and Mexico! I shall have time to receive a letter before I set out for Ohio—OHIO!''

It took Wilkinson the rest of the night to decode Burr's letter. The code was not a difficult one, but the process was tedious. A key word revealed the page and line of words in the little dictionary which the general kept locked in his portfolio. Burr's letter read:

Your letter, postmarked thirteenth May, is received. I, Aaron Burr, have obtained funds and have actually commenced the enterprise. Detachments from different points and under various pretenses, will rendezvous on the Ohio, first of November. Everything internal and external favors views. Naval protection of England is assured. Truxton is going to Jamaica to arrange with the admiral on that station. It will meet us at the Mississippi. England, a navy of the United States, are ready to join, and final orders are given to my friends and followers. It will be a host of choice spirits. Wilkinson shall be second to Burr only; Wilkinson shall dictate the rank and promotion of his officers. Burr will proceed westward first August, never to return. With him goes his daughter; her husband will follow in October, with a corps of worthies. Send forthwith an intelligent and confidential friend with whom Burr may confer; he shall return immediately with further interesting details; this is essential to concert and harmony of movement. Send a list of all persons known to Wilkinson west of the mountains who could be useful, with a note delineating their character. By your messenger send me four or five commissions of your officers, which you can borrow on any pretext you please; they shall be returned faithfully. Already are orders given to the contractor to forward provisions to points Wilkinson may name; this shall not be used until the last moment and then under proper injunctions. The object is brought to the point so long desired. Burr guarantees the result with his life and honor, with the lives and honor and the fortunes of hundreds of the best blood of the country. Burr's plan of operations is to move down rapidly from the Falls on the fifteenth of November, with the first five hundred or one thousand men, in light boats now constructing for that purpose; to be at Natchez between the fifth and fifteenth of December, there to meet you; there to determine whether it will be expedient in the first instance to seize on or pass by Baton Rouge. On receipt of this send Burr an answer. Draw on Burr for all expenses, etc. The people of the country to which we are going are prepared to receive us; their agents, now with Burr, say that if we will protect their religion, and not subject them to a foreign power, that in three weeks all will be settled. The gods invite us to glory and fortune; it remains to be seen whether we deserve the boon. The bearer of this goes express to you. He is a man of inviolable honor and perfect discretion, formed to execute rather than project, capable of relating facts with fidelity, and incapable of relating them otherwise; he is thoroughly informed of the plans and intentions of Burr, and will disclose to you as far as you require and no further. He has imbibed a reverence for your character, and may be embarrassed in your presence; put him at ease, and he will satisfy you.

Wearily the general leaned back in his chair. Here were the dates of Burr's projected movement, but where was the assurance of funds, supplies, munitions?

Dayton's note, predicting the general's removal as commander-in-chief was bad enough, but between the lines of Aaron Burr's letter Wilkinson must have read an ominous meaning. Burr couldn't succeed. And if James Wilkinson were publicly connected with his conspiracy, disaster would be complete.

Conversely, if James Wilkinson were to reveal the plot to the President, he would receive the grateful plaudits of the nation. He might even be retained as commander-in-chief of the Army. But the praise of his countrymen, as pleasing as it would be, might be supplemented by something more substantial—gold from Spain, for instance. The Spaniards would also profit from an exposure of Burr's intentions. Thus, he would have to do more than reveal Burr's duplicity to President Jefferson.

Eight weeks would be required for answering instructions to come from Washington. To circumvent Burr and to advance his own interests, Wilkinson should be at the head of his troops in New Orleans when Burr arrived and so receive credit for capturing him. But he could not leave this frontier open to Spanish penetration. A way must be found to free his troops and himself for service in New Orleans. If Spain could also be persuaded to reward him fittingly, so much the better.

It had been a long night for James Wilkinson. As the morning light filtered through the muslin which served as a mosquito bar at the windows, he walked out upon the wide gallery which ran the length of the officers' quarters. There Colonel Cushing greeted him.

General Wilkinson began to tell all—or as much as should be told—to the colonel. The young man of the night before, Samuel Swartwout, was no mere volunteer, the general said. He was a courier from Aaron Burr, bearing a letter in cipher, so long that he had not bothered to decode it in full. There was no doubt that Burr was plotting treason. The letter had offered the general the command of Burr's Mexico-bound invading army. The plotter had boasted that he had won the backing of the navy at New Orleans.

Colonel Cushing asked the general if the government knew of the plot. Wilkinson replied that it did not. He would let Washington know at once, but as Burr planned to descend the Mississippi early in December there was no time to wait for instructions. Instead, the Americans must go to the Sabine and come to an agreement with the Spaniards. Then Cushing must go downriver to New Orleans with the greater part of the American force.

Not for twelve days did General Wilkinson write the President of the United States to inform him of the stupendous plot of which, so he said, he had only recently learned. Coincidentally, on October 20, the day when he did write the President, the Cabinet was in session.

Among the topics the Cabinet discussed were charges which had been made against the general, including his failure to obey the orders "to descend with all possible dispatch to . . . take command at Natchitoches." Fortunately for Wilkinson, consideration of the charges was postponed.

For the entire twelve days, young Swarthout remained in the officers' quarters. Wilkinson explained to Colonel Cushing that he was keeping Swarthout there to drain him of all that he knew. During those twelve days the general also began some delicate negotiations with the Spaniards.

Near the end of October, General Wilkinson sent his aide, Major Walter Burling, with a message to Governor Cordero at Nacogdoches. He proposed that the Spaniards remain west of the Sabine and the Americans east of the Arroyo Hondo, thus establishing a neutral ground until such time as the governments of the two countries agreed upon the line of demarcation. When Burling was about to depart, a messenger arrived from Commandant General de Salcedo with a note refusing to make any concessions. Without regard to the adamant attitude of the Salcedo note, Wilkinson ordered Burling to proceed.

After crossing the Sabine, Burling left with Herrera a copy of Wilkinson's proposal for the neutral ground. At Governor Cordero's headquarters, which he reached on November 1, Burling did more, undoubtedly at the general's orders, than hand over General Wilkinson's letter. He dwelt upon the danger to New Spain from Aaron Burr's conspiracy, thus adding to the image of James Wilkinson as protector of Spain's interests. But Governor Cordero had his orders. Despite the dangers presented by Burling, he refused to commit himself to an agreement on the proposed neutral ground. Burling remained overnight and resumed the debate with Governor Cordero the next day, to no avail.

Discouraged, he rode back along the *camino real* to the Sabine. Here Governor Herrera again gave him a cordial welcome, and more. The lieutenant colonel had now read Wilkinson's proposal. He declared to the American officer that had he known of its contents he would have dissuaded Burling from going to Nacogdoches. He, Simón de Herrera, charged with the defense of the Province of Texas, was prepared to act even without authorization. The Burr conspiracy represented a threat so great that officers at the frontier could not wait three weeks for Salcedo to change his mind. Therefore, he would undertake a neutral ground agreement with General Wilkinson, an American whom he knew had been friendly to Spain in the past. The Burr plot must be circumvented.

On November 6, 1806, General James Wilkinson and Lieutenant Colonel Simón de Herrera signed an agreement under which the

30-mile wide strip of land between the Arroyo Hondo and the Sabine was declared a neutral ground between Louisiana and Texas—an area which neither Spain nor the United States would claim and into which no one could legally move until a permanent treaty had been drafted. A year later, at San Antonio, Herrera was to tell Lieutenant Pike that his decision to act had antagonized Governor Cordero for a while. The coolness had lasted until, contrary to Cordero's expectations, Herrera received the congratulations of Salcedo and the viceroy, José de Iturrigaray, even though he had flaunted explicit orders.

Soon, in General Wilkinson's camp, rumors spread that $120,000 in pieces of eight had arrived by mule train from San Antonio. Such a consignment would not have been surprising to General Wilkinson. But no such shipment reached him, despite an urgent request which Walter Burling, traveling under a passport from Herrera and ostensibly looking for mules for the American army, bore along the *camino real* to the viceroy. Wrote Wilkinson to the viceroy:

> *So far as I am concerned, I am risking my life, my good name and my property by the means I have adopted; my life by the change I have made in the military arrangements without the knowledge of my government; my good name by offering without orders this communication to a foreign power; and my fortune or possessions by draining my private purse and those of my friends in order to elude, frustrate and, if possible, destroy the nefarious schemes of the revolutionist.*

Wilkinson affirmed that he had already spent 85,000 pesos to shatter Burr's plans and destroy the bandits "now being enrolled along the Ohio, and 36,000 pesos in the discretionary dispatch of supplies and counter-revolutionists, which sums I trust will be reimbursed to the bearer, for whose safe return I ask Your Excellency to furnish a suitable escort as far as the immediate neighborhood of Natchitoches."

The viceroy declined to grant the extraordinary request. Perhaps he felt General Wilkinson had already received enough gold from Spain. The general had better luck in his own country. He sent to President Jefferson a bill for $1,500 for the expenses which Burling occurred while scouting the road to Mexico. It was promptly paid.

Meanwhile the general had sent Colonel Cushing and most of his troops to New Orleans. He himself arrived somewhat later, put the city under martial law and dealt severely and extralegally with suspects in the Burr plot. The President, upon receiving Wilkinson's delayed report of Burr's intentions, issued a proclamation warning all citizens not to participate in the illegal expedition. Surrendering to Acting Governor Cowles Mead, Aaron Burr denounced James Wilkinson as a perfidious villain who had frustrated any plans he might have had.

Almost certainly Burr intended to conquer all Mexico as far as the Isthmus of Darien. In this undertaking many Americans would have supported him. Neither Thomas Jefferson nor later Presidents nor Governor Claiborne of the Louisiana Territory were secretive about their hopes for American expansion to the west.

The charges of treason brought against Burr—and he was acquitted of them—were not that he dreamed of empire. But Wilkinson testified that the former vice president intended to separate the western states from the Union and seize the government and bank at New Orleans. Again, in the realm only of probability, Wilkinson's role could have been to create an incident at the border which would bring about war and give Burr the opportunity to march at the head of the Louisiana Creole dissidents, American frontiersmen, militiamen and whatever regular troops would come over to him.

Neither man profited from his public or private behavior. Aaron Burr lived a tragic and too-long life, hounded by the spectres of his failures and by terrible grief. Never did he set foot on the *camino real* so important in his plans for power and wealth and glory.

James Wilkinson's subsequent career was hardly more rewarding. His wife, to whom he was devoted and who ever believed in him, died at New Orleans on February 23, 1807, while he was still under severe public censure. He served as chief witness at Burr's trial in Richmond, Virginia, but the grand jury came close to indicting him too. Andrew Jackson publicly denounced him, Washington Irving savagely caricatured him. Young Swarthout, the bearer of Burr's coded letter to Natchitoches, insulted him and challenged him to a duel.

A Congressional inquiry looked into his entire career disapprovingly. In July 1811, at Wilkinson's request, President Madison ordered a court-martial to try him and, though the verdict was "not guilty," the wording was such that the President approved it only regretfully. Only Thomas Jefferson was prejudiced in his favor. Restored to his command in New Orleans, he fought in the War of 1812, but was relieved from regular duty because of his part in the failure of American troops to take Montreal. He was never to be reinstated to the service.

The Mexican lodestar beckoned him to the end of his days. In 1821, James Wilkinson, now 64, went to Mexico to plead for a Texas land grant, and finally secured an option. He died in Mexico City before he could meet the required conditions of occupancy.

CHAPTER FOURTEEN

THE CRY OF DOLORES

FROM NEW SPAIN'S BEGINNINGS, most of the ingredients for rebellion were present: tyranny, exploitation, hunger and discrimination by reason of caste, race or place of birth. Yet not until the half-century that began with the revolution of the English colonists in North America did the fusing elements of distant example and indigenous leadership complete the formula. The outcome of the bloody first phase of the revolution of the people of New Spain was determined along the *camino real*.

The voice of revolution was Miguel Hidalgo y Costillo, priest of the Church and the father of Mexican independence.

Miguel Hidalgo, the priest who became a general and died before a firing squad—all within eleven months—was a fifty-seven-year-old Creole who had gone into the priesthood as one of the few professions open to a person of Spanish ancestry not born in Spain. The priesthood, rich from enforced tithes, provided more than a comfortable living for even so lowly a priest as the curate of the village of Dolores, some 25 leagues northwest of Querétaro.

In his seminary days, Father Hidalgo had learned to read French. He had become dean of a college, but promotion was denied him, partly because he was a Creole rather than a Spain-born *gachupine* and greatly because of his liberal tendencies. There was also the matter of his two sets of *mestizo* children, who lived with him, though in this respect he was not singular. And he was suspected by his religious superiors because of his library—which was eventually condemned by the Inquisition—and suspected politically because he directed the

Indians of his *pueblo* to plant mulberry trees and olives and vineyards, to spin silk and press oil and make wine, enterprises reserved by law for Spain. In his cooperative pottery at Dolores a hundred worshipful Indians worked.

But Father Hidalgo was no organizer. The meanings of the orchards, the vineyards, the silk factory, the pottery interested him. He didn't enjoy the details of management such operations required. The stoop-shouldered, green-eyed priest with the white hair enjoyed far more the convivial evenings with his friends, gambling at cards, drinking, singing to the accompaniment of the little Indian orchestra he had organized in Dolores or listening to the regimental band he would hire to come over from the provincial capital, Guanajuato.

A fairly taciturn man, Father Hidalgo became animated and heated in intellectual discussions, especially in such debates as those in which he participated in Querétaro. There, in the city from which all roads to the Interior Provinces started, a hotbed of dissenting intellectuals dreamed of liberty. Some sixty of them were banded together in one of the so-called literary discussion groups—in reality made up of idealistic plotters of revolt—which abounded in Mexico. Among its dominant members were the *corregidor* of Querétaro and his wife, a number of Creole army officers from the dragoon regiment stationed at San Miguel El Grande and Father Hildalgo. They talked of many disturbing matters. They dared even to talk of independence.

The time was ripe. In 1808, the weak Charles IV of Spain, who had long since turned over all power to his wife's favorite, the minister Godoy, abdicated the Spanish throne. Forthwith Napoleon Bonaparte sent his brother, Joseph, to rule the Spanish people. Some members of the Spanish court were glad of the change of monarchs, others accepted it passively. But for most of the Peninsulars the name of Ferdinand VII, the son of their deposed monarch, became a rallying cry. *Juntas,* inimical to Napoleon, were set up in Sevilla and Oviedo so that Spanish land could be governed by Spaniards, whether France liked it or not, until such time as their legitimate king returned to them.

The colonies of the chaotic empire were also loyal to Ferdinand VII. But to the Creoles of those distant lands, most of whom had never set foot on European soil, loyalty to a monarch was one matter; the dictation of far-away Peninsular *juntas* was another. Someday these distant *juntas* might choose to deliver them to Napoleon and a France they considered atheistic or even to make a deal with Great Britain, which was giving the *juntas* military aid. Why should not the provinces establish their own *juntas* to rule in the name of Ferdinand VII?

Not a few of the Creoles were wealthy owners of mines and *haciendas,* but because they had not been born in Spain they had almost no chance for political advancement. Since 1535 only three Creoles had served as viceroys; only eighteen others had risen to ranking civil and military posts. A *junta* in New Spain, established by Creoles in the name of the king, would put the Spain-born *gachupines* in their proper place—and the Creoles in theirs.

Many of the Creoles were animated also by political doctrines born of the French Revolution, concepts declared "manifestly heretical" by the Holy Inquisition. These doctrines were even worse than heretical to the *gachupines,* who realized that self-government and rule by provincial *juntas* would end their control. They had no intention of having Creoles contest their sole right to serve as viceroys and commandants and governors.

None of this made any difference to the masses of Mexico—the Indians and the *mestizos* and the mulattoes. They exchanged their debts to the *haciendas* for lifetime bondage to Creole and *gachupine* alike. They hated both. With stoic anticipation they awaited a day of reckoning.

In New Spain, the *gachupines* forestalled effective Creole action by deposing the viceroy Iturrigaray, who had tried to assure his own continuance in power by affiliating himself with the Creoles. By the time the two *juntas* in Spain formed the Supreme Junta and dispatched a new viceroy, Francisco Xavier Venegas, to Mexico City, a civil war between *gachupines* and Creoles was all but assured. In the tense and divided provinces, intellectuals saw the opportunity to achieve independence.

Father Hidalgo and his fellow Creole conspirators in the club at Querétaro had talked revolution along with their discussion of books banned by the Inquisition. But what the army members really meant was simply a shift in power from *gachupine* to Creole. And there were no arrangements with the secret societies in other parts of the country, no coordinated plan of action. The Querétaran club's plan was simply for one of its members, thirty-one-year-old Captain Ignacio Allende, a popular bull-fighting officer of the royal regiment of dragoons quartered at San Miguel el Grande, to pronounce for independence on December 8, 1810, when the fair opened at San Juan de los Lagos, northwest of Querétaro. Other clubs would raise the cry and the revolution would be on. So believed the conspirators. They convinced themselves that the Creoles and *mestizos* and Indians would rise as one and establish a government of America—as they called their land—for Americans, owing allegiance directly to Ferdinand VII rather than to the Spanish *junta.*

But, through the confessional, the *audiencia* got wind of the hazy plot. On September 13, 1810, soldiers arrested several members of the Querétaran club. Informed by the wife of the *corregidor,* Captain Allende eluded the troops, mounted his horse and galloped to Dolores to warn and confer with Father Hidalgo. Captain Juan Aldama arrived by a different route. They reached Father Hidalgo at the conclusion of a gay evening at a *hacienda* on the outskirts of Dolores. The plotters decided that they could not wait until December, for the cat was already out of the bag. Now, tonight, the revolution must begin.

At two o'clock in the morning of Sunday, September 16, 1810, Father Hidalgo tolled the chapel bell which customarily summoned his Indians to Mass. It was the liberty bell of Mexico.

In response, fifteen Indians stumbled into the chapel, rubbing their eyes, to listen to what the historians and the people of Mexico speak of as the *grito de Dolores,* the cry of Dolores. What Father Hidalgo told them was that the *gachupines* were about to deliver their country and their holy religion to the infidel Joseph Bonaparte, to atheistic France.

"Save our country!" he exhorted them. "Save our land for Ferdinand VII! Protect our Holy Church!"

The Indians ran out of the church, to be joined now by the night watchmen and the entire *pueblo.* They opened the prison and added the prisoners to their ranks, put the local *gachupines* into the cells and took over their jewels and silver as the start of the revolution's war chest.

Armed only with pikes and machetes and axes, the *mestizos* and Indians followed Father Hidalgo and the captains out of Dolores, moving toward San Miguel el Grande, where the regiment would come over to them. At the church in Atotonilco, Father Hidalgo seized the standard of the Indians' patron saint, the Virgin of Guadalupe, from her altar, and raised it as the flag of the revolution. The cheers were deafening: Viva Ferdinand VII! Viva la Independencia! Viva Nuestra Señora de Guadalupe!

No commissary existed to feed the growing army. But corn in the fields was ripe for the harvest; barn doors were no deterrent to hungry men; oxen could be slaughtered and barbecued where they stood in the pastures. The Indians' wives and children moved with their men, adding to the swarm which spread like locusts over the plains.

The night of the 16th, Father Hidalgo's forces, already a thousand strong, entered San Miguel.

By the 20th his army had grown to a horde of 50,000. Whole *pueblos* rose to follow the deliverer. Before Celaya, Father Hidalgo, accompanied by Captains Allende, Abasolo, Aldama and Arias— Creoles all—each now heading units of the Indians, sent in word to its defenders that unless they surrendered he immediately would put to death his seventy-four *gachupín* prisoners.

The military commander surrendered as the town's *gachupines* scurried through the far gate to safety, and his regiment came over to the insurgents. That night Hidalgo entered Celaya. The flag of the Virgin of Guadalupe led the conquerors into the town. Behind it came Allende's regimental band and 100 dragoons with Ferdinand VII's standard, then thousands of shouting *vaqueros* with lances. All around the horsemen swirled the tens of thousands of all-but-naked Indians on foot, brandishing bows and machetes. By their *vivas* the Indians acclaimed Father Hidalgo Captain General of America.

Like an irresistible tide, the great *tumulto* flowed over the plain of Guanajuato, northward toward the richest mining town in Mexico, Guanajuato. Don Juan Antonio Riano, the intendent, rallied the Spanish troops, organized the militia, barricaded the streets. And on the night of September 24 Riano made the mistake which solidified the revolutionary aspect of Hidalgo's movement.

Here, at Guanajuanto, the Intendant Riano had built some years before a large rectangular stone granary 80 varas (240 feet) long and stocked it with a year's supply of grain for the 80,000 persons who lived in the city and worked the rich mines nearby. Its windows, small and high, its flat-topped roof crenelated with reddish and greenish stone, its massive doors, combined to make of it a fort which Riano was certain could hold out until the viceroy sent help. During that fateful night, Riano moved into this Alhóndiga de Granaditas the tax and tithe money and silver bars, the official provincial papers, the regular troops, and the most prominent *gachupín* and rich Creole families. By his act he separated class from class.

In the morning, the masses of Guanajuato, who had helped build the barricades and who had promised to fight to the finish, found themselves abandoned to the oncoming horde. Riano realized his mistake too late.

When Hidalgo's army arrived on September 28th, the Indians of Guanajuato, whom Riano had abandoned in the town, added their hatred to the flame of the revolution. The first Indians who sought to storm the granary were slaughtered by cannon fire. But a sharpshooter on a nearby hill killed Riano with a shot through a window. The demoralized defenders debated over who should replace him. As they argued, the attackers, unmindful of the dead bodies piling up in front of the Alhóndiga, attacked again.

Repulsed, the tide flowed again to the bottom of the wall. An insurgent soldier snatched up faggots of fat pine used in lighting the mine shafts and set the massive wooden door of the granary afire. Machetes and axes cut a passage through the embers. The Indians poured through the breach, screaming the dreadful slogan which took over the revolution: *"Muertan los gachupines!"*—Death to *gachupines!*

Most of the *gachupines* inside the Alhóndiga died there. The survivors were marched naked to the jail. Blood-mad, the victorious rebels sacked the city and went on to wreck the mines. It was two days before Hidalgo was able to establish any authority over his followers in the violated city.

Drunk with success, the barefooted conquerors swept on again in mid-October, with the assurance which came of a war chest of more than three million pesos and with the scapulars of Our Lady of Guadalupe affixed to their sombreros, but still lacking guns. At Valladolid—today's Morelia—there was no resistance. The well-armed regiment came over to Hidalgo. Mexico City lay ahead.

Friars and bandits, muleteers and peons seized the provincial cities in the name of Hidalgo and the Virgin of Guadalupe. The Royalist General Félix María Calleja struck at San Luis Potosí, hoping to retake it for Spain. In Mexico City, Viceroy Venegas scraped together troops and volunteers, and sent them under General Torcuata Trujillo to block Hidalgo's entry into the Valley of Mexico.

General Trujillo had been ordered by the viceroy to hold at the Monte de las Cruces, which controlled the road to Mexico City. On October 30 he turned tail with his 7,000 men as Hidalgo's great revolutionary horde of 80,000 looked down from the mountainside upon the golden capital.

Panic possessed the city. Every cloud of dust on the mountaintops presaged the coming of the insurgents. Father Hidalgo had counted greatly on a plebeian rising in Mexico City under the leadership of the intellectuals, to whom he sent word that he was preparing to enter the city. This did not occur.

At his vantage point at the Monte de las Cruces Father Hidalgo hesitated. While he vacillated, word spread among his Indians that the Church had excommunicated Father Hidalgo. They were the foes of the *gachupines* but not of the Faith. Torn between the Church and the Church's disowned representative who led them, the Indians also wavered. The army began to melt away. Irresistible momentum turned to inert disorganization. Father Hidalgo, the Captain General of America, with Mexico City his for the taking, turned back for Guanajuato.

On the way, Hidalgo's army and that of General Calleja, who had turned south to protect Mexico City, unexpectedly encountered each other at Aculco. The insurgents had the numbers and enough equipment to defeat the Royalists, but the sight of Calleja's five columns executing their military maneuvers in complete silence unnerved the untrained rebels. When an ammunition wagon turned over, exploded and set ablaze the winter-dry grass of the field, the terrified Indians fled through what seemed the fires of hell. Father Hidalgo took the road to Valladolid. Generals Allende, Abasolo, the Aldama brothers and Arias, headed for Guanajuato. The retreat from Las Cruces and the loss of all the insurgents' artillery at Aculco disgusted the officers with Hidalgo's leadership.

At Guadalajara, where Hidalgo established himself, he put one of the few printing presses in New Spain to work issuing his proclamations. He recruited a new army and organized the beginnings of a civil government. Allende, rejoining Father Hidalgo, tried to discipline the army and supervised the manufacture of crude cannon and hand grenades as substitutes for muskets and modern armament. At Guanajuato, General Calleja hung in groups the citizens who had sided with Hidalgo from gallows erected at the principal crossroads.

Four citizens died for each *gachupine* slain. At Guadalajara and at Valladolid Father Hidalgo reciprocated by killing batches of captured *gachupines.* The civil war in Mexico was no longer a war for independence, but a proletarian revolution contaminated by blood hatreds.

As the new year began, General Calleja, with 6,000 well-armed, well-organized regulars, and Creole and *gachupín* militia, marched upon Guadalajara. Despite the military disparity, Father Hidalgo and his 80,000 rebels should have been able to hold the city. His decision to stand at the Bridge of Calderón outside the city was well taken. General Allende placed his jerry-built cannon on the hillsides pointing down on to the plain through which Calleja's troops would march.

But his premature firing disclosed the location of his emplaced artillery and the areas of the plain they controlled. As Calleja's dragoons galloped toward the bridge, the insurgents' artillery slaughtered their own men on the field. On that frenzied day of January 17 the insurgents broke and retreated toward Zacatecas as Calleja entered Guadalajara. Captain Allende assumed command of the disconsolate rebels. Father Hidalgo became the virtual prisoner of his generals.

The tide had turned in the south in favor of the established authority. But in the north the insurgents held the countryside, the road to Saltillo and from Saltillo northward into Coahuila and across Texas.

The gay and productive annual fair at Saltillo, where imported goods and the produce of New Spain were bought and sold and traded, had only just opened in the past September when word came of the *grito de Dolores.* Merchants and farmers and clerics, *gachupines* and Creoles, and the Tlaxcalan Indians alike were aroused variously according to their personal or group or racial interests by the clarion summons of the soldier-priest. Of them all, none reacted more swiftly and energetically than did Coahuila's *gachupín* governor, Antonio Cordero, who was present for the opening of the fair. Promptly, he summoned the lancers of Monclova and of the Presidio del Río Grande to join in the Royalist defense of the province.

By early January, as Governor Cordero prepared to go south to assist General Calleja, he learned that Mariano Jiménez, a young graduate engineer whom Hidalgo had commissioned a general, and Raphael Iriarte, a one-time bandit chieftain, were approaching Saltillo from the south with 8,000 men. Governor Cordero was confident that his 2,000 men and six cannon could control the field at Aguanueva, south of Saltillo.

As General Jiménez faced Governor Cordero's troops, the insurgent sent the governor a courteous note, suggesting that he surrender to superior force and join the revolution. Cordero refused to treat with the enemy, but his Creole officers saw Jiménez' message. They went over with their men to the insurgents. Cordero fled toward Saltillo, but was overtaken and captured the same day. The next day the revolutionaries entered Saltillo in triumph to the shouted *vivas* of the people.

On February 24, Ignacio Allende ordered what was left of Father Hidalgo's army into Saltillo. The priest, a sick man now and a figurehead only, followed him in. And here, at Saltillo, after a conference of the ranking officers of the rebel army, Father Hidalgo was forced to turn over to Allende formally the command he had already relinquished.

From one end of Coahuila to the other the insurgents held that province. Nuevo León had also succumbed. And in Nuevo Santander the fiery young propagandist, José Bernardo Gutiérrez de Lara, a *mestizo* blacksmith, had won over the townsmen of the Río Grande by words rather than the sword.

With Jiménez' defeat of a Royalist force put in the field by Nemesio de Salcedo, Coahuila, Nuevo León and Nuevo Santander were safely in the hands of the revolutionists. Then, early in March, a communication from Béxar, addressed to Father Hidalgo and delivered to his generals, reported that in Texas too the revolution had triumphed. However much the conflict had gone against the insurgents in central Mexico, the sky in these eastern Interior Provinces was bright.

Allende and his generals shaped their plans accordingly. The eastern Interior Provinces would have to be the rock on which the revolution would be rebuilt. So long as Saltillo held at the south and the road to Texas and the United States was kept open, aid could reach the beleaguered revolutionaries. It was imperative, they concluded, that the principal chieftains themselves should speed to the United States and buy from the North Americans the desperately needed ammunition out of their war chest of two million pesos. If earlier emissaries, Father Salazar and Marshal Aldama, had already reached the border, the chieftains might stop at Béxar if they heard good tidings and await there the expected reinforcements from the United States. Afterward they would regroup for another assault on Mexico City.

As the leaders charted their course in the last hours before they left Saltillo, Bernardo Gutiérrez de Lara arrived from Nuevo Santander, where he had triumphed without bloodshed. He begged to be used more militantly now in the cause of the revolution. The revolutionary council commissioned him a lieutenant-colonel and ordered him to raise troops in Nuevo Santander and to be ready at Presidio del Río Grande on their return.

Late into the night of March 16 the council continued its planning. Ignacio Rayón would remain at Saltillo in charge of the remnants there of the Army of America. At Monclova, Aranda—Jiménez' second in command—would serve as insurgent governor of Coahuila.

Already the insurgent generals who would travel the *camino real* north from Saltillo were doomed men. The governor of Texas would see to that.

Manuel de Salcedo, nephew of the commandant general and since 1807 governor of Texas, was no stranger to the western hemisphere. As aide to his elderly father, the last Spanish governor of Louisiana, he had been present at New Orleans for the formalities in which Louisiana was retroceded to Spain prior to being turned over to the United States. He had returned to Spain and, after receiving his commission as governor of Texas, he and his wife and their child, his chaplain and his servants sailed from Cádiz for Boston. They visited the principal eastern cities, then embarked on flatboats for the trip down the Ohio and the Mississippi. At Natchitoches he had been entertained by Dr. Sibley before continuing to his post at Béxar.

In 1810, Governor Manuel de Salcedo returned to Nacogdoches to inspect its defenses, taking with him his wife and child, whom he left there. Then, in the fall, the tale of the *grito de Dolores* reached Béxar, was borne east to the Trinity and on to Nacogdoches and Natchitoches, and from there to the newspapers of the United States.

To San Antonio rode the revolutionary Lieutenants Francisco Escamilla and Antonio Sáenz, as agents of Gutiérrez de Lara, bearing the inflammatory doctrines. Governor Salcedo ordered that they be seized and imprisoned in the quarters occupied by the soldiers from the Alamo de Parras company in the old Mission San Antonio de Valero, secularized in 1794 and now called The Alamo. Early in January, Salcedo and Lieutenant Colonel Herrera, still charged with the miltary defense of Texas, announced that the presidial soldiers would soon leave for the Río Grande to fight the revolutionists.

The men did not want to leave their families exposed to Indian attacks. It was an unprecedented move. Were Salcedo and Herrera expecting grave trouble? Why had Governor Salcedo left his wife at Nacogdoches? Was there more than coincidence behind the crating of all Governor Herrera's household goods? What of the rumor that, when the troops moved out of the barracks at The Alamo, the buildings would be burned?

The ferment of Father Hidalgo's revolution had begun to intoxicate the *mestizos* and Indians and mulattoes, citizens and soldiers alike. Bernardo Gutiérrez' two agents had not remained free long after they reached San Antonio. But before they were arrested they had talked to some ready listeners, and these talked to others, and the others talked to others, and most listeners found truth in what the lieutenants had said. The lieutenants themselves escaped from The Alamo but were recaptured.

As the spirit of mutiny and the flame of rebellion grew, Salcedo canceled the scheduled departure of the troops. This was no time for the presidials to leave Béxar. Then, on January 21, he and Herrera posted notices that field exercises would be held in the opposite direction, on the Cíbola or the Guadalupe or the Colorado. Again rumors aroused the people and the troops.

And now another facet of intrigue.

Soon after the outbreak of the revolution, the Cabildo of San Fernando de Béxar had issued a proclamation of loyalty, and later another proclamation commending the governor for the recapture of the two prisoners of The Alamo. But *Alcalde* Francisco Travieso, who would supervise the defense of the city if the militia went on maneuvers, was uncertain of his ability to protect the town from Indians or from the schemes of agents of insurrection.

And truly the isolated town was ripe for revolution. Of this, Captain Juan Bautista Casas, a retired Creole militia officer, was certain. Moreover, he also believed in home rule by the American-born. From what he had heard, the revolution was going well below the Río Grande. Here at Béxar the soldiers were sullen. The Creole sergeants and lieutenants in the Alamo de Parras company, who could rise no higher in the army only because they were born in New Spain, might listen . . .

Captain Casas decided to find out. Through the day of January 21 —the day the notices of field exercises were posted—rumor followed rumor. That night, *Alferez* Vincente Flores, a militia ensign, paid a call on the jittery *alcalde,* Travieso. The visit was not a long one, but sufficiently long for the ensign to tell the *alcalde* that the troops were determined not to leave the city and were ready to follow Captain Casas. The insurrection could easily succeed here. The *alcalde* followed the ensign to the captain's home.

They were not the only guests of Captain Casas that night. All through the evening low-voiced instructions were given. *Alcalde* Travieso did not go home until midnight. Just after reveille he and the ensign, each swathed in heavy capes as protection against weather and recognition, accompanied Captain Casas, a sergeant and a corporal to The Alamo barracks. Travieso stationed himself at the door of the captain of the guard, Nicolas Benites, a rifle in hand.

A sentinel challenged the intruders and summoned the guard. But the guard, recognizing Captain Casas, permitted him and his party to enter Captain Benites' quarters. There they demanded that he surrender his troops. The captain refused. The conspirators overpowered him. Outside, the troops had lined up in military formation for the morning report. When Casas boldly announced to them that he had taken over command, the soldiers cheered.

Willingly they obeyed his orders to follow him to the governor's palace to arrest Salcedo and Herrera. The rebels marched out of The Alamo at the double, but when they arrived at the Military Plaza, they learned that the governor and commandant, having somehow received word that all was not well, had left to find out what might be happening at the barracks. The troops hastened back.

As they entered The Alamo plaza, Commandant Herrera, Governor Salcedo and four or five officers came out of the barracks. Herrera asked Casas what the meaning of his usurpation of authority was. Casas told him that resistance was useless, and he ordered the arrest of the royal officers. On being given their word that they would not try to escape, he put them under house arrest in the governor's palace.

A government *junta* was formed immediately, Captain Casas

at its head. He released the imprisoned agents of the revolution—Lieutenants Sáenz and Escamilla—and other political prisoners, and ordered the arrest of all *gachupines* and the confiscation of their property. Fourteen officers, the *gachupines* and a few Creoles who sided with the Royalists were among those arrested.

Late in the afternoon Lieutenant Sáenz started for Nacogdoches to complete the revolution in Texas. With him rode eighty mounted soldiers, *Alcalde* Travieso and Gabino Delgado, a member of the Cabildo who had participated in the plot. Their orders were to protect the interests of the king, safeguard "our holy religion and the country," arrest the commandant and all *gachupines* and confiscate their property, and bring back the governor's wife and child. Casas also sent a courier to La Bahía, with instructions to Captain Luciano García to proclaim the revolution there and take over the command of the *presidio*. The next day, not knowing that Father Hidalgo no longer led the revolution, he wrote him a long letter recounting what had been accomplished.

Early in February, Casas received from the revolutionary *junta* at Saltillo a commission as governor *ad interim* of Texas. Shortly afterward, orders arrived from Aranda in Monclova to send Governor Salcedo, Commandant Herrera and the other imprisoned officers to Presidio del Río Grande.

The Casas uprising had taken the government of Texas from the hands of the *gachupines* and given it to the Creoles, but without cruelty or any appreciable individual rancor. But the orders from Insurgent Governor Aranda were couched in the no-quarter spirit which had followed reprisals. The prisoners must be placed in chains and move under heavy escort at maximum pace so as to cover the 51 leagues to the river in three-and-a-half days, the time usually taken only by fast-riding couriers.

Early in the morning of February 12, Vicente Flores, promoted now from ensign to captain, and thirty mounted men set out from Béxar with the captives. Governor Salcedo and a loyal Creole, Captain Miguel de Arcos, who were considered the most dangerous, were burdened with chains. The other twelve prisoners were only handcuffed, the humiliation of these officers of the king weighing more heavily upon them than their manacles. The journey to the river took twice as long as the orders had specified. It may have been that the revolutionists of San Antonio were more humane than the general at Saltillo and the governor at Monclova. At the *presidio*, another escort took over. The procession moved toward Monclova, on the way to Saltillo for the trial of the prisoners and what seemed certain death.

But the forces of counter-revolution were already at work in Coahuila and in Texas.

At Monclova, the Sánchez brothers—descendants of Urdiñola and Aguayo, and owners of the historic *hacienda* of Santa Rosa near today's Músquiz—were among those who pretended to be loyal to the revolution and affected friendship for Governor Aranda. The governor was a simple man who desired the good opinion of the *hacendados* and the other ranking men of Coahuila. He had turned over the military aspects of his governorship to Lieutenant José de Rábago, a professional soldier, and so was free to enjoy the balls he organized as governor and to imbibe, copiously and impartially, *pulque* and imported wines.

Now Sánchez Navarro suggested that he and his brother would be happy to take care of such important prisoners and thus relieve the governor of this responsibility. The wealthy Creole said that at the distant Sánchez *hacienda* of Santa Rosa little more than house arrest would be required; he would be responsible for the captives. And so a surprised and delighted Governor Salcedo, Governor Herrera and the other political prisoners soon relaxed at the Sánchez *hacienda*, their chains removed and their jailers more than friendly.

In charge of the prisoners was a Creole rebel, Captain Ignacio Elizondo, whose most recent prior responsibility had been the guarding of the royal treasurer, Royeuela, who had been captured with his treasure trove in flight from Saltillo, then imprisoned in Monclova. Elizondo was the owner of the rich *estancia* of Santa María. Royeuela had assiduously encouraged his fears as to what would happen to him and his lands if the Royalist forces were to triumph. The persuasive prisoner also had frequent opportunity to talk with Lieutenant Rábago, to whom the high-living governor had turned over military authority.

By the time Captain Elizondo rode north as escort to Royeuela and to assume supervision of the highly-placed prisoners from San Antonio, the seeds of self-interest had been well planted. Elizondo had made up his mind to change sides. Lieutenant Rábago was already in touch with other officers who would turn against the insurgent government. So, at Monclova and at Santa Rosa the overthrow of the revolution in the eastern Interior Provinces began.

But to make certain the success of counter-revolution, allies must be found at the *presidio* at Béxar and at the outposts in Texas. They were there. Unbeknown to Governor Salcedo, the San Antonio *junta,* as well as many citizens and soldiers, was beginning to find fault with Casas. He was ruling Texas in as dictatorial fashion, many complained, as had the *gachupín* governors. Moreover, although he had not been the only person in the *coup,* he now ignored his fellow conspirators, and he had made the serious mistake of publicly reprimanding men who had stood beside him in the uprising. One such was Lieutenant Sáenz.

By now Sáenz had returned from Nacogdoches, having accomplished his assigned objective of taking over east Texas for the revolutionists. This had been easily done. The garrison at Trinidad de Salcedo was more than ready. The men of the little outpost cheered on hearing of the triumph of the revolution at Béxar. In Nacogdoches he had seized and put in irons the special military guardian sent there to protect this eastern outpost. He had arrested the *gachupines* and confiscated their property, conducted the election of a *junta* to govern in the name of the free and independent people, and after only seven days had set out for Béxar with six prisoners.

It was to be more unfortunate for Captain Casas and the revolution than for Lieutenant Sáenz that the captain heard a story that the lieutenant had also pocketed the Nacogdoches commandant's silver-filled money belt and some 500 pesos from other *gachupines* without reporting their taking to the revolution's chief. Casas imprisoned Sáenz, though for only a few days. It would have been better for the revolution had he kept him there indefinitely. Sáenz, too, decided to change sides.

Gabino Delgado was also dissatisfied. A prominent citizen of San Antonio, he had risked his position and fortune to champion the *coup.* Casas, in his success, ignored him. Another proponent of discontent was Juan Manuel Zambrano, a retired subdeacon—a 6-foot tall, broad-shouldered, pink-cheeked cleric who was more interested in politics than in the Church, and who, at his ranch 20 leagues from San Antonio, learned of the growing discontent in San Antonio. A Royalist, he came to town to see what he could do to help return the government to the officials constituted by king and Church. Sáenz and Delgado had honestly believed in the revolution. Zambrano, pretending to share their beliefs, skillfully played upon their hatred of Casas.

Before the insurgent generals decided to go to the United States themselves, General Jiménez had dispatched two emissaries, Father Salazar and Marshal Aldama, to solicit aid for the rebels. At this juncture they arrived at Béxar, Aldama resplendent in a uniform with heavy gold epaulets and fourragéres. Zambrano wondered whether these emissaries might not also be turned to use against the Texas revolution. He went in secret to Father Salazar and, as cleric to cleric and as a pretended fellow revolutionary, unburdened himself of the grievances which so many held against the acting governor, Casas. The man was hurting rather than helping the cause of the revolution, Zambrano told Salazar. He should be replaced. Father Salazar replied that he had no authority to act and that besides he was subordinate to Marshal Aldama.

Now it was Lieutenant Sáenz' turn to act. Probably at the prodding of Zambrano, he went to Marshal Aldama and, producing the diary of his Nacogdoches mission to prove his loyalty, begged Aldama to appoint some other Texan as governor. Aldama replied rightly that the appointment of a governor was not in his power. Zambrano, Lieutenant Sáenz and Delgado next circulated the tale that Aldama's uniform was suspiciously French-looking. They insinuated that perhaps the man was actually a French agent, or if he and his fellow emissary, Father Salazar, were not French agents, they were probably taking to the United States an offer to trade Texas for aid for the revolution. In either case they should be halted.

On the night of March 1, Zambrano, Sáenz and Delgado achieved a *coup* made possible by Zambrano's skillful weaving together of the various threads of discontent. It was done in the classic fashion. First the barracks were taken over, then a *junta* was elected. Its members swore to support Ferdinand VII, to protect the Holy Faith, and— going further than Sáenz had probably expected—to obey only officers appointed by the *juntas* of Spain. When Casas awakened the next morning in the governor's palace to loud noises, he found 400 troops assembled outside, shouting for his resignation. He surrendered meekly and turned over copies of his correspondence with General Jiménez. They contained incriminating evidence which would cost him his life.

For another week Zambrano tactfully continued the masquerade of local self-government. The people under Casas had savored the idea if they had, in fact, not experienced it. Zambrano would not repeat Casas' mistakes. His *junta* posted frequent notices telling the citizenry what was being done in their behalf. The people were impressed.

On March 8 the *junta* sent out two representatives, Captain José María Muñoz and Captain Luis Galan, to confer with Commandant General Nemesio de Salcedo. The men bore two messages—an oral one to deliver to the commandant general, assuring him of the loyalty of Texas; the other in writing, addressed to General Jiménez, to be used as a safe conduct pass if any revolutionists confronted them between Béxar and Chihuahua.

At Presidio del Río Grande the two captains learned that while the officers were Royalists, the people were insurgents. For their safety the commandant assigned fifteen soldiers to guard the home of the postmaster, in which they were lodged. The next day he furnished a protective escort to lead them to San Fernando de Austria, where one Captain José Menchaca, formerly of San Antonio, was in command of the *presidio*.

The captains were reassured to learn at San Fernando de Austria that Texas was not the only part of the eastern Interior Provinces in which the counter-revolutionaries were busy. The charm and persuasiveness of Governor Salcedo, still technically a prisoner at the Sánchez Navarro *hacienda* near Santa Rosa, was giving heart to Royalists and was even converting some who had not found in the revolution what they sought. Salcedo had not only won over Lieutenant Colonel Elizondo; he had persuaded him to go to San Fernando to make overtures to Captain Menchaca. Elizondo had been accompanied by Captain de Arcos, like Salcedo still technically in Elizondo's custody as a prisoner of the revolution.

The story the Béxar envoys told further encouraged the Royalists at San Fernando. During a convivial evening, the Texas captains expressed their fervent hope that Texas and Coahuila might unite, the better to protect His Catholic Majesty's kingdom. At the Sánchez *hacienda* Elizondo, Arcos, Muñoz and Galan soon brought over to the Royalist cause such officers as were still wavering. Elizondo was certain that the counter-revolution could not fail. With the *presidios* of Béxar, San Fernando and Santa Rosa firmly in the hands of the Royalists, Governor Salcedo could soon take open control.

On the afternoon of March 13 Salcedo and Elizondo left for Monclova. Salcedo would continue to play the role of prisoner; in actuality he, not Elizondo, gave the commands. Elizondo and his "prisoner" entered Monclova without challenge. There they met secretly with Lieutenant Rábago, whom Governor Aranda still thought to be his trusted second in command. In a later secret meeting with his *junta* that day on the hill of the hermitage of Nuestra Señora de Zapopán, Rábago appointed the useful Captain Vicente Flores to entice Governor Aranda into a home where a ball was to be held that night.

Flores met Aranda early in the evening as the governor drove through the streets of Monclova with a group of guitarists and four guards, singing lustily in concert with cronies who followed him in other carriages. Flores offered the governor a flask of *aguardiente* and invited him to the ball with the promise of unlimited food and drink. Later in the evening, when the besotted Aranda and his friends were frolicking in sodden delight, Captain Elizondo and a picked force captured them all. By morning the sure troops had been assembled at a hill near the town. Monclova fell to Governor Salcedo and Captain Elizondo without a shot being fired.

Among Aranda's papers, the Royalists found the letter from the insurgent chieftains which revealed that the generals and a convoy intended to leave Saltillo on the morning of March 17, and asked that a military escort meet them at the Acatita de Baján. Within the hour a messenger spurred down the *camino real* bearing the assurance of Elizondo that the escort would be awaiting the generals, as requested. All had been done except the springing of a trap which reeked with the odor of betrayal.

The seventeen generals and their disorderly convoy and the mule train with a million dollars in silver with which to purchase arms and supplies in the United States left Saltillo, by an almost sickening coincidence, on the very day that Governor Salcedo arrived in Monclova with the treacherous Elizondo for his bloodless takeover. The *coup* contained some of the elements of *opéra bouffe*. There would be no comedy in the bloodstained sequel.

Father Hidalgo, the Generals Allende and Jiménez and their fellow insurgent chieftains were unsuspecting and careless. In the cavalcade, soon to be broken up into separate groups, trailed a rabble of perhaps a thousand soldiers, the women whom many of them brought with them, and friars and priests and muleteers, mingling among the cannons and carriages, the mules and burros and carts. The mules, behind their well-mounted *arrieros,* who rode at the head of the train, alone could have displayed any discipline.

The generals were aware only of the need for haste. They knew that to the south and west the Royalists were approaching from San Luis Potosí and from Zacatecas and Durango. The destination fixed for their first stop was Elizondo's *estancia* of Santa María—15 miles or some 6 leagues away. Knowing nothing of the counter-revolution in San Antonio and the subsequent collapse at Monclova, they were so certain that the road north was safe that no guards were placed and discipline vanished. Neither did they have any way of knowing that their pretended friendly guide, the Baron de Bastrop, who rode in the very carriage of General Allende and General Jiménez, had been informing his Royalist friends at Monclova and Santa Rosa through Indian spies of everything he could learn.

Father Hidalgo left Saltillo shortly after midnight with a guard of 200 horsemen. He arrived at Santa María at ten in the morning. Allende and Jiménez and their betrayers didn't reach the *estancia* until dusk. Behind the chieftains, along the dusty valley road, the main body trailed in separate, disorganized segments.

On the 18th the insurgents passed through the rocky hill country of Cabrito, 6 leagues to the *hacienda* of Mesillas, with another 6 leagues to Anaelo, the rendezvous for the night. But only a small number of the tiring travelers reached Anaelo. Most of them slept

along the road, the women under the carts. Horses and mules were permitted to pasture without being hobbled. In the morning forty horses were missing. On the next day the cavalcade traveled an amazing 14 leagues, most of it through the pass of Espinazo, goaded by the knowledge that there was no water along the way until La Joya would be reached.

The spent revolutionists, their throats parched from thirst, found little water at La Joya, and that brackish and putrid. Throughout the night the stragglers continued to arrive; many of them did not catch up with the leaders until the next day. No one was fit to go on.

But during the early hours of the 21st they set out again. Ahead, raising choking dust clouds, rumbled the mule-drawn coaches of the principal chieftains and clergy and the more favored women. Spread out behind them followed officers and soldiers in meaningless groupings. After these trod the more than a thousand mules loaded down with leather packs of silver bars and silver money, and other droves of mules; then came the artillery, wheels wobbling, axles breaking, and the ox carts in which rode women and children. In the rear, the horsemen of General Raphael Iriarte formed a feckless rear guard. The lone caravan stretched out for 10 miles. Only the belief that at Baján friendly troops awaited them kept them going.

General Allende, the professional soldier who directed the forced march, didn't take even the most elementary precautions. Neither pickets nor reconnaissance patrols preceded the travelers. The care-

lessness of Allende—joined to the lack of foresight of the bumbling, bibulous Arenda—made certain the sequel of ambush and death, and an end to the beginning of the long Mexican revolution.

As the sun appeared, the first small group approached a hill which would live in history as *La Loma del Prendimiento,* the hill of the capture. Its members were a mixed and inconsequential lot: a Carmelite friar with a twelve-year-old boy, Lieutenant Rodriguez and a second lieutenant, one-time Royalist officers at Presidio del Río Grande who had deserted to the insurgents, and a soldier. Their hearts must have lifted at the sight of the hill around which the road wound to the nearby, yet hidden wells of Baján, whose huge impounding trough could assuage the thirst of a multitude.

The hill also hid the troops of Captain Elizondo. But all that the vanguard could discern as it approached the hill was the expected detachment of officers and soldiers idling in their saddles on the right side of the road. The two lieutenants gave no trouble at all; instead they put themselves under the orders of Captain Elizondo and subsequently collaborated with the Royalists.

An hour later a small insurgent squadron under a Saltillan lieutenant named González reined in their horses. Captain Flores, a one time insurgent himself, demanded their arms. González refused and the adversaries drew their pistols. González fell wounded from his horse and was killed by the soldiery. They dragged his body off the road.

The first three of the seventeen coaches were approaching, bearing priests and friars and women. These were indiscriminately tied up with lassos and taken around the hill out of sight. In the fourth coach were Father Hidalgo's brother and some women; they too were seized and sent ahead.

The fifth coach bore the big game, for in it rode Allende and his young son, Jiménez; Juan Ignacio Ramón; General Arias and a woman. At Elizondo's command, Lieutenant Rodríguez, the turncoat who had been the first rebel officer captured, identified them. Elizondo called out to them to surrender. Allende, shouting that he would die before submitting, drew his pistol and fired at Elizondo, but missed. An answering volley killed General Allende's son. Arias was shot and killed as he leaped from the coach in a forlorn attempt to escape. The Royalist troops lifted the body to the floor of the coach where General Allende was leaning sorrowfully over his dead son.

Allende and his remaining companions were bound and the coach went on its way toward the wells. From the carriage just behind it, a spectator watched with a certain satisfaction. He was the Baron de Bastrop, the bellwether.

Father Hidalgo had been riding in the next coach, behind five oxcarts, but he had transferred a short time before to a horse and, with another priest, was riding at the head of some forty soldiers. Elizondo and his men let them pass, then fell in behind them. When they rounded the hill where the main body of the ambushers waited, Father Hidalgo, aware too late, drew his pistol at the command to surrender, but he was seized and his hands bound behind his back.

By five o'clock in the evening Elizondo had used up the 300 lassos which he had brought. Halters took their place. There had been almost no resistance from the rebels. One or two artillery pieces had been fired from a distance, but General Iriarte fled back toward Saltillo with the rearguard. For his cowardice the insurgents later were to put him to death.

The roundup was virtually complete. No one of importance, save Iriarte, escaped. Captors and captives made camp near the wells of Baján, where Governor Salcedo arrived with 200 soldiers at nine in the evening. He divided his and Elizondo's soldiers into five guard details, one for the generals and the clergy, one for the women, one for some 800 rebel prisoners, one for the mule train bearing the fortune in silver and one for the horses and mules.

In Monclova the prisoners were dispersed. Some were lodged in the presidial company's barracks, some in a chapel, some in church buildings, some in the military hospital. On March 25 Governor Salcedo conducted Father Hidalgo and the principal generals out of Monclova, under heavy guard, to march to Chihuahua, headquarters of the commandant general, to go on trial for their lives. There Father Hidalgo and the top generals were condemned to death. So were Captain Casas, Father Salazar and Marshal Aldama. Governor Aranda and the remaining officers were sentenced to varying terms in the presidial cells at Chihuahua, Aranda receiving ten years. The common soldiers were put to work in the *haciendas* and mines of Coahuila.

Father Hidalgo was the last of those condemned at Chihuahua to die. He had been a priest and had to be turned over to the Church for unfrocking before the firing squad could fire the volley which would kill him. Before his death the Father of the Mexican Revolution repented before the Inquisition for the rivers of blood for which he took responsibility and begged forgiveness, not so much for espousing a cause in which he believed, but for the manner in which he had sought to advance it. He was taken out and shot on the morning of July 31, 1811. Seated in a chair, he placed his right hand over his heart the better to indicate its location to the soldiers of the firing squad. With the first volley he toppled over. A second volley fired into his prostrate body killed him.

The heads of Father Hidalgo and Generals Allende, Juan Aldama and Jiménez were soon hung in iron cages from the four corners of the Alhóndiga at Guanajuato. Their bodies were buried in Chihuahua.

The jubilant Royalists toasted the success of their cause. They had destroyed the revolution.

But had they? Far to the south another priest, José María Morelos, lifted again the banner of revolt. His contribution to the gaining of independence ten years later lies beyond the purlieu of this story. Soon along the *camino real* would rage ruffians and cut-throats, Mexican patriots and American filibusters who followed an implacable revolutionist, José Bernardo Gutiérrez de Lara. We have glimpsed him before. Now we meet him again.

CHAPTER FIFTEEN

A FILIBUSTER FAILS,
BUT A CAUSE ENDURES

YANQUIS WHO HAD FOUGHT beside Bernardo Gutiérrez de Lara would curse him as a bloodthirsty killer. Mexican Creole historians would almost ignore him. He would lose faith in his American friends and they in him. He would lose faith in himself. But Bernardo Gutiérrez, the *mestizo* blacksmith from Nuevo Santander, never lost faith in the justice or the eventual triumph of the revolution whose flames he so devotedly fanned for so long.

The forge at Revilla, today's Guerrero in Tamaulipas, was Bernardo's pulpit. Beside it, and months before the *grito de Dolores* echoed across the Sierra Madre Oriental and down the Río Grande plain, he had plied his *ranchero* patrons with *pulque* to encourage their response to his demand for a free country for free men. Bernardo had read much. He talked even more. The call of Father Hidalgo inspired him to act, not at first as an armed revolutionary but as a man who fought with his pen. Borne by *rancheros* and peons, officers and common soldiers who shared a desire to be free from Spain, his incendiary pamphlets were read throughout the eastern Interior Provinces. He convinced many who doubted or wavered, among them his brother who was a priest. He won over the captain of the troops at the capital of Nuevo Santander. The Indian *alcalde* of the pueblo at Revilla distributed the hand-written bulletins in adobe huts and grass jacales as he herded his sheep along the dusty trails. The Holy Inquisition and the Bishop of Nuevo León would excommunicate him. The Royalists would put a price on his head. But the swarthy peasant persevered.

In the early summer of 1811, the head of Captain Casas rotted on a pole in the military plaza at San Antonio. Father Salazar and Marshal Aldama lay shackled in the guardhouse at Béxar awaiting death. Father Hidalgo and the generals were prisoners in Chihuahua. The revolution was at ebb tide. Someone had to find arms and fighting men to continue the fight Hidalgo had begun.

The thirty-six-year-old Bernardo considered himself the representative of the revolution commissioned to seek aid. With the vacillating Captain José Manchaca, a fugitive hiding in his home, for a guide and with ten other insurgents as escorts, he left his wife and two children and on August 1 set out for the United States, crossing Royalist-held Texas far to the north of the closely watched *camino real*. The journey was uneventful until they reached the neutral ground. There a Spanish patrol captured two of the patriots. Bernardo, Manchaca and the rest eluded the troops and fled to the woods near Bayou Pierre. Soon, armed American volunteers from Natchitoches guided them into the friendly American settlement.

Their wide sombreros and vivid sashes, the bright serapes across their shoulders were usual sights in Natchitoches. But for Bernardo, the countryman from Revilla, who had never been outside his homeland, Natchitoches presented much that was new. He admired the stoutly built, wide-galleried homes of wood. The canoes and barges and keelboats alongside the wharves resting on the banks of the Red River underscored for him the advantages of free trade. He attended the strange Methodist Church which, perhaps most of all, represented the cultural difference between his own Nuevo Santander and this heretical but democratic land.

Without credentials or money, Gutiérrez was of such pleasing personality and so convincing in his sincerity as to find friends among these *Americanos heréticos*. One of them was the ubiquitous Dr. Sibley, the Indian agent, whose friendliness was usually purposeful. The doctor introduced the *mestizo* emissary to the officers of Camp Claiborne, lent him $200 and put him on his way to Washington with letters in his pocket to prominent citizens in Tennessee and Kentucky, and an introduction to the Secretary of State.

Everywhere Bernardo Gutiérrez found ready and sympathetic listeners as he pleaded for succor for the dying revolution. Idealists believed as fervently in the right of the American-born Spaniards to govern themselves as they and their fathers had believed in freedom for American-born Englishmen. Angry rivermen along the Mississippi and the Ohio hated the kingdom of Spain because of the hellish dungeons which swallowed up such Americans as Philip Nolan's adventurers. Traders and merchants and innkeepers and farmers were more than ready to fight for what they considered to be a fairer boundary and promised support to a new Mexican nation in return for trading and land privileges. The Burrites dreamed still of the Halls of Montezuma. The agents of Bonapartist France were prepared to direct and finance a revolution to gain the vast territories which Joseph Bonaparte had not won when he assumed the Spanish crown, British agents foresaw the usefulness of Vera Cruz and a Texas port in the event of a war with the United States.

Only the day before Gutiérrez arrived in Washington, Congress passed a resolution setting forth the United States' friendly interest in the establishment of independent governments in the neighboring Spanish colonies. And there was the Secretary of State himself, James Monroe, a far-sighted schemer in his own nation's behalf, with whom the fervid *mestizo* would confer three times between his arrival in Washington on December 11 and his departure from the eastern seaboard a few weeks later.

In their talks, Monroe explained why his country had a practical interest. If war with England came, as seemed most probable in this winter of 1812, the United States would want a friendly nation to the west. Spain was Britain's ally. The United States could and would send 50,000 men to fight for the revolution, said the secretary, if war were declared. In exchange, the United States wished a favorable boundary with the independent nation. Monroe suggested a line west of Texas.

The blacksmith neither approved of such a bargain nor did he have the authority to make it. Texas, he said, was not his to give. Its future would have to be decided by the revolutionaries and, in any event, a decision could be made only if his side won. Those 50,000 men could mean everything. Might he himself command them?

The secretary changed the subject. But, on his instructions, John Gresham, the chief clerk of the State Department, gave Gutiérrez a letter of introduction to Governor Claiborne at New Orleans.

Among the many whose acquaintance Gutiérrez made in Washington was one man whose friendship would have unhappy consequences. He was José Álvarez de Toledo y Dubois, a Cuban-born revolutionary who had reached the United States three months earlier as a fugitive from Spanish wrath. His father, captain of the port of Havana, had been well enough off to send his son to the Naval School of Cádiz.

He had served with distinction in the Army of Galicia against the French and fought them at sea as a Spanish officer attached to a British squadron. Afterward, during the short period in which Ferdinand VII's *Cortes* at Cádiz admitted delegates from the colonies, Toledo represented Santo Domingo. While holding that position he wrote Santo Domingo friends a warning that the colonies would have little power in a government centered in Spain, no matter what the promises of the *Cortes*. The letter was intercepted. With the help of the American consul he fled for his life to the United States. He carried with him a singular authority, a commission from the other *Cortes* delegates from the western hemisphere to lead a revolution in northern New Spain and create there an independent nation.

Toledo and his fellow colonial delegates had been convinced by Miguel Rámoz Arizpe, of Saltillo, delegate from the *Provincias Internas,* that the surest way to win independence for Cuba and Santo Domingo and the other islands of the Caribbean was to set New Spain free, beginning with its most vulnerable section, the Interior Provinces and especially Texas.

Gutiérrez knew he could learn much from such a man. Their goals were identical. The two revolutionaries agreed that Toledo should remain in the eastern United States to raise money, procure arms and enlist American volunteers. Gutiérrez would return to the neutral ground, after a meeting with Governor Claiborne in New Orleans, and do what he could to keep the revolution alive.

At a dinner in the home of Governor Claiborne, Bernardo was introduced to William Shaler, an American sea captain whom Secretary Monroe had appointed consul for Vera Cruz with instructions to find out all he could about what was happening in New Spain. The Spaniards had turned him back at Havana. He had come to New Orleans, hoping to enter Mexico by way of the *camino real*. The impressionable Gutiérrez took an immediate liking to the American agent. As for Shaler, he heard with interest that Gutiérrez' letter of introduction from the State Department to Claiborne had directed that the Louisiana governor "expedite his return" to Mexico. Shaler decided to be the expediter.

When Bernardo Gutiérrez started upriver for Natchitoches, a

twenty-day journey by keelboat, Shaler embarked with him. Daily the American gave information and counsel. War with England could come any day. Governor Claiborne and Shaler himself believed that this would automatically mean war with England's ally, Spain. Shaler advised his pupil to make no overt move until the United States and Britain were at war. When the time came, Shaler promised to give him guidance. Meanwhile, in any event, Bernardo should beware of foreign agents who had no real concern for the Mexican people.

Bernardo and Shaler found in Natchitoches and in the neutral ground a disparate aggregation of Americans itching to march into the Interior Provinces. Among the adventurers were men who looked to receiving land for their services, men who really wanted to fight for liberty, men caring for neither liberty nor land as much as for a scrap for the scrap's sake and men of pitiful avarice, who came in answer to advertisements in the New Orleans newspapers that put it bluntly: "Cash!—for those who will fight for it!... There is a great deal of money at San Antonio, and the property of the Royalists collected there is immense."

Samuel Davenport, expatriate American who was the official purveyor of supplies for Spain at Nacogdoches, was imbued with the revolutionary spirit. Also, as a businessman he envisioned the benefits to Texas, his adopted homeland, in open and wider trade with the United States, a goal which could be achieved only through freedom from Spanish restrictions. Samuel Davenport persuaded others, among them Dr. Sibley in Natchitoches.

Dr. Sibley, who had wined and dined Bernardo and given him the letters of introduction the year before, conferred with the Mexican revolutionary frequently upon his return to Natchitoches. He talked also with Captain Shaler, who was worried. Obviously, because of his lack of military experience, Gutiérrez could only be a figurehead. A military man was needed to lead and keep under control the fractious, turbulent volunteers who tented beneath the pines and oaks of the neutral ground. Perhaps it was Dr. Sibley who found the kind of man whom Shaler wanted.

His name was Augustus Magee, a brilliant Bostonian who had finished third in his class at West Point and was now 33 years old. The tall, sinewy regular had both the appearance and the background of a leader. His superiors had considered him one of the best informed young officers in the United States Army. He had come to Natchitoches as a lieutenant of artillery with Colonel Pike's regiment; from there he had scourged the desperadoes of the neutral ground. He was tough.

General Wilkinson had lately given an endorsement for Augustus Magee's promotion, but the War Department had turned it down. The lieutenant smarted under the rejection, and he had also a genuine desire to help the people of Texas rid themselves of the *gachupín* oppressors.

Samuel Davenport talked with him; soon Augustus Magee had the confidence of Shaler and Gutiérrez. They asked him to weld the raiding volunteers into an army. The republic which such an army would bring into being could become either a part of a federal republic of Mexico, when freedom for all of New Spain had been achieved, or it could join the United States, whichever its people willed.

On June 22, 1812, Lieutenant Magee resigned his commission in the United States Army. A month later the eagerly awaited word reached Natchitoches. The United States and Great Britain were at war with each other.

Gutiérrez and Shaler and Magee had already mapped their campaign. They would first take La Bahía, then invest and storm Béxar, declare Texas free and independent and unite with the insurgents still fighting in New Spain. To their bravely named Republican Army of the North would flock almost every native Texan; of this they were certain, too certain.

For two months supplies for the army had been coming from New Orleans to the warehouses in Natchitoches. For weeks Bernardo's spies had been circulating his handwritten broadsides among the people of Nacogdoches and Béxar. That which Governor Claiborne and Shaler called "the business" was at hand.

In August, Augustus Magee entered Wilkinson's no-man's land to rendezvous at the saline near the Sabine River with the men he was to command.

A filibuster patrol, which Magee had sent across the river into Texas itself, came upon a train of 200 mules loaded with fine wool and specie, and moving cautiously under the protection of a small Royalist detachment commanded by Juan Manuel Zambrano, the clerical intriguer and now a lieutenant-colonel in the Royalist army. The Spaniards wheeled and headed west on the red clay trail, beating their mules until they galloped. The filibuster patrol, too few to give chase, also turned around and raced back to the Sabine for reinforcements with which they could capture the rich prize.

Zambrano feverishly directed the defense of Nacogdoches. The bales of wool which his mules had carried were piled across the *camino real* atop the first long hill to the east of the town. Captain Bernardo Montero, the commandant, ordered a parade of his troops. But within many a home, the families of the troops and citizens of Nacogdoches congratulated themselves that the filibusters were on the way.

Soon Captain Montero realized that his men would not stand and fight. He ordered an immediate departure for Béxar. Only 100 yards down the road a militia captain called the troops to an unauthorized halt. He told Zambrano that the soldiers had left their wives and families at Nacogdoches unprotected and helpless, with an advancing army almost at their doors. They must return. The furious Zambrano, shouting that he would go on to San Antonio alone and return with enough rope to hang them all, spurred his horse down the *camino real* toward the west. Only Captain Montero, three loyal lieutenants and twenty soldiers followed him. Sixty presidial officers and men and every militiaman turned back to Nacogdoches, but not to fight.

Five days from the time they crossed the Sabine, Lieutenant Magee and Bernardo Gutiérrez and their troops strode past the breastworks of baled wool, already pushed to the right and left of the road by the cheering citizens of Nacogdoches. With them rode Samuel Davenport. His influence and Bernardo's propaganda had been effective.

The filibusters and the citizens loaded the specie and silver bars and wool upon the mules, and tallied the quantities of presidial powder, lances, spears and flour which had fallen into their hands. The loot was worth more than $60,000. The filibusters formally elected Gutiérrez as commander-in-chief, Magee his second in command and Samuel Davenport quartermaster.

Bernardo's volatile spirits soared. At his desk in Nacogdoches he scrawled lengthy proclamations to his "Beloved, Honorable Compatriots" in the Province of Texas and to "The People of Mexico" and to "The Officers, Soldiers and Residents of San Antonio de Béxar." Exultantly he wrote that an army of men descended from heroes who had fought for and won independence for themselves was on the way to help liberate Texas and Mexico and to obtain for them the blessings of liberty. He exhorted the people to rise, to abandon the

tyrants and join the ranks of free men. At the risk of their lives, his
agents carried his appeals to Béxar and all the way to the Río Grande.

His propaganda bore fruit. Soon refugees from Trinidad de Salcedo and deserters from Béxar swarmed into Nacogdoches. Magee
formed these newcomers and the men of the Nacogdoches district into
three companies of mounted troops. Davenport himself equipped each
man who could not provide himself with two horses and the necessary
supplies. From the United States came more recruits, many of them
in response to Gutiérrez' promise of land grants in Texas, until the
number of filibusters had risen to 450. Day long Magee drilled and
disciplined these and the 150 Spanish-American volunteers. He was
resolved to mold them into an army. Shaler was delighted with the
lieutenant's progress and with the animation of the members of the
expedition. He wrote Monroe:

> *The business of volunteering for New Spain has become
> a perfect mania; I hear of parties proceeding thither from all
> quarters, and they are constantly passing thro' this village
> from Natchez: several young gentlemen of very respectable
> character and acquirements have gone on. I suppose the vol-
> unteer force cannot now be rated under 600 Americans: gen-
> erally good soldiers, and there is every appearance of its be-
> coming very respectable in a short time: equal even to the
> intire conquest of the Province of Texas.*
>
> *The volunteer expedition from the most insignificant be-
> ginning is growing into an irresistible torrent that will sweep
> the crazy remains of Spanish Government from the Internal
> Provinces, and open Mexico to the political influence of the
> U.S. and to the talents and enterprize of our citizens . . .*

Looking eastward from Béxar, Governor Salcedo and Colonel
Herrera were not so much afraid of this "irresistible torrent" as they
were of their own troops. From the San Antonio River to Nacogdoches
soldiers and civilians in undetermined numbers had been corrupted
by revolutionary propaganda. Frantically Salcedo and Herrera appealed to the viceroy, the commandant general and the governors of
the Interior Provinces for loyal reinforcements. But the rulers of New
Spain had their hands full, for the rebel General Morelos was winning
victory after victory in the south. Only Governor Cordero of Coahuila
promised to send the governor of Texas a few militia units.

Early in October, the invaders moved to the Trinity. Without opposition they occupied Trinidad de Salcedo, the high bluff where the Spaniards had previously had a post. The exuberant Gutiérrez and Magee declared Texas a republic, with borders at the Sabine and the Trinity, and hoisted a green flag as its emblem. Between the two rivers scarcely an able-bodied man had not joined the Republican Army of the North.

The commanders decided to wait at the Trinity for cooler weather before marching down the La Bahía Road to the strategic *presidio* which the Americans called and spelled Labardee. But the men were impatient. They believed the time was propitious to strike directly at Béxar. The captains called for a ballot. Overwhelmingly the troops voted to advance immediately against Béxar.

In the seesaw of chance, a Royalist deserter reached Gutiérrez as the filibusters crossed the Colorado and warned him that Salcedo had learned of the filibusters' plans and was waiting with 1,400 troops at the Guadalupe. Gutiérrez and Magee summoned their captains. La Bahía, as originally planned, not Béxar, would be their objective.

The stone fortress at La Bahía, 40 leagues away and on the far side of the San Antonio River, was formidable. Strategically located and constructed upon a rocky elevation, it boasted a stone wall some 10 feet in height and 3 feet thick which enclosed more than 3 acres of presidial grounds. A sufficient number of determined troops would have had no trouble defending La Bahía. But Governor Salcedo had ordered all but 160 of the garrison to the Guadalupe.

As the filibusters approached the mission *pueblo* across the river from the *presidio,* they were greeted joyously by its residents. The watching Spanish soldiers, who had spent the previous day at Mass praying for strength, fled in terror through the door in the south wall and hid in the woods. Royalist stores of dried beef, salt and flour and enough silver to pay the army its overdue wages fell into the conquerors' hands.

Sure now of victory, Magee wrote Shaler to join him at La Bahía and there claim all of Texas to the Río Grande for the United States. Bernardo Gutiérrez, apparently unsure of his own ability, asked Shaler to help him establish the republican government which to him was the only reason for the expedition.

But the fighting was far from over. Governor Salcedo and Herrera led 800 men down the San Antonio River. At La Bahía, after two or

three inconclusive skirmishes, the Spanish commanders divided their
forces into three groups, posting one on each side of the *presidio*
and one directly across the river. Their fourteen field pieces were
trained on the *presidio* itself. Magee knew what to expect. A siege was
in store.

Salcedo and Herrera settled down for the siege, awaiting reinforcements from Coahuila. It was mid-November.

Bernardo was not impressed with Magee's conduct of the war.
No military man, he took his title of commander seriously, outlining
the strategy he had devised and becoming indignant when Magee paid
no attention. Within the *presidio* the men who had come to fight, not
to undergo the inaction of a siege, grew sullen. Many of the Mexican
volunteers lost their will to fight and many left by the back door as
had their predecessors.

Bernardo's belief that the Royalist army would come over to the
republicans had been only wishful thinking. The rank and file of the
Yanquis were all but mutinous. Magee concluded bitterly that he
could trust no one except his American officers. He called a meeting
of his officers, conspicuously ignoring Gutiérrez. They agreed unani-
mously that the commander should send a messenger to Salcedo under
a white flag with tidings that the Americans had entered Texas on the
false assumption that they were wanted and would be joined by the
people. Perhaps Salcedo would permit the Americans to withdraw
and return home. During a three-day truce which Salcedo declared,
Lieutenant Magee dined with the Spanish officers and returned with
the governor's proposal that if the republican army surrendered the
presidio, the Anglo-Americans would be permitted to leave, without
their arms but with enough food, to be provided by the governor, to
meet their needs. But no Mexicans would be pardoned.

The next day, Lieutenant Magee drew up his men in parade
formation, read the terms of surrender and ordered all who approved
of them to shoulder their rifles. To a man, American and Mexican
alike, the troops showed their disapproval by striking the butts of their
guns against the ground. The Mexicans had no wish to be sacrificial
lambs. The Americans voted "to die with their arms in their hands
rather than deliver up a single individual ... that had taken up arms
with them." They would fight on together.

The siege dragged on. In January, Lieutenant Magee was bed-
ridden and delirious. His officers became panic-stricken. They voted

to retreat, packed up to leave, then changed their minds. When Augustus Magee died in his tent on the night of February 6, Bernardo Gutiérrez and most of the Spanish-Americans believed that he had committed suicide by taking poison. He probably was a victim of tuberculosis.

Bernardo Gutiérrez' spirits rose after the death of Lieutenant Magee, whom he had come to hate and mistrust in the few weeks before the American's death. Now the gigantic Samuel Kemper, who had succeeded the dead Magee as commander of the army, agreed to the proposal of Gutiérrez that the invaders force the Royalists to fight in the open.

Shrouded in the fog that rolled off the river and covered the plains near the fort, seventy men under Captain Miguel Menchaca crept in the early hours of February 15 toward the main camp of the enemy. As the fog lifted shortly after dawn, the Royalists sighted the inferior force and charged them, which was just what Gutiérrez had hoped for.

Menchaca retreated according to plan. The Royalist regulars pursued the rebel decoys almost to the walls of the *presidio*. Within the *presidio* every cannon had been trained on the open field; every porthole was manned by a waiting rifleman. Not until the Royalists were within almost point-blank range did the riflemen and cannoneers fire.

Colonel Herrera's troops held steady and drove Captain Menchaca's company into the fort, even charging to its very walls. Gutiérrez got the fight he wanted. In a sense, the encounter was a victory for the Royalists, but one achieved at high price.

The dead and wounded lay thick upon the ground outside the *presidial* walls. And Governor Salcedo did not have men enough to take the fort, put down Comanche raids elsewhere and quell a possible new uprising of the people. He bowed to Colonel Herrera's military decision to lift the siege. The Royalists loaded their wounded on wagons and returned to Béxar. The revolutionary army, waiting for reinforcements, did not pursue. Bernardo Gutiérrez resumed at La Bahía the writing of revolutionary propaganda.

When the republican army did move up the left bank of the river, it counted 800 volunteers. At the crossing of the Salado the army was joined by a Captain McFarland with 300 Alabaman and Coushatta Indians, who had only recently migrated to Texas from Louisiana and had no traditional ties with the Spaniards.

The rebels ran into an ambush at El Rosillo, 9 miles below Béxar.
Despite Herrera's artillery, the filibusters' charge broke the Royalist
line.

Bernardo Gutiérrez established his headquarters at Mission Concepción. Recruits from Béxar flocked into his camp. Now, before Salcedo could obtain reinforcements, was the time to strike again. On
April 1 Gutiérrez and Kemper led their men to the walls of Béxar
and prepared to storm the defenses. Salcedo and Herrera made the
only possible decision. They sent three envoys under a white flag to
Mission Concepción with the conditions under which they would surrender.

Gutiérrez and Kemper held two of the emissaries as hostages; the
third was sent back with a rejection of the terms and a demand for
unconditional surrender. So, on the afternoon of April 1 Don Manuel
de Salcedo, lieutenant colonel of infantry of the Royalist forces, and
political and military governor of the Province of Texas and the New
Philippines, surrendered the whole of Texas to the revolutionary
army.

That night the Spanish-Americans and the Anglo-Americans celebrated, but separately and in different manner, the winning of Texas
and the capture of the Royalist who had been the moving spirit in the
capture of Father Hidalgo and the generals. Gutiérrez and Miguel
Menchaca and the other Mexican officers feasted at the refectory table
in the mission of San Antonio de Valero, long known as The Alamo.
The soldiers reveled in the thatched-roofed alcoves where the mission
Indians had once lived.

But Samuel Kemper and Reuben Ross and the other ranking
Americans dined on silver plates at the governor's home, with Salcedo
and Herrera themselves. Such intimacy between the conqueror and
the conquered could not be kept secret.

The next day another occurrence aroused the Spanish-American
rebels. Bernardo and his pomp-loving fellow countrymen had planned
an impressive ceremony of surrender during which the enemy would
lay their arms at the feet of the conquerors in the military plaza.
Colonel Kemper ordered instead that the arms be stacked without
formality in the barracks; moreover, he gave the Royalist officers their
freedom under parole. This was too much.

Were the oppressors to be wined and dined and given their freedom? Few among the Mexicans approved of such leniency. There

were also many among the Anglo filibusters who agreed that this was not the way to treat Spanish tyrants whom they had come so far to kill.

Discontent mounted throughout the afternoon so greatly that Bernardo concluded that the prisoners could not be protected in San Antonio. That afternoon he announced to the troops at parade that the political prisoners would be conducted to San Bernardo Bay, from whence they would be sent to New Orleans under parole. No officer or enlisted man protested audibly.

That same afternoon other men bent on terrible vengeance held a mock trial. As night fell, Antonio Delgado, formerly a corporal in the militia company of Béxar, and Pedro Prado of The Alamo company, headed 100 Mexicans and Anglo-Americans who, mounted and heavily armed, rode to the house on the main plaza where the *gachupín* officers were quartered under parole. Delgado told the guards that he and his confederates had come to take the prisoners to San Bernardo and demanded that they be brought out. Without question or delay, the guards handed over Salcedo, Herrera, Lieutenant-Colonel Geronimo Herrera, who had brought reinforcements from Coahuila, Captain Miguel Arcos, Captain Bernardo Montero and twelve fellow officers. The horsemen surrounded their victims. The silent cavalcade forded the San Antonio and rode on for a mile and a half below the town to where a low ridge ran down to the east bank of the river.

Here—the place was called La Tablita—the killers and their victims dismounted. The hands of the Royalist officers were tied behind them. With a sickening casualness, the assassins whetted their swords and knives on the soles of their boots. When they were satisfied that their weapons were fit for the work at hand, they hacked off the heads of their bound prisoners. Afterward, they stripped the bodies of rings, clothing and all other valuables, and abandoned the corpses, unburied, in a clump of mesquite for coyotes and buzzards to devour. The murderers rode into San Antonio the next morning to announce that the tyrants were dead.

The butchery at La Tablita would bring about the displacement of Bernardo Gutiérrez as leader of the army. It would also cause many American officers to go home, some of them to report that Bernardo was responsible for the massacre. But the fault was only indirectly his.

He knew well the oppression under which his people had lived, the harshness of the Inquisition and the civil courts, the urge to retaliate. Remembering the course of the revolution under Hidalgo, he should have placed a stronger and more reliable guard around the house from which the *gachupines* were taken. But no evidence exists that he connived in or approved of the ghastly slaughter.

Gutiérrez and Kemper should have marched at once for Monclova or Monterrey; the murder of the *gachupines* made immediate retaliation certain. Bernardo undertook instead to draft a declaration of independence and a constitution for the State of Texas: an essential part of the declaration would deny him further help from the United States.

His Declaration of Independence, promulgated on April 6, mirrored the revolutionary spirit of the day. It echoed much of what had been proclaimed for the North American colonies on July 4, 1776, and it antedated the first Mexican Declaration of Independence of the rebel Father Morelos in the fall of 1813. Its opening paragraph had a familiar ring:

> *We the People of the Province of Texas, protesting the rectitude of our intentions before the Supreme Judge of the Universe, declare that the chains which bound us under the domination of European Spain are forever dissolved; that we are free and independent; that we have the right to establish our own government; and that henceforth, all legitimate authority shall emanate from the People to whom alone this right belongs; that henceforth we are forever absolved from our duty and obligation to any foreign power.*

The Anglo-Americans had no quarrel with this much of the declaration, but Bernardo was a mistrustful and single-minded man. In the body of the text he made explicit what the opening paragraph of the declaration implied: the people of Texas should work to "free themselves from all foreign domination, to organize their own government, and through wise laws seek the prosperity of our country."

The meaning was clear. Texas was to be for native Texans alone. From where was to come title or office or reward for the North Americans who had led the victorious army into San Antonio de Béxar? Gutiérrez and his Mexicans had been glad enough of their prowess. With victory, Gutiérrez seemed to have forgotten his debt to them.

The provisional government authorized a *junta* of six men. Four were of Spanish extraction, a fifth was Louis Massicolt, a Frenchman. Only one was a citizen of the United States. Gutiérrez was designated the President Protector of the Provisional State of Texas. When Governor Claiborne and Shaler and their collaborators in the Texas adventure read the final draft of the constitution, which Gutiérrez finished on April 17, they could only assume that the wordy *mestizo* was an ingrate. The first article of the constitution stated plainly that Texas was "inviolably joined" to the Republic of Mexico, of which it was an integral part. Neither the Anglo-American officers nor the United States could hope for anything from this constitution or from Bernardo Gutiérrez—not even Samuel Kemper, who had succeeded to military command after the death of Lieutenant Magee. The star of Massicolt, the Frenchman, was in the ascendancy, and he encouraged the rumor that 600 French troops were on their way from Santo Domingo.

Three weeks after the triumph of the Republican Army of the North at San Antonio, Colonel Kemper and 100 American officers left for the United States. They took with them copies of the Declaration of Independence and the constitution, and the horrifying story of the murder of the *gachupín* officers. Gutiérrez was blamed for the declaration, the constitution and the killings. After the Americans reached Natchitoches, people talked little of the immediate freeing of Texas and much about the barbarism of Bernardo Gutiérrez.

Captain Shaler, the agent of the United States, decided that the man had to be headed off. A figurehead congenial to the United States must be found.

Shaler did not have far to look. The right man, he decided, was José Álvarez de Toledo, the revolutionary Cuban with whom Gutiérrez had reached an understanding in Philadelphia. Toledo had passed through Natchitoches recently with ten men, among them Anson Mower, an American printer, with a small printing press strapped to a mule's back. Gutiérrez knew nothing of Toledo's coming; his erstwhile confederate had not let him know. At Nacogdoches, Toledo took over command of the town in the name of the revolution but without authorization from Gutiérrez. He planted corn for the army, organized the militia and even established a public school. Shaler was impressed with Toledo's efficiency. Even his naval uniform, heavy with gold braid, implied authority.

Shaler was certain that such a man, were he willing to listen to the right people, would be a most suitable president of the Republic of Texas. Actually Toledo had little military ability; as was Gutiérrez, he was more propagandist than warrior. He kept his printer and press busy in Nacogdoches turning out proclamations and dissertations on the revolution, all without sanction from Gutiérrez. Toledo wrote the text and Mower set the type for a newspaper, the *Gaceta de Texas,* which they planned to publish in Nacogdoches on May 21, 1813, with articles in Spanish and an English translation.

But before the date of publication, Toledo received from Gutiérrez an angry letter. He had betrayed the revolution, Gutiérrez said. The best way that he could prove his patriotism would be to return to Louisiana and recruit volunteers. Toledo left quickly, taking with him the press and the type. In a few days the newspaper which was to have been the first to be published in Texas was printed in Natchitoches. Toledo had tarried in Nacogdoches only long enough to write to "Citizen Gutiérrez" a witheringly correct letter.

Captain Shaler welcomed Toledo's return to Natchitoches. Now they could conspire more easily. There was need for haste. Intercepted messages from Massicolt, the French member of the *junta* in San Antonio, to Pierre Girard, the French agent at New Orleans, made it clear that France had her own possessive plans for the future of Texas. Soon Shaler sent Henry Adams Bullard, a Harvard-educated lawyer, who was a member of Toledo's venturesome party, into Texas to persuade the Anglo-Americans to demand that Toledo take over from Gutiérrez. Bullard's companion was General Wilkinson's son, Joseph B. Wilkinson. And while Shaler plotted the overthrow of Gutiérrez, who had been his original choice as a pro-United States revolutionary, Royalist forces west of San Antonio sought to rid New Spain not only of Gutiérrez but of everything that he had worked for.

Spain's soldiers were spread thin. The better to combat insurgents and filibusters, the *Provincias Internas* were divided into two districts, eastern and western. Joaquín de Arredondo, *gachupín* governor of Nuevo Santander, who had just become commandant general of the eastern *Provincias Internas* (an office tendered Herrera, who was murdered before assuming it) advanced toward Laredo. From there he ordered Elizondo, now a general in appreciation of his capture of Hidalgo, and 700 well-armed troops to proceed from the Presidio del Río Grande to an observation post at the Frío River.

They were to wait there for Arredondo. No doubt remained of the loyalty of Elizondo to the Royalist cause in behalf of which he had lured Hidalgo and the chieftains to their deaths. Soon after he had occupied San Antonio, Gutiérrez had sent a messenger to Elizondo inviting him to return to the revolutionary fold. Elizondo's emotional answer ended "... were you to hide in hell itself as the last refuge, from there will I drag you by the hair, cast you under the flames, and when you are burnt to ashes scatter your remains to the four winds."

If he could not hope to do precisely that, Elizondo had begun to believe that the end of Gutiérrez and his revolution was near. Refugees from San Antonio told him of discord in the town, of the departure of the angered American officers, of poor morale and inadequate supplies. The betrayer of Hidalgo began to think of himself as the nemesis of Gutiérrez as well. Instead of halting at the Frío, as ordered by Arredondo, he hurried up the *camino real* to Béxar, arriving at the outskirts of the town on June 18.

The despairing Gutiérrez saw only one alternative to defeat. He must withdraw to the Trinity and from there negotiate with the United States for immediate assistance in return for Texas. He had never thought to be brought to such extremity, but independence from Spain was the all-important consideration. Reuben Ross, who had taken over command of the remaining Americans after Colonel Kemper left, also urgently counseled a retreat to the Trinity.

In these woeful hours, Bernardo's wife and two children arrived at Béxar. He could not greet them properly, for he and Ross and their subordinate officers had made a desperate decision. At ten o'clock on the night of June 19, the filibusters and Spanish-American defenders of San Antonio stole out of the military plaza and surrounded Elizondo's position at Alazán. Silently they waited through the night. At dawn, as the Royalists prepared to attend Mass for the success of their coming assault on San Antonio, the republicans fell upon the unready foemen, with all the vigor of their days of victory and, in a desperate, two-hour battle, routed them. Elizondo escaped.

Gutiérrez and the army then relaxed when they should have pursued.

In the spring and early summer a newspaper, *El Mexicano,* which Toledo was now publishing in Natchitoches, brought to the citizens and soldiers in San Antonio vicious tales of the incapability and cruelty and tyranny of Bernardo Gutiérrez.

Nor was this all. Even throughout the difficult months when the filibusters and the Mexicans had fought side by side and waited out the siege of La Bahía and marched to Béxar, friction between the two groups persisted. Differences in faith, in language, in customs and even eating habits grated upon their nerves. And there was the basic difference in goals. Gutiérrez clung to but one, the freedom of all Mexico. The American volunteers had more immediate, personal and material objectives. The government of the United States, privately, had a purposefulness of its own. And William Shaler, representing the interests of this country, had a consuming conviction: Bernardo Gutiérrez was undependable. He must be replaced.

On June 27, Bullard demanded and won a meeting of the *junta*. Gutiérrez, with his revolutionary purpose and his own position at stake, pleaded before it. Let Toledo serve under him as second in command. Forget such heretical proposals for the new republic as freedom of religion and the introduction of Free Masonry. Restrict to 1,000 the number of Anglo-American volunteers which Toledo could bring with him into Texas. Require of all of them an oath either to support and defend the Mexican government after independence was won or withdraw from the country.

But the *junta* voted to invite Toledo to come to San Antonio without any restrictions. When Toledo arrived in San Antonio on August 1 the army demanded that Gutiérrez relinquish the presidency. The Americans declared that unless Toledo replaced him, they would abandon the city. Gutiérrez and the *junta* were all too aware that without the filibusters the back of the revolution would be broken. The *junta* elected Toledo president of the Republic of Texas.

In the cool of the evening of August 26, an armed escort accompanied Gutiérrez and his wife out of the capital of the first Republic of Texas. Their destination was not their own home; Revilla was held by the Royalists. Instead, the saddened and bitter Gutiérrez turned his face to the east, to Natchitoches, to refuge in the United States, which had not been truly his friend. Yet Bernardo Gutiérrez de Lara would fight at the battle of New Orleans for that very nation against the British from whom the Anglo-Americans had won their own freedom. He would plot again and again with other filibusters for the achievement of the freedom which his Mexico would one day win. With liberty would come recognition for the blacksmith of Revilla, who had tried so hard to forge it.

But now, in less than two weeks, the republic from which he was being exiled, would for the time be obliterated.

A thousand Peninsular Spanish regulars, veterans of the Napoleonic wars and recently arrived at Vera Cruz and Tampico, came riding up from Laredo, their black boots shining, their blue uniforms smartly fringed in gold, their brass cannon gleaming in the August sun. Arredondo commanded them. Elizondo waited for them with 700 buckskin-clad militiamen from the Río Grande where the *camino real* crossed the Frío.

The bickering and suspicion did not end during the few days in which Toledo directed the republic. Perhaps it became worse. Many of the Spanish-Americans looked upon the revolutionary from Cuba and Spain as a foreigner, almost a *gachupine*. To end the ill-feeling, Toledo divided his army into two groups, one made up of Anglo-Americans and men from the neutral ground, the other of native Mexicans and Indian reinforcements—some 700 Taovayas, Tonka-wayas, Tawakonis and Lipans. His decision was catastrophic. What little coordination had previously existed between the disparate elements now came to an end.

On the morning of August 18, the army which Toledo had renamed the Republican Army of North Mexico marched into a trap.

The day was scorching. Even at nine in the morning the scrub-covered sands that extended 4 miles from the Medina River radiated a flame like heat. Toledo's army should have waited in its strong position for the onset of Arredondo's forces. Instead it fell victim to almost the same kind of enticement which at La Bahía had caused the lifting of the Royalist siege. A Royalist patrol approached within rifle shot of the Republican troops. It was fired upon and Major Perry, who had succeeded Ross, impetuously ordered his men to pursue the unscathed horsemen. His Indians and American filibusters and neutral ground bandits and Mexicans followed their commander afoot, helter-skelter to the Medina. But the river was 4 miles distant. Almost none of the pursuers thought to fill and take along a goatskin water bag.

Hidden by the mesquite patches the Royalists were soon lost sight of; the pursuers, hoping to surprise an even larger number, kept on until in scattered groups, parched and disorganized, they reached the waters of the Medina. They paused long enough to drink copiously and to wash their dust-caked faces. Then they continued down the road in search of the shadowy enemy.

The waiting Elizondo, joined by 150 men under Colonel Juan Manuel Zambrano, effectively let his presence be known. His contingent began firing at the scattered insurgents. The main body of the Spanish troops under Arredondo came up from farther down the river. The battle was brief and one-sided.

Never had the filibusters come up against disciplined and self-assured Spanish regulars. The Indians gave way first. For a few minutes Toledo's forces rallied. Then, their ranks torn by artillery and rifle fire, they fled in panic, pursued by Elizondo and 200 cavalrymen. The dazed fugitives headed, not for San Antonio, but for the distant Louisiana border. Few reached it. By mid-afternoon 1,000 men of Toledo's army lay dead or dying in the searing sands, many of them slain after they had surrendered.

Arredondo prepared for a triumphant entry into San Antonio. Out of the terrified city men and women and children began streaming eastward, their belongings piled high on mules or hastily tossed into field carts. The retaliation of the victors was even worse than the people feared. As the Royalists rode into the town, the citizens who had not fled lined the streets on bended knees. But their humility brought no compensation. Arredondo's firing squads mowed down the prisoners by scores. Insurgent wives and daughters were herded into a cramped enclosure, where many died. For fifty-four days they ground corn and made *tortillas* to feed Arredondo's men.

Elizondo, with a picked force of 200 horsemen, scoured the countryside in search of fleeing revolutionaries. Finding the Trinity in flood, he set up camp at the Lomo del Toro, 2 leagues west of the river, where the road to La Bahía branched off from the *camino real*. Refugees, seeking to escape by either road, must come his way. The river would stop them even if they eluded his patrols. But the avenging Elizondo made a distinction between Spanish-American and Anglo-American prisoners. He permitted the Anglo-Americans to retain one rifle for each five men, to assure them of game to eat on the way home, and provided them with passports which would get them past any Spanish patrols they might meet.

But no quarter was granted the Spanish-Americans who had dared question the rule of the *gachupines*. Among the first to die was

Delgado, one of the killers of Governor Salcedo, who was found hiding
in the rushes near the river. He was shot without trial. Soon afterward
eighty Mexicans, rounded up along the banks of the Trinity, were
hustled back to Elizondo's camp. Other Spaniards dug a long and deep
grave, laid a piece of timber across it, and after tying the prisoners,
stood them by tens on the timber and shot them. Not until then did
Elizondo, the betrayer, set out for San Antonio, driving before him
200 bereaved women and children. He would not reach his destination.
One of his officers became maddened by the executions, so it is said,
and stealing into Elizondo's tent, slew the butcher's tentmate and
wounded Elizondo so seriously that he died subsequently in his litter
beside the San Marcos River.

As one of his first official acts after the crushing of the rebels,
General Arredondo exhumed the moldering bodies and heads of Governor Salcedo and Colonel Herrera, and reburied them with pomp
in the church of San Fernando. He announced tempting rewards for
anyone who would kill Toledo or Gutiérrez: 250 pesos to a foreign
Protestant, 500 pesos to any Mexican or foreign Catholic. A special
reward of 250 pesos was offered to anyone, without distinction as to
nationality or religion, who would kill Samuel Davenport, the American-born citizen of New Spain who had fanned the fires of revolution.

East of the flooded Trinity the settlers used the respite to pack up
their belongings and leave for safety. Almost every family which had
dwelt there had contributed men to the cause of Bernardo Gutiérrez.
Only through flight could they survive. Nacogdoches became a ghost
town. From the Trinity to the Sabine the homeland of the Texas lay
all but deserted.

Toledo, whom the schemers of the United States had thought to
be more trustworthy than Bernardo Gutiérrez, returned to the *gachupín* fold in the summer of 1815, despairing too soon of the success
of the revolutions that raged throughout the western hemisphere.
Promised a full pardon which would make it possible for him and his
wife to return to Spain, he told all he knew. After working against
the revolutionaries as a Spanish agent in the United States, he sailed
for Bordeaux to enter upon a career as a diplomat. No moral adorns
his life story.

CHAPTER SIXTEEN

THE COMING OF THE AUSTINS

THE DEVIOUS HOLLANDER who called himself the Baron de Bastrop had a knack of remembering faces. Somewhere before he had come across this dejected, middle-aged American who in the wintry sunlight of December 23, 1820, was crossing the principal plaza of Béxar. Of a sudden, Felipe Enrique Neri, whose true name had been Philip Hendrik Nering Bögel and who had given himself the noble and spurious title of Baron de Bastrop, remembered when and where their paths had crossed. It had been 23 years before, in a tavern in Louisville, Kentucky.

Neri held out his hand to Connecticut-born Moses Austin, who had come here hoping to win approval of a scheme that might recoup the fortunes he had twice lost. Only minutes ago, Austin had been ordered to leave the *Provincias Internas*. The two reintroduced themselves to each other and chatted for a few moments over the happenstance. Perhaps, even before they left the square for a more private conversation in the baron's lodgings, Moses Austin had told him of the failure of his mission.

The chance meeting would bring incredibly favorable results for the United States. Because of the intervention and good offices of Baron de Bastrop, the *camino real* would become a legal thoroughfare for Anglo-American settlers. More far-reaching, this renewal in the plaza of Béxar of a brief acquaintanceship set the stage for the first of a sequence of events through which, in little more than a quarter of a century, the heirs of Spain in Mexico would surrender more than half of the vast territory which had been New Spain, and the United

States would have gained two-thirds as much territory as it had acquired through the Louisiana Purchase.

When the two men had first met in the Kentucky tavern nearly a quarter of a century earlier, Bastrop held a commission from the Baron de Carondelet, the Spanish governor of Louisiana, to recruit recently arrived Europeans as settlers in the Ouachita valley, where Carondelet hoped to build a buffer of contented, legitimate colonists against the encroaching American frontiersmen and the Englishmen venturing southward from Canada. Moses Austin had been operating lead mines in southwest Virginia as a subsidiary to his partnership in a dry goods importing business in Philadelphia and Richmond. In the midst of prosperity he had failed. Possibly he, like so many others, had speculated in the $20-a-thousand-acres warrants and had been unable to raise the necessary cash.

In icy weather Austin had undertaken a 2,000 mile roundtrip journey from Virginia to St. Génevieve in today's Missouri to investigate the rich lead deposits in upper Louisiana. He had made the journey in three months and had met Bastrop on the return leg. After he reached Virginia he requested and received from Governor Carondelet a grant of one square league of land and the Mine à Burton it encompassed, across the river from St. Génevieve. Perhaps the two travelers had disclosed to each other at supper time or over a casual drink something of their plans and their common dependence upon the good will of Governor Carondelet.

It is unlikely that the Dutch immigrant told much of the truth about himself. His story throughout his life was that he had left Holland when the armies of the French Revolution destroyed the Dutch Republic. The more accurate reason was that the province of Friesland, of which he had been tax collector, had posted a reward of 1,000 gold Dutch ducats for an absconder named Philip Hendrik Nering Bögel.

He also said that Frederick of Prussia had given him his title for distinguished military service. The fact was that he had never fought for Frederick and had simply chosen the title for himself as a high-sounding and useful one. He was persuasive, an agreeable conversationalist, graceful of figure and handsome, with simple and easy manners which readily won him friends.

Under his agreement with Carondelet, Bastrop was to bring 500 families, within three years, to a designated 12 square leagues on the eastern side of the Ouachita, a tract of 846,281 acres, none of which were certified for him but which were available to his colonists. In return for his services, he was to have the exclusive privilege of owning and operating a flour mill on the Ouachita River and to sell his flour in New Orleans and Havana. At the time of his first meeting with Moses Austin he had brought seventeen families to the chosen site, but despite auspicious beginnings, the colonization scheme collapsed because Governor Carondelet's treasury could not spare the money promised to provide the settlers with six months' provisions and seed for their first wheat crop.

The baron's second venture in the New World also failed. He had sold or pledged as his own Spanish grant many thousands of the acres in the Ouachita location and invested the money thus raised in a sailcloth factory in Louisville. The company went into bankruptcy because of litigation over the acres he had falsely claimed to be his own. Again he bounced back. Returning to the Ouachita with exclusive privileges to trade with the Indians, he rebuilt his mill and erected warehouses. He was prospering when the Louisiana Purchase spelled the end to his exclusive trade concession.

After the purchase, the Spanish government offered refuge in Texas for all those who were citizens of Spanish Louisiana. The baron, now forty-six, managed to sell more acres from his Ouachita "grant." Bearing a passport from Casa Calvo, and accompanied by a French valet and three slaves, he traveled through Natchitoches in August, 1805, on his way to San Antonio.

But Spain's general welcome to all former residents of Louisiana to come to Texas was not as warm as the baron must have been led to believe. The viceroys of New Spain and governors of Texas were far more suspicious of foreigners than had been the Spanish governors of Louisiana. Bastrop first came under suspicion when he asked for the privilege of trading with the Indians, always a cause for Spanish alarm, and by seeking to export horses. He had sought also to open a mine on the San Marcos and had been rebuffed with the reminder that such privileges could be given only to those who had been born in the Spanish peninsula itself. And it was most unfortunate, too, that his nebulous Spanish grant on the Ouachita had eventually been acquired by Aaron Burr, who, after his arrest, had asserted that this area was his destination.

But however suspect Bastrop had been at first, in the intervening years he had served the king well. He was interpreter for Herrera during the neutral ground agreement with Wilkinson. As pretended adviser to Hidalgo's insurgents he had counseled them not to send the captive Governor Salcedo from Monclova to Saltillo and had "guided" them north up the *camino real*. He had treated the Royalist wounded after the defeat of the Gutiérrez expedition.

Although he could trade only within the borders of New Spain, Bastrop prospered. His mule trains brought grain from Saltillo, bore from Béxar the cow hides which were a major export, and perhaps carried more 100-pound bales of tobacco than the government monopoly knew, to say nothing of silver. His fellow citizens were affectionately respectful. Twice he was elected second *Alcalde* of San Fernando, only to receive the veto of a suspicious governor. But Antonio María Martínez, who was that governor's successor, had such faith in this enterprising citizen of Béxar that, when Bastrop was again elected *Alcalde* in 1817, Martínez simply reported this information to the commandant of the eastern Interior Provinces as a routine matter. No protests were forthcoming. In 1820 Bastrop became the governor's official interpreter.

The fortunes of Moses Austin after the chance meeting with Bastrop in 1797 were as checkered. After he received the square league grant he had sought in Missouri, together with the lead mine, he moved from Austin Ville in Virginia in June, 1798, with his wife; his four-and-a-half year old son, Stephen Fuller Austin; a smaller daughter, Emily; his brother-in-law, Moses Bates; Bates' family; some experienced smelters and miners, and several slaves.

At St. Génevière he took the required oath of allegiance to the king, embraced the Roman Catholic faith as was mandatory for Spanish subjects and prepared to begin a diversity of operations. These were delayed by months of controversy with earlier settlers who claimed the mine and with frontiersmen who ranged the countryside without regard for property lines. Austin's temper was choleric and frequently got out of hand. His anger clouded the justice of his cause. But by the next summer he was operating a sawmill, a flour mill, a furnace and a manufactury for shot and sheet lead at the settlement he named Potosi after the rich silver mining town in Bolivia.

The sale of Louisiana to the United States brought to Moses Austin the honor of being the first presiding judge of the St. Génevière district court. But the transfer also meant problems to such old settlers as himself. Land titles which had never been completed under the French and Spanish regimes were questioned again. New settlers came in with claims that conflicted with the old. New taxes were imposed and new militia duties. The War of 1812 brought dismal commercial repercussions. A shortage of ready money plagued the frontier, despite the flow of new immigrants.

At his general store at Potosi, Austin bartered cloth, furniture and hardware for peltry, butter and eggs, and other country produce and lead, which he had to ship eastward to convert into money. To alleviate the shortage in specie, he and several other settlers applied to the Missouri territorial legislature for authority to open a bank at St. Louis. Their petition was granted and the bank was opened, but it failed in the national panic of 1819 and once again Austin was financially ruined. For a while his son, Stephen, now in his twenties, sought to run the mines and the businesses at Potosi. It was soon evident to him, too, that the Austins must make a new start.

But where should they go?

The price of government land had been cut from $2.00 to $1.25 an acre, but to discourage speculation Congress had enacted a law requiring the purchaser to pay the entire price at one time. The Austins and thousands like them did not have sufficient capital under these terms. They looked elsewhere, to Texas, their attention drawn to this easily accesible country by the Adams-Onís Treaty.

In February 1819, the United States and Spain had finally come to terms respecting the southwestern boundary of the Louisiana Purchase. John Quincy Adams and Luis de Onís drew up a treaty by which the United States received title to East Florida, which included today's state of Florida, and West Florida. In exchange, the United States renounced any territorial claim to Texas beyond the Sabine River.

The land-hungry westerners felt the treaty cheated them of what they believed the Louisiana Purchase included. Up and down the western rivers men talked of little else that spring. In Natchez one group decided that if a weasel government surrendered their rights, red-blooded men would seize what belonged to them. Under the handsome, swashbuckling young physician, James Long, the filibusters entered Nacogdoches that summer, ran up a Lone Star flag which Long's wife, Jane, had made and declared the independence of the second Republic of Texas. Long's republic was short-lived indeed and his scattered forces fled ahead of Governor Martínez' regulars.

But the Adams-Onís Treaty and the anti-treaty talk focused attention on the trans-Sabine country.

What made Texas especially attractive to nearly penniless men was the Spanish government's policy, in contrast to that of the United States, of giving rather than selling its open land to acceptable settlers.

Moses and Stephen Austin talked hopefully of becoming traders in Texas. As a preliminary, Stephen established a farm at Long Prairie in the newly organized Arkansas Territory. Here, thought the father and son, a profitable base for supplying emigrants moving west could be created. Late in the summer of 1820, reports of an enlightened change in Spanish policy began to reach the Arkansas frontier; in October, Moses and Stephen Austin held another family conference in Little Rock.

A month later Moses Austin mounted his gray horse and rode along the *camino real* to San Antonio. He reached Béxar on December 23, 1820.

Immediately on arrival, as demanded by Spanish authority, the newcomer proceeded to the governor's palace to make a declaration as to why he was in the country. Moses Austin stated that he was 53, a Catholic, and a former subject of the king of Spain, who, animated by the liberal constitution, desired to take advantage of the earlier

invitation to residents of Spanish Louisiana to move to Spanish territory. He hoped to settle in this land with his family and cultivate cotton, sugar and corn. He was, he said, the representative of 300 families who would also like to move.

Governor Martínez was unimpressed. This man was an Anglo-American. Up until the recent past his orders had been to keep out foreigners and especially Anglo-Americans. Since becoming governor in 1817, much of his time had been occupied in trying to do just that. The governor wouldn't even look at Austin's passport, much less let him explain his purpose in detail. Austin, who knew the governor spoke French and also spoke the language himself, tried to engage him in conversation. The adamant Martínez ordered Austin to leave Béxar and the province without delay.

A few minutes later the disappointed Austin was accosted in the plaza by the Baron de Bastrop, who perhaps was on his way to the governor's palace to serve as interpreter.

For three days the two men talked avidly in Bastrop's apartment. Bastrop was entirely sympathetic. Carondelet had sponsored his Ouachita grant as a buffer against illegal Anglo-American entry. Austin's proposal to bring in 300 Americans as settlers with Spanish citizenship might add similarly to the security of the province of Texas. Moreover, Bastrop knew that Governor Martínez himself had thought of a colonization scheme to protect the borders.

As Austin filled in the details of his plan, Bastrop became more and more enthusiastic. Three hundred families ... a town to be called Austina, preferably a port town but situated in a location suitable for growing cotton, wheat, sugar and corn.... Through such a port—and here again the old dream of trade with Mexico—goods and silver might be exchanged at Santa Fé. The Interior Provinces, their development so long blocked, would have a port of their own.

Neither Austin nor Bastrop was familiar with the coastline; neither could suggest just where the port or settlement should be. But they were certain of its usefulness. And they agreed that the only settlers whom His Catholic Majesty would be likely to permit under Austin's plan would be former subjects of Spain in Louisiana.

Enthusiastically, the two promoters drew up a detailed proposal to submit to Martínez. When it was finished Bastrop carefully edited the final draft, then called upon the governor. He urged Martínez to give another audience to the Anglo-American. The man was a former subject of His Majesty. His papers were in order. Had not the governor himself often discussed legal, controlled colonization? The governor agreed to a review of this Spanish subject's papers. He found them impressive. And on January 4, 1821, Governor Martínez placed into the official mailbag his endorsement of Moses Austin's proposal and dispatched it to Joaquín de Arredondo, commandant general of the eastern Interior Provinces at Monterrey.

The Baron de Bastrop was certain that Arredondo would act favorably, as indeed he did. On January 17, 1821, the commandant general granted permission for the introduction of 300 colonists under the terms as outlined. A port was authorized, as requested by Moses Austin, for the entry of colonists and the export of mules from the eastern Interior Provinces to the United States. The land to be granted to Moses Austin was not specifically located, but could be agreed on subsequently.

Soon word of Moses Austin's successful trip to San Antonio spread like a prairie fire. The people of Natchitoches, long the gateway to Spanish lands, listened as he talked at length to the prospective settlers. He himself planned to return to Texas as soon as possible with fifteen men, who would begin surveying the grant and preparing for the coming of the colonists.

Home again at last, he worked furiously. In mid-May he learned that the Spanish government had granted him 200,000 acres on the

Colorado and that the port had been officially opened. The only stipulations were that the colonists must be Catholics or on entering Texas must accept the Faith, that they must take the oath of fealty to the king of Spain, that they must be of good moral character and that they must be Louisianians. Moses Austin requested his son, Stephen, in New Orleans to charter a boat to carry the first settlers to the mouth of the Colorado River on the Gulf of Mexico. He hoped to be there to meet them.

But it was not to be. The privations of the arduous trip to Béxar and back to Natchitoches had taxed 60-year-old Moses Austin's strength beyond his capacities. Despite the attentions of his physician who "blistered and bled him copiously," he died of pneumonia on June 10, 1821. With almost his last breath he whispered his hope that whatever happened to him his son, Stephen, should fulfill his contract.

For nearly 130 years Spain had greatly wasted her opportunities to adapt the soils and the streams and the forests of Texas to the needs of civilized men. Grasping too tightly and greedily the cords which bound her colonists to her, she had strangled them with repressive regulations.

The liberal policies inaugurated by Spain's *Cortes* in 1820 came too late to save her colonial empire. Unbending priests and rich Creoles, frightened by laws which curtailed their privileges, were more than ready to seek Mexican independence rather than accept such proposals of the *Cortes* as freedom of the press, the abolition of clerical and military *fueros,* the special rights, and the rationalism of the French Revolution.

The handsome and able Creole general, Agustín de Iturbide, commissioned by Viceroy Apodaca to run down and destroy Vicente Ramón Guerrero, one of the few surviving insurgent generals, in his stronghold near Acapulco, made the bold gesture for unity and freedom. He paused at the little town of Iguala and there, on February 24, 1821, called for a union of Royalists and insurgents and a declaration of independence for Mexico. Negotiations with Guerrero had already begun.

The Plan of Iguala offered three guarantees: an independent Mexico governed by a Bourbon, the continuation of the privileges of the Roman Catholic Church and the equality of Creoles and *gachu-*

pines. After much hesitation, General Guerrero embraced Iturbide and the Army of the Three Guarantees took the field.

Six months later, the *Cortes'* ambassador, General Juan O'Donojú —Johnny O'Donohue his forebears would have called him—signed the Treaty of Cordova. The liberty in whose name Father Hidalgo had raised the *grito de Dolores* seemed assured. Subsequent efforts of a demoralized Spain to repudiate O'Donojú's treaty without major military intervention failed.

Independence for Texas, Coahuila, Nuevo León and Nuevo Santander, bound together as the eastern Interior Provinces under the rule of the *gachupine* General Arredondo at Monterrey, was won chiefly by the citizens of Saltillo. Arredondo feared that the city of Saltillo would not be loyal to the *Cortes* in Spain. To prevent its announcing for the Plan of Iguala, he moved grenadiers into the city, and dispatched artillery and infantry to the pass of Los Muertos, 9 leagues from Saltillo on the Monterrey Road.

But the soldiers also were infected. At midnight of July 1, with tapers burning yellow in the darkness and cannons booming, the soldiers and citizens swarmed as comrades into the military plaza and, with swelling *vivas,* swore allegiance to independence and the plan.

General Arredondo, more interested in the perpetuation of his own power, which he had exercised since 1813, than in principle, conferred with the leaders of Monterrey. They joined him in pronouncing also for independence. This done, he ordered all the principal civil and military officers of the four provinces to swear to support the plan. Governor Martínez did so at San Antonio. The rest followed suit.

But the troops at Saltillo refused to obey Arredondo's order for them to return to him at Monterrey. They had come out for independence without instructions from him, they retorted. The only reason he had declared for freedom from Spain, they said, was that he knew his troops had deserted him. Now they had elected a local *junta* to rule them, they no longer recognized his authority. In fact, they could guarantee his safety only if he agreed to leave.

Deserted by his army, Arredondo, as well as many another *gachupine* realized that safety lay only in flight. He and his daughter took ship to Havana, never to return. Other wealthy, conservative *gachupines* likewise departed New Spain by the hundreds. Governor

Martínez who had taken the oath of allegiance to Iturbide, continued as governor until ill health forced his retirement to Mexico City. More than had most of Spain's governors, he had witnessed the evil effects of the bankruptcy of Spanish administration.

For Texas was a pauper and almost a paper province.

After ten years of revolution in Mexico, the population of Texas had shrunk to fewer than 2,500 persons, including the presidial soldiers. Of the civilian population, almost evenly divided between persons of Creole and *mestizo* blood, about 800 lived at Béxar, 600 at La Bahía and the remainder on the ranches near them. Nacogdoches, 180 leagues from Béxar—before the Gutiérrez-Magee expedition a town of 1,000 population—was an all-but-abandoned town.

San Antonio itself was infested and all but overrun by insolent Comanches. Governor Martínez was powerless to prevent the stealing of horses and cattle from the unprotected ranches. His soldiers were ill-equipped to fight them and he had no gifts with which to bribe them. The best that he could do was to advise the ranchers to abandon the ranches and move to the protection of the military plazas. Of his few soldiers, some were constantly employed to guard the convoys of the paymasters, to transport or look for grain and to give safe conduct to ill soldiers bound for the hospital at Monclova.

In the spring of 1821, Governor Martínez carried out the orders which General Arredondo, not yet a subscriber to the Plan of Iguala, had prescribed with regard to an American whom he expected to be Moses Austin. He commissioned Don Erasmo Seguín, the 39-year-old *Alcalde* of San Fernando de Béxar, to welcome the American at Natchitoches and conduct him to the bedraggled palace. For the first time in history, a commissioner of the Spanish government was to welcome a representative of prospective American settlers.

But when the steamboat Beaver, eight days out of New Orleans, tied up at Natchitoches on June 26, 1821, not Moses Austin, but his 27-year-old son, Stephen, expecting to meet his father here, walked the stageplank ashore. Stephen Austin initially had not been enthusiastic over his father's scheme. He had lived in Arkansas long enough to be named circuit judge of the territorial court. Only a few months since, he had gone to New Orleans to seek an easier way to fortune than clearing land in virgin wilderness. There, Joseph H. Hawkins, a brother of a friend, had invited him to study law in his office. He gladly accepted and found satisfaction in this new career. He was better educated than most, with two years at Transylvania University in Lexington before his father's financial straits forced him to return to Missouri. Hawkins' kind offer fitted in nicely with his inclinations and his abilities. But his father's letters were importunate.

If Stephen Austin was favorably impressed by the courteous punctilio of Don Erasmo Seguín, the governor's representative, the Spaniard was no less charmed by Austin. Béxar had not often seen this kind of Anglo-American. Small and wiry, with a scholar's head and alert eyes, Austin seemed of a different breed from the uncouth frontiersmen and contraband traders and filibusters whom the Spaniards so thoroughly detested and feared.

Stephen was aware that his father had not been well, but he still did not know that Moses Austin had died. His party, joined now by a group of men from Catahoula, went ahead to McGuffin's. Stephen himself and Lieutenant William Wilson, who had accompanied him, and their Spanish welcomers remained in Natchitoches where, on the 4th of July, they all dined with Dr. Sibley and attended a ball in honor of the day.

As a man who would become a Spanish subject after crossing the Sabine, Stephen Austin must have felt some pangs in his final hours as an American on the anniversary of his country's Declaration of Independence. He would enter Texas with the honest intent of living up to the terms Martínez had set forth. As he wrote years later: "I bade an everlasting farewell to my native country, and adopted this, and in so doing I determined to fulfill rigidly all the duties and obligations of a Mexican citizen."

Stephen F. Austin's life as a citizen of New Spain began on the *camino real*. On July 7, he and Wilson caught up with the rest of the party at McGuffin's. As they stopped there to round up a lost mule, a Mr. Barnum, whom he had left in Natchitoches to await the mail, rode in with a letter received by Dr. Sibley, with an account of Moses Austin's death. A letter to Stephen from his mother, also giving the sad news, together with newspapers and other important mail, reached him through Seguín, to whom they had been entrusted by Dr. Sibley. Stephen had feared that his father would not recover and had come with that possibility in mind. Now that Moses Austin's death was a fact the son might still have turned back. But he resolved to fulfill his father's contract. On July 16, he rode through the United States Army post, Camp Ripley, and crossed the Sabine into Texas.

A few miles east of Nacogdoches the Americans overtook Seguín, Juan Martín Veramendi and the Spanish traders with whom they would travel. Together they entered the virtually abandoned town. Seguín had been instructed to call together any former Spanish subjects still living in the area and tell them of the *Cortes'* policy of amnesty for revolutionaries. Messengers were sent out; soon Spaniards, Americans, Frenchmen and free Negroes and mulattoes appeared. Seguín appointed an American, James Dill, as temporary *Alcade* of the resurrected town.

Riding together from Nacogdoches to Béxar, Seguín and Austin became fast friends, despite the language barrier. From the Guadalupe River, Seguín sent three men ahead with a note to Governor Martínez informing him that the son was coming in his father's stead and that these Americans were people of consequence for whom comfortable quarters should be prepared. While the travelers were still in camp on a creek 8 miles from Béxar, the messengers returned at daybreak on August 12 with hampers of delicacies prepared by Señora Seguín and with the tidings that Governor Martínez and Texas had declared for the Plan of Iguala.

Just before noon of that same day Seguín escorted Austin to the governor's palace, where the governor recognized Stephen Austin as his father's successor to the contract. Then the men discussed at length the terms which should be offered the settlers and where they should settle.

Martínez accepted Austin's written suggestions as to terms. Each male settler who was the head of a family would be entitled to 640 acres, his wife to 320 acres, each child to 160 acres and each slave to 80. Austin would charge the settlers 12-½ cents an acre to cover the cost of the stamped papers and fees, the surveys, defense against Indians and Austin's own expenses in securing the land. The 12-½-cent fee also included a small profit for Austin himself. The logical place of settlement was in the vicinity of San Bernardo Bay, the contemporary name for Lavaca Bay. Martínez authorized Austin to explore that country in search of a site. It is an historic irony that the Americans were to select the same general area where the French, whom the Spaniards had also feared, founded their colony so many years before.

The terms agreed upon, nine of Austin's men returned to Natchitoches and New Orleans to publicize the colony and to make their own arrangements to return with their families. Austin himself and several of his settlers went down to La Bahía, where he requested the commandant to assign two soldiers to him as guides for a visit to the second site of the *presidio* of La Bahía on the Guadalupe. The commandant could not spare any soldiers. Austin hired a *regidor,* a member of the town government, and two Xaraname Indians to guide him. For the greater part of a month he explored the land on which his first colonists would settle.

The *regidor,* suspicious of the American whom he believed to be exploring more than his commission authorized, guided him wrong. Austin dismissed him and went on northeast until he reached the Colorado near the future towns of Columbus and Wharton. After a downstream exploration of its banks for 30 miles he then turned his small party northeast again to the Brazos and selected the site for his colony's capital, San Felipe de Austin, where the Atascosito trail to the long forgotten post among the Orcoquisa crossed the river. Here he divided his men into two groups, which separately explored both sides of the Brazos before returning to Natchitoches.

Austin was impressed by the rich lands of the river bottoms south of the *camino real.* He would request that his colonists have the right to settle from the Lavaca to the watershed between the Brazos and the San Jacinto, and anywhere from the coast to 6 leagues above the *camino real.*

Already some fifty families above Nacogdoches in Arkansas Territory were clamoring to enter his colony. Letters from a hundred more awaited him at Natchitoches. But no matter how enticing Austin's proposals were to the frontiersmen, few could leave for Texas before their corn and other crops were harvested. Twenty-two persons, however, encamped in late November on the Brazos near the trail to La Bahía and near the future site of Washington. During January and February of 1822, more families began to arrive, coming through Natchitoches or down from Arkansas Territory to Nacogdoches, then eastward along the trail.

Despite the hardships of the overland journey and the dangers of a sea voyage, Austin was able to report to Martínez in March that eight families had already settled and fifty men were clearing land on the Brazos and one hundred on the Colorado.

Now Stephen Austin was to be engulfed in the vortex of the Mexican revolution. He had been escorted into Texas by a commissioner of the royal Spanish government. On the morning of the day he arrived in Béxar, he had learned that Texas had joined the other eastern Interior Provinces in supporting the Plan of Iguala and Mexican independence. As the representative of the newly independent nation of Mexico, Governor Martínez had recognized his right to succeed to his father's contract.

But now, from Monterrey and the politically disorganized city of Mexico came disquieting news. The provincial deputation in Monterrey representing the eastern Interior Provinces had not approved Governor Martínez' acceptance of the terms set forth by Moses Austin for his colonists. Even more important, the regency of General Iturbide was discussing plans for colonizing, not only Texas, but Coahuila, Nuevo León and California. Some members of the regency suggested that Coahuila needed settlers even more than did Texas and that two-thirds of all who petitioned to settle in Texas should be sent on to Coahuila.

Governor Martínez explained to Austin sympathetically that the congress, which met for the first time on the anniversary of the Plan of Iguala, would formulate a colonization law. Meanwhile, the future of Stephen Austin's colony seemed dark. The governor, the Baron de Bastrop and Seguín alike advised him to go to the city of Mexico to seek confirmation of his contract.

Austin agreed. After designating his friend, Josiah H. Bell, to represent him in Béxar, he set out in mid-March, with a bare $400 in expense money, through the scrubby thorn bush and prickly pear country with a Dr. Robert Andrews and a man named Waters for company. Laredo was their initial destination. Just beyond the Nueces, the three men were surrounded by more than fifty menacing Comanches in war paint, who, after threatening them, seized their supplies. Austin protested to the chief of the war party that he and his companions were citizens of the United States, with whom the Comanches were at peace. The chief returned all of the seized property except a saddle, four bridles and a Spanish grammar, which Austin had taken along to study. Later the volume was traded in Missouri and because Austin's name was in it, the story spread that he had been killed.

Without further incident, the three travelers reached indolent

Laredo on the sandy left bank of the Río Grande. With understandable caution, Austin waited now until a considerable group was formed to travel southward. He accompanied the party to La Punta and from there he made his way to Monterrey.

Austin reached Mexico City on April 9, 1822. He would remain there for a difficult year during which he learned to speak Spanish fluently, became familiar with the vexatious political maze and made friends of some of the most prominent leaders in the emerging nation. These were valuable assets. He would need them all. He would also need an all but superhuman tact and patience, for there were others, also seeking grants for colonization, who sought the ears of the highly placed.

Far away in Spain, Ferdinand VII repudiated the treaty of Córdova and refused to don the crown of an independent Mexico, one of the cornerstones of the Plan of Iguala. As an alternative the clergy and the predominantly conservative Creoles talked of establishing a strong centralist republic which they, concentrated in the large cities, could dominate. The liberals in congress, intent on helping the *mestizos* and Indians, and demanding reforms, preferred the establishment of a federal republic. Conservatives and liberals alike attacked Iturbide, the leader of the regency, who sought a lone, dictatorial role.

For Agustín Iturbide had decided that Mexico needed an autocratic monarch—if not Ferdinand VII, then himself.

On the evening of May 18 a sergeant, probably acting on orders from Iturbide, raised the cry of "Viva Agustín I!" A handful, then hundreds, then thousands took up the cry, whether they understood its implications or not. Church bells clanged throughout the night. Troops paraded. The *léperos*, the dangerous beggar class of Mexico, joined in the tumult on the side of the usurper. In the morning Iturbide, with feigned reluctance, accepted from an intimidated congress the title of emperor.

Only a week before Stephen Austin had submitted a lengthy memorial to the regency. Now he had to begin again. He was a painstaking as well as a patient man. Diligently, he interviewed every member of the congress' committee on colonization. Juan Bautista Arizpe, the deputy from Monterrey and a staunch new friend of Austin, told the deputies that they had nothing to fear from a man who had complied in all respects, including that of religion, with the terms of the contract he had signed. The chances for the Austin colony began to look better.

But work on a colonization law was desultory. In a short time the congress and Agustín I were at loggerheads and at the end of October Iturbide ordered the congress to adjourn. In its stead he appointed a *Junta Instituyente* of forty men of his own choosing.

Austin promptly presented another memorial to the emperor. Fortunately for him, some of the members of the defunct congressional committee on colonization had been appointed to the *Junta Instituyente*—among them such friends and supporters as Bernardo Gutiérrez de Lara, Lorenzo de Zavala and Refugio de la Garza. The colonization law which the *junta* devised was not repressive as it related to Anglo-Americans, but one article was of especial concern to Austin. He knew that to succeed he would have to attract some Americans of substance. In the cotton South abutting Texas, these almost inevitably would be slave-owning planters. But the word "slavery" had long been loathsome in the Spanish colonies and homeland. Not surprisingly, the initial draft of Mexico's imperial colonization law included an article prohibiting the introduction of slaves into the colonies. Austin interviewed every member of the *junta*. He impressed each with the economic importance to Texas, Santander and Coahuila of permitting the American colonists to bring their slaves with them. He succeeded in having the article amended to read that slaves who were brought in could not be sold nor bought and that their children would become free at the age of 14.

The *Junta Instituyente* passed the imperial colonization law on January 4, 1823. The law was stated in general terms and did not specifically locate Austin's grant, nor did the Mexican officialdom have definite knowledge of the geography of the area which Austin was colonizing. Austin pointed out that the titles of his settlers to their property would help to delineate the outlines of the grant.

Finally, in March 1823, Austin was satisfied that all was in order and that he could return to Texas. Except for the stipulation that only Catholics could settle in the *Provincias Internas,* the law was far from repressive. It guaranteed liberty, property and civil rights. The minimum amount of land which each settler could receive was smaller than the 640 acres Austin had promised the heads of families. For farmers, a *labor* of 177 acres would be available. Ranchers would receive a *sitio* of 4,428 acres. Settlers would be required to occupy and develop the land within two years after receiving title. In accordance with Spanish custom, there was no charge for the land itself. The colonists would be permitted to bring in their own tools, machinery, implements and household goods duty-free, and would be free of taxes and church tithes for six years.

The promoters, those who introduced the settlers, were designated *empresarios*. Each *empresario* would receive three *haciendas* of five *sitios* each—67,000 acres—for each 200 families he introduced. No provision was made for any other remuneration to the *empresarios*, although the undeveloped land would have little immediate cash value and they would be out of pocket for the surveying and other costs, including their expenses in procuring the grant. If an *empresario* could wait for the value of the land to increase, he could make a fine profit. But for the short term there was no financial gain.

Then, again, political upheaval. Twenty-nine-year-old General Antonio López de Santa Anna, as malignant and conscienceless an opportunist as ever lived, a schemer who would always trim his sails to the prevailing political winds, had early identified himself with Iturbide's ambitions and was serving as military commander at Vera Cruz. But he was angered because he was receiving from the emperor what he thought to be insufficient preferment. He connived with the civil authorities of Vera Cruz. In December 1822 he and they had jointly called for the convening of congress.

The old rebel generals reorganized their Indian armies to support Santa Anna and the congress party. Early in February Iturbide's own troops at Vera Cruz announced the Plan of Casa Mata, similar to that of Santa Anna, which would return the government to congress. With the country again in turmoil, Austin's friends advised him to remain in Mexico City so that if congress were again convened, it could approve his contract.

At the end of March the congress, once more in session, vested all executive power in Nicolas Bravo, Guadalupe Victoria and Pedro Celestino Negrete—all former guerilla chieftains—and in April exiled Iturbide. In the relative calm of the spring of 1823, the congress on April 14 finally confirmed Austin in the concession he had been granted by Iturbide's government under the imperial colonization law. It also increased the number of families he would be permitted to introduce to 300. However, the congress almost immediately suspended and later annulled the law, drawing up another which gave the states the right to award grants under guide lines of policy the congress set down. Austin's contract was the only one granted under the imperial colonization law.

At last, after thirteen months Austin was able to return to his colony. He had long since exhausted his meager funds. He had pawned his watch, drawn on Hawkins in New Orleans and borrowed from Mexican friends. But his protracted stay had given him invaluable insights into the character of the Mexican people whom he had made his own and he had learned the techniques of their indirect way of doing business.

On the return journey, he stopped at Saltillo and made the acquaintance of the brilliant Miguel Ramos Arizpe, who had represented the Interior Provinces in Spain's liberal *Cortes,* and showed him a draft for a federal constitution for Mexico which he had worked upon during the weeks of inaction in March. When, in the fall, Arizpe prepared in three days the Mexican nation's first constitution, to be known as the Constitution of 1824 with which the Anglo and Mexican rebels of the Texas revolution would at first identify themselves in 1835, his draft was without doubt influenced by Austin's precise outline.

Austin not only drew upon his knowledge of the American constitution, but also on his awareness of the Mexican character. He feared for Mexico and for his colony the effects of a strongly centralized government which would put the power in the hands of the clergy and the rich who, he suspected, would serve themselves instead of the people in the appointment of provincial governors and the administration of the law. Hence, his constitution called for a federal republic in which local self-government would prevail. Austin realized that in Catholic Mexico in 1823 religious freedom was impossible, but he did prescribe limits on the legal and property rights of the clergy and the Church.

Austin's friend, de la Garza, was now commandant general of the eastern Interior Provinces. Returning to Texas through Monterrey, Austin asked him to define the judicial and military responsibilities expected of him in his colony. De la Garza assured him that, except in the case of punishment for capital offenses, his was the highest judicial authority in the colony. The commandant general also authorized him to organize militia units to keep order and combat the Indians. From these units would emerge the Texas Rangers.

In August, with the Baron de Bastrop acting as commissioner for the governor, Austin went down the Colorado to put the first settlers in legal possession of the land they had cleared. Not until he sought a permit to introduce additional colonists would the official borders of his first colony be stated. By then the Mexican government had reserved 10 leagues along the coast and 20 from international boundaries into which no foreigners could move. The Austin colony's borders accordingly commenced at a point on the west bank of the San Jacinto, 10 leagues from the coast, thence up the river to its source, north from there to the San Antonio road—the *camino real*—along the road westward to a point from which a line due south would strike the head of the Lavaca, and down this line and the east bank of the Lavaca to 10 leagues from the Gulf and then to the place of beginning. The very road by which so many colonists entered Texas would be part of the geographical border of their political rights. In several of the Anglo-American colonies the *empresarios* sought to establish, the San Antonio road—the *camino real*—would be a boundary. In time the very location of the abandoned road would have to be established by the land titles which used it as one line. But that would be long after the day when a son's tenacity and tact gave lasting meaning to a father's unrealized ambition.

CHAPTER SEVENTEEN

THE FREDONIAN REBELLION

ACROSS THE WHOLE NORTH AMERICAN CONTINENT, men were on the march—not only those of European extraction, but, unwillingly—by war, by treaty, by the clearing of fields where wild game had grazed—the Indians who had lived east of the Mississippi were forced to cross the river, there to dislocate the Caddos, the Comanches, the Apaches, the remnants of the Texas tribes and compete with them for hunting rights indispensable to some, important to all but a few.

Their father, the President of the United States, had been considerate of his children of the Cherokee Nation. They had dwelt mostly in Georgia and Tennessee until the Treaty of 1817 or, more accurately, the despoilation of 1817, had relieved them of all their lands and villages east of the Mississippi River. To aid the Cherokees, the most amiable and cultured and permanently domiciled of the Five Civilized Nations, their benevolent father, the President, had equipped each of the bewildered farmers with a rifle and ammunition, a blanket, a brass kettle and a beaver trap as full compensation for his holdings and to lessen the hardships of his search for new lands in the Arkansas country beyond the great river.

The wise old men of the Cherokee people had found the terms of the treaty as difficult to understand or to approve as did the angry younger braves. Not many years before their father the President had sent each of them a plow and a hoe with the message that it was not good for his red-skinned children to hunt. They should cultivate their land. That was in the olden days before the Appalachian mountain country began to fill up with the palefaces with long rifles, the Tennesseans and Georgians and Alabamians, men who shot straight and readily. Now the President had told them they would be happier in distant hunting grounds.

Always the Indians had a hard time trying to understand the white men. Of only two truths were they certain: the palefaces intended to rule, and each white nation had its own way of dealing with the Indians. The French had sought out the tribesmen and traded and lived with them wherever they dwelt. The Spaniards had rung the mission bells to call them to Christ and civilization, and had fathered many children among them. The only policy of the Anglo-Americans was to push them farther westward so that white men could hunt and fish and farm and trade and build towns undisturbed.

Richard Fields, the half-breed chief, was different in that he could understand the white intruders as well as he understood the Indians with whom he was catalogued. His father was white, his mother a Cherokee. His wife, Françoise Grappé, was the daughter of the notable French trader at Natchitoches. Fields had grown up in the Cherokee Nation and had been interpreter for his tribe. He had fought under Andrew Jackson. When thousands of Shawnees and Delawares and Kickapoos swarmed into the Arkansas country recently settled by the displaced Cherokees, his tribesmen followed him out of Arkansas into the east Texas lands north of the San Antonio Road. There, in 1820, because he understood the odd ways of the whites, he sought, not only legal title to the land to which the Cherokees had come, but the promise of home rule which the Cherokee Nation had always enjoyed.

The half-breed chieftain, whom the white man and his Indian intimates called Dick, believed there was more than enough land to spare in east Texas. Victims of the white man's diseases, most of the Hasinai, the Bidais and the Ais, and even the great Caddo on the Red, had wasted away. Those who survived thought to wash out with firewater, begged or stolen or traded for, the memory of all that had once been theirs.

Dick Field's Cherokees were not hunters; they were a settled folk. Spain's treatment of the Indians was manifestly fairer than that which the United States had accorded his people and Spain was opening Texas to settlement. Dick Fields vowed to win a contract for his Cherokees which would permit them to govern themselves in this waiting territory. He sought an agreement in San Antonio, and when

Governor Trespalacios told him that he would have to win the approval of Agustín Iturbide, the Emperor Agustín I, in Mexico City, the determined leader made his way to the distant capital.

While Stephen Austin negotiated with the *junta* and the emperor in 1822 and 1823, Dick Fields listened respectfully as the council of the government debated. He sought and made friends, too, becoming for the advancement of his cause a York Rite Mason, which had become, in a way, a political party in a Mexico still in the ferment of recent independence.

When Dick Fields' money gave out, the tall, dignified, middle-aged man rode back to the Trinity. He bore a letter from Governor Trespalacios which advised him that the Cherokees could remain in east Texas until all related issues were settled. Canny Dick Fields reasoned that since matters were not settled, the letter itself was a contract of sorts, a statement of a right of his Cherokees to the land.

So thought John Dunn Hunter, a mild-mannered, stockily built American of vague antecedents who had become Fields' mentor on his return from Mexico City. The thinking of this man went further. He suggested to Dick Fields that the Cherokees deserved more than simply the right of domicile and tillage. They should own their own lands and govern their own independent country.

Together with a rip-snorting Missouri fighting man and two brothers from Virginia, Dick Fields and John Dunn Hunter would raise a singular banner, the flag of the short-lived Fredonian Republic, its striping of parallel white and red symbolic of the despoiled Cherokees of Georgia and the *Yanqui* settlers who resented the abuses of Mexican officialdom.

Few others beside Dick Fields and his advisor thought of sovereignty. The would-be *empresarios* who rushed to Saltillo, the capital of the newly formed combined state of *Coahuila y Texas,* would be satisfied if the Mexican state legislature would only pass a colonization law, award them the contracts they sought and permit them to bring in the waiting families. Many of the sturdy speculators who would eventually win contracts had been twiddling their thumbs for many months.

Among these was the irascible Haden Edwards, Virginia-born and a man of substance, whose patience was almost exhausted. Edwards had come downriver from Kentucky to Louisiana in 1822. From there he went on to Mexico City. Even for Haden Edwards, Mexico was too expensive a city in which to tarry long without gainful occupation. At fifty-one, time was as vital as money. After many months of inaction he was operating a roulette table to support himself while Mexico went through the interminable changes of government which preceded the federal republic.

Stephen F. Austin's contract was the only one validated under the imperial colonization law. Congress had declared that law invalid. Not until August 18, 1824, was the national colonization law enacted, and all it did was to set a policy for the Mexican states to follow in disposing of their lands and stipulated that there could be no colonization in the border leagues. Mexico, almost as suspicious of her neighbors as Spain had ever been, would grant no lands to foreigners within these border reserves. The law guaranteed, however, that no change in immigration policy would be made before 1840 unless national security demanded a halt to immigration from an unfriendly country. The states could give title only to persons living on their lands. No individual was to receive more than 11 square leagues.

Since the several states were to make their own local land grant laws, Haden Edwards left for Saltillo, the capital of the state of *Coahuila y Texas,* as soon as the national colonization act was passed. *Coahuila y Texas* dawdled from August until late in March to draw up its own colonization statutes. Less than three weeks later, on April 15, 1825, Edwards received a contract to settle 800 families in east Texas. For each 100 families whom he brought in, the *empresario* would receive a premium of 5 leagues of land for himself, which was all the profit permitted him. To each head of a family he could offer a square league of land for grazing and 5 *labores,* about 880 acres, suitable for cultivation.

The Edwards colony was well located. It lay "beginning at the angle formed by a line 20 leagues from the Sabine and 10 leagues from the coast of the Gulf of Mexico, thence in a northerly direction, passing the post of Nacogdoches, and in the same direction 15 leagues above; then westerly at right angles with the first line to the Navasota Creek, thence along said creek until it strikes the upper road to San Jacinto, then down the said river to within 10 leagues of the coast; thence eastwardly along a line 10 leagues from the coast to the place of beginning." This was the ancient heartland of the Texas. Edwards came into no virgin land, but into a long-inhabited territory where others besides his colonists had legal or emotional ties to the land.

By 1825 an estimated 1,000 persons lived, additionally, in the reserved contiguous borderlands. They would give Haden Edwards trouble. So would some of the Spanish-Americans who had fought beside Gutiérrez and who had returned to their old homes under the amnesty offered them by Erasmo Seguín and the *Alcalde* James Dill. Few of these long-time dwellers had clear title to their holdings. The distance to Béxar had seemed too far for a special trip to fill out the complicated Spanish forms. It was enough that they were on the land. It was theirs. It had been their fathers' land before them.

Others held deeds whose wide margin on the left hand side and the large scrolls and waxed seals gave them the appearance of old Spanish documents. Most of them were forgeries, prepared by clever counterfeiters in Nacogdoches. And also within the limits of the Edwards grant lived Richard Fields' Cherokees and the remnants of the Hasinai and other ancient tribes.

As Haden Edwards rode from Saltillo toward his east Texas grant, he might have been aware that out of these complexities disputes were sure to arise, especially when such a peremptory man as himself was involved. There was no denying that he had to know what land was legally occupied. But he was in a hurry. And he was short-tempered.

Edwards spent the summer of 1825 in Louisiana seeking colonists. To Stephen F. Austin he sent his younger brother, Benjamin, then living in Jackson, Mississippi, to learn something of the difficulties an *empresario* might face and how to deal with Mexican officials. Austin shared with young Edwards what he had learned through experience. He warned him that the *empresarios'* remuneration must come from the premium land; the government had rebuked him when he charged 12-½ cents an acre to cover his costs. He emphasized that all land to be granted belonged to the government, not to the *empresario*. The settlers would not even pay the surveying fees to the *empresario* but to the state.

Austin's counsel went unheeded. No sooner did Haden Edwards arrive in Nacogdoches with his family at October's end than he posted a notice in the square and on the main streets. It read that "by this notice I order that no person shall settle within the limits of my territory without my permission." Furthermore, it enjoined "all those who claim to have a right to any part or parts of the land or lands of said territory" to come with their titles to him, not to the *alcaldes*. "If they do not do this the said lands will be sold, without distinction, to the first person who occupies them."

None of this set well.

A second notice, warning that their lands would be sold, alienated those later Americans who lacked legal documents to prove ownership. And Edwards' notice also infuriated all who had any smattering of Mexican law. He had no control over the assignment of land; only a land commissioner could award titles.

Especially affronted were Luis Procela, *alcalde* of Nacogdoches, and José Antonio Sepulveda, the *sindico*. Who was this *Yanqui* to question the traditional rights of their friends to their lands? Procela and Sepulveda did what they could to validate the titles, among them the title of Edmund Quirk, who in 1801 had acquired the Leal land on either side of the Ais Bayou. This was probably the richest land in the Sabine district. Here Father Margil had established the mission of Nuestra Señora de los Dolores de los Ais. Procela sent Quirk's papers to José Antonio Saucedo, the top civilian authority, whose title was political chief of the department of Texas in the state of *Coahuila y Texas*, at San Antonio. Saucedo validated the Quirk deed and the deeds to the equally valuable Quinalty, Sims, Elisha Roberts and other improved tracts.

And now Edwards, coveting those fertile fields for his colonists, made his second mistake. Roughly he questioned Procela's act and accused Saucedo of forgery, treating both men as troublesome and even dishonest bureaucrats. Those bearing the titles of *alcalde* and *sindico* were accustomed to more respect. Procela denounced Edwards to Saucedo. Saucedo was already angry with the interloper, for Edwards had returned to Texas in October and had not until January even notified Saucedo, the highest ranking representative of the state of *Coahuila y Texas*, that he had taken up residence. Worse, when Saucedo wrote Edwards about Procela's complaints, Edwards had the effrontery to question the political chief's right to intervene.

Every settler whose improvements were threatened or seized by Edwards wrote impassioned letters to Saucedo or to Stephen Austin, asking what he should do. Soon the Mexicans and the descendants of the earliest Anglo-American settlers presented resolutions of protest to the state legislature at Saltillo. They had borne arms for their country, they said. Were they now to be commanded by a man they didn't even know and, worse, a man whom they could not trust?

With the area in turmoil, Edwards had the temerity to call for the election of a captain of militia. He had no authority to arrogate such military and political power to himself, but the settlers voted anyhow. They elected Sepulveda, the *sindico,* who was their friend. Having learned his lesson, Edwards called another election, this time for *alcalde* of the Sabine District, which included Nacogdoches. He put up Chichester Chaplin, his son-in-law. The original settlers turned for leadership to James Gaines, who had returned under the amnesty to his home at the lower crossing of the Sabine. There he had resumed operation of the ferry which he had bought from Vicente Micelli in 1810.

Gaines put up his brother-in-law, Samuel Norris, to oppose Chaplin. When Chaplin received a majority of the votes, Gaines demurred, protesting that Chaplin had won through the votes of unqualified squatters in the border reserve. Saucedo upheld Gaines and ordered Chaplin to turn over the official records to Samuel Norris. He also upheld Ignacio Sertuche's right to operate a ferry between the banks of the Trinity. The rivermen had made a laughing stock of Haden Edwards.

Stephen Austin became alarmed at the events in the neighboring *empresario* grant. He offered Edwards friendly and all too prophetic advice: "You do not understand the nature of the authority with which you are vested by the government, and it is my candid opinion that a continuance of the imprudent course you have commenced will totally ruin you, and materially injure all the new settlements."

The arrogant *empresario's* behavior had also disturbed the authorities of Mexico and of the state of *Coahuila y Texas* as Austin knew it would. Even before Edwards had fulfilled his contract to bring in 800 families, he was making what they would describe as "a direct attack upon the sovereignty of his Nation and his State." The government ordered Saucedo to station regular troops at Nacogdoches "to confine each citizen within the bounds of his duty." Saucedo did not have enough soldiers to comply. Finally, in secret meeting on June 3, the federal government annulled Edwards' contract. He would not hear of it until much later.

Toward the end of May, Edwards had gone to Louisiana to recruit colonists and to raise money to finance his operations until he could acquire the premium land. Again he left his brother Benjamin in charge.

Benjamin Edwards learned only in September that his brother's grant had been annulled. To Governor Victor Blanco of *Coahuila y Texas* he dispatched a vigorous protest. Governor Blanco thought the letter a sarcastic one; his reply was curt and to the point. Haden Edwards had returned from the United States to start introducing families, he wrote, and "without presenting himself to the civil local authority [Procela] nor reporting his arrival to the Political Chief of that department, or notifying the government, he declared himself on his own accord Military Chief of that District, considering himself competently authorized," had issued an abortive proclamation and called an election of military officers and an *alcalde* and sold land. All these powers belonged to the supreme authority and not to a foreigner who "by favor has been admitted to colonize and not to dictate laws." Governor Blanco said in conclusion that after the Edwards brothers had left the country they might apply to the supreme government for redress.

A few days before this letter came, Haden Edwards returned to Nacogdoches. At the end of October, Haden Edwards received from Governor Blanco what amounted to eviction orders:

"In view of such proceedings, by which the conduct of Haden Edwards is well attested, I declare the annulment of his contract and expulsion from the territory of the Republic in the discharge of the supreme orders with which I am invested."

Haden Edwards had induced colonists to take up land in his grant. He had assured them of the validity of their titles. They had abandoned their homes in Louisiana and Mississippi and Alabama. They had undergone the expense of the journey, the costs of moving themselves, their families and their slaves. They were basically solid men, the kind Texas needed. Wrathfully, Haden Edwards resolved to fight for his rights and theirs. He would accept what help he could from whoever would give it.

One of his staunchest allies from the beginning was Martin Parmer, a fellow Virginian who, after several years of trapping and hunting and farming in Missouri, where he had been a member of the Missouri Assembly, had only recently moved to the reserved lands. A hot-tempered man with a roving eye, he was known to his friends as the "ring-tailed panther." He was 48 years old when he rode into

Nacogdoches at the head of thirty-six men, and seized and barricaded the *alcalde's* office. He and his companions arrested Samuel Norris, the unfriendly *alcalde*, and Captain Sepulveda of the militia, constituted themselves a temporary court-martial until a new *alcalde* could be elected and selected Joseph Durst a Nacogdoches resident of German extraction, *alcalde* ad interim. The officials of this rump court also posted a reward of $100 for James Gaines, dead or alive.

At the first meeting of the court-martial, as its members shouted loudly for anyone who had charges pending against him to appear, Haden Edwards stood up. Obviously, no Mexicans would make representations before such a court-martial. No witnesses testified against him. The charges were dismissed. The Edwards and their followers, against whom Gaines and his followers had brought a variety of charges, seized the moment to settle a few scores.

They accused *Alcalde* Norris of collecting for stamped papers though they had understood that the settlers' exemption from taxation included the exemption from this fee. Norris had imprisoned a man for "ironically calling Sepulveda an honest man," they said. He was guilty of corruption and oppression, treachery to the people and murderous intent. They charged Sepulveda with forgery, swindling and being a person of infamous character, who had persuaded a Mexican to steal a mule for him, promising that if the culprit were caught he would "clear him with his pen, as he had done many a one before." Solemnly the rump court found the *alcalde* and the *sindico* guilty alike, but released them with the admonishment that they were never to hold office again. Then Martin Parmer, "the ring-tailed panther," and his own regulators rode home, feeling much better.

But neither Stephen Austin nor the Mexican authorities shared their jubilation. Austin saw clearly that such stupidly illegal acts would aid the enemies of Edwards and endanger all American colonists. Again he gave warning to the intemperate Virginian. Edwards' only recourse, said Austin, would be to go to the political chief and "acknowledge at once and without any reserve or stiff and foolish republican obstinacy that wrong steps were taken, that the attack on the *alcalde* was totally wrong—that you were misled by passion or something else (for it puzzles me to frame excuses for such conduct) and petition the governor to order a general court of inquiry in which the conduct of the *alcalde* and Gains [sic] and all others and your own should be fully and fairly and openly investigated.... Let the

Americans put aside their rifles and be guided by more prudence and reason than they have been. . . . No matter what Norris may have done, the parties who entered Nacogdoches have done as bad.''

But the frustrated Edwards had already determined to enlist allies, whatever allies he could, even among the exiled Cherokees of Dick Fields. His decision to pit Indians against white men insured his destruction.

The Cherokees felt as aggrieved as did Haden Edwards. Early in October, John Dunn Hunter had returned from Mexico to Dick Fields without the promise of sovereignty for which they had hoped. Around the council fires Fields and his chieftains and Hunter made war talk. Dick Fields told them that he was an old man. If the Cherokees did not win their land soon, he would not live to see them happily settled in their new homeland. The tribesmen must take and hold the land by force. Hunter told the Cherokees that they were not the only east Texans to have a reason to rebel. Many of the whites were disaffected too. He had heard much as he went through Nacogdoches. Perhaps among the white men allies could be found for the Cherokees. Together they could create a free nation. Fields and his chieftains nodded approval.

Hunter went to Haden Edwards with a proposal for an alliance of white man and red, and the formation of an independent republic in which both races would live as equals. Never before had such an alliance been proposed. Never again would it be.

Now appeared the many-lived Colonel Ellis Peter Bean as the bane of the rebels. Once he had been a rebel himself.

Twenty-five years had passed since Ellis Bean had first walked the *camino real,* a youthful prisoner in chains after the debacle of the Philip Nolan expedition. In the intervening quarter century he had escaped from prison and had served under the patriot chief, Morelos, in the mountains of Mexico. Twice Morelos had sent him to New Orleans to implore aid for the revolution. Late in 1817, harried by Royalist forces, he had fled across the border, but not before placing his dark-eyed wife, Anna Gorthas, in the care of her uncle near Jalapas.

In 1823 Ellis Bean and the American girl, Candace Midkiff, who, believing him a bachelor, had wed him in Tennessee, took up land on the Neches. As the years passed, blunt and curious friends asked him from time to time about the rumor that he had two wives. Bean always answered that the woman with whom he was currently living was his wife; the one elsewhere was only his woman.

And he was a friendly man. His boat on the Neches provided a convenient ferry across the river. Among the users were Cherokees who had settled near his home. He came to know them so well that the Mexican authorities sent him among them as an agent.

The paths of Ellis Bean and Haden Edwards might have crossed in the late spring of 1825. Edwards was journeying from Saltillo. Bean was on his way to Mexico to seek recognition and preferment as a fighter for independence. He was away from home for more than a year. He returned to east Texas with the rank of colonel and an appointment as special agent for the Nacogdoches district.

Waiting in east Texas, Candace knew only that he had not troubled to write. Perhaps, as was generally rumored, he was dead. Perhaps she wanted to believe so, for "the ring-tailed panther," Martin Parmer, had moved in as husband to "the widow Bean" only the day before Ellis Bean, returning, strode across the porch of his Neches home. It may be that Ellis Bean thought himself at fault, or perhaps a more pressing and immediate concern put this personal affront in the background. He simply ran Parmer from the house, but he would taunt Candace with her infidelity for the rest of her life.

His immediate assignment was to go among the Cherokees and upset whatever schemes Edwards had concocted with them.

John Dunn Hunter and Haden Edwards had been negotiating even before "the ring-tailed panther" had seized the *alcalde's* office the past November. Twenty-three tribes, among them the Delawares, Shawnees and Kickapoos, were ready to unite with the Cherokees, Hunter told Edwards, and take by force from the white man what they had not received peaceably. Hunter had made Edwards his bold and breath-taking proposal: Edwards and his followers should join with the Indians in the creation of a republic.

Hunter even suggested a name: Fredonia. There had been a time, soon after the American Revolution, when many educated people in the seaboard states had considered naming their new country Columbia. Others had thought of Fredonia, a play on the word freedom, which was suggested by a Dr. Samuel L. Mitchell.

Haden Edwards thought the name would do; it really didn't matter. He must win over the settlers to the idea of an equal alliance of white man and red. He knew the task would not be easy. Heretofore the whites had made subordinate allies of the Indians only to advance their own causes. But the offer had come from a representative of the Indians, who wanted equality as the price of a united front. But Edwards thought the plan had merit. He, too, had feared a Cherokee attack upon the colonists. In alliance with his faction, the Indians would attack only the enemies of Haden Edwards.

The Edwards brothers began talking to their compatriots. In the log cabins of the Ayish Bayou district and at the Sabine, the settlers let them talk. Few promised anything. The Edwardses should not have been surprised. Most of the men in the reserved leagues had grown up on the frontiers; an Indian was an ever present threat to property and life. Also, the settlers hoped that if they waited long enough the Mexican government would give them title to the lands on which they lived. It was one matter to excoriate or bully minor officials; revolution or even talk of revolution was something else.

But Haden Edwards convinced himself that the colonists' silence bespoke cooperation. He went to Natchitoches, where he was certain he would find recruits. Benjamin turned back to Nacogdoches. Near the Attoyac an excited Martin Parmer found Benjamin. Spanish troops—they were Ellis Bean and thirty-six Mexican soldiers—were approaching Nacogdoches, Parmer related. Unless the Fredonians struck now, it would be too late.

The banner of the Fredonian Republic was ready by late afternoon—a flag of red and white cloth sewed horizontally in two stripes of equal size to represent the united races. Across the base of the white upper stripe appeared the word *Independence;* beneath it, in somewhat smaller lettering, *Freedom and Justice.* Under the banner, Benjamin Edwards, Martin Parmer and fifteen men rode toward Nacogdoches through the night of December 15–16 against a numbing Texas norther. On the morning of December 16, 1826, they seized the stone fort, raised the Fredonian flag and proclaimed the Republic of Fredonia. Some 200 Anglo-Americans cheered.

The revolutionaries proclaimed a formal government. They elected Parmer commander of the Fredonian army in the field and Haden Edwards commander-in-chief.

Hunter and Fields and several subordinate chiefs arrived four

days later at Nacogdoches to create "a solemn Union, League and Confederation in Peace, in War," and "to establish and defend their
mutual independence of the Mexican United States." Around the
campfire at Sandy Springs, the Edwards party and the Cherokee
delegation agreed to the division of Texas between white and Indian
settlers in return for the support of the Cherokees. Texas above the
camino real—due west from Sandy Springs, the treaty read—would
go to the Indians; Texas below it to the white men. The Fredonian
flag would wave from the Sabine to the Río Grande. No *empresarios*
who co-operated with the republic would forfeit their lands.

Despite the rumors which Saucedo heard again and again in
Béxar and at San Felipe de Austin, few Americans were on the way
to help the Fredonians. In Mexico, where Joel Poinsett, the American
minister, was seeking to purchase Texas, the supreme government
feared that the revolt of Edwards and his colonists was a planned
incident which the United States would use as a pretext to seize what
Mexico would not agree to sell. The Mexican government announced
grandly that it was sending a thousand men by ship to the Texas coast
and another 10,000 by land. The boast was empty.

But so was the report that 800 men were crossing the Sabine to
join the rising of the Edwards and the Indians. Haden Edwards succeeded in enlisting only a few hotheads in the old neutral ground and
fewer at Natchitoches. At no time did the Fredonians muster more
than 200 men in the field.

The new republic, lying across the Spanish Trail, needed firmer
support than flags and treaties could provide. It required daring
friends in the field. These it could not win.

Colonel Bean had been active and effective in the Indian camps.
A talk with two principal war chiefs, Bowles and Big Mush, revealed
to him that they had not been consulted by Fields and Hunter; they
provided fertile grounds for the seeds of discord which he sowed.
Bean counseled patience, promised land. When Hunter and Fields
returned to the Indian villages, they found the war chiefs hostile,
the warriors reluctant. On their entry into Nacogdoches a week later
only thirty braves rode with them. At the headquarters in the stone
house, Parmer and the small force of white Fredonians occupying
the strongpoint were drunk and brawling. Quietly, about fifteen of
the braves slipped away.

Meanwhile, Bean had gone also into the border leagues. There he warned the white settlers of the futility of waging war against the government and promised that title to their homesites could be arranged for loyal citizens. When he was done, his own count convinced him that seventy men in the Ayish Bayou section opposed the Fredonians and only thirty supported the revolt. And whatever side they were taking, most of the white men were moving their families across the Sabine, away from the danger of Indian attack. For the most part these colonists in the border reserves and in Nacogdoches did not openly oppose the Fredonians; they bided their time until Mexican troops would arrive to deliver them.

In January, Norris did round up a force of eighty volunteers to storm the stone fort, from whence he planned to drag out the rebels and "take the Fredonians in chains to San Antonio." Most of his recruits were Mexicans; the others, so Edwards said, were "mostly his [Norris'] relatives." The besiegers dismounted when they approached to within 200 yards of the stone house and took positions behind some old dwellings. Inside the fortress Parmer called for a charge. He and Hunter, eleven Americans and eight Cherokees emerged from the building and routed the enemy handily. Norris' force left behind one man killed, ten or twelve wounded and half their horses.

Even though Norris' attack on the stone house failed, he frightened the Fredonians into stationing more men at the fort. Benjamin Edwards was now elected colonel and commander-in-chief. Adolphus Sterne, a German Jew recently come to Texas, supplied needed arms and ammunition. He would play later a more telling part in Texas history.

Benjamin Edwards probably still hoped that his impassioned letters, written the day after Christmas, asking support from the principal men of Pecan Point on the Red and from Austin's colonists on the Colorado and the San Bernardo and the Brazos would be heeded. "We are Americans, and will sooner die than submit to slavery and oppression," he had written. "We have now planted the standard of liberty and independence, and, like our forefathers, will support it or perish by it. Are you not Americans, too, and our brothers? Will you not rally around this glorious standard and aid us in support of this holy cause? To arms, then, like free men and the sons of those departed patriots who fought and bled for freedom." He also asked the settlers to send two delegates to Nacogdoches.

No delegates came. Stephen Austin had also been writing letters and publishing proclamations. The growth of his own colony depended on a liberal Mexican land policy. Such a policy would be jeopardized by assaults upon the sovereignty of the nation. As he wrote a Missouri friend living in Nacogdoches: "I do not wish any person basely to submit to oppression, but it is not submitting to oppression to submit to the laws, especially when we have voluntarily pledged ourselves to obey those laws by moving to the country." He asked his colonists what they, back in the United States, would have thought if foreigners had settled among them and declared their independence soon thereafter because of the injustice of some petty official.

From Austin and Saucedo and Colonel Mateo Ahumada, military commandant of the department, sped couriers and representatives eastward, bearing eloquent, rational pleas to Fields and Hunter and Haden Edwards to submit to authority. Colonel Ahumada besought Fields and Hunter to meet him either at the Trinity crossing of the *camino*, near the Lomo de Toro, or at San Felipe. Here they could discuss their problems with Saucedo and Austin. The commandant argued that the Cherokees had been invited to visit the state of *Coahuila y Texas*, select lands and apply for grants. If they had failed to do this, he said, it was not Mexico's fault that they were not legal landowners. On the other hand, their occupation had been peaceful, and if "they precipitate commencement of hostilities [it] will produce evils of the greatest consequence."

In his letter to Hunter, Austin was more circumspect:

> *My dear sir, Let us examine this subject calmly; let us suppose that the Indians overrun the whole country and take possession of it for the present as far as the Rio Grande, and drive out or massacre all the honest inhabitants; what will they gain? What kind of government will they establish? How will they sustain themselves? Do you know how the Indians sustain themselves? Do you know the Indians well enough to know that so many different tribes of differing habits and languages cannot be organized into anything like regular government, or government of any kind, and could not long agree among themselves? When the Spaniards and Americans are driven out and there is no common enemy to contend with, they would fight among themselves, and nothing but confusion and massacre and plunder would be the consequence.*

Austin argued also that if an Indian uprising succeeded, the United States and Mexico would probably unite to crush the rebels. Or, if Mexico ceded Texas to the United States, as many expected, the United States would soon sweep away the Indians as it always did. He warned that now was the time, before a treaty of cession to the United States was ratified, for the Indians to get legal titles from the Mexican government. Pithily he commented: "You know the government of the United States and its policy as it respects Indians." He said that, on the other hand, the Mexican government had promised a full hearing of all matters in complaint. "Come, therefore, and bring the Cherokee chief and the Edwardses and see the chief of department and commandant of arms; come quickly and without hesitation."

Austin did more than write. He sent a commission composed of Judge Richard Ellis, formerly of Huntsville, Alabama, James Cummins from the Colorado and James Kerr, who had come from Missouri with Parmer and who now lived on the Guadalupe, to investigate for themselves and carry to the rebels a proclamation of amnesty, which he induced Saucedo to indite.

When the commissioners reached the Neches River, they discovered that Ellis Bean's ferryboat and property had been seized by a small Fredonian contingent. Its members vowed that all the countryside from the Neches to the Sabine had gone over to the revolution. Even so, the insurgents permitted the three delegates to proceed to Nacogdoches. There they held secret talks with the Edwardses and Hunter, and a representative of the Indians identified only as Bassett. Mostly they talked of the proffered amnesty which the emissaries described, according to their later report, as "a highly benevolent act on the part of our Mexican government, and one which must place it [the Mexican government] on high and very exalted ground in the eyes of all the republics of earth and gives at one view every assurance of a warm-hearted and affectionate stepmother."

The Fredonians' answer was that "we will never concede one inch short of an acknowledgment by the government of our entire, free and unmolested independence from the Sabine to the Rio Grande." The adamant Hunter refused to permit the commissioners themselves to go to the Cherokees, nor did he ever tell the Indians of Saucedo's offer.

Negotiations had failed. On January 23, Saucedo and Ahumada

marched out of San Felipe de Austin for Nacogdoches. On the way 250 members of Austin's militia—a cavalry unit with a four-pounder —joined them. Before starting east, the political chief addressed a proclamation to the inhabitants of the Trinity, the Neches and the district of Nacogdoches:

> *The people complained that Haden Edwards, the* em-presario, *was practicing speculations on them by exacting ex-orbitant fees, and by turning off their places old settlers and giving them to new emigrants, who would pay the price re-quired.... It therefore became the duty of the government ... to interpose its arms to protect the innocent immigrants, ignorant as they were of the language and laws of the coun-try, from any further act of injustice or oppression ...*

The Mexican government had annulled Edwards' contract, he explained, but had offered him an impartial hearing, even after he took up arms, and full amnesty, both of which Edwards had refused. Saucedo called on the inhabitants to "rally around the standards of your country and unite your efforts with the national troops and militia of this colony to crush this most unjust and unnatural rebellion in its infancy." He sent ahead Lawrence Richard Kenney to call on all persons "to take up arms under the national standard." To those living in the reserved lands he promised to recommend to the president of Mexico that they be given titles. Saucedo's proclamation and appeals and promises were directed alike to the latecomers, resentful at Ed-wards' demands upon them, to the long-time settlers he had evicted or who feared eviction and to the squatters in the border reserves. He already had the support of the Mexicans.

The Fredonians were in desperate straits even before the approach of the Mexican troops and Austin's militiamen. Ellis Bean had done his work well. Big Mush and Bowles, the Cherokee chiefs, had ousted Dick Fields as their leader. Neither he nor Hunter could persuade the Cherokees to rally to the Fredonian Republic. Instead the Ed-wardses could count only on a handful of Anglo-Americans, among them the adventurers who had answered Haden's call for volunteers in the United States and the few who had supported them from the out-set. They now sent half of these, about 100 men, into the Ayish Bayou country with an ultimatum. On a certain date the settlers would have to join the Fredonians or suffer confiscation of their properties.

There was almost none to threaten. Most of them had fled when the Cherokees, the Shawnees, the Delawares and Kickapoos and Sacs began moving into the region. The few remaining were hardy, ready to fight for their rights.

Young Alexander Horton, who lived with his mother on Moral Creek just west of the Ayish Bayou, looked out of the cabin door one dawn and saw some eighty Indians, armed and in war paint, swarming outside the hut. He recognized among them Stephen Prather, a white man who ran an Indian store on the Angelina in the oldest Texas country. Prather and some other white men had resolved to dislodge a group of Fredonians from an encampment at the brow of a hill west of the ford on the Carrizo. They had persuaded the native Indians to accompany them. Gladly young Horton picked up his rifle and went along. Prather's party converged on the Fredonian camp. Awakening to chilling warwhoops, the unnerved rebels surrendered.

Later in the day most of the remainder of the Edwards' forces rode eastward down the Nacogdoches road, intent on evicting the settlers who had failed to co-operate. Prather's whites and Indians ranged themselves on either side of the road near the crest of the ridge. As the unsuspecting Fredonians rode by they were captured without bloodshed. Before nightfall Haden Edwards had only the few men who were with him at the stone house. He and Benjamin Edwards and their last-ditch followers spurred for the Sabine.

Within the month, the Cherokees tried and convicted Richard Fields of insurrection against Mexico and sent his papers and the Fredonian flag to the commandant general of the eastern Interior Provinces at Monterrey. The tribesmen put old Dick Fields, who wanted freedom for them, to death. The Edwardses themselves escaped with their lives but nothing else.

The fate of John Dunn Hunter remains something of a mystery. The *Natchitoches Courier* of June 21, 1827, printed a story from a New York paper which reported that Hunter had been murdered by an Indian who accompanied him when he quit the Cherokees.

The editor of the newspaper which carried the report believed Hunter to be an ignorant man and an impostor. There were others who said he was British and a British agent. Some Easterners, who said that they had known him, related that he had returned to his father's home in Massachusetts, resumed his right name and lived out his life working in his parent's factory for the manufacture of razor straps, penny royal, peppermint water, cough drops and macassar oil.

So ended the Republic of Fredonia, the product of the fantastic notion which clouded the brain of John Hunter and animated the exasperation of Haden Edwards, a proud, impatient and high-handed member of the Virginia gentry.

Dr. John Sibley, who knew more than a little about border revolutions, wrote an epitaph which was more penetrating than kind: "There never was a more silly, wild, quicksotic [sic] scheme than that of Nacogdoches, and all sober, honest thinking people here view it in the same light."

But the government in Mexico City would view the late Fredonian Republic in another and more menacing light.

CHAPTER EIGHTEEN

A FUSE IS LIT

THE FREDONIAN REVOLT had failed ingloriously. Few Anglo-American settlers and fewer Indians had rallied beneath the red-and-white flag which signified a biracial republic of free men. Stephen Austin and his colonists had remained loyal to Mexico, their country by adoption. The government in Mexico City should not have become uneasy because of the abortive uprising, but it did. Its punitive reaction lit a fuse of counter-action which led to an explosive keg of rebellion. The rebellion would not end until the Republic of Texas was born in massacre and terrorism, in cowardice and courage and panic and indecision and, at the last, in an unbelievable eighteen minutes of avenging, one-sided slaughter on the battlefield of San Jacinto.

By one of the curious quirks of history, the two men who were perhaps the most responsible, indirectly and directly, for the lighting of the fuse had patriotic if different reasons for the scotching of any revolution which would remove Texas from the Mexican orbit. One was a British agent, the other a loyal Mexican who himself had helped win freedom from Spain.

Henry George Ward was the British *chargé d'affaires* in Mexico City at the time of the Fredonian uprising. His assignment was to do anything that would advance the interests of Great Britain in Mexico and hinder the United States. If the Mexican nation needed a loan, as it frequently did, he was ready to assure that his country would be so kind. He also sought trade concessions for British textile mills and importers, and to stay on the right side of the right Mexicans who, his country's diplomats had agreed, were the conservative centralists.

Ward's principal adversary was Joel R. Poinsett, the American *chargé d'affaires*. An incidental aspect of their gentlemanly competition gives insight into the role which the Masonic orders played in the revolutions of the eighteenth and nineteenth centuries against authoritarian domination. Members of the secret order, so detested by the Roman Catholic Church and the monarchists of Europe and the New World, were active in the cause of human freedom. Every signer of the American Declaration of Independence save one had been a Mason. Masonry permeated the revolutionary bodies of France. Samuel Kemper, who had marched with Gutiérrez and had returned home after the murders of Salcedo and his officers, had used the cloak of Masonry to bring together one-time British Royalists and libertarian Americans to plot against Spain and wrest from her weakening grasp the territory of West Florida.

Now Joel Poinsett brought together in his own parlor a group of liberal federalist leaders and formed them into a body of York Rite Masons as answer to the Scottish Rite Masons made up of conservative centralists and dominated by Ward.

Ward did more than try to influence Mexicans through the secret brotherhood. In 1825 he suggested to the first president of Mexico, Félix Fernández, who emotionally had assumed the sobriquet of Victoria Guadalupe when he fought for Mexican independence under the banner of Our Lady of Guadalupe, that the republic should take a closer look at what the Americans were doing in Texas. Why not send a commission to Texas? And what better man could be put in charge of the investigation, asked Ward, than José Manuel Rafael Simeón de Mier y Terán, hero of the revolution?

The president approved of the idea. Possibly he welcomed a chance to put out of the way for a while the fellow revolutionary, Mier y Terán, who had once laughed at him because of the grandiose name he had assumed. But not until after the abortive uprising of the Fredonians did Victoria Guadalupe, a *mestizo* of little learning, and congress put into effect the recommendation of the suave English representative.

Victoria Guadalupe appointed a commission, under the direction of Mier y Terán, to make a political, scientific and military study of Texas. Not so general were the instructions given by Gómez Pedraza,

the minister of war, who ordered Mier y Terán to investigate the
defenses of Texas against such internal enemies as Indians and dis-
loyal colonists, as well as external enemies. He should study the
terrain where the Sabine border, agreed upon by the Adams-Onís
Treaty, would run if the encroaching Americans would ever get around
to sending a commission to mark it.

When that would be was uncertain. Joel Poinsett had lately made
what Mexico considered an insolent offer to purchase Texas, her "inalienable heritage from Spain," for a million dollars. The republic's
cabinet officers reminded Mier y Terán just before he left Mexico City
on his mission that "the Romans conceded lands to the tribes of the
North and by so doing destroyed the foundation on which during many
centuries they had built the most extensive empire that had ever
governed the world."

The admonition was prophetic.

Mier y Terán was a good choice for the assigned task, perhaps
too good. As a graduate of the College of Mines at Mexico City, with
a marked flair for engineering, he had served the revolution under
Ignacio Rayón in the desperate years and became, after his enlistment
in the spring of 1811, one of the most effective *caudillos*. Later he
accepted the clemency offered all who had shared in the seemingly
hopeless guerilla warfare. He returned to combat upon the announcement of the Plan of Iguala. The still young revolutionary hero became
a member of Mexico's first constituent congress in 1822. He supported
the liberal federal constitution of 1824 under which, after the overthrow of the self-proclaimed emperor Iturbide, Guadalupe Victoria
became the first president of the Republic of Mexico. He was a punc-
tilious, brilliant, moody and patriotic man, and, by the time he set out
for Texas, a sick man, too, stricken probably with tuberculosis.

The ill man rode in a carriage. His companions were a Swiss
botanist named Louis Berlandier, a minerologist, three army officers
and an escort of sixteen dragoons. Two heavy wagons were loaded
with scientific instruments and books and tents and supplies. In addition there were the coach, horses for the commissioners to ride when
they wished and remounts. What Mier y Terán saw and his inter-
pretations of what he saw would change the course of American
history.

In San Fernando de Béxar the head of the commission conferred with Ramón Músquiz, the political chief. There his education with respect to Texas began.

The Americans were taking over. Mexicans in appreciable numbers could be found only at Béxar, at La Bahía, which the legislature had recently renamed Goliad as an anagram in honor of Father Hidalgo, and at Nacogdoches. The *malditos hereticos,* in contrast, were pouring into the colonies of Stephen Austin and Green Dewitt below Béxar. They were encroaching by the hundreds, even thousands, upon the border leagues reserved to the federal government. The best estimates placed the number of Anglos at 20,000. They were clearing fields, building log hutments, improving their appropriated land. In contrast to their industry, the approximately 1,500 inhabitants of San Antonio, most of them Mexicans, were interested mainly in dancing, he observed. To them the worst punishment was work.

The commission had come to Béxar by the southern, more direct route. It now left, not directly for Nacogdoches, but to swing south of the old *camino real* to the area where Dewitt's and Austin's colonists had cut trails which were already far more important.

A ferry bore the travelers across the pale blue Guadalupe river. On the far side lay Dewitt's capital of Gonzales, composed of six wooden cabins inhabited by three North American men, two *Yanqui* women, two *Yanqui* girls and only one Mexican. Beyond the Colorado they passed treeless hills, crossed aggravatingly muddy ground, then they entered Austin's capital of San Felipe de Austin, a settlement of about fifty wooden houses on the western bank of the Brazos.

Here Stephen Austin's secretary, Samuel M. Williams, did his best for the distinguished guests. Rooms were ready; the best fare was offered. Mier y Terán and his companions were not impressed with the food. They nibbled indifferently at salt pork, corn bread and homemade cheese. They warded off the proffers of whiskey. The Americans were heavy drinkers, the Mexicans noted. One of the two stores which catered to the 200 townspeople and 2,000 rural settlers in the area sold only whiskey, rum, sugar and coffee; the other dealt in rice, flour, lard and cheap cloth.

Mier y Terán and Stephen Austin conferred for more than two weeks, in part because the rising Brazos made travel difficult but principally because the Texan *empresario,* still indisputably loyal to Mexico, had much to tell the commissioner. Mier y Terán quit San

Felipe with the conviction that Austin was as staunch a Mexican citizen as was he. He was not so sure of most of the rest.

To his dying day Mier y Terán would not forget his departure. A drunken American and three Negroes at least equally soused, all singing loudly, ferried his party across the Brazos in a flatboat, finally landing 2 leagues downstream, where mosquitoes made of the general's face a swollen mass that looked like flayed meat.

When he reached the long hills covered with live oaks, pines, walnuts and laurels, the gnats he had never seen before caused the general to cover his horses' ears with his handkerchiefs. What worried him more was that at San Pedro Creek and at the Neches he found more American families settled without government consent. Everywhere these *Norteamericanos* were clearing their homesteads without the permission of anyone! And he wondered what kind of people these might be when he found two little girls alone in one of the houses, their mother gone to Nacogdoches.

At the Angelina, a poor American treated the Mexican party with considerable courtesy, "a very rare thing among individuals of his nationality," commented a member of the expedition.

Only Nacogdoches was reassuring. Here were adobe houses, in straight lines, in which dwelt Mexicans. But not enough of them. Mier y Terán was welcomed to the Mexican outpost by Lieutenant Colonel José de la Piedras, the commander of the 12th Permanent Battalion, who had taken command of this frontier strongpoint a few months after the Fredonian revolt.

Out of Nacogdoches in every direction which promised information, Mier y Terán ranged, guided by Peter Ellis Bean. Even before his conscientious inspections were ended, he sent to President Victoria a pessimistic analysis. If the supreme government intended to wait for a detailed and final report, the situation would be beyond remedy. The Americans were out of hand. He wrote:

> *As one covers the distance from Béxar to this town [Nacogdoches], he will note that Mexican influence is proportionately diminished until on arriving in this place he will see that it is almost nothing. And indeed, whence could such influence come? Hardly from superior numbers in population, since the ratio of Mexicans to foreigners is one to ten; certainly not from the superior character of the Mexican*

*population, for exactly the opposite is true, the Mexicans of
this town comprising what in all counties is called the low
class—the very poor and ignorant ...*

*It would cause you the same chagrin that it has caused
me to see the opinion that is held of our Nation by these foreign Colonists, since, with the exception of some few who have
journeyed to our capitol, they know no other Mexicans than
the inhabitants about here, and excepting the authorities
necessary to any form of society, the said inhabitants are
the most ignorant of negroes and Indians, among whom I pass
for a man of culture. Thus, I tell myself that it could not be
otherwise than that from such a state of affairs should arise
an antagonism between the Mexicans and foreigners, which
is not the least of the smouldering fires which I have discovered. Therefore, I am warning you to take timely measures.
Texas could throw this whole Nation into revolution ...*

But Mexico had more immediate concerns than Texas. Internal
politics again were driving the country dangerously close to civil
war. The votes of the several state legislatures indicated that Gómez
Pedraza, the secretary of war who commanded the army, had been
elected the second president of the republic. But the country had to
reckon with the cynical young opportunist from Vera Cruz, Santa
Anna, who for most of his long lifetime would greatly contribute to
Mexico's near-continual turmoil.

Santa Anna, a participant in the Plan of Iguala, declared in
favor of Vicente Guerrero, the illiterate *mestizo* patriot who, with
Iturbide, had signed the plan. Guerrero had received a majority of
the popular vote and he won out after a mutiny of some soldiers in
Mexico City, a three-day riot of the *léperos* of the slums and his
espousal by the respected liberal, Lorenzo de Zavala. With inexplicable
generosity, Guerrero asked his opponent's running mate, the reactionary Bustamante, to serve as vice-president. Soon thereafter Mier
y Terán was appointed commandant general of the eastern *Provincias
Internas* in Bustamante's stead.

And Mexico was beset. Taking advantage of the disintegration
brought about by the protracted civil war, Fernando VII dispatched
an armada of five ships from Spain by way of Cuba with orders to
retake Mexico. Yellow fever, and not the Mexican troops under Santa

Anna, defeated them at Tampico, where the survivors of the dread disease surrendered.

Just before the invasion the supreme government voted dictatorial power to Guerrero. One of his first decrees unequivocally abolished slavery in Mexico. The transplanted Southerners in Texas were distraught. From the Sabine to San Felipe, couriers bore frantic letters from the colonists whose previously granted special rights to retain their slaves were apparently wiped out by Guerrero's decree. Those rights had been stated in a specious statute, which the Baron de Bastrop, the settlers' first legislative representative, persuaded his fellow *Coahuila y Texas* lawmakers to enact.

Mier y Terán advised Austin to ignore Guerrero's decree; it did not apply to Austin's colony, he said. Later the decree was quietly annulled.

In the fall of 1830 Vice-President Bustamante, supported by the army, drove President Guerrero from Mexico City. The president had refused to relinquish the dictatorial powers he had assumed when the Spanish expeditionary force landed at Tampico. The uncompromising revolutionary was captured aboard an Italian merchantman in Acapulco harbor, the captain of which literally sold him to his pursuers. After a semblance of a trial Mexico's second president was executed for treason.

It was hardly a stable country to which the American colonists and the earlier Texans had sworn allegiance. But as long as the constitution of 1824, with its insistence on the right of states to govern themselves, received even token support from the central government, Stephen Austin hoped that the political problems of his adopted country need not affect those settlers who remained aloof from them. But the day was not distant when at Turtle Bayou on the lower Trinity a providential expression of interest in Mexico's politics would buy time for the *Norteamericanos*.

The American colonists would blame Mier y Terán for the turmoil which precipitated this declaration of concern. Actually, he had nothing to do with the most obnoxious of the articles in the law of April 6, 1830, which came to be called the Stamp Act of the Texas Revolution. But Mier y Terán sent his recommendations concerning the Texas problem to the government early that year. The arch-conservative, Bustamante, was serving as acting president; his secretary of foreign relations—brilliant, bespectacled Lucas Alamán—was a monarchist at heart.

The lengthy report emphasized three points: no new garrisons should be established in Texas, but more soldiers should be sent to the three long-established *presidios;* to offset the overwhelming majority of Anglo-Americans in Texas, every effort should be made to settle Mexican and non-Anglo Saxon foreigners there; sea trade should be developed between the coastal towns of Texas and other Mexican ports so as to bind all sections of the country together.

Much of the report became law almost without being legally phrased. But Lucas Alamán proposed two additional articles. They were approved. One of them, Article X, set forth that no change should be made "with respect to colonies already established nor with respect to the slaves which they contained."

But this was not reassuring enough to offset the construction which the Anglos placed upon Article XI of the act. It asserted the central government's superseding authority to review any contracts the several Mexican states might make with *empresarios*. It also denied to any citizens of the United States the right to colonize Mexican lands contiguous to their own country and, ambiguously, it provided that "those contracts of colonization, the terms of which are opposed to the present Article, and which are not yet complied with, shall consequently be suspended."

Alamán wanted to make certain that the North Americans would be halted. He had reason enough. In the preceding March, Andrew Jackson had become President of the United States. The Mexican minister in Washington had written at the time that Jackson had said that the way to handle Texas was to seize it first and negotiate afterward, as he had done with Florida. The quotation was not reassuring; whether the President had made the statement or not was unimportant. The minister and Alamán both believed that such was North American policy. Moreover, the United States Secretary of State, Martin Van Buren, had instructed Joel Poinsett's successor to raise the offer for Texas from one million to five million dollars at a time when the Mexican government was desperately seeking funds to use against Fernando's invaders. The timing seemed ominous.

To the American colonists in Texas the Law of April 6 was inexcusable. More troops would be quartered among them. They could no longer hope to increase their own numbers through immigration from the United States. But to the Mexicans the Law of April 6 was an expression of the innate fear of the trespassers from the north.

The signs of North American assertiveness were everywhere to be found. Lieutenant Colonel Piedras wrote from Nacogdoches that the United States was moving troops into the cantonment at Fort Jesup on the old *camino* and that money was being raised to recruit men in New Orleans for a filibuster raid.

The Haden Edwards land grant, which had been reassigned to three other *empresarios,* including the patriot Zavala, had been turned over by them to land promoters—the Galveston Bay and Texas Land Company—and the promoters were selling scrip for 5 and 10 cents which the purchasers believed entitled them to an acre of land in Texas. Actually the *empresarios* had no land to sell. Moreover, the American newspapers which supported Andrew Jackson were declaring that the American boundary was the Río Grande because of La Salle's long-ago establishment on Matagorda Bay.

Mier y Terán, as commandant general, increased the size of the garrisons in The Alamo, at Nacogdoches and at Goliad. He established strongpoints at five other places, three significantly given names from ancient Mexican history: Tenoxtitlán, above the *camino real* crossing and near the falls of the Brazos; Anáhuac, near the mouth of the Trinity on Galveston Bay; Lipantitlán, at the mouth of the Nueces; Terán, on the Neches, with Colonel Ellis Peter Bean in charge; and Lavaca on the Lavaca River. The legal settlers in the Austin and Dewitt grants found themselves ringed by military installations. The families in the border reserves resented the virtual isolation from their kinsmen in the legal settlements.

Aggravation piled upon aggravation. Mier y Terán, from his headquarters at Matamoros, the recently opened port on the Río Grande, sought to pacify the settlers in the Austin and Dewitt colonies. He assured Austin that the anti-colonization provisions did not apply to his or Dewitt's colonies, since they were already "established" within the meaning of the law. Austin in turn sent passports to various American cities and some to Nacogdoches so that immigrants already on the way to Texas could use them as proof that they were coming into the established colonies.

But this meant they could enter only Austin's or Dewitt's colonies. Other *empresarios,* whose colonies were not yet established, would assert later that Austin had sponsored the hated anti-colonization article for his own good. Settlers from Nashville, without passports, cut a tract around Nacogdoches in a by-pass that later arrivals also used.

The settlers began to suspect everything that the government did or did not do with respect to Texas. President Victoria Guadalupe had confirmed Ellis Bean's promise of legal title to lands in the border reserves on which lived settlers who had remained loyal to Mexico during the Fredonian rebellion. But as time passed and no official arrived to draw the boundaries, the North Americans suspected that the government was reneging.

They were unaware that the delay was in part caused by the reluctance of a self-important commissioner, Juan Antonio Padilla, the secretary general of *Coahuila y Texas*, to leave Saltillo until Austin had sent a carriage for him and his wife. And when Padilla was arrested for homicide and jailed in Nacogdoches soon after his delayed arrival, the colonists construed the event as a ruse to put off fulfillment of Mexico's promise. They were mollified when another envoy, José Francisco Madero, placed a statement in the *Texas Gazette* at San Felipe that he would proceed to the Trinity to assign lands.

And then a short-tempered, blustering autocrat who was appointed the Mexican commander at Anáhuac at the river's mouth precipitated all but open strife. This man, Juan Davis Bradburn, was, ironically, a Kentuckian by birth and rearing, and an entrepreneur who in 1830 held a government contract to operate horse-propelled vessels on the Río Grande.

A fighter in one of the expeditions for Mexican freedom, Bradburn had become a Mexican citizen. The Anglo settlers hated him from the time he took command of the Anáhuac garrison, not only for his personality, but because he had impressed slaves to build barracks without compensating their owners.

Now, three months after his arrival, and upon learning of Madero's promise to assign the lands on the lower Trinity, he sent Madero a peremptory message that the law of 1830 contravened such assignments to the reserve settlers. He threatened to arrest Madero and his surveyor if they attempted to assign the lands. After an exchange of angry letters he did arrest both of them. Mier y Terán stood behind Bradburn, agreeing that federal and not state officers were the proper officials to assign the littoral reserves. Madero then agreed not to assign any land and on Mier y Terán's instructions Bradburn released his prisoners.

Madero made one more effort to help the settlers. He legally constituted their settlement on the Trinity crossing of the Atascosito Road the municipality of Villa de la Santíssima Trinidad de la Libertad, a lengthy name which the Americans promptly shortened to Liberty. Jealous of the prerogatives of the central government, Bradburn dissolved the Liberty *ayuntamiento* organized by the Coahuila state officer and set up another, answerable to him, at Anáhuac.

Not yet clearly, but in essence, the Bradburn-Madero controversy represented a conflict between state and central governments. The settlers had fared better under the authority of the state of *Coahuila y Texas* than when the supreme government gave the orders. Soon they began talking of making Texas a state separate from Coahuila. Its population would be overwhelmingly Anglo-American.

Then came a calamitous coincidence. Nervous over their future and furious at Bradburn's highhandedness, the insecure Anglos were subjected to an inevitable but highly irritating change in their tax status. Under the national colonization acts of 1823, they had been given seven years of freedom from payment of duties. But the seven years were up. Not only would they be taxed for importation of luxuries but for the most vital of necessities, such as furniture, wagons, iron and steel, cotton bagging and cotton-bale rope.

Mier y Terán installed tax collectors. The chief collector, a Serbian-Mexican named George Fisher, soon made himself unpopular —any tax collector would have—and Mier y Terán removed him on a technicality. The payment of duties was postponed. But in September 1831, unable to delay collections any longer, Mier y Terán himself came to Anáhuac to establish the collector's office and authorize a sub-office at Brazoria, 30 leagues up the Brazos, for the convenience of the Texans and ship captains. When he returned to Matamoras he left Fisher in charge at Anáhuac.

The payment of duties on needful household items seemed an intolerable burden, especially to the more recently arrived colonists. Like all frontiersmen they were short of cash. They asked themselves why the government did not reduce its garrisons if money was lacking; the custom duties was a device to make them pay for the forces quartered among them to keep them in subjection. George Fisher made things worse by ordering that boats going up the Brazos must first come up and register at Anáhuac at the top of Galveston Bay and that their captains must get clearance at Anáhuac before leaving the Brazos, which meant overland trips.

Even the loyal and conciliatory Stephen Austin lost his head over the inconvenience, which he thought insufferable. He wrote Bradburn that the law was unenforceable; more, he warned him not to try to enforce it.

Soon thereafter two ships left Brazoria without proper clearance. When Mexican troops tried to stop them, one soldier was killed. Austin promptly wrote Mier y Terán a calm version of the affair. He emphasized that the killing of the soldier was the result of Fisher's impractical order and that no disloyalty was intended.

The commandant general's answer was a frigid one. All men paid duties, from Hudson's Bay to the Horn; only at Brazoria was their collection considered reason for violence. He told Austin that he had been as conciliatory as he could be when he postponed establishing the customs offices and took upon himself the opening of suboffices, an act which might be construed as the opening of ports, a prerogative reserved to congress. He also had some harsh personal words for Austin.

But he reprimanded Fisher and soon thereafter accepted his resignation. Then to avoid further friction Mier y Terán opened more convenient customs offices, such as the one at Velasco at the mouth of the Brazos, easier to reach than was Brazoria. But the very existence of the customs post made the colonists more conscious of the hated duties.

Those January days of 1832 were hard on Mier y Terán. His illness was making him almost an invalid. He was fearful that any day the Texans might get out of hand. And at Vera Cruz, the same Santa Anna who had helped place President Bustamante in power had enunciated a new plan which threatened the Bustamante government itself. The garrisons at Vera Cruz and San Juan de Ulúa came out for the so-called Plan of Vera Cruz, which would remove Bustamante's centralist cabinet. The garrisons "requested" Santa Anna to lead the federalist movement.

Santa Anna himself had concocted the whole scheme in order to assume power, for the national elections were approaching and the Bustamante government had decided upon Mier y Terán as its presi-

dential nominee. If Santa Anna was to become president he must
switch political horses. It was as simple as that. The conscienceless
Santa Anna had turned upon benefactors and political allies before.
He would do it again. Within four years, the Mexican bugles would
sound the *deguello* at The Alamo and his name would become a syno-
nym for merciless butchery. He was on his way to becoming, through
trickery, the president-dictator of Mexico.

Stephen Austin had been gravely ill during the previous autumn
of 1831. The disturbances brought about in that fall by the presence
and behavior of Fisher, the tax collector, took place during his convalescence. The illness gave him a welcome reason not to go to Saltillo
to take the seat in the legislature to which he had been elected as soon
as he had lived long enough in Texas to be eligible. The situation
being what it was, he had not wished to leave his colony. However,
with the dismissal of Fisher, he believed that conditions in Texas
would be quieter. With a doctor's excuse for his absence in his pocket
he set out for Saltillo.

But the bullying Colonel Bradburn remained as chief of the
garrison at Anáhuac. He was constantly interfering with the colonists, even to the point of explaining to the slaves whom he had impressed without paying for their time that under Mexican law they
were really free. When two runaway slaves from Louisiana were
caught, he refused to send them back to their masters.

At this juncture a brilliant 23-year-old lawyer from Alabama
rode into town. His name was William Barret Travis, and he had
been in Texas less than a year. Sensitive, high-spirited and moody,
he had left behind him a wife whom he had married before his twenti-
eth birthday and whom he believed to be unfaithful. He had entered
into the practice of law at Anáhuac. The owner of the two slaves
whom Bradburn refused to return retained him. Travis called on
Bradburn and demanded their release. Bradburn ended the discussion by having the young lawyer thrown into jail.

There, among the other prisoners, he found congenial spirits.
One of them was Patrick C. Jack, a lawyer from San Felipe. Others
were American regulators who had tarred and feathered an American
colonist who failed to aid a woman whom some presidial soldiers had
seized and raped. The Bradburn soldiers had tried to break up the
regulators. A free-for-all ended with the beating of some of the

soldiers and the capture of four members of the mob. Bradburn announced he would court-martial them. It was then that Jack, heading a self-constituted militia, sought to rescue them and was captured. Bradburn then announced that the whole group would be court-martialed.

Many of the colonists were now ready to fight; the substitution of military court-martial for civilian court procedure was too much. At Brazoria, John Austin—no kin to Stephen Austin—was elected commander of some 200 men. The force marched on Anáhuac to demand the release of the prisoners. As they streamed through Velasco, at the mouth of the Brazos, Lieutenant Colonel Domingo de Ugartechea saw that it was impossible for his own small force to halt them. Instead he sent along with them one of his own subalterns with a letter to Bradburn recommending the release of the men.

The band reached Anáhuac on June 10. John Austin entered the *carcel* and demanded of Bradburn, in the name of the colonists, the release of Jack and Travis. The legend is that he found them both pinioned to the floor, with Bradburn, a gun in his hand, standing guard. When the colonel threatened to kill the two men unless Austin left, so the story goes, Travis cried out to let the shooting start. Bradburn won time with a request for a meeting of his officers before making a decision. Austin withdrew his men outside the town. Bradburn's officers backed their commander in refusing to yield to force and prepared to resist any attack.

The colonists knew that they must have heavier weapons to capture Bradburn's stronghold. Someone suggested that two cannons at Brazoria be impounded. Austin sent a small party to fetch them. Perhaps, as they waited near Turtle Bayou in the vicinity of Anáhuac, some of the more moderate colonists considered the impropriety of bearing arms against the government they had sworn to uphold.

In any event, William Jack, brother of Patrick and himself a lawyer, drew up some resolutions which put the uprising on surer grounds. In these statements, which came to be known as the Turtle Bayou Resolutions, the colonists disclaimed any disloyalty to the government. Instead, they proclaimed their loyalty to Santa Anna's federalist Plan of Vera Cruz. Their revolt against Bradburn, as the representative of the centralists, was, so they said, their own patriotic participation in the Mexican convulsion.

Meanwhile, Colonel Piedras at Nacogdoches had been informed

of the trouble. While the colonists waited for the cannon, he rode up at the head of sixty infantrymen and fifty cavalrymen, but instead of attacking the colonel patiently listened to the account of grievances which the colonists presented. He subsequently ordered Bradburn to pay for the use of the private property—namely the slaves—and to release the prisoners to the civil authorities for trial. Piedras also promised the colonists that he would seek Bradburn's removal; soon thereafter he persuaded Bradburn to resign. The prisoners were released and the colonists disbanded and returned home.

Nevertheless, fighting had begun in earnest. At Velasco, Lieutenant Colonel Ugartechea refused to permit the colonists, who had obtained the cannon at Brazoria, to sail with the prized artillery to Anáhuac. The colonists attacked. After three days of fighting, Ugartechea, his ammunition expended, surrendered and was permitted to capitulate with the honors of war. He agreed to sail with his soldiers to Matamoros. Of the 150-man Mexican garrison, five soldiers were killed and sixteen wounded. Seven Texans were killed and fourteen wounded.

Austin was as concerned as was Mier y Terán over this shedding of blood. In May he had left the cool of Saltillo and had ridden to the Mexican commandant's headquarters 20 miles from Tampico. Mier y Terán and his centralists had retreated there before the federalist troops supporting Santa Anna. Austin found the general ill and preoccupied with the many military decisions he had to make. He was depressed because Mexico was again involved in civil strife and plagued with the situation in Texas. The commandant general told Austin that he favored repeal of the offensive Article XI in the law of 1830 and duty-free importation of necessary household items. Austin, on his part, again assured the general of the loyalty of the colonists.

Then, at Matamoros, from where he intended to return to Saltillo to pass the summer before the autumn legislative session, Austin wrote to his colonists to observe "a dead calm." He had the illusion that a more democratic government was about to come to power under Santa Anna and that if the colonists would remain quiet they would obtain fairer treatment from that scheming pretender to liberalism than they had under the autocratic centralists. But the news of the hostilities at Anáhuac and Velasco caused him to change his plans.

At the end of June, Colonel José Antonio Mexía, a Santa Anna adherent, and his troops occupied the city of Matamoros. Soldiers loyal to President Bustamante were encamped nearby. There would have to be an armistice in the civil war for the nation's good. The opposing officers came to an odd if practical agreement. Their own conflict could wait. Texas needed looking into. So Colonel Mexía, with 400 troops, sailed to investigate the alarming events in Texas. Austin accompanied him, by invitation.

At the mouth of the Brazos, Colonel Mexía questioned John Austin as to his reasons for leading armed colonists against Colonel Bradburn. If his intent had been to cast off the authority of Mexico he had acted treasonably. If he had risen in support of Santa Anna, the act was praiseworthy. John Austin's answer was the obvious one. *Viva Santa Anna!* Fortunately he had the Turtle Bayou Resolutions to back him up. At Brazoria, Stephen Austin and Colonel Mexía attended a "Santa Anna dinner and ball." At Anáhuac the garrison declared for Santa Anna's Plan of Vera Cruz and departed for Tampico to fight Bustamante's centralists.

Colonel Piedras, still steadfastly supporting Bustamante and the centralists, was attacked by the American colonists a week later. This time a more urgent matter than trial in civilian court was involved; it had to do with the right to bear arms.

When Piedras returned from Anáhuac to Nacogdoches he discovered that during his absence some citizens had talked of joining the Turtle Bayou encampment; they had decided against doing so only for fear of exposing their undefended homes to Cherokee raiders. The colonel demanded that the local militiamen surrender their arms. Forthwith, the *ayuntamiento* of Nacogdoches, composed of the *Alcalde* Encarnacion Chirino, two other Mexicans and two Americans, called upon the settlers at the Sabine, on Patroon Creek, on Ayish Bayou and in other communities to rise.

Some 200 men from the Ayish Bayou district and all of the country to the Sabine answered the call to arms. They elected as colonel James W. Bulloch, a veteran of the battle of New Orleans. On August 1 they encamped in the pine hills to the east of Nacogdoches. From there Bulloch sent a committee to demand that Colonel Piedras either declare for Santa Anna and the Federal Constitution of 1824 or surrender. Piedras replied that he would defend his position. His 350 well-disciplined soldiers were quartered around the stone house in long low wooden barracks daubed with the red clay of the hills. Prudently he kept them near the fort, commanding the road from the east, and waited for the citizens to make the first move.

He did not have long to wait. Colonel Bulloch and his men forded La Nana above the road and grouped north of the fort. At about eleven o'clock that morning, the Americans, impatient for action, moved down North Street, which intersected the *camino real*. Piedras ordered his cavalry to charge; 100 horsemen galloped upon the advancing line, discharging their muskets almost at point blank range. The return fire of the Americans forced the Mexican horsemen to retire but not before *Alcalde* Chirino fell. He was the first man to die for constitutional government in a settlement on the *camino real*.

Some of the Americans, unused to military engagements, broke and ran. But most of them continued to advance upon the Mexicans in the square to the northwest of the stone house. The Mexicans retreated toward the stone house in house-to-house fighting that lasted for the rest of the day. By nightfall the Mexican losses were forty-seven killed and fifty wounded; three Americans were dead and five wounded.

During the night the Americans built timber breastworks across North Street. There were no corresponding sounds of activity from the stone house and the barracks. At daybreak the Americans discovered why. One colonist, emboldened by the whiskey he had drunk during the night, announced he was going to "knock and see if there was anybody at home." Carrying a heavy timber he walked under the gallery of the stone house and bashed the door open with the timber. The building was undefended. During the night Piedras, unsure of the loyalty of his men to the Bustamante cause, had ordered a withdrawal to the west. Behind him he left his dead and wounded.

Most of the Americans were willing to let well enough alone. But James Carter, a long-time citizen of Nacogdoches, called for volunteers to harass the Mexicans to the Brazos; other Americans would certainly join them there. Fifteen men responded. They sniped intermittently at the Mexicans retreating down the ancient trail, then skirted the army and hid themselves at the Angelina. As the Mexican cavalrymen drew rein to let their horses drink at the ford, Carter's riflemen began picking them off. The Mexicans sought to withdraw, but Colonel Piedras, riding up, urged them on and forced a crossing to the west side. Unable to oppose so large a force, Carter's patrol hastened down the road to wait for the next appearance of the enemy.

They were still waiting at ten o'clock the next morning. The puzzled men from the redlands decided to return to the Angelina to find out what happened. As they approached a house near the ford they were astounded to see a white flag waving from a window. Afraid of trickery, Carter rode carefully toward the house. Before he reached it, Colonel Piedras and his officers came out and surrendered. They explained that during the night the officers under Piedras had decided to go over to Santa Anna and had forced Piedras to turn over his command to them. Their present wish was to join their brothers in the cause of Santa Anna and the constitution.

Carter returned to his volunteers. If the Mexicans discovered how few were the Anglos they might decide to fight on. After a conference, Carter and four of the men rode back to the house, where they announced that they were a committee sent to accept the surrender. They would accompany Piedras and his principal officers to Nacogdoches, where terms could be worked out. However, since the woods were full of armed Americans, still hankering for more fighting, the rest of the Mexicans would be wise to remain where they were. The Mexicans were glad to oblige.

That night at Nacogdoches, the victors celebrated with feasting and drinking; the lonely Piedras sat apart, unnoticed until a citizen brought him food and drink. Then, under the terms of surrender, he was escorted to Velasco, from where he boarded a ship for Matamoros. In time he was killed defending the centralist cause.

The 250 officers and men he left behind were to have a legendary guide to San Felipe. He was a naturalized citizen of *Coahuila y Texas*, the son-in-law of the vice-governor of the state, and at the time he was only passing through from Nacogdoches on his way to San Antonio. His name was James Bowie. He was six feet tall, a mild-spoken man with grey eyes that seemed to see everything, and he carried in a silver mounted scabbard a great ivory-handled knife of his own or his brother's design. It bore his name, the Bowie knife.

Jim Bowie was a living legend. Only nine months earlier he had taken part in as notable an Indian fight as Texas history would ever record. He and his brother, Rezin T. Bowie, seven other Americans and two slaves had been attacked by more than 150 Caddo and Tuacana Indians near the old fort of San Sabá, where they were planning to seek the lost silver mines. In a fight which raged from sunrise to sunset, they held off the Indians, killing or wounding forty-eight of the attackers and losing but one of their own men. Bowie was a smuggler—some said in partnership with the pirate, Jean Lafitte—a slave dealer, adventurer and knife fighter, and he was known throughout Texas and the United States as a man not to be balked. His wife, a beautiful blonde Mexican aristocrat of wholly Spanish descent, Ursula Veramendi, adored him, and he loved her as he did nothing else in life. She bore him two children, but they and she were to die of cholera in Monclova before James Bowie, a deathly ill and broken-hearted man, himself died at The Alamo.

After he escorted the Mexican troops from east Texas, that part of the state which bordered the United States lay open to uncontrolled American immigration.

Colonel Ellis Peter Bean, in command on the Neches, and José Francisco Ruíz at Tenoxtitlán alike declared for Santa Anna. Colonel Mexía, satisfied that the Texans were supporting Santa Anna and the constitution of 1824, sailed back to fight the centralists. Early in September the legislature of *Coahuila y Texas* voted to support the insurgents. The remaining garrisons in the state soon joined up.

A few weeks earlier Mier y Terán, despondent over the future of his revolution-torn country and the loss of Texas, which he clearly foresaw, dressed himself in his most formal uniform, donned the medals and insignia of his brilliant career, tied a bright silk handkerchief around his throat and, behind an ancient church in Padilla, in Tamaulipas, drove into his body the sword which he had lifted for the cause of Mexican independence. The last message of this patriotic, perceptive soldier was:

En qué parará Texas?, en lo que Dios quiera.

How will things end in Texas?, as God wishes them to end.

CHAPTER NINETEEN

REVOLUTION

WITHIN THREE YEARS after the rout of Colonel Piedras at Nacogdoches, hundreds of armed men from every state in the American Union and from the nations of western Europe rode and walked the *camino real*. Some were young and adventurous. Not a few were true mercenaries, professional warriors ready to gamble their lives for money or land. Many more were political idealists, believing passionately that tyranny and despotism must be confronted wherever their ugly faces frowned upon freedom, self-government and religious liberty. They found in Texas other resentful but more settled men, most of them reluctant to take the ultimate and irrevocable road of revolution.

Together with the established folk, the newcomers with the rifles and pistols and Bowie knives cursed the name and the turncoat treachery of Santa Anna, the president-dictator of Mexico who had suborned and betrayed the cause of liberalism which he had so persuasively espoused only three years before.

To understand the coming of the volunteers and the Texas Revolution for which they fought and were massacred, it is necessary to be better informed than were most of the men who in 1835 began swarming by water and on horseback and afoot into a Texas in ferment.

Except at San Antonio and Goliad, the former La Bahía, no Mexican garrisons remained in Texas by the end of August 1832.

Santa Anna, whom Stephen Austin and almost every Anglo supported for reasons that may have been different from those they publicly offered, was sweeping the authoritarian centralists of Bustamante before him. Victory for Santa Anna was certain. He had promised certain reforms. The Texans decided to ask for them. From Austin's capital of San Felipe a call came for a convention to meet there on October 1, 1832.

With Austin as president, the fifty-eight delegates from sixteen settlements adopted a number of resolutions embodying the requests that to them were almost mandatory. They asked that tariff exemptions be granted for three years and that the restrictive law of April 6, 1830, be changed to permit much greater immigration from the United States. They urged that the irritating problem of clear title be settled through the appointment of a land commissioner to issue titles to the settlers. They besought the founding of primary schools where both English and Spanish would be taught. Most important of all, they asked permission to organize Texas as a single state, free of Coahuila.

But the resolutions were not presented to the government of Mexico. Santa Anna had not yet defeated Bustamante. Nor did full accord exist among the Texans themselves, for the Spanish-descended leaders in heavily Mexican San Antonio had not joined in the convention. Moreover, although the political chief thought the requests were fair, he held that the convention was unauthorized and illegal. Austin himself doubted the wisdom of offering the resolutions, particularly the one asking for statehood.

Ever the conciliator until the final breaking point, Austin sought instead to bring the Mexican and American settlers together. He persuaded the Mexicans at San Antonio and Goliad to protest by resolution the more onerous aspects of government.

This approach got him nowhere. Nor did another convention, called by restless settlers while Austin was in San Antonio, succeed. On the same day of the convention's opening, April 1, 1833, Santa Anna became president of Mexico. The date was to prove to be a grim April Fool's Day for the Texans who believed in Santa Anna. Their convention itself was noteworthy because of the appearance of the renowned Sam Houston, lately come to Texas, as a delegate from Nacogdoches. The aggressive convention repeated the requests of the gathering of 1832. A committee, with Sam Houston as chairman, drew up a state constitution to submit to the Mexican congress; it was purported to resemble the constitution of Massachusetts.

Three delegates were chosen to take the petition to Mexico City, but because of lack of funds Stephen Austin went alone, leaving in April and reaching Mexico City on July 18. Hopeful at first for the acceptance of the constitution, Austin in time despaired. The Mexican congress had adjourned, the people of Mexico City were dying by the hundreds of the cholera epidemic and Santa Anna was in the field putting down another of the unending insurrections. The scourge of cholera was also claiming the lives of many of Austin's own friends in Texas.

He was an unhappy man when he petitioned congress as it met late in September; perhaps his state of mind contributed to a reckless act. He wrote a letter to the *ayuntamiento* at Béxar urging the Mexican leaders there to form a state government without waiting for the central government to act. This was so contrary to Mexican procedure, so revolutionary that the *ayuntamiento* revealed the contents of the letter to agents of Santa Anna.

But before the government knew of the letter, Austin won repeal of the anti-immigration section of the law of April 6, 1830, a promise of an investigation of the tariffs and a recommendation by Santa Anna for legislative reforms of the court system in *Coahuila y Texas*. His request for separate statehood was turned down. The legislature of the state of *Coahuila y Texas* subsequently enacted several reform laws. The number of local courts for Texas was increased, an appellate court was created and trial by jury for criminal and civil cases was made mandatory. A modicum of religious freedom and the use of English in official documents were also granted, as was Austin's request for more local self-government in Texas.

Pleased by what he had accomplished, even though statehood had been denied, Austin left for Texas in December 1833. A few days after his departure, the central government learned of his letter to the council in San Antonio. He was overtaken at Saltillo on January 3, 1834, and brought back to Mexico City as a prisoner.

His treatment for the next eighteen months represented much of what the Texans resented. He was refused bail, although no specific charge was made against him; was placed in solitary confinement in the old Inquisition prison; and was denied permission to write to friends or even receive visitors. He had to pay his living expenses. His small cell was windowless, a single skylight admitting light for reading from ten in the morning to three in the afternoon. In April,

he was released from solitary confinement and transferred to another prison, and from there to the more comfortable city jail.

Back in Texas his compatriots raged but did not retaliate because they feared that any popular uprising would endanger his life. They did send two lawyers to Mexico City with petitions for his release and an intercessory letter from the governor. The American lawyers enlisted a Mexican attorney.

On Christmas Day, 1834, Austin was released on bond and permitted to move freely within the federal district. His passport was not approved for more than six months, although he was never charged before a court. It was finally granted when the authorities decided that his case came under a congressional general amnesty law. By the time he reached Velasco, by way of New Orleans, after an absence of two years and four months, he was convinced that Santa Anna sought naked dictatorship.

In Texas, Austin found his fellow citizens ready to fight. They had remained quiet throughout 1833 and 1834. A Mexican agent reported in 1834 that Texas would remain orderly if the settlers could win political stability.

But Santa Anna, who had been backed by the Mexican liberals and the Texans, soon deserted the groups which had supported him and allied himself with the reactionary centralists, the authoritarian churchmen and political leaders who scoffed at the idea of self-

government. The Mexican garrisons were re-established in Texas, with General Martín Perfecto de Cós, brother-in-law and appointee of Santa Anna, as commander of the eastern *Provincias Internas*. A detachment of troops was sent anew to Anáhuac and customs collectors to Brazoria in January 1835.

When a courier arrived with an announcement from General Cós that the state government had been dissolved and the governor arrested, the citizens of San Felipe seized the messenger. A letter in his pouch revealed that more troops were on the way. Hotheaded William B. Travis, with 25 men, forced the surrender of the Mexican detachment under Captain Antonio Tenorio at Anáhuac on June 29, 1835.

Even so, a majority of the Texans were not yet ready for revolution; in seven towns resolutions criticizing the capture of Captain Tenorio and his men were approved. General Cós arrested a number of abettors or participants in the capture of Tenorio. He also announced that the garrison at San Antonio would be greatly strengthened.

Inevitably those Texans who were loosely grouped together as the war party issued from Columbia a call for a convention, which was to be known as the Consultation. The peace party opposed the meeting, certain that Stephen Austin would agree with them. But soon after Austin reached Velasco on September 1, to the cheers of his fellow Texans, he announced that he favored the Consultation so that the settlers could decide in concert what course to follow. He was sure in his heart that the decision would be to fight.

The issue was simple for the war party—abandon Texas or fight for Texas. But not all Texans were yet positive that no other alternative existed. It is all but certain that between September 1 and the scheduled Consultation on October 6, 1835, Stephen Austin concluded that the Texans had no other recourse save revolution. When the Consultation set up a provisional government for the separate state of Texas it created, its headquarters were at San Felipe.

Two weeks before the Consultation was to be held at San Felipe and a week before the arrival of General Cós at San Antonio, Colonel Ugartechea issued a peremptory command to the people of the hamlet of Gonzales, Dewitt's capital on the Guadaloupe. They must surrender a brass cannon they had obtained four years before as protection against Indian attacks. The settlers refused. Ugartechea ordered a lieutenant and a hundred men to march to Gonzales and seize the cannon. They were defied at first by fewer than twenty Texans who jibed, ''Come and take it.'' Soon the number of Texans had grown to some 160 volunteers. The cannon, which had been buried in a peach orchard, was dug up.

The men of Gonzales—the Lexington of the Texas Revolution—attacked the Mexican soldiers early on the morning of October 2. Within a few minutes the troops fled, leaving behind one dead man. No Texan was hurt. The cannon itself, loaded with iron balls and pieces of chain, was fired in the skirmish, but apparently injured no one.

The issue had now been resolved. On October 9, the same day that General Cós reached San Antonio, a band of Texans captured Goliad, killing one Mexican. Random and inconclusive fighting broke out in other places. Within a few days after the affair at Gonzales, the volunteer Texan forces there had risen to some 300 men, lacking both discipline and a commander-in-chief, and with many seeking the post for which few were qualified.

The destiny of Texas might have been different had not Austin reached the encampment at Gonzales before the so-called army disintegrated. Because of his popularity and despite his lack of military experience, the unruly factions listened to him and elected him their leader. His first decision was to attack General Cós at San Antonio before he had a chance to invade the American settlements.

On October 12, Austin, with some 600 men, set out for San Antonio. Among his officers were Jim Bowie and James W. Fannin, Jr., a Texan for a year, a one-time cadet at West Point and intermittently a slave trader and Texas planter.

Bowie and Fannin headed ninety Americans in the first clash with the Mexicans on the road from Gonzales to San Antonio. With the loss of one Texan killed and another wounded, they put to flight 400 Mexicans and captured the enemy artillery. To the jubilant Texans, the routing of Mexicans was child's play, but hundreds of those who were converging now upon San Antonio would prove with their very lives that they were wrong.

In November the Texans lay siege to San Antonio. Austin decided against an assault because he lacked sufficient artillery.

It is important to remember that the besiegers who surrounded San Antonio, while their officers debated whether to starve out the Mexicans or to attack, were almost all Americans who had taken Mexican citizenship and who had lived in Texas for periods ranging up to thirteen years. They knew why they were in revolt. The volunteers under Jim Bowie knew. Fannin knew. Ben Milam, raging up from the Río Grande, knew. They had found Mexican tyranny unbearable.

But the breed of volunteers from the United States and abroad who began to stream into camp during November and December were not versed in the details of what had gone before. They had come to fight for the independence of Texas, for land, for a fresh start, for their own place in the sun, not for something with which they had previously identified themselves.

Among the arrivals in the Texan camp was a 17-year-old German lad, Herman Ehrenberg, the son of a royal official in Prussia, who had come under suspicion in his student days at Jena because of his liberal political philosophy. His was to be a charmed life.

While the Texas army shivered in the late November cold at San Antonio, all but persuaded that with the onset of winter it must abandon the siege because the men had no tents, the Texas Consultation had been seeking to do its disorderly best.

The delegates had convened at San Felipe on October 16, only to adjourn for the lack of a quorum; too many of the members were themselves at San Antonio. On November 3 the Consultation began its work. Cleavages among the members were deep and immediate. The members of the war party fought for a declaration of independence. The peace party, of which Sam Houston was the principal leader, and which generally listened to Stephen Austin, insisted that the Consultation declare that Texas was remaining loyal to Mexico itself and that the Texans were fighting to restore the constitution of 1824, which Santa Anna had abolished. When a vote was taken on November 6, fifteen delegates supported a declaration of independence; thirty-three voted to declare for the constitution of 1824 and continued allegiance to Mexico.

Out of the decision of the majority came what was known as the Declaration of November 7, 1835. In it the Texans vowed loyalty to the federal constitution of 1824, while proclaiming their opposition to Santa Anna's military dictatorship. They asked Mexican liberals to join them and asserted their intent to govern themselves only until a republican government could topple Santa Anna. They also offered land and citizenship to any who would join them in the conflict, meaning American volunteers.

The delegates then drew up a vague constitution, which they termed the Organic Law, prescribing the powers and organization of a provisional government. It was composed of a governor, a legislative body called the General Council and a court system. The worst mistake which the members of the Consultation made, and a tragic one, was to deny to the provisional government control over the volunteer army at San Antonio. The delegates designated Sam Houston commander-in-chief of the regular army when it was formed, an all-but-meaningless decision, for no standing army to speak of was enlisted during the life of the provisional government.

At San Antonio a council of war decided that the army should withdraw to Gonzales and go into winter quarters. But "Old Ben" Milam—who was 48—had a different idea and one that was pleasing to the young German, Herman Ehrenberg.

What drew Herman Ehrenberg to New Orleans, to which he worked his way after landing in New York City sometime in 1835, is unclear. Perhaps the boy heard tales of Texas in the West.

He could not have come down with the intention of fighting in a
revolution. The call had not been sounded when he reached the New
World. But on the night of October 11, 1835, drawn by 2-foot-high
posters on the streets of New Orleans, he found himself one of a
crowd of young and older men who packed Bank's Arcade coffee house
in answer to an appeal by New Orleans' Committee for Texas. The
listeners cheered the speakers, and especially the Texas representative
from Nacogdoches, Adolphus Sterne, prosperous planter, trader and
the sometime gunrunner, who had brought guns, packed in barrels,
to the Haden Edwards faction during the Fredonian rebellion.

Men who were not Texans made impromptu appeals. At the end
of the frenzied meeting $10,000 was contributed. But more than money
was needed. Members of the Committee for Texas posted another
sheet, on which volunteers were to sign. Squire Sterne, whom Herman
was pleased to discover was a native of Germany, offered to supply
rifles to the first fifty who signed up; it had been stipulated that each
volunteer should bring his own rifle, pistols and Bowie knife. Herman
was among the fifty.

The next afternoon, October 12, 1835, Herman boarded the
steamer *Washita* with the first company of the New Orleans Greys,
the initial party of volunteers to leave New Orleans for Texas. As he
later wrote in his observant, colorful memoirs:

> *Our plan was to sail up the Mississippi and the Red
> rivers, then to march or ride across country to San Antonio,
> in Texas. Although we went aboard shortly after we had en-
> listed, we had had time to provide ourselves with ready made
> clothes suitable to prairie life. The greyish color of these
> garments, which we had found in the warehouses of the city,
> accounts for the name of our company. The weapons of each
> man consisted of a rifle, pistols and the Bowie knife, famous
> in Indian wars.*

In Natchitoches the Greys were made welcome. They camped in
the thick forest beyond the town, where the citizens of Natchitoches
descended upon them with staple provisions and delicacies, and ar-
dently invited the Greys to dine with them in their homes.

But the volunteers feared that unless they hurried they would
not reach Texas in time to help the colonists. They had heard that
an early attack on San Antonio had been planned. They broke camp

in a few hours and moved along the *camino real* through woods that
were a hunter's paradise. By nine o'clock that night the Greys had
marched 42 miles. On the third day they had to skirt American troops
occupying Fort Jesup. Mexico and the United States were at peace.
The commanding officer was under orders to halt volunteers at the
border.

They spent the night at the home of a friendly planter, not far
from the border and beyond the fort's sentries, and on the next day
reached the Sabine. Cheering Texans from plantations across the
river gathered at the riverside. Among the welcomers was a pretty
Texas girl who presented the Greys with a silk banner with the inscription "To the First Company of Volunteers Sent By New Orleans
to Texas." The volunteers then transformed themselves into Texans
by kissing the soil of their new country.

Everywhere they were greeted like deliverers. At San Augustine,
on the Ayish Bayou, newly laid out on the American plan around a
courthouse square, the Greys feasted on huge beefsteaks and roasts
at big fireplaces constructed for the occasion on the streets.

Herman was the guest that night of an old settler. Outside, the
first norther of the autumn howled. Inside, before a great open fire,
the old man, his two wood-whittling sons and five of the volunteers
gathered. The young men listened while their host, a Kentuckian
and a veteran of the battle of New Orleans, regaled them with tales
of American wars. Afterward the guests slept on piles of bear and
buffalo skin, continuing their journey the next day separate from the
main body. A few weeks afterward the veteran and his sons, rifles
slung across their shoulders, caught up with the group. They had decided to fight for Texas too.

The horses they had expected awaited them at Nacogdoches. As
always, they were welcomed as saviors. But, except for the official
banquet which welcomed them, they declined all invitations, so great
was their hurry to reach San Antonio in time for the fighting.

They were forced to rest their exhausted horses and themselves at
the new settlement of Washington-on-the-Brazos just below the mouth
of the Navasota. It had a "thriving and prosperous look ... several
coffee houses, an inn and a few shops where every kind of article was
on sale from brass tacks to groceries and ready made garments" as
well as a court house and a smithy. And on and on across prairie and
through forest until the last American settlement, at Mina, later called

Bastrop, on the left bank of the Colorado on the old *camino real,* lay behind them. Between them and San Antonio stretched a hundred miles of Indian country, the land of the raiding Comanches.

The Greys encountered no Indians. But a great and destructive prairie fire threatened them; the ride across the burnt prairie where "the wind drove dark eddies of dust and ashes against us filling our eyes, mouths and noses so that we could scarcely breathe or see" was the most unpleasant part of the journey to San Antonio.

Young Ehrenberg's lively account must be skimmed over, which is unfortunate, for he wrote vividly and in detail of all he saw and heard. He and those of his companions who emigrated from Europe were amused by the easy-going soldiering of the Texans who invested San Antonio. Herman wrote:

> *There is no special regulation for the alignment of the huts or tents; each party has set up its own according to its own taste. The drum is rattling; this is the signal for the calling of the roll. Most of the volunteers are gathered around the fire, roasting raw meat at the spit. Soon a few soldiers, half-dressed, stand in line before their sergeant who, list in hand, awaits the arrival of the others. The men are without their firearms; several hold in one hand a domestic looking wooden spit, hung with a piece of roast meat, in the other the famous Bowie knife. Quite a few volunteers have failed to take their places in the line, as the position of their meat over the fire or the stage it has reached in its cooking forbids even a temporary absence. Sometimes the threatening antics of the coffee poured into the boiling water rules out attendance at the military performances now in process . . .*

However, many of the officers and men had been urging General Burleson, who had replaced Austin when the *empresario* left to raise funds in the United States, to storm San Antonio and The Alamo. His refusal spread dissatisfaction in the ranks. In his memoirs, Herman makes no bones about his contempt for Burleson who, he says, placed himself in command of the reserves when the decision to attack was finally made. Many a Texan militiaman had already packed up and left, so Ehrenberg related, before the storming of San Antonio.

The day after the decision to go into winter quarters was taken, Ben Milam, the hero of the siege, stirred the Texans and the volunteers with his summons: "Who'll follow old Ben Milam to The Alamo?" Three hundred men shouted their acceptance of his challenge. In two columns, one commanded by Ben Milam and the other by Frank W. Johnson, they broke into the town before dawn of December 5. The Mexicans offered stubborn resistance in the house-to-house battling.

Ben Milam was killed on the third day of the attack, one of two Americans killed and twenty-six wounded, so Frank Johnson, upon whom full command devolved, was to report. The Texans and volunteers slew about 150 Mexicans; into the hands of the besiegers fell badly needed supplies.

On the day that Ben Milam fell, Ehrenberg recounted that the volunteers also lost one of their best artillerymen, a former English marine named Cook:

> *The death of our Valiant Colonel Milam on the same day was another and greater tragedy. He was struck in the head by a bullet while he was standing in the yard of the house occupied by the first detachment and died instantly. We buried the two bodies quietly at night. Their funeral march was the loud, monotonous boom of the enemies' cannon while the black and idle muzzles of our silent artillery were the only tokens of grief and esteem we could give to the two brave men who had died in action.*

General Cós capitulated on December 10, the sixth day of the attack. He must have been surprised at the terms. He and his officers were required to swear that they would not interfere with the restoration of the constitution of 1824; his troops were permitted to keep their arms and enough ammunition to protect themselves against possible Indian attacks on their return to Mexico. All except convict soldiers were given permission to settle in Texas if they wished, but very few chose to do so.

Cós and his defeated army crossed the Río Grande on Christmas Day. For the time being Texas was free of Mexican troops.

Almost every Texan and volunteer knew that Santa Anna would surely invade Texas with the coming of spring, but, over-confident and quarreling, the provisional government, split by rivalries, did not get ready for him. And the self-styled Napoleon of the West came quicker than anyone believed he could, complete with mistress and silver chamber pot.

Politically paramount still was the issue of whether or not to declare independence from Mexico. During December 1835, the citizens of several Texas towns voted for independence—among these the ninety-one men of Goliad, who, on December 20 signed the Goliad Declaration of Independence. In January 1836, Austin and Houston themselves came out for independence; and on March 1, 1836, a convention at Washington-on-the-Brazos made up of fifty-nine delegates issued the Texas Declaration of Independence.

The hour was late. By then Santa Anna was already besieging The Alamo. Sam Houston, delegate to the convention, was again elected commander-in-chief. He left the convention on March 6 to take command of whatever troops were in the field.

That day The Alamo fell. By forced marches, which attested to the endurance of his thinly-clad Indians and *mestizos,* and after elaborate preparations, Santa Anna had crossed the Río Grande on February 12. His army's vanguard reached San Antonio in an incredible eleven days.

Texas was about to enter upon its darkest hours. Not many of the first volunteers who followed the *camino real* lived to see the dawn of freedom. Herman Ehrenberg was one. He was not among the defenders of The Alamo, but he did survive the butchery of the unarmed prisoners of Goliad.

The Alamo . . . Goliad . . . massacre, panic and a day of triumphant reckoning.

CHAPTER TWENTY

ALAMO COLLOQUY

THERMOPYLAE...the Vale of Roncevalles...Balaclava ... Chapultepec...Little Round Top...Verdun...Stalingrad...Tarawa ... Chosen Reservoir.

They are not simply episodes in man's political and military history. They, and many another moment in eternity, endure as reminders of the magnificence of the human spirit. They inspire and reassure and give commonality to courage. And none more so than the siege of The Alamo at dilapidated San Antonio from February 23 to March 6, 1836—The Alamo that was a Franciscan mission, Spanish *presidio* and American fort, and now is a shrine to man's willingness to die for a good cause or a poor one or because he won't be pushed around. The Alamo speaks for each of these reasons why men will themselves to stand and kill, and be killed.

No American folk tale or legend or historical fact is more memorable or more remembered, none was more contributory to the inevitable spanning of the American continent. So often has the tale been told that nothing can now be added.

The situation—a small and determined body of men surrounded by overwhelming forces—was not unusual. Unconditional surrender was demanded; the alternative was death by the sword when the fort was taken. In the final assault, perhaps 1,800 Mexicans stormed into The Alamo.

The besieged Alamo garrison had been increased on March 1 by the arrival of thirty-two men and boys from tiny Gonzales, who broke through the Mexican lines in the nighttime and took their places on the parapets; and by the return of a gallant courier, James Butler Bonham, who had ridden out of The Alamo to bear William Barret Travis' desperate plea for aid and whose honor made him return to what he knew was certain death.

One man inside the fort, an English veteran of the Napoleonic wars named Louis Rose, took a different course. He availed himself of the offer of Colonel Travis that any man could try to escape who wished to do so. He did escape. Some fifteen non-combatants, mostly women and children but also among them Joe, Travis' Negro slave, were spared; so too, incredibly, was one Mexican defender who pretended to have been held in The Alamo under duress.

The bodies of all of the men who died within The Alamo were burned save one, that of a Mexican who was buried out of respect to his kinsmen. No one knows the number of Mexicans who lost their lives at the hands of the last-ditch defenders. General Antonio López de Santa Anna, president of the tyrannous Republic of Mexico, who could lie as deliberately as he could murder or switch sides, made a face-saving report that fewer than a hundred were killed and 223 wounded. Texans then and later claimed up to 1,500 killed and wounded. The number was probably somewhat under a thousand.

But numbers are not important here. Before they went down at the end of the thirteen-day siege under the joint command of Colonel Travis and Colonel James Bowie, Texans made casualties of at least one-third of the attacking Mexicans.

Such is the stark outline. It is not enough.

Question now the men on the roll of The Alamo dead.

Who were you? Rich man, poor man, beggar man, thief, doctor, lawyer, merchant?

We were all there, and others; clerks, a hatmaker, a shoemaker, a blacksmith, a painter, a poet, down-at-heels immigrants, adventurous boys, farmers, vagabond hell raisers. Until the men and boys from Gonzales came, fewer than a dozen of us were citizens of Texas. We came from eighteen states, from England, from Ireland, from Wales, from Scotland, from Denmark, from nowhere that we would talk about. Not all of us were Anglo-Americans or Nordic. Men in whose veins ran the blood of Spaniard and Indian died beside the men of the northern countries. Whatever else had brought us to Texas, we died in a common cause and, whatever the other considerations, for a common love—the love of freedom.

Why were you so few; why did not reinforcements come?

We had come in answer to a call. That is why there were so few
of us. At first, only the few answered the call. Here at The Alamo
there might have been more, but Colonel Fannin changed his mind
and returned to Goliad to die in a massacre greater in numbers and
more deliberately savage than that of The Alamo. Santa Anna was
taking no prisoners. Yet there were thousands of Anglos in Texas—
three Texans out of four—and others, not Anglos, to whom freedom
or license had also become precious. These waited until they could
wait no longer, until we of The Alamo and the men of Goliad were
dead. The Republic of Texas then was all but surely dead also. Many
fled and some remained to fight under Sam Houston at a place called
San Jacinto.

Why did you not leave when you could?

That's hard to tell, all in one breath. Most of us thought we had
to make a stand, and San Antone was the only fortified place anywhere in Texas. Besides, we thought more of our folks were coming.
We didn't believe that the Mexicans could come so far so fast. Sam
Houston sent word that we ought to evacuate and we might have paid
attention until Jim Bowie came along with his men. Then we knew
we'd stay in The Alamo and fight. We counted on more help than
we got. But some people don't like to run, and we were amongst them.
And maybe we were a mite cocky too.

Living, how did you live at The Alamo?

Different ways, you might say. Some of the boys were highstrung
and hotblooded. There were pretty girls in the town. Some of us were
hard drinkers—Jim Bowie was one of them when the spell was on
him and he thought of his dead family—and there was plenty enough
to drink, pulque and raw whiskey and beer and wine. And cards and
dice. There was big McGregor with his bagpipes—wasn't but a few
of us that had heard bagpipes, and they from foreign parts—and
Davy Crockett with his fiddle and his everlasting jokes and tale-
spinning. He kept us laughing almost to the last. For some there was
the Bible to read and some had brought books along. Colonel Travis,
he mostly wrote messages and they were good ones. Jim Bowie mainly
tried to keep alive. A lot of us practiced at things we didn't know
much about before, like sighting a cannon and building parapets.
Some of the young ones had to be cautioned, and some of the older
ones, too, about staying out all the time with the Mexican girls and

taking on liquor and trading anything they had for whatever they
wanted. You might say it was generally fun until hell broke loose.

Dying here, how did you die?

Dying hurts. There was grunting and groaning, some screaming
too and praying here and there at the end. But none of that takes
away from us. You might say we died like men, leastways almost all
of us. Some tried to get away at the very last. They didn't make it.
You can't rightly call that cowardice. There was talk later that Davy
Crockett and some of his boys tried to surrender. We'd call that a
damn lie. He didn't strike us like being that kind of man, no matter
what some of those Mexicans said. It was their business to low-rate
our best ones. But dying comes hard to any man unless it takes him
unawares, so he don't know what hit him—musket shot or artillery
shell or bayonet. It must have been hardest for Jim Bowie, already
dying, sitting in bed with a pistol in each hand, waiting. But he didn't
wait long. It didn't take long, whichever way you look at it, not even
for the six who were found alive, hiding under some mattresses.

You volunteers of Gonzales, why did you enter The Alamo?

Somebody had to go. Our leaders wanted to. We all wanted to.
We had a thirteen-year-old boy, a fifteen-year-old boy, a sixteen-year-
old boy along. They knew why. We didn't go just to get ourselves
killed. We thought others would come along. We reckon there was
reason why they didn't. But we wish they had. The Alamo fellows
was glad to see us that night when we sneaked through the stunted
mesquite. Our women wasn't glad when we left. Before it was all
over we wasn't glad either. Still, like you say, somebody had to do it.
So we did.

Did all of you men of The Alamo die fighting?

Not all, but nearly all, more than Santa Anna expected. None
died at all until the storming. The pickets went first, surprised. The
few who tried for a getaway in the last minutes, with everyone blasted
off the parapet, were caught. They were shot. Some say a few others
tried to surrender. That was Mexican talk, mostly. Don't believe it.
We don't. Only one quit before the fight was over. An English fellow.
He took the chance that Travis gave him. He got away. He'd done a
lot of fighting before, even against that Frenchman, Napoleon. We
reckon he thought he could fight again another day.

What of the enemy?

They kept coming, them little fellows, under their red, white and green flag with the eagle. God, they kept coming. The foot soldiers in their dirty whites, the cavalrymen and the grenadiers, artillerymen dolled up like tin soldiers, only they weren't. Looked like most of them knew how to die; we taught them that didn't. We've got to admit that they were brave *hombres*. But that Santa Anna. Him and his red flag and his bugle calling. He liked to see men die. He liked to see them after they were dead. God damn his soul.

And to what avail?

Ask Santa Anna. At San Jacinto he remembered The Alamo.

Let us summon now the shadows of the 182 men, or it may have been 183, who fell before the Mexican musket and bayonet and cannon shot—weapons wielded by men who also were brave and willing to die, with the terrible shrilling of the *deguello,* the no-quarter trumpet call, insistent in the ears of the slayers and the slain, and all about them the prairie awaiting the lush spring grasses and the primroses and violets.

Beat, drummer, the roll call of the dead. Bugler, sound the requiem.

Juan Abamillo—He was a Mexican of San Antonio. He must have loved freedom.

R. Allen—Where he came from or why he was here is not recorded.

Miles De Forest Andross—He turned up from San Patricio. Only this is certain.

Micajah Autry—A poet, musician and artist, this one, and a teacher and lawyer too. A year earlier he had written his wife back in North Carolina: "I will go the whole Hog in the cause of Texas." He died at the stockade with Crockett's Tennessee Volunteers.

Juan A. Badillo—Another San Antonio Mexican and enemy of tyranny. That is all.

Peter James Bailey—They knew only that he hailed from Kentucky and Arkansas.

Isaac G. Baker—He trudged to The Alamo with the men of Gonzales.

William Charles M. Baker—He was a Bowie man, a Missourian and a member of the Volunteers, whose last home was Mississippi.

John J. Ballentine—Nothing except that he was there and had come from Bastrop.

Richard W. Ballentine—A farm boy from Marengo County in Alabama, he had hurried as fast as he could. It was fast enough.

John J. Baugh—A captain, a dreamer from Virginia. He was the adjutant. It was he who from the north wall shouted the first alarm in the darkness. He commanded the last stand in the barracks.

Joseph Bayliss—They say he came from Tennessee.

John Blair—He too hailed from Tennessee.

Samuel B. Blair—Back in Tennessee he had been handy at improvising. He was 29 and chief of ordnance. He chopped up horseshoes for cannon shot.

William Blazeby—He had sailed for New York from England to seek his fortune. Somehow he got to Texas in time.

James Butler Bonham—He was one of the giants, this handsome, rebellious aristocrat of South Carolina and Alabama. He had formed and led the Mobile Braves to Texas. He died beside the twelve-pounders on the high platform of the church. He and William Travis were two of a kind. He rode out to fetch James Fannin and his men. He need not have ridden back to death. But he did.

Daniel Bourne—If he tarried between England and Texas, it is not set down. Perhaps he just liked the smell of trouble.

James Bowie—He was the heroes' hero, the tall, redheaded alligator rider, slaver and speculator. Did he think at the end, as the musket balls entered his body and the bayonets dipped, of the golden hair of María Ursula de Veramendi?

Jesse B. Bowman—He was a Red River man.

George Brown—He may have come with Daniel Bourne. He was English too.

James Brown—They put down that he was a Pennsylvanian.

Robert Brown—Perhaps he told some where he came from, but no one remembers.

James Buchanan—Did someone mourn in Alabama?

Samuel E. Burns—He was an Irishman who came a long way looking for a donnybrook.

George D. Butler—Beside his name, only Missouri.

Robert Campbel—Count him among the one in six who came from Tennessee.

John Cane—Pennsylvania ... Here.

William R. Carey—He was a volunteer from Maryland, a gay captain of artillery with an eye for the señoritas of San Antonio. At the last he was in the barracks and his weapon was a rifle.

Charles Henry Clark—He was a Missouri man.

M. B. Clark—He knew Texas. He came from Nacogdoches.

Daniel William Cloud—The practice of law hadn't been easy in Kentucky nor in Illinois or Missouri. It was better in the Red River country of Arkansas. But Sam Houston had called for good men with good rifles and a hundred rounds of ammunition. And to Daniel Cloud "the cause of philanthropy, of humanity, of liberty and human happiness throughout the world calls loudly on every man who can aid Texas." They remembered him with a prideful resolution in Russellville, Kentucky.

Robert E. Cochran—There was nothing in Texas to put him in mind of New Jersey.

George Washington Cottle—He was Wash Cottle from Missouri and a good Indian fighter.

Henry Courtman—He was a young German, as was Herman Ehrenberg, and he had come on a Pittsburgh steamboat by way of the Ohio and the Mississippi to join the Volunteers in New Orleans. Best of all he liked a mug of beer and clear Rhine wine.

Lemuel Crawford—South Carolina . . . Here.

David Crockett—"I have come to your country, though not, I hope, through any selfish motive whatever," he had said in February in San Antonio. "I have come to aid you all that I can in your noble cause. I shall identify myself with your interest, and all the honor that I desire is that of defending as a high private, in common with my fellow citizens, the liberties of our common country." He was already a rip-snorting legend. He was the man in the coonskin cap and buckskin shirt, the bear hunter who joked and sang and told tall tales and became a Congressman from Tennessee. The Democrats licked him in 1835. He decided to come to Texas to look around, and get away from Washington and Tennessee. He didn't come to fight for Texas, but he stayed for her, he and his twelve Tennessee boys—and they liked their name, the Tennessee Company of Mounted Volunteers.

Robert Crossman—He was a Massachusetts Yankee who had moved to Louisiana.

David P. Cummings—His Pennsylvania father was a friend of Sam Houston's and well enough off to give the boy a box of rifles. David

turned them over to the Texas government. He had been off pros-
pecting land when Santa Anna struck, but he made it back to the
fort with the men of Gonzales.

Robert Cunningham—A New Yorker born, he journeyed south by flatboat from his solid family's Indiana home to join up in New
Orleans.

Jacob C. Darst—He had left his Missouri farm with his wife and two
children in August 1830 by oxcart, seeking the promised land. He
found it at Gonzales, and from Gonzales he marched to The Alamo.

Freeman H. K. Day—He too signed up with the men of Gonzales.

Jerry C. Day—Missouri . . . Here.

Squire Daymon—Tennessee . . . Here.

William Dearduff—Tennessee . . . Here.

Stephen Denison—He was a friendly Galway Irishman who glazed
and painted and odd-jobbed his way to Louisiana with no thought
at first of volunteering.

Charles Despallier—A Louisiana Creole, one of two of his breed who
was there, and a brave man who helped to burn the slums of La
Villita, where The Alamo soldiers' families had lived, under the
walls of The Alamo, the better to see to shoot.

Almeron Dickinson—Tennessean by way of Pennsylvania, blacksmith
and natural born artilleryman, he had helped defend the cannon at
Gonzales in October. He died beside his own cannon on the high
platform. In the last minutes of his life he embraced his wife,
Suzanna, huddled with their little daughter, Angelina, in the
sacristy. "If they spare you, Sue, save my child," he had said.
His widow and baby lived.

John H. Dillard—Tennessean, in search of adventure.

James R. Dimpkins—It was known that he was an Englishman.

Lewis Duel—It was the Texas fever that brought this Manhattan
plasterer here, perhaps in search of work.

Andrew Duvalt—He was an Irishman of no long residence in the
New World.

Carlos Espalier—He is down as a San Antonian. What of Charles
Despallier of Louisiana? A kinsman? The same man? The answer is
lost in the haunted air.

Gregorio Esparza—His family bore a good name in San Antonio. The
Esparzas were loyal to Santa Anna, all but Gregorio. The troops
from Matamoras bayoneted him within the church, but his family,

for their allegiance, were permitted to inter him. He was the only defender to receive Christian burial. All the other bodies were burned.

Robert Evans—He was Irish born, a New Yorker. In the last minutes, wounded, he crawled with a torch toward the powder room. He didn't make it.

Samuel B. Evans—Kentucky . . . Here.

James L. Ewing—Tennessee . . . Here.

William Fishbaugh—Gonzales . . . Here.

John Flanders—His Massachusetts father determined to foreclose a mortgage on a friend's property. Young John objected. He decided to leave home, drifted from New Orleans to Gonzales and liked it there.

Dolphin Ward Floyd—He was a bored North Carolina farm boy who went West to catch a rich, old widow and caught the Texas fever instead. He settled down in Gonzales with a widow neither old nor wealthy. He was happy.

John Hubbard Forsyth—He never cared about anything much after his wife died on Christmas Day in 1828 and he hadn't taken to the study of medicine. So he left his baby boy with his upstate New York father and he reached The Alamo with Travis on February 3, just in time, eight years later.

Antonio Fuentes—He was in jail in San Antonio that February, but drunken Jim Bowie got him out over Travis' objection, which seemed, at the time, like the deliverance of God.

Galba Fuqua—He was sixteen, a Gonzales youngster. The Gonzales boy died fighting, his jaws already shattered by a bullet, and Sue Dickinson never knew what it was he tried to tell her in the final moments. Something about her husband, perhaps.

William H. Furtleroy—He drifted in from Kentucky and Arkansas. Maybe he hoped for a farm of his own.

William Garnett—He was a wandering Baptist preacher from Virginia who left The Alamo for Velasco to clean up some business. He got back for the rendezvous with his Maker.

James W. Garrand—Louisiana . . . Here.

James Girard Garrett—Tennessee . . . Here.

John E. Garvin—Gonzales . . . Here.

John E. Gaston—He was sixteen. In Gonzales they called him Johnny. He had watched the fight for the cannon from a perch in a live oak tree. Some knew him as Johnny Davis because his mother had married again to a man named Davis. It didn't matter to him.

James George—Gonzales ... Here.

John Camp Goodrich—His was a good family in Tennessee. His brothers, Benjamin and Edmund, kept away from the trouble.

Albert Calvin Grimes—Georgia ... Here.

James C. Gwynne—He was an Englishman. He had come to Mississippi and so identified himself.

James Hannum—Refugio, Texas ... Here.

John Harris—Kentucky ... Here.

Andrew Jackson Harrison—If he told anyone where he came from, it was not recalled.

William B. Harrison—Ohio ... Here.

Joseph M. Hawkins—He was an Irishman who had made Louisiana his home.

John M. Hays—Tennessee ... Here.

Charles M. Heiskell—Tennessee ... Here.

Thomas Hendrix—From no one knows where ... Here.

Patrick Henry Herndon—Virginia ... Here.

William D. Hersee—New York ... Here.

Tapley Holland—Grimes County, Texas ... Here.

Samuel Holloway—Pennsylvania ... Here.

William D. Howell—Massachusetts ... Here.

William Daniel Jackson—He was an Irish sailor without a ship, and the liquor and girls of San Antonio were reason enough to stick around.

Thomas Jackson—Kentucky ... Here.

Green B. Jameson—He was a Kentucky lawyer who was good with tools and the Texas fever struck him, too. He was proud of the motley force which he served—they called him Benito—and he turned engineer for them and made The Alamo something of a fort. Bowie sent him to parley with Santa Anna, but the general wouldn't talk.

Gordon C. Jennings—Missouri ... Here.

Lewis Johnson—What was a Welshman doing in Texas?

William Johnson—Pennsylvania ... Here.

John Jones—New York ... Here.

Johnnie Kellogg—He was 19 and a Gonzales boy too. He had taken pretty Sidney Gaston, who was Johnny Gaston's sister, away from her husband. The jilted spouse marched along with Johnnie anyway.

James Kenny—Virginia . . . Here.

Andrew Kent—He and his wife, Elizabeth, had left the Missouri farm years before. They had five children now.

Joseph Kerr—Louisiana . . . Here.

George C. Kimball—He was a hatter by trade from New York and his little factory was doing well in Gonzales. He was happy with Prudence Nash, the widow he made his wife, and he could think of the baby son and another baby on the way. The Gonzales men made him their leader. He died with the Gonzales remnant in the barracks.

William P. King—He was 15. But at Gonzales he persuaded George Kimball to let him go in his father's stead. After all, there were nine children.

William Irvine Lewis—He was a Philadelphian and 23, and he was visiting in North Carolina when the call came from Texas for volunteers.

William J. Lightfoot—Virginia . . . Here.

Jonathan L. Lindley—Back in Illinois his father had heard that Mexico awarded 160 additional acres for every child of a settler. The old man had eleven. Jonathan was a surveyor in Gonzales when the time came.

William Linn—He had set out from Boston for Texas alone. He joined up with the New Orleans Greys before they left the city.

George Washington Main—Virginia . . . Here.

William T. Malone—He was 18 when he got drunk in Georgia and the next day he decided on Texas instead of facing his father. The pleasures of San Antonio were much to his liking.

William Marshall—Arkansas by way of Tennessee . . . Here.

Albert Martin—A captain, a Gonzales man who, with George Kimball, led his fellow citizens out of the town. He had helped repulse the Mexicans at Gonzales, in fact, had buried the disputed cannon. He bore Travis' message from The Alamo "to the People of Texas and all Americans in the world." He rode from The Alamo to Gonzales, with Travis' message, and he rode back with the men of Gonzales.

Edward McCafferty—San Patricio . . . Here.

Jesse McCoy—He was with the Gonzales men when they taught some Comanche raiders a lesson. He had been sheriff before he went out to The Alamo.

William McDowell—A Pennsylvanian, he rode down from Pennsylvania with his friend, John Purdy Reynolds, after the call to "come forward and assist your brethren." Before Texas, they had founded a settlement in Tennessee; they called it Mifflin after their home county. He entered Texas with Davy Crockett's Tennessee company.

James McGee—Ireland . . . Here.

John McGregor—A Scotsman from Nacogdoches, he was a braw man on the bagpipes and he taught the girls of San Antonio to dance to them. He and Crockett kept spirits up with their fiddle and bagpipe duels.

Robert McKinney—Ireland . . . Here.

Eliel Melton—He was the quartermaster, this South Carolinian, a good hand at butchering cattle. He and a few others tried to get away, jumping from the palisade when the Mexicans stormed over the walls. It was no use. The Mexican lancers ran most of them down. The rest were found later and executed.

Thomas R. Miller—He came from Virginia and he was the richest man in Gonzales, and middle-aged. Young Johnnie Kellogg had taken his wife away from him.

William Mills—Tennessee and Arkansas . . . Here.

Isaac Millsaps—His was a good name in Mississippi and in Gonzales. He was forty-one, with a wife who was blind and seven young ones. But he went.

Edward F. Mitchusson—Kentucky . . . Here.

Edwin T. Mitchell—Kentucky . . . Here.

Napoleon B. Mitchell—No one put down where he was from.

Robert B. Moore—He was the oldest at fifty-five, a Virginian who joined the Greys in New Orleans.

Willis Moore—Raymond, Mississippi . . . Here.

Robert Musselman—He had just finished fighting the Seminoles, but he didn't want to go back to Ohio. So he had set out for Texas.

Andres Nava—San Antonio . . . Here.

George Neggan—South Carolina . . . Here.

Andrew M. Nelson—South Carolina . . . Here.

Edward Nelson—South Carolina . . . Here.

George Nelson—South Carolina also. Were they brothers?

James Northcross—Virginia . . . Here.

James Nowlin—Ireland . . . Here.

George Pagan—Mississippi . . . Here.

Christopher Parker—Mississippi . . . Here.

William Parks—San Patricio . . . Here.

Richardson Perry—Here.

Amos Pollard—The Texas call was strong. Young Dr. Pollard quit his practice in New York and wound up in New Orleans, well before the call. He was The Alamo's surgeon and he tried to cure Jim Bowie. He was killed treating the wounded in his hospital on the second floor of the long barracks.

John Purdy Reynolds—He was William McDowell's friend. They came down together from Pennsylvania and he had held the rank of major before the fighting ever began.

Thomas H. Roberts—Here.

James Robertson—Tennessee . . . Here.

Isaac Robinson—Scotland . . . Here.

James M. Rose—He was a high-spirited nephew of the James Madison who had been President. It was he who stammered out the news on February 26 that Santa Anna's cavalrymen were in sight. He was Davy Crockett's friend and, when the Texans burned the slums of La Villita, he came close to being the first man to die.

Jackson J. Rusk—Ireland . . . Here.

Joseph Rutherford—Kentucky . . . Here.

Isaac Ryan—Louisiana . . . Here.

Mial Scurlock—Louisiana . . . Here.

Marcus L. Sewell—English and a shoemaker. He had been doing well in Gonzales.

Manson Shied—Georgia . . . Here.

Cleland Kinloch Simmons—He was a Charleston aristocrat who had pledged himself "to defend our brethren at the peril of our lives, liberties, and fortunes." He and his dismounted cavalrymen died in the barracks.

Andrew H. Smith—Tennessee . . . Here.

Charles S. Smith—Maryland . . . Here.

Josiah G. Smith—North Carolina and Tennessee . . . Here.

William H. Smith—Nacogdoches . . . Here.

Richard Starr—England . . . Here.

James E. Stewart—England . . . Here.

Richard L. Stockton—Virginia . . . Here.

A. Spain Summerlin—Tennessee and Arkansas . . . Here.

William D. Sutherland—His Alabama mother wrote to her sister: "Oh, yes he is gone. My poor boy is gone, gone from me. The 6th day of March he was slain in The Alamo..."

Edward Taylor, George Taylor, James Taylor—They were brothers from Liberty, Texas, and inseparable.

William Taylor—Tennessee ... Here.

B. Archer M. Thomas—Kentucky ... Here.

Henry Thomas—Germany ... Here.

Jesse G. Thompson—Arkansas ... Here.

John W. Thomson—North Carolina and Tennessee ... Here.

John M. Thurston—Pennsylvania and Kentucky ... Here.

Burke Trammel—Irish, from Tennessee ... Here.

William Barret Travis—We have met him before. "I shall never surrender or retreat," he wrote. He had been a braggart and a gambler and lover, a flashy dresser, but not here.

George W. Tumlinson—Missouri ... Here.

Asa Walker—So great was this Tennessee youngster's hurry to reach The Alamo that he borrowed a benefactor's overcoat and gun without consent, leaving his clothing as security.

Jacob Walker—He was a gunner, a Nacogdoches man who liked to talk about his young ones. Four Mexican soldiers shot him and hoisted his body on their bayonets like a bale of hay in Sue Dickinson's room while she watched.

William B. Ward—Ireland ... Here.

Henry Warnell—He was different from all the rest, a redheaded, hard-drinking, tobacco-chewing, loud-mouthed jockey who left a girl and a baby behind him in Arkansas. He said during the siege, thinking perhaps of the wild nights in San Antone: "I don't like to be penned up like this." But he was a good artilleryman and he talked horses almost until the end. Some even say he escaped, grievously wounded, and made his way to Port Lavaca, where he died.

Joseph G. Washington—Tennessee ... Here.

Thomas Waters—England ... Here.

William Wells—Georgia ... Here.

Isaac White—Kentucky ... Here.

Robert White—He was a Gonzales man ... Here.

Hiram J. Williamson—He was a fiddle-footed bachelor from Philadelphia with talent as a drillmaster.

David L. Wilson—Scotland . . . Here.

John Wilson—Pennsylvania . . . Here.

Antony Wolfe—He was a gunner and English-born. The Mexican bayonets didn't overlook his two little boys.

Claiborne Wright—North Carolina . . . Here.

Charles Zanco—He was a long way from Denmark when he died.

So with the roll. And in it every manner of man save professional soldier. They died well, almost all of them, in what Santa Anna pretended to dismiss as "a small affair."

A week after New Orleans learned of the fall of The Alamo this poster, adorned with twin cornucopias of plenty, was plastered along the city's streets:

TEXAS!!

Emigrants who are desirous of assisting
Texas at this important crisis of her affairs
may have a free passage and equipments
by applying at the

NEW-YORK AND PHILADELPHIA HOTEL,

on the OLD LEVEE, *near the Blue Stores.*

Now is the time to insure a fortune in Land:
To all who remain in Texas during the War
*   will*
Be allowed 1,280 Acres.
To all who remain Six Months, 640 Acres.
To all who remain Three Months, 320
*   Acres.*
And as Colonists, 4600 Acres for a family
*   and 1470 Acres for a Single Man.*

New Orleans, April 23, 1836.

Before the settlers came in numbers, the Texans would know terror and mad flight and, at the providential last, vengeance and victory at a place named San Jacinto.

CHAPTER TWENTY-ONE

THE TORTURED ROAD
TO FREEDOM

AFTER THE FALL of San Antonio, the puppet government of Santa Anna had issued, on December 30, 1835, a punitive decree the ferocity of which would in the end make it fail of its purpose. All armed foreigners who entered Mexico with the intention of attacking the government would be executed as pirates upon capture. This was calculated terrorism, its purpose to deter the onrushing volunteers or, if the American invaders persisted, to put them to the sword. Between the departure of the New Orleans Greys and the Tampico Blues and the Texan retribution at San Jacinto, no fewer than 800 volunteers died. Some fell in no-quarter fighting, as with Travis and Bowie and Crockett at The Alamo; most of the rest were executed in cold blood after being taken prisoner.

The first invaders to be murdered, and this even before the edict, were twenty-eight men of the Tampico Blues, three companies of whom had been recruited at Banks Arcade in New Orleans on October 13, 1835, the night after the New Orleans Greys came into being. They sailed on the *Mary Jane* from New Orleans on November 6 under the command of the liberal Mexican general, José Antonio Mexía, whom Stephen Austin had convinced of the loyalty of the Texans to the constitution of 1824, and were bound for Tampico, from where Mexía hoped to arouse the eastern *Provincias Internas* to insurrection.

The *Mary Jane* ran aground off the Tampico bar in mid-November. A premature uprising of the Mexican garrison and the arrival of loyalist reinforcements influenced Mexía to attack Tampico on November 15. Defeated, he withdrew to an American schooner with most of his troops. Thirty-one men were left behind as prisoners. Three of these died of their wounds. The others were tried as pirates and shot on December 14.

Next came the turn of the Matamoras expedition. This was a foolish and fateful foray, entered upon by mostly idle, reckless and plunder-bent men—a majority volunteers from the United States who had found time heavy on their hands after the fall of San Antonio and who listened to Dr. James Grant and other American speculators in land below the Río Grande.

An attack upon Matamoras had also been urged by Mexican liberals and military men, and by Texas' first American governor, Henry Smith, and General Sam Houston, who on December 17 sent an order to James Bowie to take command of the venture. Later the general council itself requested Houston to lead the invaders. Bowie never received the order and Houston, impatient and discouraged over the lack of discipline and the bickering among the political leaders, refused the command. Small bands of volunteers and some Texans under the command of Colonel James W. Fannin, Jr., Francis W. Johnson and Dr. Grant went their several ways toward Matamoras.

James Fannin's Goliad campaign was a tragic bumble from beginning to end, its sequel more tragic still. Operating separately and aloof from the smaller components of the Matamoras expedition, he landed at Copano, the port to the south of Goliad, on February 2, 1836, three weeks before the beginning of the siege of The Alamo. Under him were some 200 men, four companies of the Georgia battalion of volunteers and a lesser number of Texans.

Another 200 men were standing by at Refugio, site of the last Spanish mission established in Texas and now settled by an *empresario*. The ill-fated Grant and Johnson, with their sixty volunteers, were encamped at San Patricio, an Irish and Mexican town on the Nueces. Captain Jack Shackelford's company of Red Rover and other volunteers, to the number of eighty, waited Fannin's summons on the Lavaca. One hundred men in two companies, commanded by Captain Amasa Turner, camped at the mouth of the Brazos, ready to report to Fannin at Copano. The New York Battalion of 190 men was delayed. The British had held them in their brig, the *Mattawankeag*, in the Bahamas, for two months on charges of piracy, but they entered the mouth of the Mississippi on February 12. The rest of the force-in-being was composed of a company of regulars, occupying the old *presidio* of Nuestra Señora de Loreto at Goliad, under Francis W. Thornton.

Back at The Alamo this early February were also 150 men under James C. Neill, charged with the defense of Béxar and The Alamo. Brought together they would have made up a formidable force for the times and place.

Sam Houston was on furlough. Fannin, in Copano as agent of the provisional government to organize the Matamoras expedition, was Texas' senior army officer. On February 4 and 5 he marched his men to the Texas camp at Refugio. There he learned the next day that Santa Anna was already on the march to destroy Texas.

Fannin removed his headquarters to Goliad, leaving behind him John Chenoweth with a few mounted men to guard Copano, and Amon King and his minute company at Refugio. Shackelford joined Fannin at Goliad with the men of Lavaca.

Now came the first disaster. The schooner carrying Amasa Turner and his 100 men and a great supply of munitions, clothing and shoes for Fannin's volunteers, was wrecked on February 5 on the Brazos bar. Turner and his men occupied themselves in trying to salvage the desperately needed cargo.

Fannin had decided to withdraw to Goliad because of his "conviction of its importance, as being advantageously located for a depot of reenforcements, clothing, provisions, and military stores." It commanded the seacoast and protected the only convenient landing for sizeable vessels. And certainly Goliad was a vital key to the invasion of Texas. The decision was literally fatal.

Meanwhile, Santa Anna had collected his men and mules, and four-wheeled wagons, and 200 two-wheeled carts for the advance upon The Alamo.

Late in January, Santa Anna's right wing under General José Urrea, an honorable soldier, had concentrated at Matamoras for provisions and reenforcements. On February 13, ten days before Santa Anna reached The Alamo, Urrea threaded toward San Patricio in search of Johnson's and Grant's raiders, who were now reenforced by William G. Cooke's two companies. Cooke notified Fannin on February 9 that Johnson and Grant and their sixty men had left on a rash foray into Tamaulipas, declining to serve under Fannin. The defectors left behind three cannon and some ammunition. Fannin sent Captain Burr H. Duval to fetch the artillery and ammunition, with orders to

Cooke to return with the party to Goliad. The group reached Goliad on February 19.

It was then that Travis sent from The Alamo the heroic James Butler Bonham to Goliad to request support from Fannin. Fannin played with the thought of removing his headquarters to Béxar or of reenforcing the garrison. But he did nothing, thereby insuring the massacre of The Alamo and, as it turned out, of his own men and himself at Goliad.

Fannin continued instead to direct his men in the refurbishing and strengthening of the ancient fort. He was still working when Travis' second appeal for help reached Goliad on February 25.

It must be said in Fannin's behalf that he planned to march for The Alamo the next day with 320 volunteers, leaving behind Chenoweth's mounted riflemen from Copano to hold the Cíbolo crossing, and summoning Captain King's company from Refugio to strengthen Goliad. But the relief expedition got no farther than 2 miles from the Goliad fort, where a wagon broke down, oxen wandered off and provisions proved scarce. Fannin returned to Goliad to continue its strengthening.

Fate struck again the next day. Johnson had returned to San Patricio on February 26 from his foray into Tamaulipas. His thirty-four men, with a hundred fresh horses, were scattered at five separate sites within the village. The fast-moving Mexican General Urrea surprised them before daybreak and all, save Johnson and four others who escaped, were killed. On March 21 Grant's party, which had accompanied Johnson on the freebooting expedition, was ambushed at Agua Dulce creek. The Mexicans killed Grant and thirteen of his men and captured six others. Only six escaped.

Much too late, Fannin realized that his little army could aid no one by remaining within the walls of the fort at Goliad. Copano had been sealed off. Travis was beleaguered in The Alamo. Fannin at last saw clearly what lay ahead. His only reasonable course was to withdraw from Goliad. He wrote on March 1 to James W. Robinson, lieutenant governor and acting governor:

> *I learn from several sources that as soon as Bexar is retaken [by the Mexicans], they next march here and thus complete their chain of communication to the interior and the Gulf. I am resolved to await your orders, let the conse-*

*quence be what it may.... I should be pleased to have one
more express from Washington [on-the-Brazos] and if we
are not to be sustained in a proper manner, and in good
time, receive orders to fall back to the provisions and on the
colonies, and let us all go together.... I have orders from
you not to make a retrograde movement, but to await orders
and reenforcements. If a large force gets here, and in possession of the provisions in stores now on Matagorda, being all
now in Texas, it will be a desperate game for us all.*

Here Fannin glossed over the situation. Robinson's order not
to retreat was accompanied by other orders to hold his position at
Copano and, if possible, at San Patricio. Fannin essayed the defense
of neither. Nor was Robinson's directive mandatory in case superior
forces attacked Fannin. It is more than likely that he gave in to the
spirit of his men who, having made of Goliad a fort they believed
impregnable, wanted to defend it. And Fannin believed that a letter
of his own to Robinson on February 7, telling of the advance of Santa
Anna, would bring the Texas settlers pell-mell to Goliad. But he did
not realize that the convention of 1836 was living in a fool's paradise,
believing, even as late as March 5, that he and Travis had united and
that The Alamo was secure. A day later The Alamo's defenders
were dead.

So, within Fort Defiance, as Fannin had renamed his stronghold,
he and his men prepared for siege. Ammunition and provisions were
alike scarce.

Travis' appeal of March 3 did not reach the convention until
after The Alamo had fallen. Upon reading it, Houston and his military
staff left for Gonzales. Ignorant of the fate of the men of The Alamo,
Houston ordered Neill at Gonzales and Fannin to proceed to the beleaguered men of Bowie and Travis.

And then on March 12, Amon King, with some thirty men, on
a roundup of settler refugees, stumbled upon a Mexican cavalry outpost. He gathered together the Texas ranchers and dispatched a rider
to Fannin asking for help. As soon as Fannin received the summons, he sent William Ward and some Georgians and other volunteers
to King's rescue. They found them at Refugio on the afternoon of
March 13, besieged in the old church by fifty or sixty Mexicans.

Sam Houston had arrived on March 11 at Gonzales, where he

learned that The Alamo had been overwhelmed on March 6. Captain Francis J. Dusanque set out for Goliad with the grim tidings together with Houston's orders to Fannin to retreat to the Guadalupe, to the new town of Guadalupe Victoria, immediately with whatever artillery could expeditiously be removed.

Dusanque reached Fannin on March 13. Most of the Goliad defenders' carts and mules were at Refugio, to where Ward had marched to the relief of King. At Guadalupe Victoria, Captain Samuel A. White was assembling transport. Nearby were Albert C. Horton with some forty men, most of them on horseback, on their way to join Fannin. Philip Dimitt's small company, summoned to Gonzales by Houston, stood ready, and the New York Battalion was reforming on Matagorda Bay. Fannin did not know that William P. Miller and 75 mounted men were heading for Copano and were near Aransas Pass.

Then came a third fatal mishap. On March 14 Fannin sent couriers to Ward and King, fighting at Refugio, and to Horton and White at Victoria. The couriers were captured. Their messages informed the Mexican general of Fannin's condition, his plans and his strength. And Fannin, lacking horsemen, was stumbling in the dark.

Late in the afternoon of March 14 Albert Horton led his carts and mule teams into Goliad. Now was the time to retreat to Victoria. The elusive Ward, anticipating such a withdrawal, avoided Urrea and struck out for Victoria where he expected Fannin would be waiting. But at Goliad Fannin tarried on the 15th and 16th "in vain anticipation of Ward's return." On the afternoon of the 17th he learned of the annihilation of King and his men. He should have retreated to Victoria. Instead, he took his time, discussing military measures throughout March 18 with his officers.

The die was cast on March 18. The Mexican cavalry cantered before Goliad that morning, wearing out the pursuing Horton's horses. Inside the fort the oxen, the only means for removing artillery and baggage, lowed in the corrals for unobtainable fodder.

Fannin made plans to retreat the night of March 18 with the darkness for his shield, but Horton, guarding the San Antonio ford, persuaded him that the night was too black. Fannin agreed to wait until the next day, unwisely disregarding Houston's order to sink the extra artillery in the river. Instead he brought off nine brass cannon and 500 spare muskets.

The retreat began late and was confused from the start. Hard-come-by provisions were burned and there was insufficient food for the march. Hours were lost ferrying a howitzer across the river. Oxen wandered off in search of grass. And Fannin paid no attention to the advice of Duval and Shackelford to push on to the woods near Coleto Creek. Instead the Texans camped on the open prairie between Manahuilla and Coleto Creek. Urrea overtook the Texas force on the prairie, a broken ammunition wagon delaying escape to water and woods until too late. The 300 volunteers, inexperienced as they were, gave a rugged account of themselves, fighting off the thousand Mexicans through a desperate afternoon, losing nine men killed and fifty-one wounded while killing fifty of Urrea's soldiers and wounding 140. The unwounded might have escaped at nightfall but they would not leave their wounded comrades. The next morning Urrea's artillery, which had been brought up, opened fire, a twelve-pounder outranging Fannin's cannon and riflemen. The Texans huddled in makeshift trenches, helpless against the barrage, lacking food and water and unable to come to grips with the foe superior in artillery and numbers.

Fannin had no choice but to surrender. Thornton, who had gone ahead with about thirty mounted riflemen to guard the Coleto crossing, escaped. Ward, heading for Victoria, tried to join up with Fannin on the 19th when he heard the sounds of battle. Urrea pressed on to Victoria and surprised Ward, killing and capturing a number of his men as they sought to enter the town. Ward and the remainder retreated to the Guadalupe woods. Some of the men left the party and eventually ten of them escaped.

Ward and his remaining men headed for Dimitt's Landing. Two miles from the landing, the all-but-defenseless volunteers were surrounded by Urrea's cavalry and surrendered. Few lived long. Urrea had protested the cold-blooded murders from their outset, but Santa Anna was adamant. Of the thirty-three Americans captured at Refugio, Urrea shot Captain Amon King and fourteen others, setting free the rest on the grounds that they were colonists or Mexicans and not volunteers from the United States and subject to the law against pirates.

But Urrea had assured Fannin that he could expect clemency. So William Ward and his men who surrendered on March 27 were also certain of it. But of the 342 men of Fannin's command only twenty-eight survived the Mexican firing squads; twenty others were spared for use as interpreters, nurses, mechanics or physicians. They owed their lives to the entreaties of the beautiful wife of a Mexican officer, whom they knew as Señora Alvarez, and a sympathetic officer, General Francisco Garay, who intervened for them. Santa Anna's army was taking no prisoners.

One of the survivors was Herman Ehrenberg, the young German, whose life was a charmed one. He was to relate of his captivity at Goliad:

> The first night of our captivity passed away in discomfort. A burning thirst tormented us, and although we asked repeatedly for water we had to wait until eight o'clock in the morning before six of our men were allowed to go to the river and get water for themselves and the other prisoners. ... There was no distribution of food on that day, only a second allowance of water in the evening, and another dreadful night came upon us. The heat had become much greater, and was much more stifling than during the preceding night. Nor was food offered the second morning. The Texans protested violently and loudly but they could do nothing else. The Mexican sentries stood by loaded cannon trained upon the prisoners with lighted wicks in their hands. That evening the Texans got six ounces of beef to a man with the promise of another distribution when a herd of cattle arrived. Most of the men ate the meat raw. Even the smallest cooking fire added too greatly to the unendurable heat.

On the sixth day the prisoners received their third and last ration, a pound of beef. By now the Mexicans had taken all their personal belongings. Then came the departure from Goliad:

> On the morning of the eighth day of our captivity great clouds hung over the horizon and the air was hot and sultry. The artillery which earlier in the week had commanded the gate was now leveled at our camp. The gun was ready to fire at the first signal. Several companies of Mexican soldiers stood in front of us, wearing their parade uniforms, which I must confess looked very shabby and seemed to be made of the coarsest material. ... After the roll had been called an order to march was given. The Greys, led by a volunteer called MacMannemy, passed through the sombre gates of the fort.

There two lines of Mexican soldiers, some 700 men, were drawn up on either side of the prisoners, who believed that they were being taken to an eastern harbor to embark for New Orleans.

Fifteen minutes later the massacres began:

> *A command to halt given in Spanish struck our ears like the voice of doom, for at that very moment we heard the distant rattle of a volley of musketry; almost instinctively we thought of our comrades who had been separated from us and most probably taken in the direction from which those shots came.*
>
> *Bewildered and anxious, we gazed inquiringly now at each other, now at the Mexicans. The Mexican officers shouted to us again and ordered us to kneel; the few of us who understood would not and could not obey this command. Meanwhile, the Mexican soldiers, hardly three feet away from us, pointed their rifles at our chests.*
>
> *Our surprise was as deep as it was ghastly. The idea that they had planned to shoot us seemed unthinkable. If we had known how desperate our situation was, what would we not have done to sell our lives as dearly as possible? Unarmed though we were we should have followed Winkelried's example and, wresting bayonets and spears from the hands of the foe, should have avenged our deaths with the blood of our assassins . . .*
>
> *With menacing gestures and drawn sword, the leader of our murderers yelled once more the command to kneel. A second volley of musketry came to our ears from another direction; [the victims had been divided into three columns and led out in these separate groups to their deaths]. This time a wail of distress followed it, probably from those victims whose deaths had not been instantaneous. These sounds startled our friend [who had been rendered speechless] from the spell of silent staring. Fully roused now and with blazing eyes he cried out boldly, "Comrades, did you hear those shots? They were directed against our friends. Did you hear those cries? They were their last protest. No hope is left; the last hour of grace is come. Therefore, Com-*

rades . . ." then a fearful crash interrupted him, then all was quiet; thick clouds of smoke rose slowly toward the river. The blood of my lieutenant squirted on my clothes and around me the last convulsions of agony shook the bodies of my friends.

Close to me Matten and Curtman were struggling with death. I saw no more; quickly making up my mind, I sprang up and took advantage of the thick smoke which hid me to rush around the hedge and make for the river. I heard and saw nothing; the murmur of the water alone guided my steps. A heavy blow on the head from a sword made me reel; the small form of a Mexican lieutenant emerged from the smoke in front of me and a second thrust of the sword hit my left arm, with which I tried to parry it. I had nothing to lose, everything to gain. It was a matter of life and death. Behind me I had the bayonets of the Mexican soldiers, in front of me the effective weapon of a coward who blocked my way to the river in safety. In a moment I was on him. I could not go back. He did not put up any fight, but fled. My path was cleared, safety was in sight. Shouting "The Republic of Texas forever!" I jumped into the waters of the stream, and swam slowly and wearily to the other side with bullets flying over my head as I steered my course through the current of the river. It was then that I had the ill luck of losing the faithful dog of our company; he had been with us from the beginning of our campaign and following me in my dash for safety, had jumped with me into the river. The thought of retaining him as a companion during my flight to the prairie was already cheering my depressed spirit when a bullet hit him and he sank under the water. As soon as I reached the other bank, I looked back at the place where my friends lay bleeding to death. The enemy was still shooting and yelling, and it was with a sorrowful heart that I listened to these shouts of triumph which in my fancy were mingled with the groans of pain of my dying friends.

The Mexicans . . . stripped the bodies of their fallen foes of everything they wore or possessed and left them naked on the field.

So did Herman Ehrenberg escape, one of the miraculously blessed of the 28 who survived the orgy of murder.

Even before the dreadful news of The Alamo and Goliad seeped through the Texas settlements and farms, the panicky flight of civilians eastward, which would later be described with wry and sheepish humor as the Runaway Scrape, had begun.

The exposed citizens of central Texas—at San Patricio and Refugio and San Antonio and the surrounding countryside—were the first to leave, beginning in mid-January when they heard that the Mexicans were on the Río Grande in force. Pell-mell, panicky departures mounted after Sam Houston arrived in Gonzales on March 14 and there, learning of the fall of The Alamo, determined to retreat to the Colorado. With his decision went an order to the inhabitants to accompany him; hard-riding couriers bore the news to the people of Texas.

The start of Houston's retreat marked the real beginning of the Runaway Scrape. On March 17, Washington-on-the-Brazos was emptied and two weeks later all the settlements on both sides of the Brazos were uninhabited. As Houston continued on toward the Sabine, the unprotected settlers between the Colorado and the Brazos joined in the flight toward Galveston Island or Louisiana. Before mid-April, east Texas as far as Nacogdoches and San Augustine was empty.

The plight of the fugitives was pitiful. They fled not only before Mexicans but in fear of Indian uprisings. Beset by cold, rain and hunger, hundreds died and were buried—or, in extremity, lay unburied—where they collapsed. Disease ravaged the living.

Private Robert Hunter, who had helped take San Antonio in December, wrote to his family of what he saw. Here is one observation:

> *That same morning [March 14] we seen two women with five children with bundles of clothing on thare head. The Capt. ast theme which way are you going? We are trying to git a way from the Mexicans. Thare husbands was kild in the Alamo. The Capt. ast theme, why are you walking don't you have no waggons? They said yes but their horses was out on the prire and we could not find theme. We left our supper on the table, we took what little clothing we could carry and our children and left a foot ...*

The settlers feared that Spanish agents had promised the Indians, notably the Cherokees, an unlimited right to plunder if they would help destroy the Texans. The easternmost settlers begged the United States to send troops. There is no doubt that they would have been sent had the Indians risen. General Gaines marched eight companies of the 6th Infantry and five companies of the 3rd Infantry to the Sabine, where they went into camp on the site of Wilkinson's one-time encampment and the American general sent word to the Indians that they would be punished if they attacked the inhabitants.

Noah Smithwick, who as a blacksmith had prepared arms for the patriots, left his own indelible description of what he saw from Bastrop to Cole's Settlement:

> *The desolation of the country through which we passed beggars description. Houses were standing open, the beds unmade, the breakfast things still on the table, pans of milk moulding in the dairies. There were cribs full of corn, smokehouses full of bacon, yards full of chickens that ran after us for food, nests of eggs in every fence corner, young corn and garden truck rejoicing in the rain, cattle cropping the luxuriant grass, hogs fat and lazy, wallowing in the mud, all abandoned. Forlorn dogs roamed around the deserted homes, their doleful howls adding to the general sense of desolation. Hungry cats ran mewing to meet us, rubbing their sides against our legs in token of welcome. . . . There were broken down wagons and household goods scattered all along the road. Stores with quite valuable stocks of goods stood open, the goods on the shelves, no attempt having been made to remove them.*

Sam Houston learned of Fannin's surrender on March 25. There was no chance now to turn against the Mexicans on the Colorado. The retreat was resumed. On April 12 the Mexicans reached the Brazos downstream from the Texans. Again retreat.

Santa Anna was enjoying himself chasing Texans evermore to the east. He and his generals—Sesma and Morales, Tolsa, Gaona and the others—were in high spirits, so high and so confident, in fact, that they ignored the basic military rule not to divide themselves into smaller and smaller components. The empty streets of Gonzales echoed the tread of Mexican feet on April 26. San Felipe fell without fighting on May 7. At the Brazos, there were no boats.

Here Colonel Juan Almonte tried to trick the Texans with his American accent, shouting over to the American pickets on the eastern bank: "Bring over that boat—the Mexicans are coming!" A few days later Santa Anna led his troops 30 miles down the bank to Thompson's Ferry, where on April 11 a terrified Negro showed the Mexicans a hidden canoe. A small vanguard made it to the east bank. The next morning they captured a Texan outpost at Thompson's Ferry, together with another canoe and a flat boat. On April 14, the last of the Mexicans were on the eastern side.

Soon was bruited news of big game. David Gouverneur Burnet ad interim president of the Republic of Texas, and some of his key men were at Harrisburg, only 20 miles away, so a loyal Mexican related. With 700 infantrymen, fifty horsemen and a six-pounder, Santa Anna plunged headlong toward Harrisburg. The rest of the army was left behind. All the next day the vanguard hurried, reaching the village at midnight.

But nobody of importance was at home. Burnet and his aides had escaped to Galveston. Three printers whom Santa Anna threw in jail —they were publishing the *Telegraph and Texas Register*—let it be known that Houston was on the Brazos, his army swelled to 800 men. There rode the cavalry under Colonel Juan Almonte under orders to check possible concentration points.

Almonte reported to Santa Anna on March 17 that Houston was about to cross the San Jacinto River at Lynch's Ferry.

This is what Santa Anna had been waiting for. Without pausing to collect his scattered forces, he marched toward a rendezvous with Almonte at New Washington, thence to Lynch's Ferry. Houston would be cut off.

The vain, basically incompetent Santa Anna had committed a cardinal military sin, that of dividing his forces when unity was needed. General Sesma waited at Thompson's Ferry with 1,000 men. General Urrea, the conqueror of Goliad, was at Matagorda with another 1,200. Filisola followed somewhere in the rear with 1,800 troops. Gaona fumbled with two battalions somewhere near the town named for his late excellency, the so-called Baron de Bastrop.

With New Washington behind him, Santa Anna ordered a Cap-

tain Barragon to scout ahead for Texans on March 19. On the morning
of the 20th the astounded Captain reported that Houston was between
7 and 8 miles away and apparently ready to face up to the Mexicans.
This was good news for Santa Anna. He would wipe the *Yanquis* off
the map.

The forthcoming battle should have been a pushover. Santa Anna,
had he not scattered his army, could have counted six Mexicans to one
Texan. But the actual odds at San Jacinto were only four to three.

And those 900 Texans and volunteers were ready to kill. The
Alamo and Goliad were in their minds. And some were also ashamed.

The Mexicans were actually ahead of Sam Houston's army,
though few knew it. On April 18 the Texans came upon Buffalo Bayou
near Harrisburg; in the gloaming, unerring Deaf Smith brought to
General Houston a happy gist of news. Santa Anna, the butcher, was
himself in command of the Mexicans ahead. He was east of Vince's
Bayou and moving down San Jacinto Bay. Unwittingly, the Texans
had come between him and the larger body of the Mexican army trail-
ing behind. At dawn of April 19 Sam Houston spoke to his men. They
had bisected the Mexican army. Houston shouted: "Victory is certain!
Trust in God and fear not! And remember The Alamo, remember The
Alamo!"

It is improbable that at any other place or at any other time did
men assemble with such bloodlust pulsing through their veins, pulsing through their hearts. The Texans were blood-mad. They had the
weapons for slaughter, the rifles, the immense Bowie knives which
three out of every four men bore, the two beautiful six-pounders—the
Twin Sisters—which had been sent to them from the people of Cincinnati. The only good Mexican would be a dead Mexican ...

All night they marched, across Buffalo Bayou and Vince's Bridge
in the moonlight. At two in the morning they fell to the ground for
brief napping. At dawn they were up, breakfasting at seven o'clock,
when they were spied by a Mexican scouting party, which warned
Santa Anna. After an inconclusive skirmish in which a boatload of
flour was captured at Lynch's Ferry, the Texans spread out to await
the Mexicans.

The first fighting was desultory. The Twin Sisters menaced the
advancing Santandistas. The Mexican charge died almost aborning.
A Texan mounted foray took a licking. Santa Anna was irritated. The
Texans didn't fight like professional soldiers. Instead they fought as

did their forebears at Lexington and Concord and King's Mountain.

On the morning of April 21 Santa Anna's army was strengthened by 400 men under General Cós. The volatile Latins celebrated their arrival. But after noon they took their *siesta*.

It took the Texans just eighteen minutes—eighteen minutes of slaughter and scalping, and the slaying of prisoners by men who remembered The Alamo; eighteen minutes from the time 731 men raced behind Sam Houston and his white charger to the camp of the sleeping Mexicans, a fifer and drummer playing the favorite, "Will You Come to the Bower I Have Shaded for You?"

Nine Texans died and fourteen were wounded. Santa Anna's army was wiped out, with 630 dead and wounded, and 730 captured. And in the hands of the Texans, with only Houston standing between him and their revenge was Santa Anna, captured hiding in the grass in a blue cotton jacket and red worsted slippers for disguise and pleading that he was only a private in the Mexican army.

For the Republic of Texas began an uneasy ten years of truce broken by frequent and inconclusive armed clashes on land and sea with the Mexicans who refused to recognize the reality of the new nation.

CHAPTER TWENTY-TWO

TO THE HALLS OF MONTEZUMA

THE ALMOST COMICALLY SHORT-LEGGED and stocky Lieutenant Zachary Taylor had selected the site for Cantonment Jesup twenty-two years earlier, in 1822—a mile square of land straddling the *camino real* and a day's march east of the Sabine. Here, at America's farthest western outpost on the trail to Mexico, American troops, following the treaty of 1819, could control lawlessness in the former neutral ground and protect emigrants moving West into the *empresario* grants.

Lieutenant Taylor had ordered the pine trees cut near the ever-flowing spring of potable water in this land of salines. He had seen to their felling and planing on two parallel sides, and supervised their use in the construction of white-walled, long, single-storied barracks, raised-galleried headquarters, mess halls and storage sheds for the cantonment. The structures were rebuilt in 1836, using the same heart pine, and together were given the more pretentious name of Fort Jesup. The future of the young Republic of Texas was too much in doubt to leave the United States border unprotected.

Here, in the summer of 1844, by a quirk of fate, this same Kentucky-raised son of Virginia, "Old Rough and Ready" to his men since the Seminole War three years before, had returned as a brigadier-general, at the head of an "Army of Observation."

General Taylor's orders were simply to protect the Republic of Texas from any Mexican invasion during the long months in which her annexation to the United States was being negotiated. His command included seven companies of the 2nd Dragoons, eight companies of the 3rd Infantry, and eight companies of the 4th Infantry, too many men to quarter at Fort Jesup. Taylor established a tent city, protecting the flimsy canvas from the direct summer sun by thin lath latticing, and called it Camp Salubrity.

Camp Salubrity on the Red River at Grand Écore was at the very end of the trail which had always, legally or illegally, extended to the Red. Ten years before, the river had cut itself a new channel, away from Natchitoches, passing before Camp Salubrity near Grand Écore, a mighty, three-humped bluff on the bright red river. Here, at the port for Natchitoches and the San Antonio trade, and at nearby Camp Wilkins, the regulars whiled their time away, waiting for orders, playing brag for silver quarters, and losing a lot of them to a certain Brevet Lieutenant Ulysses S. Grant.

This was the year that the Senate of the United States, weighted with Abolitionists, failed to pass by the necessary two-thirds majority a treaty annexing Texas to the Union as a slave state. That summer, a Whig, Henry Clay, ran for President on an anti-Texas-annexation platform. The Democrat, James K. Polk, and his running mate campaigned with gusto under the banner of "Polk, Dallas, Texas, and Oregon." Mexico, which had never recognized the independence of Texas, warned President Tyler that annexation of what Mexico considered an inalienable part of her territory would be considered an act of war.

In November, Polk won less than half of the popular votes for President but the electoral college gave him a majority of sixty-five votes. Slavery or no slavery, constitutional or not, Texas would be invited into the Union. A deciding factor for many people was the fear of a Great Britain which had shown too much interest in protecting Texas, the young republic whose Gulf shores threatened the mouth of the Mississippi River. Besides, if there was to be war over Texas, it would be better to wage it against Mexico instead of Britain.

Given its mandate from the people, Congress prepared in December a joint resolution, requiring only a majority vote of each house to annex Texas. On March 1, 1845, just before President Polk's inauguration, the United States Congress voted to invite Texas to annex itself.

The Republic of Texas had wearied of earlier rebuffs of its requests for annexation, and had all but decided to accept Britain's proffers of aid. Now, while Texas discussed the United States' offer,

Mexico raised money and troops for the invasion of Texas. She then belatedly offered Texas recognition as an independent country in return for a promise to accept no offer of annexation.

President Anson Jones called a special session of the Texas Congress at the capital, Austin, which quickly turned down the Mexican offer and voted for annexation. At a subsequent convention on July 4, 1845, the sixty-one delegates voted overwhelmingly for annexation, as did the people in Texas' first plebiscite in the fall. On December 29, 1845, President Polk approved Congress' joint resolution and said that all formalities had been completed; Texas was officially a part of the United States.

The Congressional bill provided that Texas might later become five states rather than one, that she could keep her public lands and that the United States would adjust all boundary questions.

The matter of a boundary contained the immediate cause of war. But, as President Polk pointed out, it didn't matter whether Texas' western border was the Nueces, as Mexico said, or the Río Grande, which the Texas republic declared it to be in 1837, and which earlier American Presidents had proclaimed as a border of the Louisiana purchase. Mexico, which had never ratified a treaty of delineation with the United States, still claimed all the land to the Sabine and intended to fight for it. And in the ears of many people of the United States rang a self-vindicating watchword. Our manifest destiny, they told each other, entitles us to what we can take of the North American continent.

In January, Mexico rejected Polk's offer in which he was prepared to go as high as $40 million in return for California, New Mexico, a Texas border at the Río Grande and the $3 million owed to Americans for damages during Mexico's continuous political turmoil. The Anglo-Americans didn't seem to understand that pride was also at stake in Mexico's abrupt refusal—pride and years of emotional denunciation of the *Norteamericanos.*

A year after General Taylor returned to Fort Jesup, and while Texas awaited its convention of July 4, 1845, an express rider from Natchitoches brought new orders to him. His former instructions had been simply to be ready to defend Texas if it were attacked during its negotiations with the United States. Now he was to occupy a port which he would select, near the Río Grande, as soon as annexation was assured.

As soon as the Texas convention made its decision for annexation, the general marched his eager infantrymen out of Fort Jesup, along the old Spanish trail toward Camp Salubrity and on to Grand Écore. There steamers waited to carry them, their blue fatigues moist from perspiration, down the Red to New Orleans. At last, in the summer of 1845, American soldiers were on their way to the Halls of Montezuma. New Orleans, which so often before had been the point of departure for filibusters, was now the staging area for the officially sanctioned invasion. Taylor had selected Corpus Christi at the mouth of the Nueces for his camp.

Behind at Fort Jesup only the seven regiments of the 2nd Dragoons tarried. Soon they too were gone. Under the command of robust, red-faced Colonel David E. Twiggs, their red sashes bright against their blue coats and tassels hanging against their cream-colored trousers, the horsemen rode smartly westward to the Sabine along the short-cut which American soldiers had cleared. At the river they were again on the trail which St. Denis had known.

They passed through a cheering Nacogdoches about the time General Taylor arrived by ship at the mouth of the Nueces. At the Trinity they turned south toward Goliad and the flourishing towns along the old La Bahía Road and newer trails the Texans had made. They rode each day from midnight until early morning to avoid the penetrating summer sun. Like Aguayo's troops long before, they knew the extremes of Texas weather, not cold this time but heat which kept them bivouacked eight days along the way. These troopers were the first American soldiers to cover the whole way from Fort Jesup to the Río Grande by land.

By late August General Taylor had some 4,000 men under tents at Corpus Christi. There the dragoons joined him.

The President's orders to General Taylor were to be conciliatory as long as American negotiations with Mexico for peaceful settlement of the territorial and indemnity questions continued. But with no one to fight, discipline waned. When the army moved again six months later, in February—this time 196 miles to the left bank of the Río Grande opposite the Mexican army at Matamoros—the very march was a tonic, though sunburn and thirst and prickly chaparral were ramrods the men would gladly have foregone.

Despite the advance through "Wild Horse Country," the name of the area according to American maps, Taylor's orders continued to be conciliatory. Diplomatic negotiations proceeded. But at the river,

General Pedro de Ampudia—hated by the Americans for executing a filibuster named Sentmanat, then boiling his head in oil the better to preserve it for its public exhibition—ordered General Taylor to withdraw at once to the Nueces or take the consequences. Taylor stood his ground, on land claimed by Texas and the United States, strengthening the earthworks he had already begun, later called Fort Brown and in time Brownsville.

In late April, General Mariano Arista replaced General Ampudia and brought with him orders from the Mexican government, dated April 4, to attack the Americans. That onslaught was not long delayed.

On April 25 a squadron of sixty of the 2nd Dragoons, under Captain S. B. Thornton, was ambushed by a larger Mexican force in the contested borderland. Some Americans were killed, others were wounded and the survivors surrendered. This was no simple border skirmish but an implementation of Mexican governmental policy.

On May 11, 1846, President Polk announced to Congress that "War exists by the act of Mexico," for "American blood has been shed on American soil." The war "to conquer a peace" was on.

A cheering Congress promptly authorized enlistment of 50,000 volunteers for twelve months and voted $10 million for the Mexican War. Throughout the nation the fever for enlistment was great, especially in Sam Houston's Tennessee. Here, instead of the 3,000 volunteers called for, 30,000 signed up. Those permitted to go from "the Volunteer State," as it would henceforth be known, had to be selected by ballot. This was the war the frontier had wanted since rivermen's blood had coursed hotly at the thought of Philip Nolan's men in distant Chihuahua's prison. General John Ellis Wool directed recruitment in Ohio, Indiana, Illinois, Kentucky, Tennessee and Mississippi. Within six weeks he had dispatched 10,000 men to succor Taylor, with more to follow, and reserved 3,000 for an expedition planned by the President, which Wool himself would lead.

In the meantime, Taylor's regulars and the earlier volunteers who had enlisted for three to six months defeated the Mexicans in the Battle of Palo Alto and the next day at Resaca de la Palma, routing the Mexicans, who drowned by the hundreds as the ebullient *gringos* chased them into the Río Grande.

On May 18, General Taylor occupied Matamoros on the right side of the river.

But despite these operations, it was obvious to all in the field, and even perhaps to the general himself, that he was not competent to organize an army for victory. Indian fighting was one thing; what lay ahead, another. And yet, in a few weeks, with thousands of recruits and newspaper reports of his great "successes" arriving from the East, the volunteers and officers began to misdoubt the evidence of their senses. Besides, there was something about this foreshortened man, so calmly disdainful of danger, that inspired those he could not properly lead. A soldier could love a man he didn't feel to be his superior.

At Corpus Christi, Taylor had made no reconnaissance to determine conditions farther west. At Fort Brown he had taken no measures to protect adequately his supplies at Port Isable. And now at Matamoros, with the volunteers pouring in, several hundred of his men died from measles, mumps, dysentery and from polluted water and bad latrines. The raw recruits whiled away valuable training time at fandangoes, or playing Old Sledge, Chucklcluck, monte or faro, or just brawling for lack of something better to do.

There was another cause of attrition. While most of the regular officers were West Pointers and native born Americans, almost half of the volunteers were recent immigrants, many of the Roman Catholic faith. As the two armies lay across the river from each other, the Mexican commanders skillfully played on religious prejudices and spread tales of European condemnation of the United States' actions against Catholic Mexico. Additionally, brightly dressed sirens tempted the unkempt men across the river. In the subsequent weeks at Matamoros, the psychological warfare worked and desertions mounted. Many of the Irishmen would find themselves in action again, fighting for Mexico in defense of Mexico City as the San Patricio Company. They would be shot as traitors in time, with the Stars and Stripes waving over them.

Taylor planned now the conquest of Monterrey and an attack on Saltillo. He moved his Army of the Río Grande up the river by steamer. At Camargo almost continuous salutes honored the dead who succumbed to the unsanitary camp conditions which no one had taught them to correct.

At Cerralvo, Taylor's reconnaissance greatly improved. It was here that Captain Ben McCullough's Texas Rangers came riding into camp on their tough little horses with a braided lariat at the pommel along with a bag of parched and pounded corn. They were jaunty in

their coarse red or blue shirts tucked into wide-belted trousers, their
protective leggings, their buckskin caps and soft felt hats. Familiarity
with their armament made them casual with their heavy rifles and
bullet pouches, their large powder horns and Bowie knives. Many of
them carried Colt revolvers, the six-shooter patented the year the
Texas Republic was born. More important to Taylor than their appearance was their knowledge of the countryside and of Mexicans.

Taylor was on his way to take Monterrey and Saltillo in the manner he had destroyed the Indians in the Everglade swamps, relying on
steel. But ahead, at Monterrey, rose the fortified ramparts of the
ancient city of Léon, cradled for defense in the steep spurs of the
Sierra Madre and resting on the swift-running Santa Catarina
River.

It took the Americans five days of hard fighting to achieve Taylor's victory. On the fifth day General Ampudia conferred with General Taylor. The result was the withdrawal of the Mexicans with their
arms, accoutrements and six field pieces, and an armistice and promise
by General Taylor on September 25 not to go beyond Rinconada Pass
on the way to Saltillo for eight weeks, or "until the orders of the re-
spective governments can be received." The armistice gave Mexico
time to recuperate. The conquest of the city made a national hero of
General Taylor.

From the point of view of politics, a hero was one thing. A Whig
hero, General Taylor, was not exactly what a Democratic President
wanted. General Winfield Scott, ranking general of the American
Army, was also a Whig. But, a second Mexican front with General
Scott in the field might provide a second hero and would detract somewhat from the first. The President had achieved, moreover, a clearer
understanding of what the Mexican War entailed. It would not be
enough simply to invade and hold Mexico's northern states. A drive
straight to her heart would be needed to bring the sister republic to
her knees. If, at the north, Taylor would hold at Monterrey, Scott
could be given the bulk of Taylor's regulars and all other possible
support for an invasion through Vera Cruz.

On November 12 General Taylor received at Monterrey orders
from the Secretary of War to go no farther. Three days before he had
ordered General W. J. Worth to leave in four days for the occupation of Saltillo. Telling no one of the Secretary's order, he permitted
Worth to leave on schedule and followed himself the next day. Wash-

ington was far away and the general felt he knew better than the cabinet what should be done.

At the beginning of the month the last of the Mexican troops who had fought at Monterrey had been called in to San Luis Potosí. With no army to defend Saltillo, Taylor's forces marched into the heart of the town. General Worth established his headquarters in the main plaza, facing the church, while General Taylor set up his beyond the town at the Mesa del Ojo de Agua near the principal spring, ignoring a note from Governor José María de Aguirre of Coahuila calling this "the most unjust invasion in the history of the world." The governor and many of the most prominent people fled. The Americans jailed the vice governor and named Lieutenant Colonel W. B. Warren of the 1st Illinois Regiment governor.

Having established the American forces at Saltillo, Taylor himself returned to Monterrey, leaving Worth at Saltillo.

A few weeks after the state of war was acknowledged, President Polk dispatched an emissary to call on Santa Anna in exile in Havana. Santa Anna had returned to Mexico from Washington after his capture by Sam Houston. He helped defend Mexico against the French in 1838 and lost a leg. He would not let the Mexicans forget his sacrifice. He was acting president in 1839, helped to overthrow the president, and became dictator from 1841 to 1845. Excesses led to his banishment to Havana.

As President Polk saw it, the latest government of Mexico, that of General Mariano Paredes y Arrillaga, was too unstable to last. If a man friendly to the U.S. achieved power, the northern republic might be able to negotiate a peace. Santa Anna, who had been living outside Mexico, had made no pronouncement for war. If he returned to Vera Cruz he might declare for peace. In fact, he said that he would be glad to do so if the United States would assist him to return to Mexico. President Polk accordingly ordered the American Navy to permit the as-always opportunistic Santa Anna to pass through the blockade. Less than two years later he would again leave his country, going then into self-imposed exile in Venezuela to await another opportune moment to return.

In the summer of 1846, Santa Anna found in Mexico that the war sentiment was too strong for him to challenge. On September 17, two days before Taylor opened his assault on Monterrey, Santa Anna accepted appointment as commander-in-chief of "The Liberating

Army'' to drive the North Americans from Mexican soil. As devious as ever, he was again supporting the federalist constitution of 1824 and would soon become president under it.

After appropriate devotions at the shrine of Our Lady of Guadalupe, Santa Anna went to San Luis Potosí to take over active command of that city and of the army in October. A bankrupt government could do little to help him except make pronouncements against the army invading the homeland; dissensions within the Mexican leadership, accustomed now to revolutions whose only reason was a play for power by contending interests, promised little constructive support.

San Luis Potosí rallied fervently and, by forced levies of manpower, recruited 7,500 men from that state. Guanajuato sent 2,000 and Jalisco almost as many. But all were poorly armed, few had experience in disciplined warfare and no money could be raised to feed, clothe or equip the army of 20,000 centered at the city. San Luis Potosí alone of the states raised money, providing a total of $800,000 for the support and equipment of the army. Not until January did the central government vote a levy on church properties as a last desperate effort to wring money for the bankrupt treasury.

By then Santa Anna knew that Taylor had advanced beyond Saltillo to Agua Nueva and realized that poorly trained, equipped and prepared though his men might be, he should now move against the American Army. The timing seemed propitious. He knew that Taylor's regulars had been drawn from him to join the forces of General Winfield Scott, which were being assembled for an attack on Vera Cruz. Santa Anna believed he could easily defeat Taylor's untrained volunteers and by the victory achieve a psychological triumph for Mexico before turning to the more difficult task of repulsing the Americans in the south.

On January 23 Santa Anna ordered the director of the mint at San Luis Potosí to work day and night to coin ninety-eight bars of silver on deposit there and thereby assure his army of funds for the advance.

On January 25 General José Vicente Miñón's resplendent dragoons rode out of the city to begin their scouting operations. The rest of Santa Anna's forces began to leave on January 27. Hired mules and oxen pulled the artillery; heavy carts filled with ammunition followed close behind.

It was not the time of year for ill-equipped men to travel those shelterless miles from San Luis Potosí to Saltillo. Their rations were poor meat, their water saline. The hot sun burned them and torrential rains soaked them. At night heavy snows covered them as they lay, tentless and fireless for lack of wood, on the barren plain. Death, debility and desertions cost Santa Anna 2,000 troops before ever he faced the enemy. But he brought them to the field of Buena Vista ready to fight.

For General Wool, the responsibility of recruiting 20,000 volunteers didn't end with mustering them into service. The general was a precise and thorough technician, a martinet admired by his fellow officers for his insistence on the rules and discipline and supply which had brought success to Napoleon and to the European armies which he had visited on presidential assignment. He realized, if the volunteers did not, that a rifle, a powder horn and a few dozen bullets would not win the war. Personally he saw to the procurement of tents, haversacks, knapsacks, canteens, mess pans, kettles, wagons, horses, harness, mules, even nose bags.

But there was little about this gentlemanly, reserved, spare man of medium height to inspire red-blooded Americans who felt they had yet to settle the old scores of The Alamo and Goliad. Born in Orange County, New York, he began his career as a clerk in a store, became a merchant and was prospering when a fire wiped him out just before the War of 1812. He enlisted in the army and remained in it, serving as inspector-general from 1816 to 1841. Subsequently he undertook special missions for the President.

He completed his assignments punctiliously, just as his part in the battle of Buena Vista would be carried through competently. But he didn't understand the spirit of man. There is the story of a night after Buena Vista when the jubilant, grateful soldiers organized a serenade of General Taylor and General Wool. Such a ceremony was strictly against orders. General Taylor thanked the men warmly. General Wool reprimanded them.

But General Wool placed the men on the field to fight. Santa Anna said later that he attacked the Americans only because he thought the men he would face were raw volunteers. Wool had drilled them despite their mutterings. But it was General Taylor who somehow inspired them to successes far beyond their training.

In June 1846, 62-year-old General Wool was ordered to San Antonio de Béxar. The President's strategy called for a small column to take over New Mexico, another to secure control of California, Taylor to take Monterrey and Wool to seize Chihuahua.

But before Wool arrived at San Antonio, another American regular officer, Lieutenant Colonel William Selby Harney, without orders and with an impatience which characterized many Americans, left San Antonio and crossed the Río Grande. Harney was a tall, broad-chested, well-built extrovert whose frontier birth near Nashville in 1800 and early days developed his prowess as a hunter, spear fisherman and runner. As a young man he could outlast an Indian afoot.

Taylor had sent him to San Antonio with six companies of the 2nd Dragoons to protect the town from Indians. Acting on rumors of a Mexican troop concentration at Presidio, Harney called for "Texians" to fight Indians. Seven hundred promptly signed up. With them and three companies of the dragoons he set out on the old Presidio road to the Río Grande in mid-summer. Anxious to get going, he refused to wait for two small Texas Revolution cannon at Victoria Guadalupe, brashly promising that he would capture fieldpieces from the Mexicans at the river. "We'll go and take them; they will suit me exactly," he said.

Arrived at the Río Grande, Harney and fifteen picked men proceeded to swim their horses through the sluggish river into what might well have been the jaws of the enemy—only to find the Mexican troops gone and the *alcalde* of Guerrero, whose older designation of Presidio del Río Grande persisted among the Texans, ready to turn over the town of 2,000 and its protection from still other military "friends" to the Americans.

Carelessly, the colonel then ordered his entire force to cross. Promptly the river rose, cutting off any retreat. This also suited the colonel. He now proposed that his command storm Monterrey by surprise. But his officers, who had followed him thus far, refused to anticipate superior orders to that extent.

The river, having fallen again, a courier from General Wool succeeded in reaching Harney at Guerrero with peremptory orders for the reckless officer to return to San Antonio at once. Shortly another courier appeared. After talking to Texans clamoring to join Harney's unauthorized expedition, Wool had become apprehensive that the colonel had no intention of turning about. He sent the second messenger with an order for Harney to turn his command over to his second and return under arrest.

But Harney, obedient to the first message, was already on his way back to San Antonio and conformity to the general strategy planned by the War Department and the President. He left behind sixty men to guard the flour and grains he had collected. These panicked at the approach of a small Mexican force, fired the store houses and disgracefully escaped after a small engagement in which three men were casualties.

Mexicans thrilled to the news that American troops had been repulsed. Such American escapades might lift the hearts of impatient volunteers, but generals need reliable officers.

In San Antonio, Harney refused to shake hands with the general who had ordered his arrest for what he called "so trivial a cause." But no disciplinary action was taken. Even General Wool had to overlook the unsoldierly independence of such free-wheeling regulars as Harney. To bring the volunteers under military discipline would prove even more difficult.

Wool had arrived in San Antonio on August 14 from La Vaca, today's Port Lavaca, in Matagorda Bay. By mid-September he had 3,400 men assembled at San Antonio, of whom only 600 were regulars, and more than 2,000 horses and 1,112 wagons. Ahead, somewhere beyond the Sierra Madre, lay Chihuahua, to be reached through country for which there were only a few worse-than-useless published maps and over a route through the mountains which Pike had mentioned in 1806 but of which no one knew anything in 1846.

Rising early, retiring late, precisely and without humor, Wool worked out his plans. If he seemed overcautious about his service of supply, if he chose to bring wagons rather than depend on mules, it was his temperament to think ahead. He preferred to feed his people to making enemies by living off the country. Where the artillery would have to go, the wagons could also wheel. And no matter what way that was, it certainly led as far as Santa Rosa, which could be reached by old trails still in use.

On September 26, on orders from Wool, Colonel Harney and 1,300 men set out from Camp Crockett at San Antonio with 175 wagons and supplies for two months.

General Wool left San Antonio two days later with 144 additional troops and shortly caught up with the main party. Ahead of the main part of the column by a few days, Captain Hughes and his topographical engineers selected the route to be followed to the Río Grande, choosing approximately the one followed by the Mexican General Wohl when he made a secret approach to San Antonio north of the Presidio road. Wohl's route involved crossing rivers nearer their sources, where they were smaller, and appealed to the engineers as being more practical than the Presidio road. At Castroville, on the Medina, founded in 1844 by a Frenchman for German emigrants, they found the old Presidio road ford below town too heavily silted to be practicable for wagons. The one 3 miles above was too rocky and too full of holes. Instead they chose as the place of crossing the ford Castro had selected as the location for his town. Beyond here, Wool's army marched north of the old *camino real*. His column reached the Río Grande eleven days after leaving San Antonio.

Here, where the river flowed 3½ feet deep across the 816-foot-wide Paso de Francia, where Aguayo's swimmers had towed rafts to cross his army, General Wool's immense train of artillery, military stores, provisions, baggage and men crossed without casualty in three days on a flying bridge prepared in San Antonio by Captain Fraser and his associate engineer, a Virginia regular named Captain Robert E. Lee. While the men waited their turn to cross, Captain Lee noted "a great whetting of knives, grinding of swords, and sharpening of bayonets."

On the west side, a small contingent of Mexican lancers awaited the general under a flag of truce to tell him of the Monterrey armistice. By so doing they gave the general his first word of General Taylor's victory at Monterrey. Wool was convinced that a peaceful advance into Coahuila up to the armistice line would not be a violation of the armistice. He continued on into Presidio.

On October 11, when his column had reached the east bank of the river, the general had published an order to his men:

> *Tomorrow you will cross the Río Grande, and occupy the territory of our enemies. We have not come here to make war upon the people or the peasantry of the country, but to compel the government of Mexico to render justice to the United States. The people, therefore, who do not take up arms against the United States, and remain quiet and peaceful at their homes, will not be molested or interfered with, either as*

regards their persons or property; and all those who furnish
supplies will be treated kindly, and whatever is received of
them will be liberally paid for.

It is expected of the troops that they will observe the
most rigid discipline and subordination. All depredations on
the persons or property of the people are strictly forbidden;
and every soldier or follower of the camp, who may so far
forget his duty as to violate these injunctions, will be severely
punished.

It was the measure of the man that General Wool saw to it that
from the Río Grande to his column's rendezvous with enemy troops
below Saltillo his troops marched as a disciplined army. The towns to
which they came welcomed them as friends and saw them leave as
friends.

In contrast, as Captain Hughes of the topographical engineers
was to note, a few months later, writing from the mouth of the Río
Grande on February 1, 1847:

We have recently often heard of deeds of extreme cruelty
perpetrated by them (Mexicans) on the Río Grande; but it
remains to be seen how far they were acts of retaliation, pro-
voked (but not justified) by the outrages they have endured.
From Saltillo to Mier, with the exception of the large towns,
all is a desert, and there is scarcely a solitary house (if there
be one) inhabited. The smiling villages which welcomed our
troops on their upward march are now black and smouldering
ruins, the gardens and orange groves destroyed, and the in-
habitants, who administered to their necessities, have sought
refuge in the mountains. The march of Attila was not more
withering and destructive. It is but an act of justice to Gen-
eral Taylor to say that he did everything in his power to pre-
vent these excesses . . .

General Wool left Captains Fraser and Lee at the Río Grande
under orders to erect earthworks on each bank of the river to protect
the passage of the remainder of the column—the type of earthwork
which the General Lee of a later day would remember and adapt to
his needs.

The Americans found Presidio del Río Grande to be a town of

about 1,200 inhabitants with an abundance of corn, cotton, sweet potatoes, beans and sugar cane and fruit, thanks to irrigation from a small creek. The adobe houses were in poor condition. A mile or so away the thick walls of San Bernardo, which the Americans called a *Jesuit* mission, stood in a "tolerable state of preservation." Thanks to the efficiency of Wool's quartermaster department, fresh supplies were procured through the *alcalde*. Payment was made at the going rate.

Beyond Presidio, the army followed the circuitous *camino real* route toward San Fernando de Rosas, the San Fernando de Austria of Gutiérrez' day. For the first 23 of the 25 miles to Nava there was no water "although the whole country was obviously once irrigated and in a high state of cultivation, as we noticed everywhere dry ditches once filled with water, and frequently passed houses in ruins. As far as the eye could reach on both sides, we saw nothing but a wide-spread champaign country, bearing evidence of former prosperity. It is now nothing but a desert waste, abandoned to the dreaded Comanches, or the not less terrible Mescaleros and Apaches, who have driven the timid inhabitants from their rural dwellings, and cooped them up within the precincts of the villages, converting this once smiling garden into a howling wilderness."

Captain Hughes made no comment on the causes of such desolation—the removal of protective military arms which could control the savage Indians while Mexico fought its way to a stable democracy, and the warfare between centralists and federalists, which not only desolated the country but also gave cover to predatory bandits operating as soldiers.

Beyond San Fernando in its rich and productive valley the road began by circuitous windings but easy grades its ascent of the rough cactus-covered San José hills. From their summit the men caught their first glimpse of the Sierra Gorda, a spur of the great Sierra Madre, far across the *llano,* or plain, of San José. Through the lifting veil of mist they saw the wall of serrated mountains rising to a height of 4,000 feet, "stretching to the north and south as far as the eye could reach and apparently presenting an impassable barrier to our further progress."

At Santa Rosa, General Wool decided that the only practicable way to Chihuahua, the city he had been ordered to take, was by way of Parras, through which ran the major road from Saltillo up the west side of the Bolsón de Mapimí. Only mule trails led through the mountains and beyond them lay 90 miles of the waterless great sink.

Following the road easterly along the base of the Santa Rosa mountains, then southerly, the American column moved through rolling, dry and dusty lands on the high plateau. After two days the army came through country characterized by maguey to the Hacienda de las Hermanas, named for three small knolls between the Gachupinas and Lampasos mountains. The spring with its waters a warm 111 degrees had been walled in for a favorite resort for the fashionable of Monclova. The *hacienda* itself had some 1,000 acres in cultivation and some 160 peons working them. Its owner, Miguel Blanco of the important Coahuila family, welcomed the officers profusely.

On the other side of the pass, the road began to follow the east bank of the Monclova river, passing several *haciendas* and a number of *ranchos* on the way. Ahead, according to reports, there might well be a different welcome from that accorded Wool's forces so far. Monclova, the erstwhile capitol of Coahuila, had furnished bountiful supplies to the Mexican army. Its authorities had protested Wool's advance during the armistice. For a while a force of 2,500 under Colonel Blanco had stood ready to defend the town. Although it had disbanded, it might easily mobilize again. Wool's column encamped on the east bank of the clear, pure Monclova River, opposite the *alameda* of the town. On November 3 he entered the city with all his troops and took formal possession of it, running up the American flag over the governor's palace, which he made his headquarters.

Wool found Monclova, as described by Captain Hughes:

> . . . *a fine and rather cleanly town. The houses are well built, the better class of stone, and the principal church is a very large and imposing structure. There is here also an extensive and once comfortable hospital (now abandoned to the bats) erected by the Spanish government, and large quarters for troops. The introduction of running water through all the streets, and its numerous alamedas (skirted with long avenues of trees) and its numerous well irrigated gardens, impart to Monclova, particularly to persons who have recently traversed the dry and uncultivated plains of Coahuila, a most*

*agreeable and charming aspect. It wears, however, that melan-
choly appearance of decay and of premature old age so common to Mexican towns.*

Immediately above the city were large reservoirs of water and
three grist mills, and all around were fields principally of corn but
also of cotton, sugar, beans and figs. Wool seized 10,000 pounds of
flour, collected for the Mexican army. But he promised that if the
people remained strictly neutral they had nothing to fear.

Coming to a country more nearly hostile to his passage, Wool
took cognizance of the armistice and remained here some twenty days.
By now Wool recognized that his line of supply, extending 600 miles
back to San Antonio, was too long and impossible to maintain. He
decided to "cut the cord." He would make Monclova his supply base
and bring the stores as needed from Camargo, 200 miles away. Colonel
Churchill and the second major part of his forces caught up with
Wool's men while they waited at Monclova. Wool ordered the companies which were stationed along his march to protect the supplies
to rejoin the main body.

Wool's reconnaissance convinced him that no concentrations of
troops remained in Coahuila or to the west. All intelligence pointed
to San Luis Potosí. He feared that if he persisted in his earlier plan
of taking Chihuahua, Santa Anna would gain even further opportunity to destroy in detail the widely separated components of the
American forces.

Wool reckoned that the armistice should end on November 19.
On the 24th he got his column under way again, leaving behind some
250 men of the 1st Illinois to guard his depot. A day later he received
orders from General Taylor to occupy Parras, 180 miles away.

As the column marched from Castaño a norther dropped the
temperature from a reading of 95 in the early afternoon to 24 in the
evening. At Baján the men filled their canteens at the large stone
reservoir. On the way to La Joya the marl hurt the men's eyes and
feet. At Agua Nueva a fine new spring provided fresh water not
known to travelers along the road thirty years before. Fifteen miles
south of Agua Nueva, at the putrescent Tanque San Felipe, Wool's
column left the old *camino real* and turned west toward Parras
through an easy mountain pass.

On December 5 the army encamped before Parras, southwest of

Saltillo. The column had walked more than 750 miles from Lavaca, "transporting its supplies, medical stores and munitions of war, with a celerity and success almost unexampled in the history of modern warfare; and the day after its arrival at Parras, it was in every respect in condition to have resumed its line of march for an equal or still greater distance." Or so claimed the proud Captain Hughes. Moreover, he was impressed that all along the way people had remained undisturbed in the possession of their property, a situation the Mexicans themselves, so often visited by bandits, least expected.

Wool took military possession of picturesque little Parras in the midst of its rich grain fields. While his men relaxed, he sought provisions for the Army of Occupation and sent reconnoitering parties to investigate the enemy's movements to the south.

Within twelve days of their arrival at Parras, Wool's men marched eastward. A courier from Worth reached Wool during the *siesta*. Santa Anna and 30,000 men were reported to be within three days' march of Saltillo. Worth had but 900 men to pit against him. Within two hours, at 4:30 P.M., Wool's column, with its immense train of 350 wagons loaded with supplies, 400,000 cartridges, 200 rounds for the cannon, quartermaster's and hospital stores for a year's campaign and sixty-days' ration for his whole command, was under way. Only fourteen of his soldiers were unable to move. They were left behind with a small military detachment.

Officers and men were quickened by the fear that they might arrive too late to meet the avalanche that threatened Worth. To block Santa Anna's advance, Wool headed across country for Agua Nueva, 21 miles below Saltillo, on the great road from San Luis Potosí to that city. By getting his men up every morning at one o'clock and by two days of marching averaging 40 miles each for the infantrymen, the column covered the 120 miles in less than three and a half days.

But the enemy was not in sight.

At the dusty, windswept ranch of La Encantada, close by a miniature Grand Canyon, 7 miles behind Agua Nueva and 14 from Saltillo, where Wool had disencumbered himself of his train, Captain Robert E. Lee had returned to headquarters with the heartening news that no enemy lay immediately ahead.

Accompanied by an unwilling Mexican guide and without other escort, the 39-year-old captain had gone far south until, on a mountainside, scores of little fires implied that a mighty host lay encamped. A less courageous man would have accepted the testimony of his senses. Even the Mexican guide, sure that death would befall a peon who guided a *Norteamericano,* was afraid to go farther. But Lee picked his way toward the lights. He was rewarded by the discovery that these were the fires of humble shepherds. They assured him that their sheep and not Santa Anna's soldiers were resting. They had neither seen nor heard anything of an army's approach from the south. Lee and the guide took so long to return that Wool ordered the peon's father brought in and held as hostage for the captain's safe return.

Leaving his men encamped at Agua Nueva, Wool now rode through dense fog to Saltillo on December 22 to confer with General Worth and General Butler, whom Taylor had sent to that city with reinforcements. On the way back the next day, in clearer weather, the general and his aide were better able to examine the countryside.

Wool found that after climbing the short sharp ascent just south of Saltillo the road remained on a fairly level plain. Some 5½ miles beyond Saltillo, on the left, were the four or five adobe buildings constituting the headquarters of the Buena Vista ranch. This *estancia* lay in a valley bounded by flat-topped, pyramidical mountains on the left and saw-tooth peaks on the right.

A mile and a half down the road the high country almost came together. In the 40-foot defile—a defile which the Mexicans called *La Angostura,* the Narrows—the road and the meandering stream which flowed from La Encantada took up all the space. At right angles to the road, on the left, in the front and rear of the pass, mountain torrents had eroded two tremendous ravines through the tablelands at the foot of the mountains. The one to the south was 400 feet wide at the base of the mountain and twice that at the road. The one on the Saltillo side of the pass was longer, but narrower. In effect, they cut the land between Buena Vista and La Encantada into three segments: the north field where the Buena Vista buildings were situated, the south field near La Encantada and the central plateau, which ranged from ¾ of a mile to 3 miles wide from mountain base to mountain base.

This central plateau was itself no level plain. From the foot of the eastern mountains to the road, deep gulches had been cut through the rocky silt borne down from the level of the valley. At the blunt base of the highest and widest of these tables lay the river and the road. To the right of the road the river had formed a network of gullies whose 20-foot perpendicular sides made use of that area by horsemen or even infantrymen impossible. Beyond the gullies tall, steep hills succeeded steep hills in lines parallel and finally joining the mountains.

Reining his horse and studying the terrain, Wool observed to his aide: "This is the spot of all others I have yet seen in Mexico which I should select for battle were I obliged with a small army to fight a large one." Within two months he would be fighting exactly on this spot.

Between times there would be alarms, one of them on Christmas Day. Captain Lee wrote home that the headless turkeys, still in their feathers, and the little roasters tied to the tent posts had to wait. Within a month the Virginia engineer was ordered to join General Scott. He rode off on his diminutive mare, Creole, and so missed the battle that was to come.

If earlier alarms had been false, by mid-January it was all too clear that Santa Anna intended to come north rather than turn south for the defense of Vera Cruz. Colonel Harney, again briefly in Wool's command, made one reconnaissance far deeper into enemy country than ordered. He had found no signs of the enemy. But a few days later fifty picked men of the Arkansas regiment and some of the Kentucky cavalry sent by General Butler, who were also not satisfied with obeying limited orders, went on toward Salado and returned for shelter from the cold and stormy night to the La Encarnación *hacienda,* 30 miles beyond Agua Nueva. Here, without sentries they were surrounded and surrendered in the morning to General Miñón's cavalry. A few days after this disaster, a captain and seventeen men from the Kentucky cavalry, neglecting normal precautions, were also captured.

By now, with the return of General Butler to the United States, and General Worth's withdrawal with his troops to join Scott's forces, Wool was in full charge of the defense of Saltillo. In late January he urged General Taylor to come on from Monterrey at once with whatever units he could spare. For General Zachary Taylor the time for decision had come.

General Winfield Scott, the War Department and the President had all ordered Taylor to evacuate Saltillo and bring all troops back to Monterrey. But retreat would have a pernicious effect on volunteers.

Besides, between San Luis Potosí and Saltillo lay the dry desert from which Santa Anna could derive no sustenance. He would arrive in Saltillo with attenuated forces. On the other hand, if the Mexican general were permitted to occupy Saltillo he would be able to regroup his forces there and be in a strong position to attack.

General Taylor risked court-martial and his reputation when he left Monterrey for Saltillo. He brought with him Captain Sherman's and Captain Bragg's batteries of eight pieces, Lieutenant Colonel May's squadron, the 2nd Dragoons and Colonel Jefferson Davis' Mississippi Rifles. Davis, as a young officer, had married Taylor's daughter against her father's wishes. She had died of malaria three months after he took her to his Mississippi plantation home. Now the former son-in-law and his volunteers would contribute greatly to saving the general's career.

The Americans marched through a Saltillo where Wool had ordered the streets barricaded and the public goods concentrated. In case of enemy attack the occupying American troops would move from the plaza into the churches. Two 24-pound howitzers had been placed in the redoubt on the hillside above the town. Taylor continued on to Agua Nueva.

The American commander could not believe that Santa Anna would dare to cross the dry country which long before had blocked Spain's expansion northward. But when the people of Saltillo began deserting the city—a sign that they knew something which he didn't —General Taylor finally admitted the evidence McCullough's Texas Rangers brought him: Santa Anna had reached La Encarnación. Agua Nueva could be turned. So on February 20 he decided to fall back on the spot so strongly recommended by Wool. He left Colonel Yell and the Arkansas mounted riflemen at Agua Nueva to keep an eye out for the enemy.

On the evening of February 21 the American army arrived at Buena Vista. General Taylor proceeded to Saltillo to check belatedly on its defenses, taking with him most of the regular troops. For the defense of the pass Wool was left with the volunteers. That same evening Santa Anna reached Agua Nueva, which Yell's Arkansans evacuated in precipitate flight, lighted by great columns of fire from the stores they ignited before fleeing. By the morning of the 22nd Santa Anna had arrived at the pass.

Santa Anna had not intended to come so precipitately from Agua

Nueva. But if, as it appeared, the Americans were in flight, the general would pursue them. His infantry was exhausted. For the last 60 miles from San Luis Potosí they had marched across wastes where water and fuel were non-existent, and snow and cold rain congealed their marrow. Hundreds died of exposure. Other hundreds deserted.

At La Encarnación, Santa Anna ordered his men to carry two days' rations of salt meat, drink all the water they could and fill their canteens. No time remained to rest. A promise of the rich stores stockpiled by the *Norteamericanos* at Saltillo would have to substitute for the present non-existent necessities.

The general galloped his multi-uniformed lancers and dragoons out of Agua Nueva after the retreating Americans, whose abandoned wagons and burning stores implied confusion and haste. At 10 o'clock on the morning of February 22 he stopped short on the south side of La Angostura. The American troops were in position to fight and the site they had chosen to defend would be hard to attack. To give him time for his infantry to come up and to scout the situation, he sent his chief medical officer to General Taylor under a flag of truce with a demand that the general surrender within an hour to the 20,000 men he boasted were surrounding the American position. General Taylor's answer was not the polite one recorded by his aide, who wrote a more decorous answer than "Old Rough and Ready's" profane comments. But either phraseology meant the same thing. The Americans would fight.

During the night of the 21st, while the Americans bivouacked at Buena Vista, Wool had ordered Colonel Hardin's Illinois men to throw up a parapet on the spur in the pass to the left of the road and a parapet across the road.

The American and Mexican flags hung listlessly in a light breeze that morning of February 22. But this birthday of George Washington was the awaited day. As the band struck up "Hail Columbia," the watchword for the day spread from regiment to regiment: "The Memory of Washington!" Stationed behind the roadblock in the pass was Captain Washington's battery of eight pieces.

This pass of La Angostura was the key point in the defense of the road to Saltillo. If it held, the enemy's artillery could advance only with the greatest difficulty. Contiguous to it, on the left, and ranged on the plateau all the way back to the foot of the eastern mountain waited the greater part of the American forces. These con-

sisted of some 4,759 officers and men, of whom only some 600 were
regulars, arrayed to meet Santa Anna's 20,000. But Wool's selected
site reduced considerably the effectiveness of Santa Anna's lancers
and the maneuverability of his artillery, which together made up the
bulk of his forces. The volunteers were glad when "Old Rough and
Ready" himself rejoined the troops in the morning.

Early in the afternoon, not waiting for all his weary troops to
come up, Santa Anna ordered General Ampudia to the eastern side
of the plateau with light infantry to seize one of the higher tables
or benches of land in an effort to turn the American left. Colonel
Marshall, in command of the Kentucky and Arkansas horse, operating
as riflemen on foot, and Major Gorman's rifle battalions of the Indiana
foot tried to maneuver their way to the peak and slide down onto
the spur before the Mexicans could occupy it. From three o'clock on,
when a Mexican howitzer was fired from the road, the crackle of rifles
reverberated through the valley and far forward on the plateau.
Captain O'Brien with three of Captain Washington's eight guns and
the Second Indiana regiment under Colonel Bowles gave their support to the Americans.

Ampudia's men reached the mountaintop before the Americans,
thereby winning access to the spur. At dusk Colonel Marshall brought
his men back to the base of the mountain. Losses had happily been
trifling. During the afternoon Taylor had feared the Mexicans were
also trying to turn the American right and had accordingly sent
Colonel McKee and the 2nd Kentucky, Bragg and two guns and Albert
Pike's squadron of Arkansas horse to the western hills, which they
reached by a circuitous 2-mile route. With nightfall they remained
where they were. General Taylor, unexplained to this day, returned
again to Saltillo, taking with him the Mississippi regiment and some
of the 2nd Dragoons.

During the day General Miñón had been seen in the environs of
Saltillo and Major Warren, in charge of its defense, moved riflemen
into the towers of the church to control the bright plaza upon which
it fronted and the approaches to the city.

In the south plain beyond La Angostura the Mexicans bivouacked
without tents as they had every night since San Luis Potosí. This
night Santa Anna rallied them with a verbose speech on the atrocities
of the barbarians of the North, who had left the Mexicans no alternative to the sword. The death of their brothers who had fallen resisting

the unholy invasion must be avenged. Soon all hardships would be rewarded by the riches the men would capture from the enemy who polluted their soil. The *vivas* resounded. *Viva la Republica! Viva Santa Anna! Libertad o Muerte!*

The Americans heard the cheers as they, also tentless, settled for the night at their cheerless posts. More pleasant were the lilting snatches of Mexican music played by Santa Anna's band and carried on the light evening winds. Soon, however, the wind rose to almost hurricane proportions. No moon shone and from the dark clouds overhead cold rain fell almost continually. It was a night of fear and pain for both armies camped along the road. Only those Americans at the foot of the mountain found wood for fires. And during the cheerless night some 1,500 more of Santa Anna's infantrymen scrambled their way up the mountain to augment Ampudia's forces there.

Dawn brought little comfort to the Americans. In brilliant array, Santa Anna stretched his cavalry and infantry across the whole south field, regiment by regiment, matched horses side by side. While the Mexican bands played sacred music, priests in their bright vestments said mass, moving up and down the line of soldiers to bring the Host to reverently kneeling lancers and infantrymen. The service over, and the blessing given, Santa Anna's resplendent troops went through the evolutions and military drill which had once brought fear to the heart of Father Hidalgo's insurgents.

All this the grimy, inexperienced Americans could see as they looked southward up the valley. Behind them, for all they knew, the menace Taylor had gone to investigate at Saltillo, whatever it was, might appear.

The battle on the mountain was resumed. Colonel Marshall's riflemen, including Major Gorman's rifle battalion of four companies and augmented by Major Trail's battalion of 2nd Illinois and Conner's Texans, fought briskly and well. The discarded British army flintlock muskets the Mexicans used recoiled so violently that the soldiers fired from the hip. Because the Latins used too much powder, the guns fired high and were inaccurate. But numbers and persistence won the action and the Americans were unable to keep Ampudia's reinforced forces from turning their left.

In the meantime Santa Anna undertook to control the pivotal snub-nosed spur above Washington's artillery. Ill-fed horses and weary men pulled and pushed three cannon over the stone-studded plateau under the mountain to a position about 800 yards from the left of the American center. Under the shelter of this battery's fire, a column of lancers and infantrymen under General Santiago Blanco hastened down the road toward La Angostura. Washington's battery discharged its cannon into the closed ranks, which continued doggedly to come on though each blast felled whole columns. Then, Blanco's forces wavered, halted and took refuge in the gullies of the plateau to their right.

Now at about 9 A.M. two other Mexican columns launched their attack. Under General Pacheco and General Lombardini, their arms gleaming, their belts freshly whitened with pipe clay, 3,000 infantrymen toiled to the plateau from the base of the mountain and drove relentlessly against the American left. Their purpose was to cut through to the heavily fortified spur. Lombardini was wounded and retired, but the drive continued. The Americans resisted in hand-to-hand combat and the Guanajuato corps was all but wiped out.

Farthest out on the plateau, Bowles' 2nd Indiana withstood a withering crossfire from the Mexican artillery, assisted only by O'Brien's three guns on their right. Their position, so far removed from other American forces, was desperate. To relieve them, General Lane ordered O'Brien to advance toward them. But Colonel Bowles, seeing O'Brien's three cannon suddenly turned in the opposite direction when the horses were hitched to pull them forward, misconstrued the situation and ordered his men to retreat. In bloody, sweating pandemonium the Indiana men followed orders all too well. Their retreat became a runaway. To compound the difficulty, Bowles chose no particular place to which to retreat. Some of the Indianians ran as far as Saltillo.

As Santa Anna said later, the Americans were three times beaten but didn't know it. Here was the first time. The retreat of the Indianians opened a passage across the plateau which forced O'Brien's battery, the six companies of the 2nd Illinois and Sherman's battery, which was with them, to retire from their exposed, unsupported positions. With no horses left to pull a four-pounder and no men to fire it, O'Brien abandoned the piece. It became a Mexican battle trophy.

Nearer the spur, the 2nd Illinois under Colonel Bissell, part of the 1st Illinois under Colonel Hardin, Sherman's battery and the

2nd Kentucky under Colonel McKee, which had just returned from the fruitless round trip to the western mountainside, held against tremendous odds and forced the Mexicans back toward the mountain. Meanwhile, Marshall's riflemen, isolated from the center, could only fall back, in good order, toward Buena Vista. The Mexicans poured their masses of infantry and cavalry along the base of the mountain toward the American rear, isolated from the strategic center. Pacheco and Lombardini's men charged again.

For two hours Wool had entire responsibility for the direction of the American troops against the full power of the Mexican onslaught. The men had fought well. But now disaster threatened.

Not until then did General Taylor arrive on the scene. Escorted by Lieutenant Colonel May's squadron of 2nd Dragoons and mounted on Old Whitey, he placed himself on the spur above La Angostura, visible to all, and while bullets cut through his coat, he maintained a casual disregard of his peril. With one foot thrown over the pommel of his saddle, he unconcernedly wrote his reports.

If "Old Rough and Ready" could take it like that, so could the others. His mere appearance generated an electric communication of courage.

With Taylor's arrival, Wool left the plateau to rally the Americans in the north field. Soon he met Colonel Jefferson Davis' Mississippi regiment, their red shirts hanging free outside their white duck trousers, 18-inch Bowie knives at their belts, their rifles trailed. Following Taylor from Saltillo, they had turned off the road as they approached the Buena Vista ranch buildings. Wool saw in this fresh unit a phalanx behind which the broken regiments could regroup. Davis' first attacks against the Mexican lancers forced them back. At the *hacienda*, the Kentucky and Arkansas cavalry, and Major Trail and Gorman's riflemen turned back repeated assaults on the buildings.

There seemed no way to stop the Mexicans. By early afternoon their numbers in the northern plain were vastly augmented as a result of American successes on the plateau. There the increased American fire, followed by the close pursuit of the Mexicans by Hardin's, Bissell's and McKee's men, broke the Pacheco-Lombardini column in two. Santa Anna's horse was killed by cannister and the general, with half the column, withdrew to the south field, while the rest, in good order, filed around the base of the mountain toward Buena Vista to join Ampudia's men there or to continue toward Saltillo and join

General Miñón's cavalry. From the mountainside, the San Patricio battery of American deserters showered the American pursuers with cannister. But the central plateau was practically cleared of Mexicans.

On the northern plain the battle raged ever more ominously. Along the base of the mountain some 3,000 Mexican cavalry, in precise battle array and supported by infantry, turned west toward the road and bore down on the Mississippi regiment. Davis' men were now augmented by Colonel Bowles and some of the Indianians who had rallied, and Bragg's and Sherman's batteries. Waiting to meet the charge of the brightly caparisoned lancers, Davis spread his men into an open angle toward the apex of which the elegant Mexican horsemen galloped their horses, their lance points describing shining circles in the air. The Mexican commanding officer checked his horse to consider what were the dangers of the terrain where the Americans had formed to stop him.

Just as his bugler sounded the charge, the Mississippi riflemen's deadly fire felled the leader and hundreds of his lancers. The American artillery boomed its protective cannonades. The Mexicans reeled back in confusion. The Mississippians ran forward, grabbed the enemy's horses by their bridles and finished off many of the riders with their Bowie knives, while they sounded the blood-curdling war whoop that a later war would know as the Rebel Yell. Davis' obtuse angle had worked. When later, as president of the Confederacy, he would interfere in the military conduct of the war, his critics were heard to say that "if the Confederacy perishes, it will have died of a 'V'."

With Sherman and the Indiana men on the right, and Bragg and some dragoons on the left, the Mississippians herded the Mexican brigade toward the mountain. For half an hour a hailstorm pelted the contenders. They hardly noticed it in the overwhelming roar of artillery which reverberated in the valley. The Mexican lancers, ever more closely packed together, as the cannon fired into their dense mass, were in danger of being entirely destroyed.

At this moment, several Mexican officers who had become separated from their men rode up to General Taylor, probably to save themselves, and said Santa Anna had sent them to ask what were Taylor's wishes. It was a strange question, but Taylor, thinking it wise to investigate, sent Wool under a white flag of truce to confer with the Mexican general at the spot he was supposed to be.

It soon became obvious to Wool that although the United States forces were withholding their fire, Santa Anna was not where the officers had said he was. Nor was there any sign that the Mexican offensive was relaxing. He returned quickly to Taylor. But in the American lull, the Mexicans in the north field escaped to the plateau and by 4 o'clock were joining the other Mexicans there in a renewed and desperately strong attack on the American center.

For now Santa Anna resolved to attack from the south field again.

Taylor ordered Hardin and his six companies to go out and meet the attack being engineered by General Pérez. Bissell's and McKee's men hurried to help Hardin. O'Brien's two Texas 6-pounders blazed again and again. Unexpectedly Pérez' forces, which had been concealed in the *barrancas,* rose, their muskets blazing. The Mexican fire, accurate for once, took heavy toll. The Americans were overwhelmed by Pérez' left wing and stumbled down the gulch in headlong flight toward La Angostura. In the road Washington's artillery opened up with spherical case shot which permitted some of the men to reach the pass. But many a valiant man lay dead, including Hardin, McKee, Henry Clay's son and scores of others. Taylor himself might have been captured had not O'Brien continued to fire his two guns until not a single gunner was on his feet. Then, almost surrounded himself, he escaped, leaving behind the two cannon from Victoria, while the Mexicans hurried on toward the fortified spur.

This was the most precarious moment of the day.

At this same time, Bragg, with Sherman close behind, and the Mississippi and Indiana men following them, came breathless from the north field. Without waiting for the infantry to catch up, Bragg wheeled his artillery into battery and opened against the approaching enemy. Sherman followed suit. Volley followed volley. And still the enemy came in their thousands, though the shot played bloodily through them. Desperately Bragg turned to General Taylor for a suggestion. What order could there be? In this moment of almost sure defeat, the story goes that Taylor responded calmly: "A little more grape, Captain Bragg."

There seemed no way to keep the position from being overrun by the Mexican masses whose hands could all but tear the cannon from their wheels. Sherman's canister tore great gaps through the Mexican regiments. The exhausted Indiana and Mississippi infantry attacked Pérez' flank and rear. Before the concerted, desperate charges the Mexicans fell back to the broad ravine.

The battle was over. Shaking from exhaustion, Mexican and North American watched the darkness rise out of the valley and climb the slope of the eastern mountain.

Who had won? And what had they won? Six hundred and seventy-three Americans had died. Santa Anna had lost 1,800 in killed and wounded. The battle must be renewed on the morrow if Santa Anna hoped to gain Saltillo. The adversaries had alike shown near-incredible bravery. During the night some officers, including Wool, questioned whether the troops would be willing to fight again with daybreak.

Santa Anna answered that question by ordering the bulk of his worn men to move southward through the moonless night to Agua Nueva. A brigade, burning fires in the south field, deliberately gave the appearance of an army encamped. Taylor answered the question by welcoming the approach of Kentucky mounted volunteers, dragging four heavy guns through the Pass of Rinconada in a forced march of 35 miles in twenty-four hours, and by bringing up the fresher men from Saltillo to replace his battle casualties.

But in the morning, the unbelieving, bleary-eyed Americans gazed down the road and discovered a field being vacated by the last of the enemy's troops. Wool and Taylor, who had shared a tent that night, looked also, to assure themselves of this miracle, then fell weeping into each other's arms.

Taylor's dispatches described Buena Vista as an American victory. It won him the Presidency of the United States.

Santa Anna, with three American regimental flags and three American cannon, hurried on to San Luis Potosí ahead of the ambulatory cortege whose wounded and dysentery-ridden men did not arrive in time for the *Te Deum* honoring the great victory the general claimed.

In Saltillo, American army doctors and Mexican civilians cared for the American and Mexican wounded in churches converted into hospitals. Taylor left for the United States and the plaudits and votes of a grateful nation.

Wool remained at Monterrey to administer the country north of Saltillo until peace with Mexico was signed. In the interim, *rancheros* and bandits, operating as guerillas, slaughtered American teamsters conducting their trains of supplies until Wool's Order 11 brought surer peace to the roads of Coahuila and Nuevo Léon than they had ever known. The order made the local authorities personally responsible for any depredations in their area.

Santa Anna assembled a new army and prepared to oppose General Winfield Scott's invasion through the historic port of Vera Cruz. After his defeat he would go into exile again to return briefly to serve once more as president, long enough to solve Mexico's chronic treasury shortage by selling the Mesilla Valley to the United States in the Gadsden Purchase. Banished again, he finally returned to Mexico to die, a broken man, in 1876.

The Americans landed near the Isle of Sacrifice. By March 29 both Vera Cruz and the fortress of San Juan de Ulúa were in the invader's hands. At bloody Cerro Gordo on April 18, Colonel Harney and the sabre-swinging dragoons captured the strongly fortified hill that controlled the road to Mexico City. Four days later General Worth occupied the Castle of Perote and in mid-May captured Puebla.

From here the Americans followed the stage road which was the route Cortés had followed.

On August 18 General Scott began the assault on the Tacubaya causeway leading into Mexico City. On this day Captain Thornton of the 2nd Dragoons, who had been in the first engagement of the war, was the first man to die. At the convent of Churubusco the Irish deserters who fought in the name of Saint Patrick refused to surrender, convinced that capture meant death. The twenty-nine survivors were court-martialed. Twenty were hung. At the fortified hill of Chapultepec the *niños héroes,* the cadets of the military college on its summit, gave up their lives for their country as General Scott stormed the ramparts.

On September 13 the victorious American army entered Mexico City. Characteristically, General Harney, without authorization, left his assignment as guard over supplies at Mexicalcingo and with his dragoons escorted the bedecked General Scott into the great plaza. After General Scott's formal review and the huzzas of the troops, the Marines began patrolling opposite the Halls of Montezuma.

On February 2, 1848, the "Treaty of Peace, Friendship, Limits and Settlement between the United States of America and the United Mexican States" was signed at Guadalupe Hidalgo. The United States Senate ratified it on March 10 and in May the ratifications were exchanged at Querétaro. By it Mexico gave up all claim to today's Texas, California, Nevada, Utah, three-fourths of Arizona, half of Colorado and New Mexico, and a piece of Wyoming.

Half of the northern states of Mexico would have been happy to accept independence from a Mexico which could not protect them from Indians and brigands. In Mexico City itself there were leaders who urged the United States to take over the whole country to assure stable government and the prosperity they believed would follow. Growing public opinion in the United States supported the idea that the only way to deal with Mexico was to annex it. With such attitudes prevalent in both countries, the Mexican government thought it should sign the treaty fast.

The land Mexico lost was borderland over which she had never exerted strong control. But Mexican history teaches the inexorable growth of a North American empire, an interpretation which explains much of Latin America's fears of the United States. First the United States was confined to the Atlantic seaboard. Then came expansion through the Louisiana Purchase, followed by the acquisition of the Floridas, the annexation of Texas and finally the Treaty of Guadalupe Hidalgo. If at times there have been other suspicions, they are those which grow out of differences in cultural and religious roots.

But on both sides of the border the goal is the same, the dignity of the individual man. The *camino real* of the viceroys is no more. But many roads to friendship lead across the broad Río Grande, not the least of which should be respect for a common heritage along an ancient trail.

CHAPTER TWENTY-THREE

FOOTNOTE TO THE PRESENT

TODAY THE OLD CAMINO REAL ITSELF can be traced
or paralleled in comfort for much of its thousand miles, from Natchitoches to Saltillo—or, to be more accurate historically, from Saltillo
to Natchitoches. Its survival in Texas is much the doing of a persever-
ing gentlewoman, no longer living, and her visionary and precise
associates, who together rediscovered the road and awakened Texans
and many who were not Texans to its import.

In November, 1911, the Daughters of the American Revolution
appointed Mrs. Lipscomb Norvell of Beaumont chairman of the Texas
Old Trails and Roads Committee. The committee was a segment of
the National Old Trails undertaking of the national organization,
which would also mark the Santa Fé Trail and the Natchez Trace.

Mrs. Norvell took four years to persuade the legislature that
charting the road which had long since ceased to exist was a worth-
while undertaking for the state. In 1915 Senator Louis J. Wortham
successfully sponsored a bill to appropriate $5,000 for the necessary
survey and won permission for the erection of 123 monuments from
the Río Grande to the Sabine, the cost of which would be borne by
the Daughters of the American Revolution.

Major V. N. Zivley, whom the Governor of Texas appointed that
year to chart the road, wrote Mrs. Norvell: ''Seventy-five years ago
it was comparatively easy to trace the road, while today, in many
places for miles and miles where the road has been abandoned and
cultivated, there is not the least evidence of its original location to be
found on the ground.'' To find its route he had to use land descrip-

tions, trees as indicated by earlier surveyors, posts and mission sites, relics, the recollections of the aged, Franciscan diaries, worn wagon ruts, records of such lawsuits as one in 1840 to refix a property's southern boundary, which happened to be the *camino real.*

Throughout the winter of 1915–16 Major Zivley placed oak post markers to indicate the trail. Later the Daughters of the American Revolution replaced them with boulders of Texas granite. The Zivley markers were placed roughly 5 miles apart, sometimes a little less, sometimes a little more, depending on where they could be best seen and protected. More than once Major Zivley marveled at the engineering ability of the Spanish trail blazers. Frequently the abandoned road was shorter and on more suitable ground than the road in use in 1915. Impressed, he wrote Mrs. Norvell: "The old Spaniards who located this road ... if not engineers by education were such by bent of native genius. They selected the best crossing on the streams and the best ground, avoided the hills and sandy stretches and at the same time economized distance. The road from the Navasota to the Trinity passes over firm ground, prairies and timber alternating, missing heavy sand on either side, with considerable water holes along the entire distance." He might have included in his tribute the Indians, who first used the segments of the trail, and the buffalo, who created so much of it.

Mrs. Norvell and her associates in the Daughters of the American Revolution were not satisfied with simply marking the *camino real.* They kept after the Texas legislature until, in February, 1920, a new road—Highway 21—following as closely as possible the San Antonio road from the Sabine to Béxar, was dedicated. Highway 21 was the first state road built in the United States with the intent of bringing alive again a vanished historic trail.

A motorist in quest of history can encompass today in a leisurely, inquisitive few weeks the nearly 2,000 miles from Natchitoches to Saltillo and back, a distance which took the luckier *entradas* four months to travel. Each day of the journey, however swift or slow, can be rewarding. The visitor from east of the Red River first follows Louisiana Highway 6 from Natchitoches to the Sabine, then Texas Highway 21 to San Antonio. From there to Guerrero, the ancient Mission San Juan Bautista and Presidio del Rio Grande, there is no direct road. He could go by a variety of national and state highways to Eagle Pass to pick up Mexican Federal Highway 85 for

Monclova and Saltillo, with the visit to Guerrero as a side trip, from Eagle Pass.

It is not the shortest way to the heartland of Mexico. But history has its own rewards for those who travel the doomed road of empire that ran for 300 years and 1000 miles. The *camino real's* meaning for the Americans of the North was contained in a glib and heady phrase. That phrase was "manifest destiny."

BIBLIOGRAPHY

BOOKS

Alamán, Lucas, *Historia de Méjico*. 2 vols. In Colección de Grandes Autores Mexicanos bajo la dirección de D. Carlos Pereyra. Editorial Jus, Mexico, 1942.

Alcaraz, Ramon, *The Other Side; or Notes for the History of the War between the United States and Mexico*, New York, 1850.

Alessio Robles, Vito, *Coahuila y Texas desde la Consumación de la Independencia hasta El Tratado de Paz de Guadalupe Hidalgo*. 2 vols., N.p., Mexico, 1945.

Alessio Robles, Vito, *Coahuila y Texas en la Epoca Colonial*. Editorial Cultura, Mexico, D.F., 1938.

Alessio Robles, Vito, *Francisco de Urdiñola y el norte de la Nueva España*. Mexico, 1931. 333 pp. Index and bibliography.

Alessio Robles, Vito, *Monterrey en la Historia y en la Leyenda*. Antigua Libreria Robredo de José Porrua e Hijos, Mexico, 1936.

Alessio Robles, Vito, *Saltillo en la Historia y en la Leyenda*. A del Bosque, Mexico, 1934.

Bancroft, Hubert Howe, *History of the North Mexican States and Texas*, 2 vols. San Francisco, 1884–1889.

Barker, Eugene C., ed., *A Comprehensive Readable History of Texas*. Dallas: Southwest Press, 1929. 653 pp. Index. Short bibliography.

Barker, Eugene C., *Mexico and Texas, 1821–1835*. University of Texas Research Lectures on the Causes of the Texas Revolution. P. L. Turner Co., Dallas, 1928.

Barker, Eugene C., *The Life of Stephen F. Austin, Founder of Texas, 1793–1836*, Nashville & Dallas: Cokesbury Press, 1926. 551 pp. Index & Bibliog.

Baylies, Francis, *A Narrative of Major General Wool's Campaign in Mexico in the Years 1846, 1847, and 1848*. Little and Co., Albany, 1851.

Benson, Nettie Lee, *Report that Dr. Miguel Ramos de Arizpe presents to the*

August Congress on the Natural, Political, and Civil Condition of the Provinces of Coahuila, Nuevo Leon, Nuevo Santander, and Texas. Translation, Annotation and Introduction by Nettie Lee Benson, U. of Texas Press, Austin 1950.

Belisle, John G., *History of Sabine Parish, Louisiana.* Sabine Banner Press, 1912. 319 pp.

Billington, Ray Allen, *Westward Expansion, A History of the American Frontier.* New York: Macmillan, 1949.

Binkley, William C., ed., *Official Correspondence of the Texas Revolution, 1835–1836.* D. Appleton-Century, N.Y., London, 1936.

Binkley, William C., *The Expansionist Movement in Texas,* 1836–1850. Univ. of California Press, Berkeley, 1925.

Binkley, William C., *The Texas Revolution.* Louisiana State University Press, Baton Rouge, 1952.

Bollaert, William, *William Bollaert's Texas.* Edited by W. Eugene Hollon and Ruth Lapham Butler. Published in Cooperation with the Newberry Library, Chicago, by the University of Oklahoma Press. Norman, 1956.

Bolton, Herbert Eugene and Thomas Maitland Marshall, *The Colonization of North America: 1402–1783.* Macmillan, New York, 1936.

Bolton, Herbert Eugene, *Athanase de Mézières and the Louisiana-Texas Frontier, 1768–1785.* 2 vols. Arthur H. Clark Co., Cleveland, 1914.

Bolton, Herbert Eugene, *Texas in the Middle Eighteenth Century.* University of California Press, Berkeley, 1915.

Bolton, Herbert E., *The Spanish Borderlands: A Chronicle of Old Florida and the Southwest.* Yale University Press, New Haven, 1921.

Bolton, Herbert E., *Wider Horizons of American History.* D. Appleton-Century, New York, London, 1939.

Bonnell, George W., *Topographical Description of Texas, To Which is added an Account of the Indian Tribes.* Austin: Clark, Wing, & Brown, 1840.

Brown, John Henry, *History of Texas from 1685 to 1892,* 2 vols. St. Louis, 1893.

Bulnes, Francisco, *La Guerra de Independencia: Hidalgo-Iturbide.* Talleres Linolipográficos de "El Diario," Mexico, 1910.

Bustamante, Carlos María de, *Resumen Histórico de la revolucion de los Estados Unidos Mejicanos, sacado del "Cuadro Historico," que en forma de cartas escribió el Lic. D. Carlos María Bustamante.* Londres (etc.), R. Ackermann, 1828.

Callcott, Wilfrid Hardy, *Santa Anna: The Story of an Enigma Who Once Was Mexico.* University of Oklahoma Press, Norman, 1936.

Carleton, James Henry, *The Battle of Buena Vista,* Harper & Bros., New York, 1848.

Carrillo y Gariel, Abelardo, *El Traje en la Nueva España.* Dirección de Monumentos Coloniales. Instituto Nacional de Antropología e Historia. Mexico, 1950.

Caruso, John Anthony, *The Liberators of Mexico.* Published by Pageant Press, Inc., New York, 1954.

Castañeda, Carlos E., *Our Catholic Heritage in Texas, 1519–1936*. Prepared under the auspices of the Knights of Columbus of Texas. 7 vols. Austin, Texas, Von Boeckmann-Jones Co., 1936–1950.

Castañeda, Carlos E., *The Mexican Side of the Texan Revolution by the chief Mexican participants*. Translated with notes by Carlos E. Castañeda. Dallas, Texas, P. L. Turner Co., 1928.

Céliz, Fray Francisco, *Diary of the Alarcón Expedition Into Texas, 1718–1719*. Translated by Fritz Leo Hoffman. The Quivira Society, Los Angeles, 1935.

Chabot, Frederick C., *McFarland Journal*. Yanaguana Society, San Antonio, 1942.

Chabot, Frederick C., *San Antonio and Its Beginnings, 1691–1731*. Naylor Printing Co., San Antonio, 1931.

Chabot, Frederick C., *The Alamo, Altar of Texas Liberty*. Naylor Printing Co., San Antonio, 1931.

Chabot, Frederick C., *With the Makers of San Antonio*. Privately Published. Printing by the Artes Gráficas, San Antonio, 1937.

Chávez, Fray Angélico, *Origins of New Mexico Families*. The Historical Society of New Mexico, Santa Fé, 1950.

Claiborne, J. F. H., *Life and Correspondence of John A. Quitman, Major-General, U.S.A., and Governor of the State of Mississippi*, 2 vols. New York, 1860.

Claiborne, W. C. C., *Official Letter Books of W. C. C. Claiborne, 1801–1816*. Edited by Dunbar Rowland, Jackson, Miss. Printed for the State Department of Archives and History. 1917.

Clark, Robert Carlton, *The Beginnings of Texas, 1684–1718*. Austin, 1907. 94 pp. Bibliography.

Cox, Mamie Wynne, *The Romantic Flags of Texas*. Banks Upshaw and Co., Dallas, 1936.

Creel, George, *Sam Houston, Colossus in Buckskin*. New York, 1928.

Crocket, George Louis, *Two Centuries of East Texas: A History of San Augustine County and Surrounding Territory. From 1685 to the Present Time*. The Southwest Press, Dallas, 1932.

Crowell, Pers, *Cavalcade of American Horses*. Garden City Books, Garden City, 1951.

Cutler, Jervis, *A Topographical description of the state of Ohio, Indiana Territory and Louisiana. Comprehending the Ohio and Mississippi rivers, and their principal tributary streams*. By a late Officer in the U.S. Army (known to be Cutler). Boston, pub. by Charles William, J. Belcher, Printer, 1812.

Dobie, J. Frank, *Tales of Old-Time Texas*. Little, Brown and Co., Boston, Toronto, 1955.

Douglas, Claude Leroy, *James Bowie: the life of a bravo*. Dallas, B. Upshaw & Co., 1944.

Du Pratz, Antoine Le Page, *The History of Louisiana, or the Western Parts of Virginia and Carolina*. Translated from the French. 2 vols., London. T. Becket and P. A. de Hondt, 1763.

Du Pratz, Antoine Le Page, *Histoire de la Louisiane, contenant la découverte de ce vaste pays; sa description géographique ... les moeurs, coûtumes et religions des naturels....* Paris, 1758.

Dunn, William Edward, *Spanish and French Rivalry in the Gulf Region of the United States, 1678–1702.* Austin, 1917.

Dyer, Brainerd, *Zachary Taylor.* Louisiana State University Press, Baton Rouge, 1946.

Edward, David B., *The History of Texas; or, The Emigrant's, Farmer's, and Politician's Guide to the Character, Climate, Soil and Productions of that Country; Geographically arranged from Personal Observation and Experience.* Stereotyped and published by J. A. James and Co. Cincinnati, 1836.

Ehrenberg, Herman, *With Milam and Fannin: Adventures of a German Boy in Texas' Revolution.* Translator: Charlotte Churchill. Editor: Henry Smith. Tardy Publishing Co., Inc., Dallas, Texas, 1935.

Espinosa, Isidro Félix de, *Crónica apostólica y seráfica de todos los colegios de Propaganda Fide de esta Nueva España.* Mexico, 1746.

Field, Joseph E., *Three Years in Texas, Including a View of the Texan Revolution, and an Account of the Soil, Commercial and Agricultural Advantages, &c.* Boston: Abel Tompkins, 1836.

Filisola, Vicente, *Memorias para la historia de la guerra de Tejas,* 2 vols. Mexico, 1848–1849.

Flint, Timothy, *Francis Berrian or the Mexican Patriot.* Key and Biddle. Philadelphia, 1834. (A novel but has good color, from knowledge.)

Folmer, Henry, *Franco-Spanish Rivalry in North America, 1524–1762.* Arthur H. Clark Co., Glendale, California, 1953.

Foote, Henry Stuart, *Texas and the Texans,* 2 vols. Philadelphia: Thomas Cowperthwait & Co., 1841.

Freeman, Douglas S., *R. E. Lee, A Biography.* Four volumes. New York, 1934–1935.

Friend, Llerena B., *Sam Houston: The Great Designer.* University of Texas Press, Austin, 1954.

Gálvez, Bernardo de, *Instructions for Governing the Interior Provinces of New Spain, 1786,* ed. Donald E. Worcester. Albuquerque: The Quivira Society, 1951.

Gambrell, Herbert, *Anson Jones: The Last President of Texas.* New York, 1948.

García, Genaro, *Leona Vicario: Heroina Insurgente.* Museo Nacional de Arqueología, Historia y Etnología, México, 1910.

Garrett, Julia Kathryn, *Green Flag over Texas: A Story of the Last Years of Spain in Texas.* The Cordova Press, New York and Dallas, 1939.

Garrison, George P. *Texas—A Contest of Civilizations.* Houghton Mifflin, Boston and New York, 1903.

Garrison, George P., *Westward Extension, 1841–1851.* New York, 1906.

Gayarré, Charles, *History of Louisiana.* 4 volumes. F. F. Hansell and Bros., New Orleans, 1903.

Goodrich, S. G., editor, *The Token; A Christmas and New Year's Present.* Gray and Bowen, Boston, 1831.

Grant, Ulysses S., *Personal Memoirs of U. S. Grant.* Two volumes. New York, 1885–1886.

Gray, Col. William F., *From Virginia to Texas, 1835.* Diary of Col. William F. Gray, with Preface by A. C. Gray. Gray, Dillaye and Co., Houston, 1909.

Green, General Thomas J., *Journal of the Texan Expedition against Mier.* New York, Harper & Brothers, 1845.

Green, Rena Maverick, *Samuel Maverick, Texan: 1803–1870. A Collection of Letters, Journals and Memoirs edited by Rena Maverick Green.* Privately printed. San Antonio, 1952.

Gregg, Josiah, *The Commerce of the Prairies.* Edited by Max L. Moorhead. University of Oklahoma Press. Norman. 1954.

Guardia, J. E., *Historic Natchitoches.* Issued in new and enlarged form by The Natchitoches Chamber of Commerce, Esther Forbes, Secretary-Manager, 1936.

Hackett, Charles W., "Policy of the Spanish Crown Regarding French Encroachments from Louisiana, 1721–1762," *New Spain and the Anglo-American West.* Los Angeles, 1932.

Haggard, J. Villasana, *The Neutral Ground Between Louisiana and Texas, 1806–1821.* The University of Texas, Austin, Texas, 1942.

Hamilton, Holman, *Zachary Taylor, Soldier of the Republic.* Indianapolis, 1941.

Henry, R. S., *The Story of the Mexican War.* Bobbs Merrill, Indianapolis, 1950.

Herbermann, Charles G., ed., *The Catholic Encyclopedia: An International Work of Reference on the Constitution, Doctrine, Discipline and History of the Catholic Church.* 15 vols. The Encyclopedia Press, Inc. New York, 1914.

Hodge, Frederick Webb, *Handbook of American Indians north of Mexico.* Government Printing Office, Washington, 1907.

Hogan, William Ransom, *The Texas Republic: A Social and Economic History.* University of Oklahoma Press, Norman, 1946.

Holley, Mrs. Mary Austin, *Texas.* Lexington, Kentucky: J. Clarke & Co., 1836.

Hollon, W. Eugene, *The Lost Pathfinder, Zebulon Montgomery Pike.* Norman: Univ. of Okla. Press, 1949. 240 pp., bibliog., maps, index.

Horgan, Paul, *Great River: The Rio Grande in North American History.* 2 vols. Rinehart, New York, 1954.

Hughes, George W., "Memoir Descriptive of a March of a Division of the U.S. Army, under the command of Brig. Gen. John E. Wool from San Antonio to Saltillo" . . . in *Senate Doc. 32, 1st Session, 31st Congress.*

Humboldt, Alexander von, *Political Essay on the Kingdom of New Spain,* trans. John Black, 4 vols. London, 1811–1822.

Hunter, John Dunn, *Memoirs of a Captivity among the Indians of North America from Childhood to the Age of Nineteen.* Printed for Longman,

Hurst, Reese, Orme, Brown, and Green, Paternoster Row, London, 1823.

Jacobs, James Ripley, *Tarnished Warrior: Major-General James Wilkinson.* Macmillan, New York, 1938.

James, Marquis, *The Raven: A Biography of Sam Houston.* Blue Ribbon Books, Inc., New York City, 1929.

Johnson, F. W., *Texas and Texans,* ed. E. C. Barker and E. W. Winkler.

Joutel's Journal of LaSalle's Last Voyage: 1684–1687. With Historical and Biographical Introduction, Annotations and Index by Henry Reed Stiles. Joseph McDonough, Albany, 1906.

Kendall, George Watkins, *Narrative of the Texan Santa Fé Expedition.* Harper & Brothers, New York, 1847.

Kennedy, William, *Texas, The Rise, Progress and Prospects of the Republic of Texas,* 2 vols. London, 1841.

Kinnaird, Lawrence, "American Penetration into Spanish Louisiana," *New Spain and the Anglo-American West.* Los Angeles, 1932.

Lafora, Nicolás de, *The Frontiers of New Spain, Nicolás de Lafora's Description, 1766–1768,* ed. Lawrence Kinnaird. Berkeley: Quivira Society, 1958.

Lamar, Mirabeau Buonaparte, *The Papers of Mirabeau Buonaparte Lamar,* edited from the original papers in the Texas State Library by Charles Adams Gulick, Jr., and others... Austin, Texas (A. C. Baldwin and Sons, printers). 6 vols. (1921–1928).

Lay, Bennett, *The Lives of Ellis P. Bean.* University of Texas Press, Austin, 1960.

Lea, Tom, *The King Ranch.* Research by Holland McCombs, Annotation, Francis L. Frigate. Little, Brown and Co., Boston, Toronto, 1957.

Leutenegger, Benedict, O.F.M., *Apostle of America: Fray Antonio Margil.* Franciscan Herald Press, Chicago, 1961.

Lord, Walter, *A Time to Stand.* Harper & Brothers, New York, 1961.

McCaleb, Walter Flavius, *The Aaron Burr Conspiracy.* Wilson-Erickson, New York, 1936.

McClellan, Elizabeth, *History of American Costume, 1607–1870.* Tudor Publishing Co., 1937.

McCloskey, Michael B., *The Formative Years of the Missionary College of Santa Cruz de Querétaro, 1683–1733.* Academy of American Franciscan History. Washington, D.C., 1955.

McDaniel, H. F. and N. A. Taylor, *The Coming Empire.* New York and Chicago, 1878.

McMaster, John Bach, *A History of the People of the United States from the Revolution to the Civil War.* 7. vols. D. Appleton and Co., New York, 1900.

McWilliams, Richebourg Gaillard, *Fleur de Lys and Calumet, Being the Pénicault Narrative of French Adventure in Louisiana.* Translated from French Manuscripts and Edited by Richebourg Gaillard McWilliams. Louisiana State University Press, Baton Rouge, 1953.

Mansfield, Edward D., *The Mexican War; History of its Origin ... Despatches of the Generals.* (10th edition), New York, 1873.

Margry, Pierre, ed., *Découvertes et établissements des Français dans l'ouest et dans le sud de l'Amérique Septentrionale, 1614–1754,* 6 vols. Paris, 1879–1888.

Marshall, Thomas Maitland, *A History of the Western Boundary of the Louisiana Purchase, 1819–1841.* University of California Press, Berkeley, 1914.

Mecham, J. Lloyd, *Francisco de Ybarra and Nueva Viscaya.* Duke University Press, Durham, 1927.

Menchaca, Antonio, *Memories of Antonio Menchaca.* Yanaguana Society Publications, Vol. II, San Antonio, 1937.

Moore, Effie Missouria, *Alone by the Sea: The Story of Jane Wilkinson Long, "The Mother of Texas."* The Naylor Co., San Antonio, 1951.

Morehead, Max, *The Chihuahua Trail.* Norman: Univ. of Okla. Press, 1959.

Morfí, Fray Juan Agustín, *History of Texas 1673–1779.* Translated, with biographical introduction and annotations, by Carlos Eduardo Castañeda. 2 vols. The Quivira Society, Albuquerque, 1935.

Muir, Andrew Forest, ed., *Texas in 1837, An Anonymous, Contemporary Narrative.* Austin: Univ. of Texas Press, 1958. 219 pp. index, notes.

Myers, John Myers, *The Alamo.* E. P. Dutton, New York, 1948.

Nardini, Louis R., *No Man's Land: A History of El Camino Real.* Pelican Publishing Co., New Orleans, 1961.

Newcomb, W. W. Jr., *The Indians of Texas From Prehistoric to Modern Times.* U. of Texas Press, Austin, 1961.

Newton, Lewis W. and Gambrell, Herbert P., *A Social and Political History of Texas.* Turner Co., Dallas, 1935.

Norvell, Mrs. Lipscomb, *King's Highway.* Firm Foundation, 1945.

Ocaranza, Fernando, *Crónica de las Provincias Internas de la Nueva España.* Polis, Mexico, 1939.

Olmsted, Frederick Law, *A Journey Through Texas; or A Saddle-trip on the Southwestern Frontier.* New York: Mason Brothers, 1861. 516 pp.

Pagès, M. de, *Voyages Autour Du Monde, et Vers Les Deux Poles, Par Terre et Par Mer, Pendant les Années 1767, 1768, 1769, 1770, 1771, 1773, 1774 et 1775.* Chez Moutard, Paris, 1782.

Parkes, Henry Bamford, *A History of Mexico.* Houghton Mifflin, Boston, 1938.

Parkman, Francis, *LaSalle and the Discovery of the Great West.* Little Brown and Co., Boston, 1894.

Parton, James, *The Life and Times of Aaron Burr.* Fields, Osgood and Co., Boston, 1870.

Peterson, Charles W., *Military Heroes of the War of 1812 with a Narrative of the War.* 10th Edition, James B. Smith and Co., Philadelphia, 1858.

Phares, Ross, *Cavalier in the Wilderness.* Louisiana State University Press, Baton Rouge, 1952.

Pichardo, José Antonio, *Pichardo's Treatise on the Limits of Louisiana and Texas.* Edited by Charles Wilson Hackett. 3 vols. University of Texas Press, Austin, 1931–1946.

Pike, Zebulon Montgomery, *An Account of Expeditions to the Sources of the*

Mississippi, and through the western parts of Louisiana, to the sources of the Arkansaw, Kans, La Platte, and Pierre Juan Rivers; Performed by Order of the Government of the United States During the Years 1805, 1806, and 1807. And a Tour through the Interior Parts of New Spain, when Conducted through these Provinces, by Order of the Captain-General, in the Year 1807. Philadelphia: C. & A. Conrad Co., 1810. Illustrated with maps and charts.

Pike, Zebulon M., *The Southwestern Expedition of Zebulon M. Pike,* Edited by Milo Milton Quaife. The Lakeside Press, R. R. Donnelley and Sons, Chicago, 1925.

Portré-Bobinski, Germaine and Clara Mildred Smith, *Natchitoches: The Up-to-date Oldest Town in Louisiana.* Dameron-Pierson Co., Ltd., New Orleans, 1936.

Powell, Philip Wayne, *Soldiers, Indians and Silver: The Northward Advance of New Spain, 1550–1600.* University of California Press, Berkeley and Los Angeles, 1952.

Priestley, Herbert Ingram, *José de Gálvez, Visitor-General of New Spain (1765–1771).* Berkeley: Univ. of California Press, 1916.

Ramos Arizpe, Mignel, *Report ... to the august congress on the natural, political and civil condition of the provinces of Coahuila, Nuevo Leon, Nuevo Santander, and Texas of the four eastern interior provinces of the Kingdom of Mexico.* Trans. & ed., Nettie Lee Benson. Austin: Univ. of Texas Press, 1950. 61 pp. Latin Am. Studies #11.

Ramsdell, Charles, *San Antonio: A Historical and Pictorial Guide.* University of Texas Press, Austin, 1959.

Ramsey, Albert C., *The Other Side: or, Notes for the history of the war between Mexico and the United States.* Written in Mexico. Translated from Spanish and edited, with notes, by Albert C. Ramsey. New York, London, J. Wiley, 1850.

Ray, Worth S., *Austin Colony Pioneers: Including History of Bastrop, Fayette, Grimes, Montgomery, and Washington Counties, Texas, and their Earliest Settlers.* Published by the author. Austin, 1949.

Reavis, L. U., *The Life and Military Services of Gen. William Selby Harney.* Introduction by Gen. Cassius M. Clay. Bryan, Brand and Co., St. Louis, 1878.

Red, W. S., *The Texas Colonists and Religion, 1821–1836.* Austin, 1924.

Richardson, Rupert N., *Texas, The Lone Star State.* New York, 1943, 590 pp.

Richardson, Rupert N., *The Comanche Barrier to South Plains Settlement, a Century and a Half of Savage Resistance to the Advancing White Frontier.* Glendale, California: Arthur H. Clark Co., 1933. 424 pp. bibliog. & Index.

Ríos, Eduardo Enrique, *Life of Fray Antonio Margil O.F.M.* Translated and Revised by Benedict Leutenegger, O.F.M. Academy of American Franciscan History. Washington, D.C., 1959.

Rister, Carl Coke, *Robert E. Lee in Texas.* University of Oklahoma Press, Norman, 1946.

Robertson, David, *Trial of Aaron Burr for Treason. Printed from the Report taken in Short Hand by David Robertson, Counsellor at Law.* Vols. I and II. James Cockcroft and Co., New York, 1875.

Robertson, William Spence, *Iturbide of Mexico,* Duke University Press, Durham, North Carolina, 1952.

Rodenbough, Theo. F., compiler, *From Everglade to Cañón with the Second Dragoons . . . 1836–1875.* D. Van Nostrand, New York, 1875.

Roe, Frank Gilbert, *The North American Buffalo: A Critical Study of the Species in Its Wild State.* University of Toronto Press, Toronto, 1951.

Rourke, Constance Mayfield, *Davy Crockett.* New York, Harcourt, Brace & Co., 1934.

Rowland, Dunbar, *Mississippi Territorial Archives, 1798–1803.* Executive Journals of Governor Winthrop Sargent and Governor W. C. C. Claiborne. Compiled and Edited by Dunbar Rowland, Vol. I, Nashville, Press of Brandon Printing Co., 1905.

Shackford, James Atkins, *David Crockett: The Man and the Legend.* Edited by John B. Shackford. University of North Carolina Press, Chapel Hill, 1956.

Shea, John Gilmary, *Discovery and Exploration of the Mississippi Valley,* Redfield, Clinton Hall, New York, 1852.

Shipman, Daniel, *Frontier Life.* 1879.

Shreve, Royal Ornan, *The Finished Scoundrell: General James Wilkinson, sometimes Commander-in-Chief of the Army of the U.S., who made intrigue a trade and treason a profession.* The Bobbs Merrill Co., Indianapolis, 1933.

Simpson, Lesley Byrd, *Many Mexicos.* G. P. Putnam's Sons, New York, 1941.

Smith, Justin, *Annexation of Texas.* New York, 1911. 476 pp.

Smith, Justin H., *The War With Mexico.* 2 vols. Macmillan, New York, 1919.

Smithwick, Noah, *The Evolution of a State.* The Steck Co., Austin, 1935. A facsimile reproduction of the original orginally published by Gammel Book Co., Austin, 1900.

Stapp, William Preston, *The Prisoners of Perote, containing a journal kept by the Author.* 1845. Facsimile of the original by The Steck Co., Austin, 1935.

Steen, Ralph W., *The Texas Story, Revised Edition.* The Steck Co., Austin, 1960.

Stephenson, Nathaniel W., *Texas and the Mexican War.* New Haven, 1921.

Stiff, Edward, *The Texan Emigrant.* Cincinnati, 1840.

Stoddard, Major Amoss, *Sketches Historical and Descriptive of Louisiana.* Published by Mathew Carey, Philadelphia, 1812.

Strode, Hudson, *Jefferson Davis: American Patriot, 1808–1861.* Harcourt, Brace and Co., New York, 1955.

Surrey, N. M. Miller, *The Commerce of Louisiana during the French Regime, 1699–1763.* Columbia University, New York, 1916.

Taylor, Virginia H., assisted by Mrs. Juanita Hammons, *Letters of Antonio*

Martínez, Last Spanish Governor of Texas, 1817–1822. Texas State Library, Austin, 1957.

Texas, A Guide to the Lone Star State. American Guide Series. N.Y.: Hastings House, 1940. 718 pp., chronology, bibliography, index.

Thomas, Alfred Barnaby, *Teodoro de Croix and the Northern Frontier of New Spain, 1776–1783.* University of Oklahoma Press, Norman, 1941.

Thrall, Rev. Homer S., *A Pictorial History of Texas.* N. D. Thompson and Co., St. Louis, 1879.

Tinkle, Lon, *13 Days to Glory: The siege of the Alamo.* New York, McGraw-Hill, 1958.

Tolbert, Frank X., *The Day of San Jacinto.* New York, McGraw-Hill, 1959.

Tornel y Mendívil, José María, *Tejas y los Estados Unidos de América, en sus Relaciones con le República Mexicana.* Mexico: Impreso por Ignacio Cumplido, 1837.

Valades, José C., *Santa Anna y la Guerra de Texas.* Imprenta Mundial, México, 1936.

Warren, Harris Gaylord, *The Sword Was Their Passport.* Louisiana State University Press, Baton Rouge, 1943. 286 pp.

Webb, Walter Prescott, ed. *The Handbook of Texas.* The Texas State Historical Association, Austin, 1952.

Webb, Walter Prescott, *The Texas Rangers, A Century of Frontier Defense.* Houghton Mifflin Co., Boston, New York, 1935.

Wilcox, Cadmus M., *History of the Mexican War.* Washington, 1892.

Wilkinson, James, *Wilkinson, Soldier and Pioneer.* Printed by Rogers Printing Co., New Orleans, 1935.

Williams, Alfred M., *Sam Houston and The War of Independence in Texas.* Houghton Mifflin Co., Boston, 1898.

Wooten, Dudley G., *A Comprehensive History of Texas, 1685–1897.* Edited by Dudley G. Wooten. In Two Volumes. Vol. I. William G. Scarff, Dallas, 1898.

Wortham, Louis J., *A History of Texas: from Wilderness to Commonwealth.* 5 vols. Fort Worth, 1924.

Yoakum, H. *History of Texas From Its First Settlement in 1685 to Its Annexation to the United States in 1846.* 2 vols. Redfield, New York, 1855.

MAGAZINES

Southwestern Historical Quarterly

Almonte, Juan Nepomuceno, "Statistical Report on Texas, 1835," XXVIII (January, 1925), 177–222.

Austin, Stephen F., "Descriptions of Texas by Stephen F. Austin," contributed by Eugene C. Barker, XXVIII (October, 1924), 98–121.

Barker, Eugene C., "Notes on the Colonization of Texas," XXVII (October, 1923), 108–119.

Barker, Eugene C., "The Government of Austin's Colony, 1821–1831," XXI (January, 1918).

Barker, Eugene C., "The Influence of Slavery in the Colonization of Texas," XXVIII (July, 1924), 1–33.

Bates, W. B., "A Sketch History of Nacogdoches," LIX (April, 1956), pp. 491–497.

Benson, Nettie Lee, "Bishop Marín de Porras and Texas," LI (July, 1947), 16–40.

Biesele, Rudolph L., "Early Times in New Braunfels and Comal County," L (July, 1946), 75–92.

Blake, R. B., "Locations of the Early Spanish Missions and Presidio in Nacogdoches County," XLI (January, 1938), 212–224.

Bolton, Herbert E., "The Location of La Salle's Colony on the Gulf of Mexico," XXVII (January, 1924), 171–189.

Brindley, Anne A., "Jane Long," LVI, No. 2 (October, 1952).

Cleaves, W. S., "Lorenzo de Zavala in Texas," XXXVI (July, 1932), 29–40.

Cole, E. W., "La Salle in Texas," XLIX (April, 1946), 473–500. Maps.

Cox, Isaac Joslin, "The Louisiana–Texas Frontier," XVII (July, 1913), 1–42; (October, 1913), 140–187.

Curlee, Abigail, "The History of a Texas Slave Plantation, 1831–1863," XXVI (October, 1922), 79–127.

Davis, Andrew, "Folk Life in Early Texas: The Autobiography of Andrew Davis," contributed by R. L. Jones, XLIII (October, 1939), 158–175; (January, 1940), 323–341.

Dobie, J. Frank, "The First Cattle in Texas and the Southwest Progenitors of the Longhorns," XLII, No. 3 (January, 1939).

Dunn, William Edward, "The Apache Mission on the San Sabá River; Its Founding and Failure," XVII (April, 1914), 379–414.

Dunn, William E., "The Founding of Nuestra Señora del Refugio, the Last Spanish Mission in Texas," XXV (January, 1922), 174–184.

Dunn, William Edward, "The Spanish Search for La Salle's Colony on the Bay of Espiritu Santo, 1685–1689," XIX (April, 1916), 323–369.

Ferguson, Dan, "Forerunners of Baylor," XLIX (July, 1945), 36–65.

Garrett, Julia Kathryn, "Dr. John Sibley and the Louisiana–Texas Frontier, 1803–1814," XLIX (October, 1945).

Garver, Lois, "Benjamin Rush Milam," XXXVIII (October, 1934, January, 1935).

Hackett, Charles W., "The Marquis of San Miguel de Aguayo and His Recovery of Texas from the French, 1719–1723," XLIX, No. 2, October, 1945.

Haggard, J. Villasana, "House of Barr and Davenport," July, 1945.

Harris, Helen Willits, "Almonte's Inspection of Texas in 1834," XLI (January, 1938), 195–211.

Hatcher, Mattie Austin, "Conditions in Texas Affecting the Colonization Problem, 1795–1801," XXV (October, 1921), 81–97.

Hatcher, Mattie Austin, "Texas in 1820," Report on the Barbarous Indians of the Province of Texas by Juan Antonio Padilla, XIII, July 1919–April 1920.

Hatcher, Mattie Austin, "The Louisiana Background of the Colonization of Texas, 1763–1803," XXIV (January, 1921), 169–194.

Henderson, Harry McCorry, "A Critical Analysis of the San Jacinto Campaign," January, 1956.

Henderson, Harry McCorry, "The Magee-Gutiérrez Expedition," LV (July, 1951), 43–61.

Henderson, Mary Virginia, "Minor Empresario Contracts for the Colonization of Texas, 1825–1834," XXXI (April, 1928), 295–324; XXXII (July, 1928), 1–29.

Horgan, Paul, "The Lost Journals of a Southwestern Frontiersman," XLIV (July, 1940), 1–15.

Howren, Alleine, "Causes and Origins of the Decree of April 6, 1830," XVI (April, 1913), 378–422.

Ireland, Pat, "Liotot and Jalot, Two Early French Surgeons of Early Texas," XLIII (July, 1939).

Jones, O. Garfield, "Local Government in the Spanish Colonies as Provided by the Recopilación de Leyes de los Reynos de las Indias," XIX (July, 1915), 65–90.

Lincecum, Gideon, "Journal of Lincecum's Travels in Texas, 1835," ed. A. L. Bradford and T. N. Campbell, LIII (October, 1949), 180–201.

Love, Clara M., "History of the Cattle Industry in the Southwest," XIX (April, 1916), 370–399; XX (July, 1916), 1–18.

Manning, William R., "Texas and the Boundary Issue, 1822–1829," XVII (January, 1913), 217–261.

McElhannon, Joseph Carl, "Imperial Mexico and Texas, 1821–1823," LIII (October, 1949), 117–150.

Mezquía, Fr. Pedro Pérez de, "The Mezquía Diary of the Alarcón Expedition into Texas, 1718," trans. and ed. Fritz L. Hoffman, XLI (April, 1938), 312–323.

Morton, Ohland, "Life of General Don Manuel De Mier y Teran as It Affected the Texas-Mexican Relations," XLVI (July, 1942), and subsequent issues.

Murphy, Retta, "The Journey of Pedro de Rivera, 1724–1728," XLI (October, 1937), 125–141.

Nelson, Al B., "Juan de Ugalde and Picas-Ande Ins Tinsle, 1787–1788," XLIII (April, 1940), 438–464.

Padilla, Juan Antonio, "Texas in 1820," trans. Mattie Austin Hatcher, XXIII (July, 1919), 47–68.

Ramsdell, Charles W., "The Last Hope of the Confederacy—John Tyler to the Governor and Authorities of Texas," with an introduction by Charles W. Ramsdell, XIV, No. 1 (July, 1910).

Reeve, Frank W., "The Apache Indians of Texas," L (October, 1946).

St. Denis, Louis, "St. Denis's Declaration concerning Texas in 1717," ed. and trans. Charmion Clair Shelby, XXVI (January, 1923), 165–183.

Sánchez, José María, "A Trip to Texas in 1828," XXIX (April, 1926).

Shelby, Charmion Clair, "St. Denis's Second Expedition to the Rio Grande, 1716–1719," XXVII (January, 1924), 190–216.

Solís, Fr. Gaspar José de, "Diary of a Visit of Inspection of the Texas Missions Made by Fray Gaspar José de Solís in the Year 1767–68," trans. Margaret Kenney Kress, XXXV (July, 1931), 28–76.

Smyth, George W., "The Autobiography of George W. Smyth," ed. Winnie Allen, XXXVI (January, 1933), 200–214.

Stenberg, Richard, "The Western Boundary of Louisiana, 1762–1803," XXXV (October, 1931), 95–108.

Strickland, Rex W., "Moscoso's Journey through Texas," XLVI (October, 1942), 109–137. Maps.

Walters, Paul H., "Secularization of the La Bahía Missions," LIV (January, 1951), 287–300.

Wilcox, S., "Laredo during the Texas Republic," XLII, No. 2, October, 1938.

Williams, Amelia W., "A Critical Study of the Siege of the Alamo and of the Personnel of Its Defenders," XXXVI (April, 1933); XXXVII (July, 1933) (October, 1933); (January, 1934) (April, 1934).

Williams, J. W., "Moscoso's Trail in Texas," XLVI (October, 1942), 138–157. Maps.

Woldert, Albert, "The Location of the Tejas Indian Village (San Pedro) and the Spanish Missions in Houston County, Texas," XXXVIII (January, 1935), 203–212. Map, p. 204.

Quarterly of the Texas State Historical Association

Austin, Mattie Alice, "The Municipal Government of San Fernando de Bexar, 1730–1800," VIII (April, 1905).

Austin, Stephen F., "Journal of Stephen F. Austin on His First Trip to Texas, 1821," VII (April, 1904), 287–307.

Barker, Eugene C., "Land Speculation as a Cause of the Texas Revolution," X (July, 1906), 76–95.

Bolton, Herbert E., "Notes on Clark's 'Beginnings of Texas,'" XII (October, 1908), 148–158.

Bolton, Herbert E., "The Jumano Indians in Texas, 1650–1771," XV (July, 1911), 66–84.

Bolton, Herbert E., "The Native Tribes about the East Texas Missions," XI (April, 1908), 249–276.

Bolton, Herbert E., "The Spanish Abandonment and Re-occupation of East Texas, 1773–1779," IX (October, 1905), 67–137.

Bolton, Herbert Eugene, "Tienda de Cuervo's Inspección of Laredo, 1757," VI (January, 1903), 187–203.

Bonilla, Antonio, "Brief Compendium of the Events Which Have Occurred in the Province of Texas from Its Conquest, or Reduction, to the Present Date," written in 1772; trans. by Elizabeth H. West, VIII (July, 1904).

Buckley, Eleanor Claire, "The Aguayo Expedition into Texas and Louisiana, 1719–1722," XV (July, 1911), 1–65. Map.

Bugbee, Lester G., "The Old Three Hundred, A List of Settlers in Austin's First Colony," I (October, 1897), 108–117.

Bugbee, Lester G., "The Real Saint-Denis," I (April, 1898), 266–281.

Bugbee, Lester G., "What Became of the 'Lively'," III (October, 1899), 141–148.

Burnam, Jesse, "Reminiscences of Capt. Jesse Burnam," V (July, 1901), 12–18.

Clark, Robert Carlton, "Louis Juchereau de Saint-Denis and the Re-establishment of the Tejas Missions," VI (July, 1902), 1–26.

"Concerning Philip Nolan," VII (April, 1904).

Coopwood, Bethel, "Notes on the History of La Bahía del Espíritu Santo," II (October, 1898), 162–169.

Cox, Isaac J., "The Early Settlers of San Fernando," V (October, 1901), 142–160.

Cox, Isaac J., "The Founding of the First Texas Municipality," II (January, 1899), 217–226.

Cox, Isaac Joslin, "The Louisiana-Texas Frontier," X, No. 1, July, 1906.

Dunn, William Edward, "Apaches Relations in Texas, 1718–1750," XIV (January, 1911), 198–274.

Holland, J. K., "Reminiscences of Austin and Old Washington," I (October, 1897), 92–95.

Kuykendall, J. H., "Reminiscences of Early Texans, A Collection from the Austin Papers," VI (January, 1903), 236–253; (April, 1903), 311–330; VII (July, 1903), 29–64.

Lewis, W. S., "Adventures of the 'Lively' Immigrants," III (July, 1899), 1–32; (October, 1899), 81–107.

Looscan, Adele, "Micajah Autry, A Soldier of the Alamo," XIV (April, 1911), 315–324.

Manzanet, Don Damian, "Carta de Don Damian Manzanet a Don Carlos De Siguenza ... Sobre El Descubrimiento de la Bahía del Espíritu Santo," Translated by Lilia M. Casis, II, No. 4, April, 1899.

McCaleb, Walter Flavius, "The First Period of the Gutierrez-Magee Expedition," IV (January, 1901), 218–229.

Rather, Ethel Zivley, "De Witt's Colony," VIII (October, 1904), 95–191. Maps & charts.

Schmitt, Edmond, J. P., "Who Was Juchereau de Saint Denis?" I (January, 1898), 204–215.

Terrell, Alex W., "The City of Austin from 1839 to 1865" (October, 1910), 113–128.

Thomson, Alexander, "A Belated Colonist," II (January, 1899), 237–239.

Winkler, Ernest William, "The Cherokee Indians in Texas," VII (October, 1903), 95–165.

Wood, W. D., "Sketch of the Early Settlement of Leon County, Its Organization, and Some of Its Early Settlers," IV (January, 1901), 203–217.

Zuber, W. P., "Captain Adolphus Sterne," II (January, 1899), 211–216.
Zuber, W. P., "Thomson's Clandestine Passage around Nacogdoches," I (July, 1897), 68–70.

Other Magazines and Journals

Baker, Karle Wilson, "Nacogdoches," *Southwest Review*, XXI (October, 1935), 1–14; (January, 1936), 137–154.
Bobb, Bernard E., "Bucareli and the Interior Provinces," *Hispanic American Historical Review*, XXXIV (February, 1954), 20–36.
Bolton, Herbert Eugene, "The Mission as a Frontier Institution in the Spanish-American Colonies," *American Historical Review*, XXIII (October, 1917), 42–62.
Brooks, Philip Coolidge, "Pichardo's Treatise and the Adams-Onís Treaty," *Hispanic American Historical Review*, XV (February, 1935), 94–99.
Carreño, Alberto María, "The Missionary Influence of the College of Zacatecas," *The Americas*, VII, No. 3, Jan. 1951.
Cox, Isaac Joslin, "General Wilkinson and His Later Intrigues with the Spaniards," in *The American Historical Review*, XIX, October 1913 to July 1914. The Macmillan Co. London, 1914.
Cox, Isaac Joslin, "Hispanic American Phases of the 'Burr Conspiracy,'" *Hispanic American Historical Review*, XII (May, 1932), 145–175.
Cox, Isaac J., "The Pan-American Policy of Jefferson and Wilkinson," *Mississippi Valley Historical Review*, I (September, 1914), 212–239.
De Léon, Alonso, "Carta que se da noticia, de un viaje hecho y la bahía de Espíritu Santo, Texas; y de la población que tienen ahí los franceses," *Historical Collections of Louisiana and Florida*, ed. Benjamin French. 2nd series; N.Y., 1875, pp. 293–295.
Donahue, William H., "The Missionary Activities of Fray Antonio Margil de Jesús in Texas, 1716–1722," *The Americas*, XIV, No. 1, July, 1957.
Fisher, Lillian Estelle, "Teodoro de Croix," *Hispanic American Historical Review*, IX (November, 1929), 488–504.
Gutiérrez de Lara, "Diary of José Bernardo Gutiérrez de Lara, 1811–1812," contributed by Elizabeth H. West in *American Historical Review*, XXXIV, No. 1, October 1928 and No. 2, January, 1929.
Hamill, Hugh M. Jr., "Early Psychological Warfare in the Hidalgo Revolt," in *The Hispanic American Historical Review*, May, 1961.
King, Grace, "The Real Philip Nolan" in *Publications* of the Louisiana Historical Society, X, Proceedings and Reports, 1917. The Louisiana Historical Society, New Orleans, 1918.
McCloskey, Michael B., "Fray Isidro Felix de Espinosa, Companion and Biographer of Margil," *The Americas*, VII, No. 3, Jan., 1951.
Mecham, J. Lloyd, "The Northern Expansion of New Spain, 1522–1822, A Selected Descriptive Bibliographical List," *Hispanic American Historical Review*, VII (May, 1927), 233–276.

Murray, Paul V., "Venerable Antonio Margil de Jesús, O.F.M., Friar of the Winged Feet, 1657–1726," *The Americas,* VII, No. 3, Jan., 1951.

Pratt, Julius W., "The Origin of 'Manifest Destiny,'" in *The American Historical Review,* XXXII, October 1926 to July 1927. The Macmillan Co., New York, 1927.

"Projected French Attacks upon the Northeastern Frontier of New Spain, 1719–1721," *Hispanic American Historical Review,* XIII (November, 1933), 457–472.

"Remarks on the Condition, Character, and Languages of the North American Indians," from the *North American Review,* No. L, January, 1826.

Scarborough, Frances, "Old Spanish Missions in Texas," *Southwest Review,* XIII, No. 2 (January, 1928), 155–177; No. 3 (April, 1928), 367–397; No. 4 (July, 1928), 491–509; XIV, No. 1 (October, 1928), 87–105; No. 2 (January, 1929), 237–255.

Shelby, Charmion, "Efforts to Finance the Aguayo Expedition: A Study in Frontier Fiscal Administration in New Spain," *Hispanic American Historical Review,* XXV (February, 1945), 27–44.

Shepherd, W. R., "Wilkinson and the Beginnings of the Spanish Conspiracy," *American Historical Review,* IX (April, 1904), 490–506.

Sibley, John, "Letter of Dr. John Sibley to His Son," in *The Louisiana Historical Quarterly,* X, No. 4, October, 1927.

Stenberg, Richard R., "The Boundaries of the Louisiana Purchase," *Hispanic American Historical Review,* XIV (February, 1934), 32–64.

West, Elizabeth Howard, "The Indian Policy of Bernardo de Gálvez," *Proceedings of the Mississippi Valley Historical Association,* VIII (1914–1915), 95–101.

Whitaker, Arthur P., "The Commerce of Louisiana and the Floridas at the End of the Eighteenth Century," *Hispanic American Historical Review,* VIII (May, 1928), 190–203.

Whittington, G. P., "Dr. John Sibley of Natchitoches, 1757–1837," in *The Louisiana Historical Quarterly,* XX, No. 4, October, 1927.

DISSERTATIONS AND THESES

Bacarisse, Charles A., "The Baron de Bastrop: Life and Times of Philip Henrik Nering Bögel, 1759 to 1827," dissertation for doctorate, University of Texas, Austin, 1955. Unpublished.

Birge, Mamie, "The Casas Revolution, 1811," master's thesis, University of Texas, 1911. Unpublished.

Calloway, Carolyn Louise Covington, "The Runaway Scrape," master's thesis, University of Texas, Austin, 1942. Unpublished.

Donaho, R. C., "The History of Nacogdoches and Haden Edwards' Colony," master's thesis, University of Oklahoma, Norman, 1929. Unpublished.

Donoghue, Jack Vincent, "Washington on the Brazos," master's thesis, University of Texas, Austin, 1935. Unpublished.

Evans, Cleo F., "Transportation in Early Texas," master's thesis, St. Mary's University, San Antonio, 1940. Unpublished.

Evans, Kenneth, "The Administration of Manuel de Sandoval, Governor of Texas, 1734–1736," master's thesis, University of Texas, Austin, 1928. Unpublished.

King, Nyal C., "Captain Antonio Gil y Barbo: Founder of the Modern Nacogdoches, 1729–1809," master's thesis, Stephen F. Austin State College, Nacogdoches, 1949. Unpublished.

Marshall, Ellen, "Some Phases of the Establishment and Development of Roads in Texas, 1716–1845," master's thesis, University of Texas, Austin, 1930. Unpublished.

McArthur, Daniel Evander, "The Cattle Industry of Texas," master's thesis, University of Texas, 1918. Unpublished.

McLeod, Ruth Mullins, "A History of Natchitoches," master's thesis, Louisiana State University, Baton Rouge, 1936. Unpublished.

Moore, Wilma Harper, "A History of San Félipe de Austin, 1824–1836," master's thesis, University of Texas, Austin, 1929. Unpublished.

Portré-Bobinski, G. "French Civilization and Culture in Natchitoches," dissertation, George Peabody College for Teachers, 1940. Printed and copyright, 1941. n.p., n.d.

Walters, Paul Hugh, "Survey of the History of La Bahía," master's thesis, University of Texas, 1944. Unpublished.

Warren, Harris Gaylord, "New Spain and the Filibusters, 1812–1821," Ph.D. dissertation, Northwestern University, Evanston, Ill., 1937. Unpublished.

Wilson, Maurine T., "Philip Nolan and His Activities in Texas," master's thesis, University of Texas, Austin, 1932. Unpublished.

Wimer, Alfonso C., "Life of the Military in Texas: 1687–1731," master's thesis, St. Mary's University, San Antonio. 1940. Unpublished.

MANUSCRIPTS AND BOOKLETS

Blake, R. B., Early Spanish Missions Built in Nacogdoches County, 1716–1721, Typescript in East Texas Collection at Stephen F. Austin State College, Nacogdoches, including typescript of documents from the Nacogdoches County records upon which these findings were based.

Robert Bruce Blake Research Collection. Compiled in the Eugene C. Barker Texas History Center, Archives Collection, University of Texas, Austin, 1958–1959. Typescripts, 75 bound volumes, from the Nacogdoches Archives (1745–1835) and the Bexar Archives (1734–1835).

Robert Bruce Blake Research Collection Supplement. Compiled in the Eugene C. Barker Texas History Center, Archives Collection, University of Texas, Austin, Texas, 1958–1959. Typescripts, 17 bound volumes, from the Nacogdoches Archives (1745–1835) and the Bexar Archives (1745–1835).

Bridges, Katherine, Natchitoches in 1726, manuscript in Russell Library, Northwestern State College of Louisiana, Natchitoches.

Bridges, Katherine, The Bayou Pierre Settlement, manuscript in Russell Library, Northwestern State College of Louisiana, Natchitoches.

Carter, W. T., The Soils of Texas, Bulletin 431 of the Texas Agricultural Experiment Station, College Station, Brazos County, Texas, July, 1931.

Delanglez, Rev. Jean, S.J., The French Jesuits in Lower Louisiana (1700–1763), The Catholic University of America Studies in American Church History, XXI, Washington, 1935.

Derbanne, "Relation du poste à Natchitoches," manuscript letter written by Derbanne, *garde-magazin* at the post, June 12, 1724, in the Russell Library, Northwestern State College of Louisiana, Natchitoches.

Forrestal, Peter P., "The Venerable Padre Fray Antonio Margil de Jeśus" in Preliminary Studies of the Texas Catholic Historical Society, II, No. 2, Reprinted from *Mid-America*, III, No. 4, April, 1932.

Hatcher, Mattie Austin, The Opening of Texas to Foreign Settlement, 1801–1821, University of Texas Bulletin No. 2714, Austin, University of Texas, 1927.

Hignett, Mary LaBarre, "The Raguet Family," mimeographed typescript, Las Cruces, New Mexico, 1959, in the Russell Library, Northwestern State College of Louisiana, Natchitoches.

"Land Resource Areas of Texas," a 4-page brochure consisting of map and five pages of explanation. Prepared by Texas Agricultural Extension Service, J. E. Hutchison, Director, College Station, Texas, In Cooperation with the Texas Agricultural Experiment Station and the Soil Conservation Service, U.S. Department of Agriculture. Compiled by Harvey Oakes, Soil Conservation Service, Curtis Godfrey, Texas Agricultural Experiment Station, and Jack Barton, Texas Agricultural Extension Service.

New Spain and the Anglo-American West; historical contributions presented to Herbert Eugene Bolton. A documentary collection. Vol. I eds. Charles W. Hackett, George P. Hammond, J. Lloyd Mecham; Vol. II eds. William C. Binkley, Cardinal Goodwin, J. Fred Rippy. Priv. printed, Los Angeles, 1932.

Niles Register—Index. George L. Crocket. Typescript volume in the Archives Collection, Stephen F. Austin State College Library, Nacogdoches. 1931–1932.

Niles Weekly Register ... Baltimore, Franklin Press, 1811–1849. 75 volumes in 64.

O'Rourke, Thomas P., "The Franciscan Missions in Texas (1690–1793)," a dissertation, Washington, D.C., 1927.

Tharp, Benjamin Carroll, *The Vegetation of Texas*. Illustrated. Printed for the Texas Academy of Science by the Anson Jones Press, Houston, 1939.

Vogel, Claude L., "The Capuchins in French Louisiana, 1722–1766," Washington, D.C., 1928.

Zivley, V. N., The King's Highway, manuscript in Texas State Archives, Austin.

MISCELLANEOUS

"A Guide to Points of General and Historic Interest in Division No. 11," Texas State Highway Department, Lufkin, Texas, 1936.

American State Papers: Public Lands IV. 18th Congress, 2nd Session, No. 426: "Claims to Land between the Rio Hondo and Sabine River, in Louisiana," communicated to the Senate January 31, 1825.

"Anent John Dunn Hunter," a bound typescript made by the Missouri Historical Society. St. Louis, Mo.

Barker, E. C., ed. *The Austin Papers,* three volumes. Volume I in two parts was published by the Government Printing Office (Washington, 1924) in two parts as Volume II of the *Report* of the American Historical Association for 1919. Volume II was published in the same way in 1928 as the *Report* of the American Historical Association for 1922. Volume III was published by the University of Texas Press, Austin, 1927.

Biografiá del general Santa Anna, aumentada con la segunda parte. Reimpresa por V. G. Torres, México, 1857. No author given.

Bridges, Katherine, "Louisiana Fragments: The Fabulous Dr. Fredelizi" in mimeographed Newsletter of the North Louisiana Historical Association, October, 1960.

Forrestal, Rev. Peter P., Peña's Diary of the Aguayo Expedition. Translated by Forrestal. Reprint from the Records and Studies of the U.S. Catholic Historical Society, XXIV, October, 1934.

Forrestal, Peter P., "The Venerable Padre Fray Antonio Margil de Jesús," Preliminary Studies of the Texas Catholic Historical Society, II (April, 1932). 34 pp.

Gaines, James, Papers. Collected by Mrs. Guy Blount, in East Texas Collection at Stephen F. Austin State College, Nacogdoches, Texas.

Griffith, William Joyce, "The Hasinai Indians of East Texas as Seen by Europeans. 1687–1772," Philological and Documentary Studies, II, No. 3. Reprinted from Publication No. 12, Pages 41 to 168, Middle American Research Institute, Tulane University, New Orleans, 1954.

Hardin, J. Fair, *El Camino Real: The Road of Empire.* N.p., n.d.

Haltom, Richard W., *History and Description of Nacogdoches County, Texas.* Compiled and Published by Richard W. Haltom, editor and proprietor of the *Nacogdoches News,* 1880. From East Texas Collection of S. F. Austin State College.

"Nacogdoches: Texas Centennial, 1716–1936," Booklet, 24 pps. Printed by the *Redlands Herald,* Nacogdoches, 1936.

Norvell, Mrs. Lipscomb, "A Collection of Miscellaneous Material Relating to the Surveying and Marking of the King's Highway, Texas," Tulane University, New Orleans, Louisiana.

"Plano del Presidio de Nuestra Señora del Pilar de los Adaes, en la frontera de los Texas 1722," catálogo de Torres Lansas, Mexico 113, in Archivo

General de Indias, Sevilla. Photostat at Russell Library of Northwestern State College of Louisiana, Natchitoches.

Visit to Texas: Being the Journal of a Traveller Through Those Parts Most Interesting to American Settlers With Descriptions of Scenery, Habits, etc., New York, Goodrich and Wiley, 1834. No author.

Wilkinson, James, Gen. James Wilkinson, A Paper Prepared and Read by His Great Grandson, James Wilkinson. Read May, 1916, before the Louisiana Historical Society and reprinted in its Quarterly.

ACKNOWLEDGMENTS

So many have helped in the preparation of this book through advice, their own great knowledge and plain hard work in our behalf that it is almost impossible to single out a few for especial thanks. This book is the product of many minds and diverse effort. Our problem is with whom to begin. A chronological accounting seems to make most sense.

The first authority we consulted was Dr. William Ransom Hogan, chairman of the history department at Tulane University, whose own *The Texas Republic: A Social and Economic History* is excellent. He introduced us to Herbert Eugene Bolton's *Wider Horizons of American History,* which played a significant part in shaping our thinking about the *camino real,* and to Carlos E. Castañeda's monumental *Our Catholic Heritage in Texas.* He also put us in touch with Dr. William Joyce Griffith, chairman of Tulane's Committee on Latin American Studies. Through him we met the Hasinai Indians and learned that the word Texas means friends. Ora Wesley-Schwemmer told us precisely where the road ran and Charles Harrington, also a graduate student in history, prepared a preliminary bibliography which started us on our way. Mrs. Reba Nell Herman, secretary to the history department, was repeatedly helpful.

Even before we set foot on Texas soil, two brilliant and friendly citizens of Austin, Edward Clark and his wife, Anne Metcalfe Clark, parents of our dear young friend Leila Clark Wynn, shared with us their own knowledge and rare library. Anne Clark's gift of a copy of the two volume *Handbook of Texas,* of which the late Walter Prescott Webb was editor-in-chief, put us in possession of the basic reference tool required for this study of the Spanish trail.

The Clarks introduced us to Dr. H. Bailey Carroll, editor of the Southwestern Historical Quarterly and director of research in Texas history at the University of Texas, whose assistance was inestimable. Dr. Carroll gave generously of his time and not only opened the worlds of this Quarterly and the Texas Historical Quarterly to us but guided our next steps. One of these, a major one, took us to Miss Llerena B. Friend, librarian of the Barker Texas History Library, who taught us the relative importance of various studies and whose own life of Sam Houston was indispensable. Another step brought us to Miss Nettie Lee

Benson, librarian of the Latin American Collections, whom we had previously met through the pages of the SWHQ, and who introduced us to the pertinent and important works in those collections at the University of Texas.

Dorman H. Winfry, then archivist of the Texas State Archives and now State Librarian, dug things out of the archives we wouldn't have known to ask for. Jaime Platon, assistant part-time archivist, was most helpful.

At the University of Texas certain unpublished theses and dissertations were invaluable to us. The dissertation of Charles A. Bacarisse on the Baron de Bastrop and Maurine T. Wilson's master's thesis on Philip Nolan are the fullest sources on these two men we have found.

Benjamin Carroll Tharp at Texas Agricultural and Mechanical College most helpfully presented us with one of the last copies of Major V. N. Zivley's map of the *camino real* through Texas.

The loan of Nyal C. King's thesis on Gil Ybarbo, on microfilm, from the Stephen F. Austin State College library at Nacogdoches was but the first of many courtesies by Miss Mildred Vivian Wyatt, librarian. Mrs. Lois Foster Blount, assistant professor of history at the college and director of the East Texas Room of the library, pointed out the index of Texas references in Niles Register prepared by the late Reverend George Louis Crocket. Crocket's *Two Centuries of East Texas* is the excellent product of many years of thorough research into county history and an example of what fine work dedicated local historians can accomplish.

President Ralph W. Steen of Stephen F. Austin State College, the well-known Texas historian, made several recommendations.

Northwestern University at Evanston, Illinois, mailed us the microfilm of Harris Gaylord Warren's outstanding dissertation on "New Spain and the Filibusters, 1812–1821" which was the basic research for his popular but scholarly *The Sword Was Their Passport*.

At Natchitoches, Katherine Bridges, Louisiana Librarian in the Russell Library of Northwestern State College of Louisiana, is the prototype of the perfect research librarian. She knows her field and the books in her library and feeds you the material as fast as you can digest it. The Louisiana Room over which she presides is a joy to work in and her enthusiasm for western Louisiana lore is so contagious it could easily have limited this book to the space of the trail from Natchitoches to the Sabine. Her guided tours and those of Mrs. John Kyser, wife of the president of the college, and Donald MacKenzie, assistant librarian, conjured vivid ghosts as did our conversations with Mrs. Irene C. Wagner and Miss Gratia Smith.

Father Antonine Ribesar, OFM, Director of the Academy of American Franciscan History, and Father Finbar Kenneally, OFM, of the Academy, sent us books, magazines and suggestions, and reminded us that the habit of the Franciscans is grey—"as in *Greyfriars' Bobby.*"

We are indebted to James Wilkinson, president of the Louisiana Historical Society, for his affectionate biography of his great grandfather, General James Wilkinson.

As far as the Texas Revolution is concerned, Dr. William Campbell Binkley has forgotten more than most historians will ever know. His presence in New Orleans as editor of the Mississippi Valley Historical Society's publications, with headquarters at Tulane, made his library and guidance available and gratefully received.

Over the four year period we have worked on the book, the Howard-Tilton Memorial Library of Tulane University has had two librarians and an interim administration. Dr. Garland Taylor got us started; then Roy Kidman, assistant librarian, and Dean John Hubbard of Newcomb College, made unusual carrel space available so that typewriter and Soundscriber in a crowded library would not annoy others; and Dr. Robert Talmadge, the new librarian, authorized special dispensations for Tulane's writer-in-residence.

Mrs. Edith Bayles Ricketson, now librarian emeritus of the Middle American Research Institute library at Tulane, provided works so recently acquired that they were not yet catalogued. Mrs. William Griffith, director of archives, unlocked the library's rare book room for repeated visits. The way to the third level was smoothed by Mrs. Faye Swanson and Miss Elizabeth Beelman, library assistants. And when it came time for maps and final checking, Mrs. Robert Whittemore, reference librarian, and Miss Marjorie LeDoux, librarian of the Latin American Library, provided the impossible.

The Coahuila side of the Coahuila y Texas story was opened to us by Mrs. Dorothy Ostrom Worrell of Eagle Pass with whom our only connection was a mutual friend, Mrs. Robert Wing of Greenville, Miss., and a mutual love of the *camino real.* Her loan of the three volumes of Vito Alessio Robles' unique history of Coahuila and Texas made repeated reference to his work possible.

The loan of books recalls James W. Silver, chairman of the history department at the University of Mississippi, who guided us in our study of the Mexican War and lent us Justin Smith's two volume *War with Mexico* for the duration of our need; Francis Ingram Tucker, Nacogdoches attorney and amateur historian; Bill Hogan and Bailey Carroll.

The Office of the Chief of Military History of the Department of the Army very kindly prepared a bibliography of Mexican War books.

Not surprisingly, the Missouri Historical Society's library in St. Louis furnished excellent clues to the story of John Dunn Hunter.

The judgments of Dr. Jack D. L. Holmes, then assistant professor of history at McNeese State College in Lake Charles, Louisiana, who has done so much work in Spanish archives and Louisiana history, were important to us.

What may seem a simple problem to the knowledgeable proved a major question to a writer and researcher who couldn't decide whether Texas and Mexico should be spelled with an X or a J. We requested the opinions of Dr. D. Lincoln Canfield, chairman of the department of languages and linguistics at the University of Rochester, and Tulane's Professor Daniel Spelman Wogan, chairman of the department of Spanish and Portuguese languages, and learned that it was not until the 19th century that the Spanish Academy changed the spelling from X to J. As modern Mexico prefers the older spelling—which the people of Béxar had also known—we decided to use the X although many historians whose works we turned to write of the road to the Te*j*as and to the little *presidio* of Béjar.

Howell Jones, secretary of the San Antonio Chamber of Commerce, helped with some contemporary references in the final chapter.

Far removed from the Spanish trail, Miss Doris O. Pitcher, librarian of the public library in Camden, Maine; Mrs. Lucy Crittenden, librarian of the William Alexander Percy Library in Greenville, Mississippi, and Charles Daniel, head of the Information and Reference Department at the New Orleans Public Library, arranged for interlibrary loans from the Library of Congress and were otherwise most helpful.

As with every book we've written in the last ten years, the assistance of our friend and secretary, Ione Boudreaux Lundy, has been incalculable from beginning to end.

To all of these, and many others, we wish to express our deep appreciation.

HODDING CARTER, *author*
BETTY W. CARTER, *researcher*

INDEX

HODDING CARTER, Southern newspaper publisher, historian and novelist, was born near Hammond, Louisiana, and educated at Bowdoin College, Columbia University, and Tulane University. His ancestors were early settlers in the Louisiana Purchase territory. The story of the Spanish trail to Texas has been a project dear to Mr. Carter's heart for many years.

Mr. Carter has spent most of his life in Louisiana and Mississippi and written about his region and the South "with intimate, instinctive feeling and knowledge." Ralph McGill, editor of the *Atlanta Constitution,* said of him: "More than any other person who has written on the 'why' of the South, I believe he has come closest to an answer that can be understood and accepted as true and reasonable by all save the unreasonable."

A Pulitzer Prize winner for editorial writing, he has served on the Pulitzer Advisory Board and has held a Guggenheim Fellowship and a Nieman Fellowship, has won the William Allen White Citation and the Elijah Lovejoy Award and has been elected a Fellow of Sigma Delta Chi.

As an officer in World War II, Mr. Carter established and edited the Middle East editions of *Stars and Stripes* and *Yank.* He holds honorary degrees from six Northern and Southern universities and colleges. Mr. Carter, his wife and three sons make their home in Greenville, Mississippi, where his *Delta Democrat-Times* is published. He is currently writer in residence at Tulane University.

Mr. Carter is the author of a number of books, among them *Lower Mississippi, The Winds of Fear, Southern Legacy, Where Main Street Meets the River,* and *The Angry Scar* and some 250 magazine articles and short stories.